THE GERMAN ROAD
TO THE EAST

THE GERMAN ROAD TO THE EAST

AN ACCOUNT OF THE "DRANG NACH OSTEN"
AND OF TEUTONIC AIMS IN THE
NEAR AND MIDDLE EAST

BY

EVANS LEWIN

LIBRARIAN OF THE ROYAL COLONIAL INSTITUTE, LONDON
AUTHOR OF "THE GERMANS AND AFRICA"

NEW YORK
GEORGE H. DORAN COMPANY
1917

Printed in Great Britain

CONTENTS

CHAP.		PAGE
	INTRODUCTION	1
I.	GERMANY AND ASIA MINOR	17
II.	THE STRATEGIC IMPORTANCE OF ASIA MINOR	33
III.	THE BAGDAD RAILWAY	50
IV.	GERMANY AND THE PERSIAN GULF	78
V.	THE GERMANS IN PALESTINE	99
VI.	THE RUSSO-TURKISH WAR	115
VII.	THE BERLIN CONGRESS	128
VIII.	GERMANY, TURKEY, AND THE BALKAN WARS	148
IX.	PAN-GERMANISM AND AUSTRIA-HUNGARY	194
X.	AUSTRO-GERMANY AND THE SERBS	231
XI.	THE ADRIATIC GATEWAY	250
XII.	GERMANY AND RUMANIA	267
XIII.	GERMANY AND POLAND	280
XIV.	THE GERMANS IN RUSSIA	291
	BIBLIOGRAPHY	321
	INDEX	329

INTRODUCTION

In August 1915, a year after the outbreak of the war, Herr Rohrbach, one of the leaders of the Pan-German movement in the Fatherland and perhaps the chief exponent of colonialism as applied to Germany, wrote that " after a year of war almost everybody in Germany is of opinion that victory or defeat —at least political victory or defeat—depends upon the preservation of Turkey and of the liberty of our communications with her " *; and further, that " if Turkey is beaten and divided amongst the Allies it would be the end of Weltpolitik and Germany would cease to be a world-power." † These words, by a man who has made a life-study of the aims of Pan-Germanism and has done everything in his power to facilitate the growth of Teutonism beyond the bounds of the Fatherland, at once reveal the importance that was attached to the realization of the *Drang nach Osten*, which is the theme of this book, and demonstrate the part that was to be played by Turkey in the creation of a great Germanic world-power.

Previous to the outbreak of the war few people in this country understood the full significance of the great movement that was driving Germany upon paths of expansion and aggression. Fewer still realized that practically the whole population of the Fatherland, from the Emperor and his subservient ministers downwards, was determined to secure for Germany that place in the sun which was claimed as the right of a progressive and constantly expanding nation. The Pan-German movement, so far as it was considered at all in Great Britain, was regarded as the political toy of a set of noisy enthusiasts, who were stated to be without much influence in their own country and far less formidable to the internal

* *Das Grösser Deutschland*, August 1915.
† *Evening Mail* of New York, August 25, 1915.

and external policies of the Empire than were the Socialists. The utterances of the Pan-German leaders were regarded as so much noisy verbiage and senseless rodomontade, and the numberless speeches, books, pamphlets, and every kind of literature distributed wholesale by the Pan-German League to all good Germans, both in the Fatherland and elsewhere, were looked upon with amused tolerance as examples of literary effervescence, pleasing to the man in the street but not in the least likely to affect the main course of national policy.

The public men of Germany were practically unknown. No attention whatever was paid, save by a few earnest students of contemporary politics, to the many statements that were made regarding the aims and objects of Pan-Germanism. Whilst on the one hand most Britons looked upon the rapid economic advance of Germany, the enormous increase in material prosperity, the marvellous development of overseas trade, and the wonderful organization of German commerce as an event of little significance for this country so long as we could maintain our relative lead; on the other hand the building of the German fleet and the continuous increase of the army were regarded in some quarters with no little uneasiness.

But the nation as a whole took its cue from the political leaders who misdirected its affairs and gave little heed to the warnings of those who were patriotic enough to point out the menacing danger that threatened the peace of Europe. The historian of the future cannot fail to be amazed at the self-satisfied inertia in which all political parties in the United Kingdom were steeped. Great Britain, who had formerly led in the van of civilization, seemed not only to be deliberately closing her eyes to the pregnant possibilities of modern Germany, but also appeared to be sunk in a drowsy intellectual torpor. Such historians, in times sufficiently remote from present events, will regard with cynical amusement as well as with unqualified disdain the clumsy but successful attempts of British politicians to throw dust in the eyes of the democracy. Nor can they fail to survey with feelings akin to contempt the proceedings of a democracy which allowed itself thus to be deceived by its chosen leaders.

The amazing ramifications of the Pan-German movement, with its secret agents in every quarter of the globe, with its definite and clearly formulated policy, with its unblushing and unhidden attempts to acquire influence wherever two or three Germans were gathered together, were practically unknown in this country. No one—least of all the politicians—cared or dared to draw attention to the marvellous development of the Teutonic theories. A few ardent patriots, such as Lord Roberts, pointed out the unsoundness of the military position of Great Britain, and the danger with which she was threatened, owing to the continuous increase of the German military and naval power. But the political danger was overlooked. Few politicians studied the vital factors that underlay this growth of rampant chauvinism in the Fatherland, and fewer writers of note made available for the use of the somnolent British public the vast amount of literature that had been published in Germany describing and voicing the ideals of aggressive Teutonism.* With the exception of an anonymous book published in 1904,† which should have been in every Englishman's house and should have been consulted and read as frequently as the Bible itself, and one or two other works dealing with the subject,‡ no books were issued that revealed the inner meaning of Pan-Germanism. Even so distinguished a publicist as the late Mr. Archibald Colquhoun, whose knowledge of Germany and especially of her relations with Russia and the Balkans was extensive, wrote that " so long as Pan-Germanism means only an attempt to secure for the Fatherland the intellectual and spiritual allegiance of its children, even when their bodies owe fealty to an alien land, it is at once a great and an elevating ideal. The world owes so great a debt to German character and culture that it cannot consider such an allegiance to be otherwise than ennobling." § Mr. Colquhoun

* There were, of course, exceptions to this general apathy with regard to Germany. Mr. J. L. Garvin wrote on the subject in the *Fortnightly Review*, under the signature of " Calchas," as long ago as 1901 ; and Dr. E. J. Dillon, whose knowledge of the Near East is perhaps unrivalled, frequently called attention to German intrigues. Nor should the many articles in the *Daily Mail* and in the *National Review* be overlooked. But they had little effect upon the general public, who were persistently misled by responsible politicians.
† " The Pan-Germanic Doctrine."
‡ Such, for example, as Professor Usher's " Pan-Germanism," 1913.
§ " Pan-Mania," in the *North American Review*.

stated further that " Pan-Germanism is rather a cult than a political propaganda (except in Austria), and, as such, it enjoys popularity and support among all the different political parties, wields immense influence, and dispenses a vast amount of money for the advancement of its various aims"; and he ventured the opinion that the movement was really an embarrassment to the German Government and a thorn in the side of the Kaiser.

What even the best informed failed to realize was that Pan-Germanism was a national movement, embracing practically every element in the Fatherland; appealing alike to the militarist and the pacifist; the soldier and the merchant; the trader and the agriculturist; the producer and the consumer; the Catholic and the Lutheran; and gathering its adherents from all political parties, as Mr. Colquhoun states, but by this means controlling and directing their policy into avenues favourable to the Pan-German ideal. In fact Pan-Germanism was a vast political conspiracy far more formidable to the State than Nihilism had ever been in Russia, because its operations were in the main open and above-board, its leaders were known throughout the length and breadth of the Fatherland, and its adherents were to be found in every class of society. Only in foreign countries, where a certain amount of discretion had to be observed, were its proceedings marked with any degree of secrecy. The great strength of Pan-Germanism lay in the fact that it was catholic in its scope and appealed to different classes in different ways, and that its operations were suited to local needs and local conditions.

It will of course be asked by the future historian why it was that a movement of such potentiality, which secured the august approval of the Kaiser and the support of every German, failed to attract attention in Great Britain, which was so directly threatened by the extension of the Germanic idea. The operations of Pan-Germanism were revealed from time to time in ways that should have convinced any less self-satisfied nation that its long immunity from attack was seriously threatened. Pan-Germanism was no new and rapid growth. It was not the result of an outburst of popular effervescence, fanned by some passing wind of changing fancy, but can be traced as a national and vivifying ideal of the Germans long before the present German Empire secured political unity. Moltke, for instance, as a young officer, was one of its earliest exponents and eagerly anticipated the time when all German rivers should be under German control. The clear light of Pan-Germanism was not hidden beneath a bushel but burned as a steady and alluring flame visible by all who cared to raise their eyes.

The chief reason why the increasing illumination of modern Pan-Germanism failed to penetrate the intellectual darkness of Great Britain is to be found in two causes, both discreditable to the nation as a whole. Politicians of all parties failed in their plain duty towards the country. Those who knew the condition of affairs and realized the full significance of Pan-Germanism remained silent or made reassuring speeches. Those who did not know simply refused to believe that there was anything wrong with the body politic in Germany. No statesman was at the head of affairs and the bright flame of political genius had dwindled to a flickering and almost expiring light. It required the shock of some sudden calamity to stimulate the sullen fires of passive patriotism, and the trumpet-call of war to revivify the moribund body of contemporary political life.

If the politicians failed to arouse the nation to an appreciation of its danger, the diplomatists, who were the instruments of the politicians, seemed equally unable to cope with the new conditions by which they were confronted—or were their warnings unheeded and their reports pigeon-holed in some dark corner of the Foreign Office? But the blame cannot be equally apportioned, for the diplomatists were badly served and the victims of an antiquated machine and of a hide-bound service.

M. Chéradame, who during the last twenty years has constantly called attention to the ramifications of German policy, particularly in connexion with the Near and Middle East, has stated that one of the main causes of the failure of Entente Diplomacy, both before and during the war, was the inadequacy of the Diplomatic Service. No one with any knowledge of the arrangements made by Germany with respect to her Diplomatic and Foreign Services can doubt for a moment the superiority in almost every respect of German methods.

It is not, as M. Chéradame states, that the diplomatic agents of the Allies were personally inferior to those of the Fatherland or lacked the essential qualifications for dealing with the problems by which they were surrounded; but the organization of the foreign activities of the Kaiser included new instruments of observation and influence with which the Government at Berlin had for the past quarter of a century flanked its Diplomatic Service, without these new organs having apparently any connexion with it. In none of the allied countries of to-day have agents of observation and of action corresponding with those employed under the highly organized German system been attached, either officially or secretly, to the Diplomatic Service—that is, of course, apart from the so-called secret agents employed for specific and clearly defined purposes. As a result of clinging to antiquated methods there has been a decided inferiority in the " equipment " of the Allies which has seriously militated against the usefulness of the Diplomatic and Foreign Service.

The Pan-German plan for the creation of a great world-power, dominating not only Central and South-Eastern Europe, but controlling practically the whole of Africa, the Ottoman Empire, Persia, and large portions of the Far East, with a considerable part of South America, has been founded upon very exact knowledge acquired by means of an intense application devoted during twenty-five years to every political, ethnographic, economic, social, military, and naval problem, affecting the interests of practically every country in the world. This work has been carried on and perfected either by the agents of the powerful and ubiquitous Pan-German League and other similar societies, or by agents of the secret service, which during recent years has undergone a remarkable development.

So thoroughly has this systematic study of foreign countries been revealed during the past few months that it is unnecessary to emphasize the importance and all-embracing nature of the mission of these Teutonic reporters and intriguers. Each agent in his own sphere fitted into the mosaic of the Germanic investigation. There has been a regular hierarchy of trained investigators and reporters carrying their messages to the Fatherland and influencing, in many obscure but useful directions, the policy and political life of foreign countries. This work has been performed by the various agents, the intermediary machinery between the spies and the official diplomats (such, for instance, as Baron Schenck, who has been working at Athens, and the different agents charged with the duty of " nobbling " the Press), who have methodically studied all the basic problems of the Pan-German plan, and have prepared the means of perverting neutral opinion and directing it into channels useful to the Fatherland, of paralysing the revolt of the Slavs of Austria-Hungary, of facilitating the spread of discontent and unrest in Russia, of furthering the extension of Pan-Slavism in the Mohammedan countries of Northern Africa, of influencing the disloyal elements in Ireland and South Africa, and of directing German activities in the United States, Brazil, and the Argentine. The reports of these numerous agents have been forwarded to the Great General Staff at the Wilhelmstrasse, the operations of which have always been directed so as to correspond as much to political as to military necessities ; and to the cabinet of the German Emperor, who has not scrupled to gather the threads of this enormous activity into his own hands.

The diplomacy of the Allies has been unable to counteract these widespread preparations and has thus failed to keep in touch with social and political movements in other countries and has merely fulfilled its traditional and in some respects out-of-date functions. The British public has had an entirely false conception of what should be the duties of the agents it employs in foreign countries, who in reality should serve as the eyes and ears of the Motherland, gathering and forwarding information for the aid not only of a few privileged officials at the Foreign Office, but also for the benefit of the nation as a whole. The public has imagined that diplomatists make history by preparing mysterious and wise combinations. But the experience of centuries demonstrates that they " simply register history, but do not make it." * As Albert Sorel, a recent French historian, has written, " diplomatists are but the notaries of history." Diplomatists, like other functionaries, await and act upon instructions from higher quarters. Neither Richelieu, Napoleon, Palmerston, Disraeli, Cavour, nor Bismarck,

* Chéradame, in *La Victoire*, January 9, 1916.

who have prepared and created history, were diplomatists by profession, but were served in their great aims by men who acted not on their own initiative but under the direct instructions forwarded to them.

The diplomacy of the allied countries, especially that of Great Britain, has not been assisted and seconded by those numerous agents of observation who have kept the authorities of the Fatherland in touch with events in foreign countries; and it is still obliged to rely upon the out-of-date methods of the past which should long since have given way to more adequate and useful means of gathering information. The methods at present employed, scarcely differing from those of a hundred years ago, have been altogether insufficient to enable either the diplomatists themselves or the home authorities to follow the formation and development of political thought or the chain of events in Central Europe and the Balkans which have been the immediate causes of the present war. The information acquired by official diplomacy is nearly always obtained second-hand, for the members of the Embassy do not mix with the numerous and diverse elements that constitute the social and political life of foreign countries, but only with a select and privileged class of society. Unlike those who have served the foreign intelligence agencies of the German Government, they have not therefore been able to associate themselves with, or to understand, the numerous political movements by which they have been surrounded.

The work of the subordinate officials has frequently kept them to the grindstone in copying numerous documents which do not as a rule depart from precise and definite formulas.* Moreover, the system under which members of missions are so frequently removed from their posts, after three or four years' experience, to other spheres of work, not seldom in countries of entirely different conditions, whilst designed to give them a wider and more extensive grasp of foreign affairs than could perhaps be obtained by remaining for a long time

* Sir Maurice de Bunsen informed the Civil Service Commission that " in our Diplomatic Service all the routine work is done at most posts by the diplomatic staff. They are often for hours typewriting, deciphering telegrams, and doing work which people of less intellectual standing than theirs could do just as well." Another witness stated that " the principal duty of an attaché from the point of view of the Chancery is typewriting."

in one city, has resulted in their not acquiring that intimate and exclusive knowledge which, if properly applied, should be so useful to the Mother Country. The recent report issued in connexion with our Civil Service, whilst calling attention to this fact, has not sufficiently emphasized the real importance of a longer residence at foreign Courts. With regard to the Consular Service, the fact that British officials have frequently been foreigners without any real interest in the policy of Great Britain has been a disadvantageous factor in perpetuating our insular ignorance of foreign affairs.* Whilst many German consuls have been closely connected with the policy of the Fatherland, and indeed have not scrupled to act as spies on behalf of their country, British consular officials, on the contrary, have been almost exclusively engaged on routine work connected with their various offices. M. Chéradame, in speaking of the Diplomatic Service of the Allies, especially in the Near East, has not hesitated to state that very few of the diplomatists know thoroughly the language of the country in which they are stationed, and that fewer still have travelled extensively in that country in order to study its peculiar social and political conditions. Although this statement seems to be an exaggeration there is reason to believe that there is room for improvement in this respect. Other authorities have made similar observations on the inefficiency of the service due to the special conditions under which its members have to work.

The diplomatists of the Entente have not had at their disposal the agents of observation such as have been attached to the German service, in order to attend the numerous Pan-German meetings; to procure and translate the pamphlets and

* It is only amongst the unpaid officials of the Consular Service that there are foreigners. But in this connexion it is only just to notice that other nations, even Germany, have appointed foreigners to their unpaid services. The percentages of the unsalaried officers of foreign birth in the foreign Consular Services were as follows: France 78, Germany 70, United States 55, Great Britain 46. In this respect, therefore, our own Service does not make a bad showing. Strong representations, however, have been made upon this aspect of the Consular Service. As the unsalaried officers in our own Consular Service are rather more than twice as numerous as the salaried officers there is ample room for reform. At such important posts as Bremen, Lübeck, Düsseldorf and Frankfort-on-Main the British Consuls were unpaid—at the last city the Consul-General was Mr. Beit von Speyer.

publications issued by the Pan-German League and by other propagandist societies; to enter into personal relations with the leaders of the Slav or Latin parties in Austria-Hungary, who were frequently without any parliamentary standing and more often without social rank, but who were nevertheless the real forces that were influencing the internal policy of the Dual Monarchy; to mix with the numerous racial and political groups in the Balkans and in Turkey; and to report their observations to headquarters.* In the absence of this indispensable organization, Entente diplomatists have been obliged upon many matters to rely upon superficial and incomplete information, and the result has been that our diplomacy in the Near East has not been able to appreciate or to diagnose correctly the course of events in that troubled part of the world.

In a previous book I have described the plans of Pan-Germanism in connexion with Africa.† I have there shown that after years of careful preparation, political and economic, the Germans were ready to appropriate the greater part of Africa and that it was their intention to found there a great German African Empire, which was to have been a tropical storehouse from whence the Fatherland was to have received the main portion of the raw products needed for its industries. That the German plans miscarried was not due to any want of careful and systematic preparation, but to the fact that the German, with all his theoretical knowledge, is a poor psychologist and did not correctly gauge either the meaning or the strength of the Pax Britannica, or the loyalty of the natives of Africa generally, and completely failed to understand that the Dutch in South Africa would appreciate the benefits of their connexion with Great Britain. The desire to found this great tropical dependency was one of the subsidiary causes of the war.

But there can be no doubt that the main cause of the

* Sir Arthur Hardinge, British Ambassador at Madrid, admitted the difficulty of keeping in touch with these political elements. "I think it is exceedingly difficult," he informed the Civil Service Commission, "both for foreign embassies in London and for the British embassies abroad to have any real or close touch with democratic movements in the modern world."

† "The Germans and Africa," 1915.

present upheaval is to be found in the Near and Middle East. For many years Germans have been endeavouring persistently to extend their influence over the Balkans, European Turkey, Asia Minor, and Mesopotamia, in order that the great plan of a highway from Hamburg and the shores of the North Sea to the Persian Gulf, and from thence a German waterway to India and the Far East should be realized. No opportunity has been lost that would conduce to the success of this enterprise.

Every country that stood across the Germanic path to the East or threatened the consummation of the *Drang nach Osten* was subjected to German influences; and Serbia, the most formidable obstacle that had to be surmounted, was either to be completely crushed and swept out of the way or else brought within the Germanic sphere. For this purpose King Milan was bought as the agent of Vienna. For this purpose Queen Draga, the wife of the impossible Alexander, was finally won over to the Teutonic cause. For this purpose Austria attempted to crush, and with German help has succeeded in so doing, the opposition of Serbia. M. Chéradame has stated emphatically that "the part of the Pan-German plans concerned with Austria-Hungary, the Balkans, and Turkey, that is to say, Central Europe and the East, constitutes the essential and principal part of the Pan-German plans." *

It will be shown in the following pages that there were three principal roads for the accomplishment of this design, each leading to and ending at a point, probably Koweit, on the Persian Gulf. These three avenues were through Trieste and down the Adriatic to Alexandretta on the coast of Syria; through Serajevo and the Sanjak of Novi-Bazar, or through Belgrade and Serbia, to Salonika; and through Belgrade and Nish to Constantinople. To carry the forces of Germanism through Asia Minor and Mesopotamia the Bagdad railway, that prime instrument of German expansion in the East, was planned and rapidly pushed forward. The influence exerted by Germany at Constantinople and the close relationship between the Kaiser and Abdul Hamid were intended to secure the triumph of Pan-Germanism in this part of the world and eventually to strike a deadly blow at British influences in the Eastern Mediterranean, Egypt, Mesopotamia, the Empire of

* *La Victoire*, January 18, 1916.

the Shah, and the Persian Gulf, and to place the Indian Empire in a position of strategical peril.

The plans of the Pan-Germans were known to every inhabitant in the Fatherland, and in view of recent events it is quite impossible to look upon the utterances of the most advanced leaders of this movement as irresponsible and idle verbiage. Even the apparently ludicrous statements of such writers as Tannenberg, Hasse, and Class, representing as they do the extremes of German chauvinism, were symptomatic of the extraordinary national megalomania which had attacked the greater part of the German people. The German nation in its arrogant pride literally applied to itself the Kaiser's dictum, " We are the salt of the earth," and regarded other nations as subservient tools in the great schemes of German aggression. The German Emperor voiced the prevailing national opinion as long ago as the year 1896, when on the twenty-fifth anniversary of the foundation of the Empire he stated that it had become " a world-power, the inhabitants of which dwell in all quarters of the globe, bearing with them everywhere German knowledge and German culture. The time has arrived to link this greater German Empire close to the home country." " The German nation," he said on another occasion, " alone has been called upon to defend, cultivate, and develop great ideas," and yet again he stated that " our German nation shall be the rock of granite on which the Almighty shall finish his work of civilizing the world."

There is no cause for surprise therefore that when the sovereign of a great people indulges in such language his subjects should work for the consummation of the Pan-German ideal. Under the patronage of the Pan-German League there was published in the year 1895 a pamphlet entitled " Grossdeutschland und Mitteleuropa um das Jahr 1950 " (Great Germany and Central Europe in the year 1950), in which the author said : " Without doubt the Germans will not alone people the new German Empire thus constituted ; but they alone will govern, they alone will exercise all political rights ; they will serve in the navy and in the army ; they alone will be able to acquire land. They will thus have, as in the Middle Ages, the sentiment of being a race of masters ; nevertheless they will so far condescend that the less important work shall be done by the foreigners under their domination." This was the direct outcome of the movement which at first arose out of Moltke's riverine policy. The German Empire was to become a replica of the Roman system and Germans were to be a nation of slave-drivers. In fact a few years later the Emperor himself, when laying the foundation-stone on October 4, 1900, of a Museum of Roman Antiquities at Saalburg, set the seal of his august approval upon the Roman system. " May our German Fatherland," he said, " in the future, by the co-operation of princes and people, of armies and citizens, become sufficiently powerful and so strongly united, as extraordinary as the universal Roman Empire, that at last in the future one may be able to say, as was said formerly *Civis Romanus sum*, I am a German citizen."

The war has had one profound and long operating cause: the intense activity displayed by the Pan-German party due to the ever-increasing belief in the invulnerability of Germany and the knowledge that of all the countries with which Teutonism would have to reckon in her fight for world-supremacy that which should have been the most formidable was the least prepared. As we know, the intense and almost grotesque hatred of Great Britain manifested at the opening of the war was entirely due to the realization by the Germans that they had made a mistake in believing that the British lion was fast asleep, and that this serious miscalculation was likely to upset their carefully matured plans. It is interesting to have a competent French opinion as to the falsity of the German claim that Great Britain caused the war, and to read a French view of the *laissez-faire* attitude of the British Government previous to the outbreak of hostilities. " During recent years," states M. Chéradame, " the rulers of Great Britain have been exclusively guided by the seducing but entirely inaccurate idea that since they desired peace there would not be war. British foreign policy has been inspired throughout by this conception. This alone explains the attitude of extreme conciliation adopted by the British Cabinet towards Germany at the period of the Bosnian annexation, during the Balkan Wars, and with respect to the Bagdad railway which so manifestly threatened communications with India. The Liberal Cabinet reflected the prevailing British opinion which absolutely believed in the assurances of Lord Haldane, who passed for a perfect connoisseur of Germany and affirmed that she had not the least thought of attacking Great Britain. Up to the declaration of war, Sir Edward Grey, always inclining to a belief in the judgment of his friend Lord Haldane, had extolled every conceivable combination that might have maintained peace had William II been willing. Finally, does not the total want of preparation for a Continental war that was evident in Britain from the commencement of the conflict constitute the best proof of the sincerely pacific intentions of Great Britain before the war?" M. Chéradame then proceeds to discuss the position of France. "Actual military events," he states, "prove that if France had allowed herself to be cajoled by the flatteries of the tempter of Berlin, an efficacious coalition of the Great Powers against Germany would have become impossible. If France had believed the Kaiser, she would not have been at war, since that would have been useless. In effect, without fighting, France would have been reduced practically to a state of absolute slavery, which in the course of history has never come about except as the consequence of a totally disastrous war. If we had trafficked with Berlin nothing would have been able to arrest the pacific penetration of France by Germany. Little by little France would have ceased to be mistress of her own house." These words are profoundly true, for Germany would have secured by peaceful means the paramount position she desired, had not public opinion in France and Russia become thoroughly awake to the insidious nature of the German plans. This resolute and unexpected opposition determined the Kaiser to throw in his lot with the Pan-Germans and to adopt the programme of a party that had fully decided upon war.

This determination was no recent or hastily conceived decision. So long ago as 1898, Admiral von Goetzen, an intimate friend of the Kaiser, informed Vice-Admiral Dewey, then in command of the American squadron at Manila, that " in about fifteen years my country will have commenced its great war. In two months we shall be at Paris. But this will only be the first step towards our real end—the overthrow of England. Everything will happen at the chosen hour, for whilst we shall be ready our enemies will not be prepared." * In fact German military circles have for years been counting upon the certainty of war with France and Russia and had ardently desired the outbreak of hostilities —a fact which is admitted even in Germany itself, for Maximilien Harden wrote four months after the outbreak of war, in his review *Zukunft*, that "this war has not been imposed upon us by surprise. We have wished for it: we ought to have wished for it. Germany has brought it about through the unchangeable conviction that her work gives her the right to a larger place in the world and to larger outlets for her activities." † In the following pages an attempt has been made to show that German ambitions, although embracing many parts of the world and seeking the extension of German territory to the North Sea by the absorption of Holland and Belgium and of a considerable portion of Northern France, were mainly centred in the *Drang nach Osten* and in the creation of a great Central European State, including Austria-Hungary and considerable portions of Russia, with an economic, if not political, suzerainty over the Balkan States and Turkey, both in Europe and Asia. In order to make the story a more or less coherent whole it has been necessary to deal with many subsidiary topics, but it is hoped that the main theme has been so sufficiently indicated that it will not be overlooked in the necessary mass of detail.

The key of the whole situation is to be found in the East. The Allies, in coming to their somewhat tardy decision that it is above all things necessary to stem the German eastward advance, have arrived at the only possible solution of the German problem. The destruction of the Hamburg–Persian Gulf scheme is an object common to all the Allies; for the realization of this idea would threaten the integrity and the safety not only of Russia and the British Empire, but also the economic and political interests of France and Italy. The results of the activity engendered by the long and close alliance between the Wilhelmstrasse and the Porte depend absolutely upon what the Allies are able to do with their

* *Echo de Paris*, September 24, 1915, quoted from the *Naval and Military Record*.
† *Le Temps*, November 20, 1914.

present base at Salonika, which is the only geographical point whence they can threaten and destroy the Turco-Germanic junction and put an end, once and for all, to German enterprise in Asia.* An offensive from Salonika will be a necessary prelude to the overthrow of the Teutonic Powers and will contribute directly to final victory in Europe itself.

* The entry of Rumania into the war on the side of the Allies has undoubtedly been directly furthered by the presence of the Allies at Salonika. Without that *sine qua non* Great Britain would have waited in vain for a favourable solution of the Balkan situation.

CHAPTER I

GERMANY AND ASIA MINOR

IT has been stated—although no definite proof has as yet been produced for the statement—that it was the great imperialist Cecil Rhodes who was the first British statesman to suggest to the Kaiser that Germany might find ample compensation in Asia Minor and Mesopotamia for diplomatic defeats elsewhere. No one was better acquainted with the ramifications of German policy and with the secret operations of Teutonic agents than Rhodes; and he doubtless foresaw the inevitable clash of interests between Great Britain and Germany, and the consequent economic and possibly military struggle if Germany were to be enclosed permanently within the boundaries of the new Empire and were to be prevented, as seemed only too possible, from further expansion in Asia, Africa, and the South Pacific.* The ubiquitous agents of the Kaiser, whose activities in every part of the world, and especially in South Africa, were well known to Rhodes, by their unceasing endeavours to undermine British prestige and to create in tropical and sub-tropical Africa a great German dependency with the aid of the Boers,† had convinced him that only by meeting this movement half-way could any satisfactory understanding be reached.

Rhodes believed that an attitude of opposition in every quarter of the globe would produce an explosion of the pent-up forces of Teutonism and would bring Great Britain and Germany into irreconcilable conflict.

* Dr. G. W. Prothero, the editor of the *Quarterly Review*, alludes to this statement in his pamphlet, " German Opinion and German Policy before the War " (March 1916), in the following words : " It is also not improbable that the self-restraint exercised in Berlin is partly traceable to Mr. Rhodes's visit in March 1899, at which some sort of an understanding is said to have been reached by the Emperor and his visitor respecting Imperial plans in Mesopotamia and those of Rhodes in Africa."

† On this question consult " The Germans and Africa."

Germany was like an engine filled with tremendous forces for which there was no safety-valve. Sooner or later the expansive energy, political, economic, and military, that had been generated inside the German machine would burst aside all artificial barriers and sweep in a devastating current throughout the world, or, if mishandled by German statesmen, would produce a national uprising within the newly formed Empire, which would be disastrous for Germany and Britain alike. To prevent this catastrophe Rhodes, although he himself was in active conflict with the Germans in Africa and found his own plans thwarted by the expansive tendencies of German Colonial policy, wished to bring about some *modus vivendi* whereby the activities of the two Empires might still continue through legitimate avenues of expansion.

Only in two portions of the world did there seem to be any possibility of such an understanding. In South America, where German influence was rapidly increasing and where there existed vast plains suitable not only to colonization but also for plantation, the Monroe Doctrine, supported by British statesmen and alone guaranteed by the power of the British fleet,* seemed to create an insuperable but nevertheless a purely artificial barrier against German political expansion. Only with the goodwill of the United States and Great Britain could this obstacle be overcome, and both, standing for the inviolable integrity of American territory and for the unassailable

* The value of the Monroe Doctrine has been questioned by several American authorities, whilst responsible British critics, who are naturally averse from expressing any opinion upon this question, have also discovered that although American friendship is of great value to this country it may have been secured at too great a price. The support of the Doctrine, so far as Great Britain is concerned, is a matter of expediency rather than of sentiment. On the American side Mr. Clive Bigham's clever little book should be read, but a greater authority, the late Admiral Mahan, has also questioned the utility of the Doctrine. " South of the point whence influence can be effectually exerted upon the isthmus," he wrote, " the Monroe Doctrine loses much of its primacy. If national honour demand, we can continue to assert it in its utmost present extent; but in view of the rapid pronounced transfer of the world's ambitions and opportunities to Asia, it is undeniable that the centre of interest has shifted afar, for us as for others. If the new stake be as large and as imminent as is believed, it is to be pondered whether we do not weaken our power for efficient action there by continuing pledged to the political—that is the military—protection of States that bear us no love." (" The Problem of Asia," p. 80.)

sovereignty of the Latin States, were indisposed to modify their traditional attitude on this question.

In Asiatic Turkey, on the other hand, under suitable and efficient guarantees that British interests would be respected, there were no insuperable objections to German expansion; for although Great Britain had always opposed the final partition of the Sultan's dominions, mainly to prevent the undue growth of the Russian Empire, it had become sufficiently evident that the eventual break-up of the Ottoman Power could only be delayed at the expense of western civilization generally.

The Sick Man of Europe, who had been cleared out of Bulgaria, bag and baggage—who was no longer even suzerain of Rumania, Serbia, Montenegro, and Greece; whose hold over Macedonia and Albania was becoming more and more enfeebled; who exercised but a shadowy influence over Bosnia and Herzegovina; whose power over a great part of Arabia and over the nomad tribes of Mesopotamia was almost nominal; and whose control over Egypt was reduced to a political absurdity—might well give place to stronger political influences even as he would have to submit to the economic control exercised by the great financial and banking interests of Western Europe. The territorial integrity of Turkey having once been assailed could be attacked a second time without any sacrifice of principle—if it could be proved that such an operation would be for the benefit of mankind generally. Britain, France, Russia, and Austria have each on various pretexts lopped off branches from the rotting tree, ostensibly for the benefit and safety of those who had clustered in its shade; and there seemed no insuperable objection to Germany also protecting the interests of her own nationals by similar salutary measures.

Moreover, in putting forward this suggestion, Rhodes took a leaf out of a political book which had only lately been closed. He, and in this matter are included all who believed in the possibility of some arrangement, doubtless remembered that it had been the deliberate policy of the greatest of German statesmen to divert the activities of possibly aggressive Powers into directions likely to cause the minimum of inconvenience to the Fatherland. Bismarck, for example, had supported

French colonial enterprises in the well-founded hope that the Gallic temperament for adventure would cause the French to turn to Africa rather than to Alsace-Lorraine; to cherish new ideas of national expansion upon the Mediterranean and the Atlantic rather than to nurse secret designs for revenge; to advance into the sandy wastes of the Sahara rather than to hanker after the flesh-pots of Metz and Strasburg, or to long for the vineyards of the Rhine. He believed that by turning the current of political thought towards Africa he might also create French difficulties with Great Britain and thus keep the French imagination busily employed upon problems less dangerous to Germany than any policy of *revanche*.

Bismarck's policy was unscrupulously opportunist, but it was sound. Russia, France, and Italy might well be kept occupied with their political toys in order that Germany might have time to consolidate her position. Russia, for example, might be encouraged in the Balkans. "It would be a fortunate thing," he said to Prince Hohenlohe, "if Russia obtained Constantinople and the Balkan Peninsula, for then she would be weakened." * The French might go ahead in Tunis and not trouble themselves about the Italians,† whilst the Italians might be encouraged in Tripoli.

To create a balance of expansive interests was Bismarck's set policy, and it is doubtless this underlying idea that appealed to Rhodes when he suggested Asia Minor as a field for German influence. In that quarter, at any rate, were possibilities that did not exist elsewhere, and there seemed no reason why Great Britain, Russia, and Germany should not come to some satisfactory arrangement about Turkish Asia. Rhodes did not realize perhaps that the Teuton is essentially a glutton and that half a loaf in Asia would not necessarily compensate him for the loss of a banquet in Africa and South America. It is not of course possible to decide whether he were right or wrong in this respect for the experiment was only tried in a tentative fashion by the British Government owing to the impossible nature of the German demands; for the Imperial

---

* "Memoirs of Prince Chlodwig of Hohenlohe-Schillingsfürst," 1906, vol. i, p. 350.
† *Ibid.*, p. 275.

epicure at Berlin desired to secure the delicacies of the Asiatic banquet whilst the Pan-German gluttons were prepared to swallow the whole dish.*

It is obvious, however, that although Rhodes may have made certain suggestions to the Kaiser, the idea of German expansion in Asia Minor was no new thing, for German policy had long been gravitating towards the Middle East and at the time of Rhodes's visit to Berlin plans of commercial and economic penetration, as well as of political control, had been freely debated in Pan-German circles. It is not proposed to discuss in this chapter the historical basis of Germanism in the Levant, for since the days of the Hohenstaufen Emperors† and the powerful Teutonic order a profound change had come over the eastern littoral of the Mediterranean. The Ottoman Power had risen. Lands where Germanic influence had formerly been considerable had fallen under other control, and Teutonism, so far as the Levant was concerned, might be said to have lost every shred of its former grandeur. German power in the East had completely ceased and even Austria failed to exercise any decisive influence over the affairs of Asiatic Turkey.

It was natural therefore that with the growth of a national spirit in the disunited Germanic States there should arise a desire for the re-erection of the shattered edifice of Teutonic

* As is well known, Rhodes returned from his visit to Berlin full of enthusiasm for the German Empire and filled with a desire for a better understanding between the two nations. Sir Lewis Michell, Rhodes's official biographer, stated that " Rhodes came away with a vivid impression of the Kaiser's great personality, and ever afterwards spoke of him with respect and admiration, and as a memento of his visit founded scholarships at Oxford for German students, leaving the selection entirely in His Majesty's hands." Sir Lewis Michell adds that the respect was mutual. A correspondent wrote to him stating that at a visit which he paid to Sir F. Lascelles in April 1899, the latter mentioned that the Emperor was delighted with Rhodes " and expressed strong regret that he was not his Prime Minister, called him a reasonable man, and said he offered every guarantee before it was required, and thus left nothing to be demanded." (Michell's " Life of Rhodes," vol. ii, pp. 250-1.) Although, as has been indicated, there is no official confirmation of the statement that Rhodes spoke about Asia Minor during his visit to the Kaiser, I have good reason to believe that the matter was discussed—such, at least, is the opinion of those entitled to know something of the inner history of that momentous meeting.

† It will doubtless be remembered that the greatest of the Hohenstaufens—Frederick Barbarossa—who defeated the Moslems at Philomelium and Iconium, died in Cilicia in 1190.

influence in the East, and that contemporaneously with the quickening and vivifying of the feeling of racial solidarity which characterized Germans even when all political bonds had been loosened, there should be a revival of interest in, and a renewal of communication with, countries over which Germans had formerly exercised such decisive control.

It was doubtless this idea that influenced the future Field-Marshal von Moltke, then a young officer, full of enthusiasm for his profession but deeply convinced of the dangers of militarism, to devote his attention to Asia Minor and to suggest that in that country Germans might find ample scope for their energies. Moltke, the brilliant strategist, perceived that it was towards the highlands of Anatolia and Armenia and the plains of Mesopotamia that the attention of Europe would be directed; that here close at hand was the future highway of the East, binding Europe to Asia by a natural avenue of direct communication; that, as he was constantly stating at a period when the value of railways was scarcely realized even by the most advanced students of strategy, some day it would be possible to place an iron arm across the Asiatic dominions of the Sultan, the shoulder of which would be a united German Empire, whilst the fingers would stretch towards Persia and India on the one side and towards the southern limits of Persian waters on the other. It was the vision of a seer, but it is nevertheless undoubted that just as Moltke was constantly endeavouring to demonstrate the value of railways [*] and believed that "from a military point of view every railway is welcome, and two are still more welcome than one,"[†] so he recognized that the time was not far distant when the political and economic status of Asia Minor would be profoundly changed.

It is easy, of course, to attribute great designs to a master-mind, but there is, nevertheless, ample evidence that Moltke in his early manhood cherished ideas of German expansion in the Levant. Syria and Palestine by the fall of Acre had just been delivered from the power of the Egyptian Viceroy, Mehemet Ali, and it was Moltke's idea that out of the Viceroy's territories a buffer State between Turkey and Egypt might

---

[*] *See* his lectures upon this subject contained in his published Essays.
[†] Pratt's " Rise of Rail-Power," p. 278.

be created, preferably under German control. Writing in 1841 * he suggested that the Holy Land should be placed under "a sovereign prince of the German nation and of genuine tolerance . . . because Germany has the negative advantage of not being a maritime Power, while it has the nearest commercial road to the East through the navigation of the Danube and the Austrian ports on the Adriatic." This idea has certainly never been absent from the minds of Pan-Germans since Moltke first threw out the suggestion.

It is necessary to call attention to the views of Moltke because, as one of the three outstanding figures of modern Germany, he exercised a profound influence over the national policy. His early views thus expressed and never subsequently modified encouraged the newly aroused aspirations of his countrymen. They show the future Field-Marshal to be one of the earliest exponents of Pan-Germanism and demonstrate that he was as well qualified for a leader of political as of military strategy.

Moltke shared the national aspiration for a homogeneous German Empire, stretching from the Atlantic to the Adriatic and the Black Sea. If the thought embodied in an article contributed to the *Augsburg Gazette* † in 1844 is to be followed to its logical conclusion, he looked for the expansion of Germany at the expense of her neighbours. The Danube, he said, was "the principal means of communication between the heart of Germany and the East," and whilst "in time of peace we must and may hope that Austria will protect the rights and future of the Danubian countries, it was also to be desired that Germany in the end will succeed in liberating the mouths of her great rivers." The waters of the Danube falling into the Black Sea, the mouth of the Rhine being in Holland, the mouth of the Pruth in Bessarabia (then under Turkish control), and that of the Elbe being between Hanover and Schleswig-Holstein (then Danish territory), it follows that Moltke looked for the inclusion of Holland, parts of Denmark, Rumania, and possibly Bessarabia in a German federation—at a period prior to the unification of Northern Germany itself. Speaking

* In the *Augsburger Allgemeinen Zeitung*.
† Quoted from the *Augsburger Allgemeinen Zeitung* in "Moltke's Essays," vol. i, p. 308.

of Rumania he said: "What German heart is not filled with sorrow at the sight of the long processions of our countrymen, who with their wives and children, their goods and chattels, go to seek a new home on the other side of the ocean? Wallachia is a country wide enough to receive them all, and even by the poorest can now be reached in a few days at small expense by the road along the Danube. If Germans were directed to these countries, German industry need no longer flee to the noxious swamps and the glowing sun of other continents, and while the German language would be heard on the banks of the proud Danube, German colonization would stretch from the Swabian mountains to the mouth of the Sulina." *

But unfortunately, as Moltke himself admits, there were then no signs of Germanic influence in the Middle East. Although the destruction of the Turkish Empire seemed imminent and only Great Britain appeared to be in earnest in preserving the *status quo*—and although France had established herself in Algeria and Russia had advanced beyond the Caucasus—Germans were unable to take advantage of this favourable opportunity owing to their political disunion. "We see the dissevered provinces," he writes, "the whole of the Ottoman country under the influence of Russia, of France, and of England, without being able to discover any trace of German influence. It is a striking fact that in Turkey one always hears of these three Powers, but never of Austria; and yet the last State should be held in the greater regard there for it is the sword of Austria which will sooner or later be thrown into the balance to decide the fate of the Empire. All the fleets of the world can neither accomplish nor prevent the partition of Turkey. Austria's armies may execute the first task and can certainly fulfil the second."†

It was with these ideas that Moltke returned from his sojourn of six years in Turkey, whither he had first been attracted in 1835, owing to his great interest in military topography. He had then received permission to make a journey through Italy, Greece, and Turkey—a furlough which was afterwards extended into a mission for the purpose of instructing and

---

* *See* his "Essay on the Military and Political Situation of the Ottoman Empire," 1841, "Moltke's Essays," vol. i, pp. 296–7.
† *Op. cit.*

organizing the Turkish troops, which were then in sore need of the advice of competent military authorities, as the Ottoman Empire seemed tottering to its fall after the attacks of Mehemet Ali and his adherents. Two years later, Moltke was joined by three other Prussian officers. His stay in Asia Minor led him to realize the immense importance of Asiatic Turkey, which being not only a peninsula but also a continent in itself forms a natural bridge for the nations who penetrate into the Western countries from the East and vice versa. He entered enthusiastically upon his topographical researches, and in the words of Ernest Curtius, the classical historian, he " employed this sojourn in the Levant in promoting the science of geography whose revival by Ritter he had so long watched in his youthful days."*

" This rediscovery of the countries of ancient civilization," continues Curtius, " is the mission of our century in which scientists have been constantly employed ever since Karsten Niebuhr recognized the old brick walls of Babylon in 1761. To this mission Moltke, a born topographer, was introduced by a wonderfully happy providence. He was the first to take his plane-table to these countries, once the home of the art of surveying. The banks of the Euphrates and Tigris, the cradle of human history, were explored by him, and in addition a great work was achieved by the drawing of the maps of Asia Minor and Turkish Armenia by von Vincke, Fischer, von Moltke, and Keipert; the first practical part taken by German research in a great work of our time." Thus, it may be added, for the Germans are essentially a practical people, was commenced that period of German activity in Asia Minor which culminated in the visit of the German Emperor to Constantinople and the building of the Bagdad railway.

In that *Drang nach Osten* which is the theme of German historians and of Teutonic political and economic thinkers, the plains of Mesopotamia and the table-lands of Asia Minor have played an important part not only as forming the stepping-stones to other and perhaps larger adventures on the path to world-domination, but also as a desirable land of promise in themselves. Germans realized that their interests lay in

* Speech in memory of Moltke at a meeting of the Royal Academy of Sciences at Berlin, July 2, 1891.

securing the economic, and finally the political, control of these regions before they were able to bring about the union of their own divided Fatherland. "More than anywhere else," wrote the anonymous author of "The Pan-Germanic Doctrine," one of the most scathing exposures of German policy, "the German sees in Turkey a field for endeavour, which he partly regards as his by right. There is the future German corn granary, the wool industry, the naphtha industry, the colonizing question, the new material for German industrial products, the fresh impetus to shipping, the opening up of the lands of "Bable and the Bible," the great railway line. . . . There is the Pan-German idea of Austria, and so Germany gravitates naturally towards the East, and acquires such an economic hold over the Turk that the three countries, Germany, Austria, and Turkey, come to form a trinity visible and indivisible. There is the idea of the Germans and the Turks swaying the East; there is the ever-present desire of emancipation from England and the attraction of Oriental colour and display, and the hope that in Turkey Germany's Nirvarna has been found—all these ideas, hopes, and reflections have at various times passed in kaleidoscopic vision through the German brain, and some of them have actually come to pass, whilst others seem near to completion." This statement, written in 1904, before Englishmen had even commenced to realize the true trend of German policy, admirably describes the magnetic attraction that compelled Germans towards the East.

Whilst the makers of modern Germany were engaged in consolidating her influence in Europe and the exponents of transmarine Imperialism were seeking outlets for German enterprise in Africa, the South Pacific, and South America; whilst German statesmen were drawing into the Teutonic net the Balkan States and were manacling the wrists of Turkey in economic and political gyves; whilst Germans were continuously pressing forward in Russia in the hope that the Muscovite giant might be securely bound with commercial bonds; other Germans were quietly surveying the theatre of operations in the Asiatic territories of the Sultan. The process of peaceful penetration, which was to precede political absorption, if indeed it were not at first a national policy deliberately engineered by the supreme rulers of the German States, was nevertheless a national aspiration and was forwarded and facilitated by the unofficial efforts of the advance agents of German civilization in the East.

The German mind intent, and rightly intent, upon the aggrandisement of the Fatherland, saw in Asiatic Turkey— an immense territory feebly held by a moribund Power, a territory where, owing to the unfortunate relations between France with her special interests in Syria and the Levant generally; Russia with her strong political position in the Transcaucasus and in the north-eastern regions of Asia Minor; and Britain with her waning influence at the court of the Sultan, but with her as yet almost unassailed commercial position at the Eastern ports, and her strategic interests in Egypt, and to a lesser degree in Mesopotamia—every opportunity for a bold and aggressive policy on the part of a fourth Power which, owing to the dissensions of the other three, might herself secure the paramount position. The opportunity in Asia Minor, so apparent to Moltke, was also realized by other German thinkers. In 1848 the economist Wilhelm Roscher, then Professor of Economics at Leipzig, wrote that Asia Minor would become in the future the portion of Germany in the spoils of Turkey,* and but a few years later, in 1853, that celebrated Pan-German idol Paul Anton de Lagarde stated that the most important task of German policy was the colonization of Asia Minor. All German people, he said, should co-operate for this desirable end, because in this task was to be found a means of linking Germans together in a common enterprise which would create a community of interest between the German States.† De Lagarde preached colonization and economic penetration to his countrymen as a means to a desirable end, and it may here be stated that undoubtedly one of the chief aims of the German expansionists, as had already been suggested by Moltke, was to turn the swelling tide of emigration into avenues where emigrating Germans would be of use to the Fatherland. It mattered little to the enthusiasts that Asia Minor was largely peopled by races of an alien creed and Asiatic civilization, or that Mesopotamia was unlikely

* *See* " La Question d'Orient," by André Chéradame, 1903, p. 3.
† *See* " Pan-Germanic Doctrine," p. 195.

to be a suitable country for extensive European settlement. The German leaven would not only gradually reform the country but extensive and homogeneous German communities would eventually cluster round the pioneer settlements. As will be seen later, this idea did not appeal to the Sultan.

Another economic writer, Friedrich List, whose reputation was by no means confined to the Fatherland, also recognized the economic significance of the East for Germany and enthusiastically supported Roscher's thesis that the current of German emigration should be directed away from America and towards " the rich portions, but little peopled, of Hungary, Moldavia, and Wallachia, towards Bulgaria and the northern coasts of Asia Minor." List believed that German unity would be achieved not merely by political means or through the deeply seated feeling of nationality and race, or even through the agency of wars, but by an economic development that would be shared by the Germanic peoples and would lead to the establishment of mutual interests and the forging of strong economic bonds. He believed that a nation is united by material interests rather than through any feeling of unity resulting from a common origin and a common language, and his programme, practical and comprehensive, has been realized in all its essential details with the exception of one —the concentration of the surplus German population in German territorial colonies. In the regions of the Near East and in Asiatic Turkey it would be possible, he thought, by peaceful penetration to create a new Germany, which would offer in grandeur, in population, and in riches to old Germany " the most solid bastion against the Russian danger and against Pan-Slavism."[*]

List's policy is worth some attention because he applied the doctrines of Adam Smith to Germany at a period when that country was divided into a number of loosely connected States without any definite political policy. "A vigorous German consular and diplomatic system ought to be established in these quarters [i.e. in Texas, Central and South America], the branches of which should enter into correspondence with one another. Young explorers should be encouraged to travel

[*] *See* " Deutschland und die Orientbahn," by Paul Dehn, Munich, 1883. Quoted by Chéradame.

through these countries and make impartial reports upon them. Young merchants should be encouraged to inspect them— young medical men to go and practise there. Companies should be formed and supported by actual share subscription, and taken under special protection, while companies should be formed in the German seaports in order to buy large tracts of land in those countries and to settle them with German colonists—companies for commerce and navigation, whose object should be to open new markets in those countries for German manufactures and to establish lines of steamships— mining companies, whose object should be to devote German knowledge and industry to winning the great mineral wealth of those countries." These ideals were also to be carried out in the East. "A similar policy," he wrote, "ought to be followed in reference to the East—to European Turkey and the Lower Danubian territories. Germany has an immeasurable interest that security and order should be firmly established in those countries, and in no direction so much as in this is the emigration of Germans so easy for individuals to accomplish or so advantageous for the nation. A man dwelling by the Upper Danube could transport himself to Moldavia and Wallachia, to Serbia, or also to the south-western shores of the Black Sea, for one-fifth part of the expenditure of money and time which are requisite for his emigration to the shores of Lake Erie. . . . Under the existing circumstances of Turkey it ought not to be impossible for the German States, in alliance with Austria, to exercise such an influence on the improvement of the public condition of these countries that the German colonist should no longer feel himself repelled from them, especially if the Governments themselves would found companies for colonization, take part in them themselves, and grant them continually their special protection." *

It would be quite possible to quote many other statements showing that previous to the construction of the Anatolian railways German attention was being directed to Asia Minor The stream of German thought, at first insignificant and almost entirely neglected, even by those who should have realized the drift of German policy, at length swelled into a mighty

* "The National System of Political Economy," by Friedrich List, p. 347.

current, especially after von der Goltz had undertaken the reorganization of the Turkish army. It was reflected in a thousand German newspapers and in numerous books and pamphlets. The tentative suggestions of Moltke and List, of Roscher and Rodbertus, the founder of so-called scientific socialism in Germany, who " hoped to live long enough to see Turkey fall into the hands of Germany and German soldiers upon the banks of the Bosphorus," were at length translated into definite schemes of commercial penetration and political control, based upon strategic considerations and upon the possibility of finally attacking Great Britain at one of the most vulnerable points of her great Empire.

The idea of a great German dependency in Mesopotamia gained many adherents in the Fatherland, where all who thought about the matter at all—and most Germans did—became convinced that Germany's destiny was to be traced along the projected course of the Bagdad railway and upon the plains of Mesopotamia. " If one can speak of boundless prospects anywhere," wrote Prince von Bülow, " it is in Mesopotamia " *
and the opinion that there was an opening " for German influence and German enterprise between the Mediterranean Sea and the Persian Gulf, on the Rivers Euphrates and Tigris and along their banks," was general throughout Germany.

The potential riches of Mesopotamia were constantly held out as a bait for the German investor. In 1886, Dr. Aloys Sprenger, the Oriental scholar, whose works on Mohammedanism are well known, published a pamphlet entitled " Babylonia : the richest country of the past and the most remarkable field of colonization of the present day," in which he stated that " of all the lands of the world there is not one more inviting for colonization than Syria or Assyria. In that country there are no virgin forests to be cleared away, no natural difficulties to be conquered, but it is only necessary to scratch the earth, to sow, and to gather the harvest. The East is the only territory in the world which has not yet been swallowed up by a Great Power. It is, moreover, the finest field for colonization. If Germany does not miss the opportunity but seizes it before the Cossacks advance from their side, she will have acquired the best portion in the partition of the world " ;

* " Imperial Germany," p. 96.

whilst a little later Dr. Kaerger elaborated the same idea in his pamphlet "Asia Minor: a field for German colonization." Like the economist List, he counselled the colonization of Asia Minor by means of large societies established in the neighbourhood of the Anatolian railway, and he demanded the immediate conclusion of a treaty between Germany and Turkey by which the Porte should be guaranteed against all aggression in return for concessions which would facilitate the directing of German emigration towards the fertile regions of Turkey, and the establishment, later, of a Customs union between the two countries.

Turkey was thus to become the political and economic vassal of the Fatherland in order that her future might be placed upon sound and solid foundations. "To create colonies and German culture in Turkey," wrote Kaerger, "is a plan which, without taking into consideration its political or commercial consequences, is of special importance for Pan-Germanism. Because of the situation of this territory not only should the German Empire but also the whole of the German people contribute to this task. The Germans in Switzerland and above all those in Austria should be called to co-operate in the work as well as those who dwell within the German Empire."* Here is expressed the idea originally formulated by Moltke. Common economic aims and co-operation for a mutual purpose would tend to establish the racial consciousness of the German people and to promote the movement for eventual political amalgamation.

This idea of political absorption was vigorously preached by the chief organ of the Pan-Germans, the *Alldeutscher Blätter*, which has on many occasions prepared the way for subsequent national action. "German interests," stated that journal on December 8, 1895, "demand that Turkey in Asia at least should be placed under German protection. The most advantageous step for us would be the acquisition of Mesopotamia and Syria and the obtaining of a Protectorate over Asia Minor. A Sultanate should be formed in the countries situated in the German sphere of influence, with a guarantee of the most complete autonomy for its inhabitants"; whilst in the next year the Pan-German League published a pamphlet

* *Alldeutscher Blätter*, 1895, p. 224.

entitled "Germany's claim to the heritage of Turkey," * in which it was stated that neither the people of Anatolia nor the Arab tribes of Syria and Mesopotamia would oppose an occupation of their lands. Mesopotamia, in the pregnant phrase of the writer, would become " Germany's India." The fundamental ideas of the organizers of *Deutschthum* in the East are admirably expressed in this pamphlet. In fact the time was rapidly approaching for Germany to advance boldly upon the path of empire. " The Anatolian lands," wrote Dr. Grothe, " as the Bagdad railway, must belong to Germany ; for in some place or other Germany must set down her foot firmly. . . . Asia Minor of all countries is the place for the German emigrant."

* "Deutschland's Ansprüche an das Turkische Erbe," 1896.

CHAPTER II

THE STRATEGIC IMPORTANCE OF ASIA MINOR

THREE factors were instrumental in directing German attention to Syria, Asia Minor, and Mesopotamia—the strategical, political, and economic. In the case of a great military and naval Power such as Germany was rapidly becoming it is natural that attention was devoted to the first of these three important considerations, and it is therefore necessary to consider what part Asia Minor was called upon to play in the strategical destiny of the Fatherland. For this purpose it will be well to consider briefly how important, if not paramount, was the position of Asia Minor, used in the widest extension of the term, in ancient times, when the vast conquering nations of antiquity were at the zenith of their power.

Mesopotamia itself, the country between the rivers, forms one of the most remarkable regions in the world. Stretching between the two mighty waterways of the Tigris and Euphrates and spreading from the foothills of the Armenian Mountains to Bagdad, and thence by extension to the head of the Persian Gulf, it forms a natural avenue between the East and the West, a strategic highway of supreme importance narrowing to a comparatively small outlet into Persian waters, and an economic road over which were carried the riches of Asia to be exchanged for the products of Europe. Held successively by the Assyrians, Babylonians, Persians, Greeks, Romans, Arabs, and Turks; the home of many of the mighty cities of antiquity, such as Babylon, Nineveh, Asshur, Edessa, Hit, Ctesiphon, and Thapsacus; crowded with the wonderful ruins of buried civilizations and holding in its alluvial lands the secrets of primitive ages—it presents a standing evidence of the frailty of all things and of the permanence of change and decay. Mighty emperors have held sway over its destinies; warriors have crossed its torrid and sweltering lands in their journeys of conquest. Here were the palaces of Sennacherib and Assurbanipal; of Nebuchadnezzar and Tiglath-Pileser. Here marched Alexander on his way to the conquest of India, Trajan, Julian, Saladdin, and the romantic Haroun-al-Raschid, who made Bagdad the centre of all the wit, learning, and art of the Moslem world; and to these regions have turned the thoughts of conquerors and warriors in all ages of the world.

It is obvious that a country which has played so important a part in history—from whose bosom have sprung many of the civilizing agencies of the past; which has attracted the adventurous from all parts of the known globe—must possess qualities and resources of an uncommon order. As will be shown later, its fertility and agricultural possibilities were remarkable, as indeed they are at the present day, resulting in an extraordinary abundance of material resources and in a profuse distribution of riches amongst its inhabitants. But in addition to its extraordinary fertility it was the highway of antiquity and the clearing-house of commerce. Germans, with their keen eye to commercial advantage and with their appreciation of strategic values, have recognized, in spite of new strategical and commercial developments, the possibility of re-erecting the ancient empires of the East and of reopening a great commercial and therefore strategical route from Hamburg to the Persian Gulf, and incidentally of attacking Great Britain in two of her most vulnerable points—Egypt and India.

Four main avenues of trade and commerce lead from Central Europe towards the East. The first of these finds its outlet at Trieste at the northern end of the Adriatic; but the entrance to this sea is commanded by the Straits of Otranto, and the rise of Italy as a naval and military Power has modified the strategic value of this route. To meet this growing danger, German attention was devoted to Corfu, where the German Emperor planned his summer residence, and where doubtless in the course of time the German flag would have flown over a territorial colony, and to Valona, the strategical pivot of the Adriatic and the key to Albania. The first of the commercial routes being threatened and subject to interruption in time of war, it became one of the main objects of Teutonic policy to obtain control over the second of these natural avenues of trade. This route passed through Belgrade, Nish, Uskub, through the gap between the western borders of the Rhodope and the coastal mountains and over the historic plain of Kosovo and by the valley of the Vardar to its outlet in the Ægean Sea at Salonika, whence by direct communication with Smyrna contact could be established with the commercial routes of the East. This highway, again the scene of bloodshed, is one of the most important avenues between east and west. "Can we wonder," writes Miss Newbigin in her book on geographical aspects of the Balkans, "that the plain of Kosovo has been time and again the scene of bloody slaughter ? Here, in 1389, the Turks routed the Serbs and made their long dominance sure ; here, in 1448, the Hungarians defeated the Turks, and made the end of that long dominance a probability of the future," * and here, it may be added, the Serbs made their last gallant stand against the onward rush of Teutonism. Through this valley runs the railway from Vienna and Budapest to Salonika, one of the destined feeders of the great Hamburg–Persian Gulf route.

The third of these great avenues of communication branches from the second at Nish, and entering Bulgaria by the junction between the Rhodope and the Balkans, near Sofia, descends to a broad valley leading ultimately to Constantinople by a road which has been traversed constantly by armed hosts proceeding across the passes of the Balkans. Through this passage runs the railway which was to be the great avenue of trade with Bagdad and the East. The fourth Teutonic outlet is along the Danube, and by the railways leading to Varna and Constantia, and thence, should the opportunity ever occur, across the Black Sea to Trebizond and the routes into North-Eastern Asia Minor. These are the natural outlets from Europe, should the great port of Odessa be left out of account, over which Teutonic influence was spreading and which were destined to join the projected Germanic confederation of States to the proposed Teutonic Empire over the Middle East.

So far as Asiatic Turkey itself is concerned there are many gateways into the rich territories that formed so tempting

* "Geographical Aspects of Balkan Problems," by M. I. Newbigin, 1915, p. 80.

a bait for the Germans, some of which are immediately available whilst others had fallen from their former great commercial positions. Of these Smyrna, with its great harbour, Mersina, and Alexandretta, a port on the gulf of that name (Iskanderum), are directly connected with the Anatolian railways; whilst Tripoli, connected by railway with Homs, Beirut, joined with Damascus, Jaffa, the port of Jerusalem, and Haifa—all communicating with the great railway from Mecca to Aleppo—were destined to form so many feeders to the German commercial system; whilst other ports, not less important, but long fallen into disuse, such as Suediah (the ancient Seleucia)* on the bay of Antioch would doubtless in the course of time have been connected with the system of railways that was to transform Asiatic Turkey. Further, the route through Haidar Pasha, on the Asiatic coast opposite Constantinople, was to be the main connecting-link between Germany and the East, and the head of the great railway system that was to bind Asia Minor in economic and strategic fetters to the Fatherland.

If we regard the position of these territories in the past we shall see that they formed the great battle-ground of antiquity. But for our immediate purposes we need only study their position as they affect the present relations between Europe and Asia. In the long struggles between Persia, Egypt, and Greece, the Mesopotamian routes were constantly used by the invading armies. The operations of the contending forces were facilitated by the valleys through which flowed the Euphrates and Tigris, of which the strategic values are not less at the present day than they were at the time of Cyrus and the Ten Thousand. They still form the connecting-links between the East and the West, dependent upon the successful application of sea-power for their greatest utility to any attacking nations with the exception of Germany and Russia, whilst

* The importance of Suediah from a political and commercial point of view cannot be doubted. "The ancients well knew the value of its position, for it was the great highway to Europe and Asia: then, as now, it commanded the road to the Northern and Western nations." ("Memoir on the Euphrates Valley Route," by Sir W. P. Andrew, 1857, p. 77.) It was this point which was fixed upon by Napoleon when he prepared to proceed to the Euphrates in 1811. The place forms the key to Antioch and Aleppo, and it has been suggested that a landing of the Allies in this neighbourhood would do much to render the Turkish communications insecure.

STRATEGIC IMPORTANCE OF ASIA MINOR

in the case of the latter country the command of the Black Sea is a factor of great value. But though it is obvious that these routes were alike the scenes of military invasion and commercial operations, it is also clear that there were causes at work that robbed them of their value, and eventually almost completely severed communication between East and West. The downfall of Persia, the decline of Egypt and Greece, the long decay of the Roman Empire, and finally the age of mediæval darkness which spread like a pall over Western Europe and was succeeded by the blighting influence of the Ottoman Power, caused the decay and ruin of the Asiatic provinces and resulted in the stoppage of all commercial intercourse.

From the close of the thirteenth century to the second decade of the sixteenth, a period of a little more than two hundred years, the rising power of the Turks constantly extended the area of their political control, until the power of the Sultan was exercised, north and south across the Levant, from the steppes of Russia to the confines of the Sudan. When the Ottoman power in Europe reached its zenith at the end of the sixteenth century, practically all Hungary, Transylvania, Bukowina, Bessarabia, the Danubian provinces of Moldavia and Wallachia, Bosnia, Serbia, the Balkan Peninsula, Greece, and most of the Ægean islands were in Turkish hands or were Turkish tributaries; whilst the Black Sea was a Turkish lake, the Crimea was in Turkish hands, and Vienna itself was threatened by the swelling Mohammedan tide. In Asia and Africa the Ottoman power extended over all the territories which had formerly been the centres of European trade and commerce. The Turkish lands thus came to intercept all the great routes which in ancient and mediæval times had carried the trade between East and West, and although the Turks were not actually opposed to commerce, they were determined that the threads of it should be held in their own hands.

A great barrier therefore existed between Europe and Asia, and intercourse gradually became less and less frequent over the trade routes of Asia Minor and Mesopotamia. But, and this is the point that is too frequently overlooked, the greatest disaster to the land-borne trade of the Levant occurred through the discovery of a new route to the East passing around Africa, and the consequent rise of the Portuguese power.

The Levantine trade forsook its old courses for the cheaper and probably safer routes around the Cape; and within a few years there was a readjustment of the economic balance in favour of Western Europe but to the disadvantage of the purely Asiatic route.

The mediæval trade routes between Western Europe and Eastern and Southern Asia fell into two groups; the northern, which passed mainly by land, and the southern, which passed mainly by sea. The former communicated with Central Asia, China, and India through the Black Sea and Asia Minor; the latter through Syria and Egypt. Each group had branches, which entered Asia Minor near Aleppo and diverged in the direction of Tabriz and Bagdad.* At the beginning of the fourteenth century there were five principal routes of commerce with the East: (a) the land route from the mouth of the River Don on the Sea of Azov, by the north and south of the Caspian Sea to China, (b) the road from Trebizond on the Black Sea to Tabriz and Central Asia, (c, d) the two ways from the Gulf of Alexandretta to Tabriz and to Bagdad and the Persian Gulf, and thence to India, and (f) the route up the Nile and thence across to Kosseir on the Red Sea. Of these routes that through Aleppo alone seemed to have survived as a great highway in the crash which followed the establishment of the Turks in Constantinople.

The mercantile travellers who followed the last-named route carried their goods as far as Bir on the upper waters of the Euphrates, where they would remain until it was possible to descend that river to Bagdad or some other point of departure for the land routes to the East, or proceed to the port of Basra on the estuary of the Tigris and Euphrates. Upon the revival of interest in the Euphrates route at the end of the sixteenth century, several European travellers made journeys to the East along this waterway. In 1574 Leonard Rauwolf, and in 1579 the Venetian merchant Gaspard Balbi, went this way, and two years later the Englishman John Newbery made the same journey. In 1583 Ralph Fitch sailed down the Euphrates, and was followed in 1599 by Sir Anthony Shirley, and at about the same period by John

* See "The Ottoman Turks and the Routes of Oriental Trade," by A. H. Lybyer, *English Historical Review*, vol. xxx, pp. 577–89.

Cartwright, the latter voyages being the first attempts to establish commercial communication between England and India by means of the Mediterranean routes.

It is therefore apparent that in the Elizabethan age the main commercial centres in what may be termed the Mesopotamian regions were at Aleppo, Bagdad, and Basra, just as at the present time the chief economic-strategic points are these cities, with the addition of Constantinople and Adana. This route, as will be seen later when the history of the Bagdad railway is examined, had peculiar strategic advantages for England, just as the alternative route from Constantinople has for Germany. Moreover it was the Aleppo-Bagdad-Basra route that Napoleon, who contemplated following in the steps of the Emperors Trajan and Julian, decided upon when he was formulating his scheme for the conquest of India. Basra, one of the most important commercial points in the East, was to be the pivot of his operations against our Indian dependency. The schemes of Napoleon have a direct bearing upon the present situation, for they show how history constantly repeats itself under various forms and combinations. Napoleon aimed not only to deliver a staggering blow against British prestige in India, but also desired to secure the domination of the Levantine route to the East. These are the two dominant aims of Germany in building the Bagdad railway and in overwhelming those Balkan States that have opposed her advance. The thrust from Belgrade means nothing less than the aim of Germany to dominate the East. An arm driven from Belgrade, whether the elbow rest upon Salonika or Constantinople, will inevitably grasp in its fist, if unopposed, the two ports of Koweit and Basra and eventually strike at the heart of India.

The policy of Napoleon in the East has been ably dealt with by several authorities, but there are nevertheless many points that still require elucidation, especially in connexion with the negotiations with the Emperor Alexander and the failure of the French plans for an invasion of India through Russia and Persia. For present purposes it is only necessary to remember that the Napoleonic scheme may be divided into three sections or periods, determined by the then political conditions of Europe and the then grouping of the Great Powers.

In each case, with the exception of the Russian plan, they were defeated owing to the inability of the French to retain command of the sea, and in this respect they differ considerably from German schemes for the domination of Turkish Asia, which do not depend upon sea-power for their successful accomplishment. As is the case with the German plans, the aims of Napoleon were not unconnected with commercial schemes; for the persistence of French designs against India was as much determined by the desire of France to seize from Britain the trade in indigo, sugar, and cotton as by military necessity. The Napoleonic schemes, although audacious in view of the fact that Great Britain was predominant on the seas, were by no means chimerical on the part of a ruler who desired to re-establish the former credit of the French name in the Levant, to utilize the resources of Egypt in order to nourish and re-create an army of invasion, and to establish once more French ascendancy throughout Syria.

The invasion of Egypt, which ended so disastrously for French arms, was in itself a part of a larger scheme for opening the Red Sea routes to French commerce and depended for its ultimate success upon a better organization of the French colonies in the Indian Ocean—the Ile de France, Réunion, and Madagascar—and better means for the support of the French fleets in the East, as well as upon the control of the Mediterranean. This plan to conquer India, through Egypt on the one hand and through the agency of the French strategic outposts in the Indian Ocean on the other, and by that means to secure a revenge against British maritime supremacy, was not in itself an original idea of Napoleon. The German philosopher Leibnitz, in writing to Louis XIV, had stated that " the possession of Egypt will open a prompt communication with the richest countries of the East, will join the trade of the Indies to that of France, and will prepare the way for great commanders to march to conquests worthy of Alexander " ; and in 1672 he was summoned to Paris to explain this plan to Le Roi Soleil. But, so far as I am aware, there is no evidence that this plan was known to Napoleon at the time of his Egyptian expedition (1798), although it was subsequently communicated to him when Mortier, commanding the army of occupation in Hanover, found a copy of the memoir in the library of that city.* The plan suggested by Leibnitz was, however, merely the formulation of a desire frequently expressed that the old trade routes across Syria or down the Red Sea should again be made available for European commerce. Various schemes of this nature were put forward from time to time, either in the name of religion or of commerce. Thus a former French Consul at Damietta, Jean Coppin, suggested in the year 1686† that France should establish protectorates over Tunis, Bona (Algeria), Corinth, Constantinople, Adrianople, Brussa (Asia Minor), and Lower Egypt, and thus anticipated in some important respects the subsequent course of French expansion in the Mediterranean; whilst an Austrian subject, Dominique Jauna, suggested in the year 1747 the conquest of Cyprus and Egypt by a coalition of Christian princes in order that the Mohammedan power might be overthrown in two places that were considered to be vital strategic points.‡

French influence was considerable in the Levant and the possibility of reopening the old trade routes exercised a peculiar fascination over many responsible authorities. Thus in the eighteenth century an alliance with Russia was suggested, during the visit of Peter the Great to Paris, for the purpose of opening a continental highway to India,§ and subsequently, in 1787, the same idea was formulated by the Marshal de Castries, who suggested the possibility of "attacking the English establishments in India with an army which should leave Astrakhan and march through Bokhara" to the confines of India.

Inquiries had been made as to the possibility of such a plan, particularly in conjunction with Russia and Persia. In 1781 the French Consul at Bagdad forwarded a memoir through the French Ambassador in Turkey on the possibility of ousting Turkey from Mesopotamia, and the Ambassador was specially instructed to furnish a comparison between the two

* A précis of this document was published at Paris in the year 1805 in the "Voyage de Hanovre," by Mangourit. See "Les Origines de l'Expédition d'Egypte," by F. Charles-Roux, 1910, p. 22.
† See his "Bouclier de l'Europe ou la Guerre sainte."
‡ See his "Histoire générale des Royaumes de Chypre, de Jérusalem, d'Arménie, et d'Egypte."
§ See "Les Colonies françaises," by Marcel Dubois and Auguste Terrier, 1902, p. 44.

journeys to India by way of Suez and Basra respectively and to supply " exact maps both of the Red Sea and its coasts and of the principal places in Egypt." *

The check to Napoleon's plans occasioned by the collapse of the Egyptian expedition led to a renewal of the suggestion for attacking India by land, but the death of the Emperor Paul in 1801 put a temporary stop to the negotiations. Paul had been greatly influenced by the secret communications of the First Consul, who doubtless did not fail to impress upon the Russian sovereign the wisdom of the supposed will of Peter the Great, which was stated to contain the following passage : " I recommend all my successors to realize this truth, that the trade of the Indies is the trade of the world and whoever is able to control it exclusively will be the real sovereign of Europe. In consequence we should never miss any opportunity of exciting wars in Persia, to hasten the disintegration of that country, to penetrate to the Persian Gulf, and to attempt then to re-establish the ancient commerce of the Levant through Syria."† The plan for an invasion of India by this route has not received the attention it deserves, partly because the tragic end of the Russian Emperor caused its immediate abandonment and partly owing to the fact that documentary evidence, save of secondary importance, is wanting.‡ Nevertheless there are two documents extant which reveal the projected course of the expedition. The first of these is entitled " Sketch of a Plan of Campaign against the English Establishments in India arranged by Bonaparte and Paul I," and is contained in the papers of the Baron de Stedingks. From this account it appears that it was the French plan to transport an army of 35,000 men from Ulm, with the consent of Austria, down the Danube, which would be conveyed by a Russian fleet across the Black

---

* A French Consul was then resident at Basra with a Vice-Consul at Bagdad. It was computed that a messenger from Marseilles to Bombay could travel over the Mesopotamian route in forty-eight days.

† This will of Peter is generally regarded as apocryphal. Indeed there is excellent testimony that the Russian sovereigns themselves did not believe in its existence, for in Prince Hohenlohe's Memoirs it is said that the Emperor Alexander stated, when staying at Livadia in 1876, that the will did not exist. (Hohenlohe, vol. ii, p. 183.) Nevertheless the ideas supposed to be formulated in this document have guided Russian policy during the last two hundred years.

‡ *See* Dubois and Terrier, p. 71 *et seq.*

STRATEGIC IMPORTANCE OF ASIA MINOR

Sea, whence it would be taken along the Don and across to Tsaritsyn on the Volga in order to descend that river to Astrakhan. There a Russian army of the same number would join the French contingents and the combined armies would advance upon India by the right bank of the Indus, through Herat and Kandahar. The second document, which was published in 1849 as an appendix to the Memoir of Leibnitz to Louis XIV, contains further details, but does not reveal the source of information. It should be specially noted in connexion with this plan that both the Don and the Volga were to play an important strategic part in Russo-French plans of conquest.

These schemes were not renewed until 1805, when General Decaen, in command at the Ile de France, was instructed to prepare the way in the Indian Ocean for a French attack upon India, which apparently was to come from two directions—through Egypt and the Persian Gulf, and by way of the Cape. The landing of a British army in South Africa rendered the position less favourable and the project was allowed to lapse until Napoleon again coquetted with the Eastern Powers, entered into a treaty with Persia—(Do we not see the same plans, *mutatis mutandis*, employed by Germany at the present day?)—and was again compelled to relinquish his plans by the state of affairs in Europe. These plans, as is well known, were favoured by the Emperor Alexander I, who succumbed to the fascination of Napoleon at Tilsit in July 1807, and during a prolonged interview in a barge moored in the middle of the Niemen agreed to divide with the Western Emperor the hegemony of the world.

But the whole scheme came to an untimely end with the rupture of the Franco-Russian Alliance and the disastrous invasion of Russia in 1812; and from that period to the present time there has been no attempt to revive these grandiose plans of conquest. That Napoleon, having failed to secure the co-operation of Russia, regarded the invasion of that country as part of a greater scheme for the conquest of India is certain. Speaking to M. de Narbonne on the eve of his departure for Russia he said: "After all, this long road is the highway to India. Alexander the Great went as far as I am going in order to reach the Ganges."

An examination of Napoleon's strategy shows that he

had determined to reach India in one of three ways : through Russia, through Mesopotamia, or through Egypt and the Red Sea. In the present era we are witnessing the revival of similar schemes on the part of another Power, by the second of the routes chosen by the great French adventurer, but with this great difference—Turkey was then hostile to France, but is to-day entirely friendly to Germany. The Hamburg–Bagdad route is merely the modern translation of an extremely ancient document.

As was the case with Napoleon, this policy of Eastern expansion has been dictated by the impossibility of a Western advance so long as Great Britain holds her present dominating position as a sea-Power. The whole of Germany's sea-commerce comes out of the small triangle of which Heligoland forms the centre, or through the narrow waters between Denmark and Norway, which, as has been seen during the present war, can be blocked by the British fleet. Ninety-five per cent. of this traffic passes through the Straits of Dover, whilst even the 200 miles broad northern passage between the Orkney Islands and Norway can be successfully held by British sea-power. Even should these outlets be passed the Mediterranean can be blocked at Gibraltar, and only at the Dardanelles and the Bosphorus does British naval power cease.* " The geographical importance of these straits to Germany," states a well-known German authority, Dr. Gerhard Schott, " consists not only in their quality as a fortified highway, but also in the fact that they are a joint bridge-head in the great trans-continental world-traffic route of the future, Berlin–Vienna–Constantinople–Bagdad–Persian Gulf–Indian Ocean, a route independent of Great Britain and controlled by the Central Powers. Here is our future. Here, even in time of war, we shall have a way open to the important oceans of the world. Its maintenance is a question of life for the Central Powers." This statement reveals the importance of Mesopotamia to Germany. The ancient highway of the East was to become the modern avenue of Teutonic commerce and is the strategic key to German schemes of aggression against the maritime Powers of Western Europe.

* *See* the Lecture by Dr. Gerhard Schott, Director of the Hamburg Naval Observatory, before the Austrian Geographical Society on November 29, 1915.

STRATEGIC IMPORTANCE OF ASIA MINOR 45

Apart from the question of the construction of railways in Asiatic Turkey, which will be discussed later, there has existed in Germany, and still exists, much confusion of thought with regard to the strategic and political value of the Sultan's Asiatic territories. Three parties, holding somewhat divergent ideas, have studied the question from the Teutonic point of view, and have formulated theories with regard to the future of these countries that it is somewhat difficult to reconcile with each other. In the first place there are those who believe that a strong Turkey, able to hold her own against all comers in Asia Minor, at least politically, would be the best guarantee of Germany's ultimate economic success in the Anatolian and Mesopotamian regions. These look to economic rather than to political absorption, though as a matter of fact it is impossible to conceive that Germany, in secure possession of economic supremacy, would be content, or even able, to refrain from also exercising political and military control. In the second place there are those who hold that the ultimate destiny of Asiatic Turkey is to become a Germanic protectorate under the direct suzerainty of the Kaiser, who would thus rule over, or at any rate direct the policies of, a confederation of States stretching from the North Sea to the Persian Gulf, and as the Protector of Islam would be enabled gradually to extend his influence over other Mohammedan countries; whilst there is a third party, exemplified by Herr Ballin and the shipping magnates, who dislike the continental policy embodied in Mesopotamian adventures and believe that the salvation of the Fatherland will only be found in " freeing the seas " from Britannic predominance. These look upon Eastern expansion as a purely subsidiary movement unlikely to be of any great service to the Empire so long as Germany is unable to counteract the sea-policy of her maritime enemies. Hamburg, and not Belgrade, should be the keystone of the German arch.

The first of these views has been expressed by Field-Marshal von der Goltz, who, more than any one else, has been instrumental in establishing German influence at Constantinople. On various occasions he has advised Turkey to abandon her European and African possessions in order to establish herself firmly in Anatolia, with Mesopotamia as a background.* By so doing

* *See* " The Pan-Germanic Doctrine," p. 209.

she would be able to consolidate her position, carry out the necessary reforms, strengthen her military power, and doubtless, under German inspiration and guidance, offer a firm front to Russian and British aggression. Germany would then seek compensation in Syria and Palestine and as a friendly neighbouring Power be able to direct and influence the policy of a re-established Turkish Empire. On the other hand, Dr. Paul Rohrbach, the German colonial expert and indiscreet friend of colonialism, who has so frequently exposed the plans of his countrymen, has stated that " a strong political and military Turkey might enable us to find in the territory of the Euphrates a strengthening of our position and an improvement of our economic situation. For a weak and feeble Turkey not a penny,* but for a strong Turkey let us give all the money that is necessary."† Possibly Rohrbach dreaded the extension of Slavic influence in the Balkans owing to the growing power of Bulgaria, and believed that a strong Turkey would be an efficient counterpoise to such disruptive tendencies. In any case his political foresight has not been justified by the course of events. But Chéradame, the French expert, writing about the same time, showed a better appreciation of the situation when he stated that " Hungary is Germany's client, Rumania her satellite, *Bulgaria a broken barrier*, Bosnia and Herzegovina the gates to the East, whence Germany will proceed over the Bosphorus to Asia Minor," ‡ and in those pregnant sentences summed up what was the general opinion prior to the Balkan Wars.

* The importance of strengthening Turkish power in Mesopotamia was emphasized in an article in the Russian newspaper *Turkestanskaya Viedomosti* on December 1, 1914, in which the writer said : " The geographical position of Mesopotamia, between the Eastern provinces of Turkey and Western Persia, affords a point of contact between the two most important Mussulman kingdoms in Central Asia. Till recently the paramount European influence, political and economic, in Mesopotamia and the Persian Gulf was exercised by Great Britain. But the German has sought to establish his influence in this region, and the railway of Asia Minor, with its terminal point at Bagdad on the Tigris, is the result. The strengthening of Turkish influence in Mesopotamia was entirely consonant with German aims. The inhabitants of Mesopotamia consist chiefly of Arabs, Kurds, Syrians, and Armenians. Of Turks there are practically none—a fact which was bound to reflect on the stability of Turkish rule. Owing to the absence of good communications within the district, the Turks are practically unable to enforce their sovereignty, which in the valley of the Tigris and Euphrates is merely nominal."
† " *Die Bagdadbahn*, 1902, p. 16.
‡ " L'Europe et la Question d'Autriche."

The whole question is of course intimately connected with the Bagdad railway and cannot be considered apart from that undertaking, which was regarded by the best military opinion to be a strategic avenue of the first importance. Whether it would eventually lead to a vast increase of Turkish or German military strength, or to both, does not affect the question of strategic values; for whilst Asia Minor is for the Sultan or the Kaiser a magnificent reserve of soldiers, its full resources, owing to the absence of routes and the impossibility of rapidly concentrating the Ottoman forces, could only be made available by its construction. "From the military point of view," stated Lieutenant-Colonel Rogalla von Bieberstein, "the railway will facilitate a more rapid concentration of the forces in Asia Minor, whether it be at Constantinople or upon the north-east frontiers of Asia Minor, against Russia." This truth is self-evident, and it matters little in the present grouping of European Powers whether Germany or Turkey rules in Asia Minor. As has before been indicated, and is also as self-evident as the strategic value of the Sultan's Asiatic domains, Asia Minor was also to be utilized as a weapon of offence against Great Britain. "If it came to a matter of war with England," stated the redoubtable Rohrbach, "it would be for Germany simply a question of life or death. The possibility that events may turn out favourably for us depends wholly and solely upon whether we can succeed in bringing England herself into a dangerous position. That cannot be done by a direct attack in the North Sea. All idea of invading England is purely chimerical. We must therefore look for another combination that will enable us to attack England at a vulnerable spot—and this brings us to the point where, as regards Germany's policy, the situation in Turkey and the conditions prevailing there decide that policy, the corner-stone of which to-day is to keep her attention riveted upon England." *

In other words, in seeking for a formula Germany recognized that only in the East could Great Britain be attacked with any chance of success—a position to which our statesmen have been singularly blind. Foreign observers realized this fact long before it was generally recognized in England. In this connexion it is only necessary to read what two keen American

* *Die Bagdadbahn*, 1911, p. 18.

observers have written upon this subject. The late Homer Lea, in spite of the absurdity of some of his views, nevertheless correctly gauged the course of Germany's Eastern policy. " As the value of Holland to the German Empire," he wrote, " lies without itself, so is it true of the extension of German sovereignty over Austria. It is not the twenty millions added to the German race or their territory that constitutes the value of Austria to Germany. It lies in Asia Minor. It belongs to the Mediterranean. Already this Teutonic race, certain of its destiny, conscious of its strength, has stepped across the Bosphorus. As Germany gains a sea by the occupation of Denmark, so Austria brings to her another. With the absorption of Austria, the Mediterranean and its littoral passes within the environment of Berlin. The destruction of Austrian sovereignty is the means to a great end. There is a savage sublimity in this thought—to use empires as stepping-stones."* The strategic importance of Asia Minor and its value both to Great Britain and Germany are more clearly expressed by the late Admiral Mahan, who, whilst stating that preponderance of political influence is conferred by commercial enterprises for the development of a country, " provided the nation by which they are undertaken supports them by its power, expressed by its wealth and, in case of necessity, by its organized military forces," wrote that " the irreversible fact remains that in the entrance of the Black Sea, in the valley of Mesopotamia, and in the table-land of Asia Minor, by virtue of their natural features, of their extent, and of their central position, rests an ultimate control of the Eastern Mediterranean resembling that exercised some centuries ago by the Ottoman Turks." He stated further that a highly developed modern State firmly planted in Turkey in Asia, with an efficiently organized army and navy, coasting the Black Sea, the Persian Gulf, the Red Sea, and the Levant, would control issues from vast territories to the outer world. " The creation of such a political entity and its development on healthy lines are as much one of the problems of Asia "—and, it may be added, of Europe—" and as important as China itself. The latter is primarily and chiefly a region simply of production ; the other, while not barren in this aspect, would fulfil the far more vital rôle of controlling

* " The Way of the Saxon," 1912, p. 146.

communications. In superiority of interests to the world at large, therefore, its power excels." *

To sum up : it is evident that Turkey in Asia, with Egypt, holds a predominating position in world-strategy; that the possession of the one entails in the long run supremacy over the other, since nothing remains stationary and empires rise and fall; that whilst Britain has established herself in the latter country she has been slow to recognize the necessary and vital connexion between the two spheres of influence; and that Germany, profiting by this weakness in the Britannic strategic chain, determined to establish herself in these regions in order eventually to dominate Asiatic communications. A strong and independent Turkey, indifferent alike to Great Britain, Russia, and Germany, might have effectually preserved the balance of power in these regions, but a weak, disorganized, and un-neutral Turkey was bound eventually to fall under the domination, military, political, and strategic, of whichever Power was prepared to stake its existence on the future control of the great Eastern highway.

* " The Problem of Asia," pp. 71–2.

CHAPTER III

THE BAGDAD RAILWAY

In the wide scope of their aggressive imperialism, the Germans, like the Romans of old, have sought to dominate the routes of land communication with the East. They have endeavoured to foist upon those nations who have been unfortunate enough to occupy the avenues of communication, first by economic, then by political, and finally by military methods, their own culture and civilization and to break down all opposition by the sheer weight of the military engine that during the last fifty years has been fashioned in the Fatherland. From the earlier conception of Pan-Germanism, as a welding together of the disunited elements of the German race into a united and homogeneous people, they have advanced by successive stages towards the dream of world-domination, and like the Romans they are now endeavouring to create a world-empire to which other nations shall be compelled to bring their unwilling tribute. One of the chief weapons in this phantasmagoria of rampant imperialism was to have been the Bagdad railway.

It would be interesting, but nevertheless beyond the province of this book, to draw a comparison between Roman, German, and British imperialism. It has long been the fashion amongst a certain school of political thinkers whose knowledge, such as it is, has been rendered useless owing to the peculiar bias of their preconceived notions, to talk of the British Empire as though it were a new and improved edition of Roman policy; to imagine that the peoples of the King-Emperor have been held in subjection by the military power of the central authority; to regard the subject races within the British Empire as ruled by the fear of the sword; and to look forward to the time when the sacred principles of nationalism shall have taught them to throw off the yoke of a foreign conqueror. In this respect the sentimentalists of Britain and the expansionists of modern Germany have been at one. Nothing, save the stern lessons of practical experience, would convince the former that the British overseas Empire was not subjected to an intolerable yoke ; nothing, save the illuminating lessons of the present war, could convince the latter that the so called subject-peoples of Greater Britain and the natives of India were not ready to rise in rebellion against the British power.

The Germans neither understood nor appreciated the special position of the overseas Dominions. They were completely ignorant of the fact that the British self-governing States were not peopled by subject races ; because in the ardent prosecution of their own imperialism they could not conceive the possibility of any colonial empire existing as an independent and almost equal unit within a greater political system. They could not realize the fact that races subject to imperial power in those provinces that did not possess representative or responsible institutions could enjoy personal liberty and retain personal rights ; because in their own overseas Empire no such phenomenon was possible.

The dangerous fallacy that the people of the British Empire have been subjected to a central military authority has been directly responsible for this startling misconception of British imperialism even by those German authorities who have been best qualified to judge the scope and achievements of British policy. The Pax Britannica has to them no special meaning. Such a system neither existed nor was possible within the area of the German Colonial Empire.

A comparison between British and Roman imperialism reveals therefore this enormous, and to the Germans startling, difference between the two systems. The Roman Empire was primarily the creation of the sword and spear ; the British Empire the product mainly of the plough and the axe. Roman policy was centred in the Mediterranean and dominated a compact and closely allied system of States, contiguous in territory, and bound together by military roads or by easily controlled sea-routes ; the British Empire was established upon all the seas, which separate but nowadays do not divide, but least of all has it been founded upon that *mare clausum* which for the Roman Empire was the main avenue of commerce and trade and represented what at one period the Thames must have been for London—the beginning and end of all trade routes. As Sir Charles Lucas has stated in the admirable survey of imperialism contained in his book, " Greater Rome and Greater Britain," " the Roman Empire was one, the British Empire is two in one ; each of the two halves of the British Empire contains the most diverse elements ; one half is a political structure which has no common ground whatever with the Roman Empire and cannot be compared with it in any way ; the other half admits of comparison but still more of contrast." *

But if we compare the Roman system with what the German Empire is, and still more with what it was intended that it should become, we shall find many and striking similarities in the mosaic of the imperial design. The framework of imperialism in both is dominance. It was the ambition of Germany to compel all who should become subject to her sway and should shelter under the protecting ægis of her superior culture to exclaim with pride in the might of the Central Empire, *Civis Germanicus sum.* It is not necessary to carry the comparison along the logical avenues that might be followed, or to study further the methods of German imperialism except in so far as they relate to the creation of those main routes of commercial and military power which are designed to bind closely together the future Teutonic system of subordinate States.

Germany as a land-empire, seeking as one of her main purposes the domination of the great land-routes to the East, had endeavoured in these modern days of rapid transit to control rail-power and gradually but persistently had worked towards the complete mastery of the routes of commerce leading to the East. The growth of railways has been contemporaneous with the increase of German military power, and the construction of the Bagdad railway and its associated lines " can best be compared with those roads which the Romans, in the days of their pride—the pride that came before their fall—built for the better achievement of their own aims as world-conquerors. Apart from the fact that the roads now in question are iron roads, and that the locomotive has superseded the chariot, the main difference between Roman and German

* " Greater Rome and Greater Britain," 1912, p. 155.

is to be found in the fact that the world which the former sought to conquer was far smaller than the one coveted by the latter." *

In considering the Bagdad railway and what it means to Germany it would be well to bear in mind that German imperialism aimed at two diverse but closely connected objects—the destruction of British sea-power and the substitution of German maritime dominion in its place, and the creation of a great land-empire, independent of sea-power, stretching from the North Sea to the Persian Gulf. Which of these two ideals was the predominating aim of German policy it is not possible to say. The complete achievement of the one was in a large measure dependent upon the accomplishment of the other; but it must nevertheless be realized that either could be accomplished with a large measure of success without the immediate execution of the other, but not less important, plan. The building of the German fleet and the creation of the German army were therefore the two chief weapons that were forged in the armoury of German imperialism to secure the ultimate control of the destinies of Europe, and consequently of the rest of the civilized and uncivilized world.

The policy which resulted in the construction of the Bagdad railway was, as has been shown, no new or impulsive movement. It was the child of Pan-Germanism begotten of the direct needs of German commercialism, of which militarism became the active and aggressive guardian. As has been seen, the idea was present in the minds of many Germans long prior to the more recent extensions of Teutonic policy, and was current in German circles even before the Fatherland was established as a homogeneous political unit. What Moltke thought others were not slow to teach, and the present Emperor, representing in his own person and correctly interpreting the desires of millions of his subjects, threw the whole of his influence into the political balance on the side of expansive imperialism. Nothing save a direct military defeat could stop the current that was welling from the deep springs of national ambition —a river that swept against the roots of the racial solidarity of other nations and threatened to overthrow the tree of nationalism in all European countries.

* " The Rise of Rail-Power," by E. A. Pratt, 1915, p. 344.

The construction of a railway through Asia Minor to the head-waters of the Persian Gulf might have been undertaken by the British Government at a period when Germany was as yet indifferent to the urgent calls of imperialistic adventure, and the political future of a large portion of the Sultan's dominions might have been directed into other channels had British statesmen been as fully alive to the importance of land-dominion as they were convinced of the superiority of sea-power. But the construction of the Suez Canal, the spinal cord of the British Empire as it was termed by Bismark, diverted their attention from the possibility of securing yet another link in the chain of communications between Great Britain and her eastern dependency, and as the guardians of the commercial destinies of the Britannic system of States they did not appreciate the political desirability of opening a way across the torrid and sweltering land of Mesopotamia to the countries of the Middle East. The commercial possibilities of such a line were not sufficiently inviting to a nation that seldom thought save in terms of money, and strategical and political reasons were not sufficiently realized by the Governments that happened to be in power. In proportion as British influence declined in European and Asiatic Turkey after the golden period when Lord Stratford de Redcliffe's nod was welcomed as law at the court of the Sultan, British attention became more and more exclusively devoted to preventing Russia from operating upon the sick man at Constantinople, and in consolidating and strengthening the sea-routes upon which the British Empire mainly depended for its existence. So long as Russia appeared to threaten the safety of India scant attention could be paid to subsidiary objects; and no thought at all was devoted to the possibility of any other nation driving a wedge through the Balkans and thrusting across the Bosphorus a military arm towards the coveted outlets upon the Persian Gulf.

The failure of the promoters of the Euphrates Valley railway was due both to political and economic causes. Although Turkey, then almost completely under British influence, was willing that the line should be built and was prepared to give every facility for its construction, both France and Russia were opposed to the extension of British interests in Mesopotamia—France thinking that her undoubted interests in Syria were seriously threatened and Russia believing that the time was not far distant when she would be able to advance across the Armenian Taurus.

The first proposals for a railway from a port in the Mediterranean to the Persian Gulf were made by Francis Rawdon Chesney, then a young officer in the British army, whose remarkable surveying work in the Euphrates Valley forms one of the most interesting episodes in Asiatic travel. Chesney, who explored this district in 1831, had learned during a visit to Egypt in the preceding year that Lord Aberdeen was making inquiries as to the best line of communication with India, and conceived the idea that a railway from one of the ports opposite to the Island of Cyprus to the head-waters of the Euphrates, and water transport down that river to Basra, would provide a quick and excellent route to the East; whilst at some later period the railway itself might be extended to the Persian Gulf. Such a railway, stated M. Jules Falkowski, "will exercise a decisive influence upon the future of the Ottoman Empire, which has its real basis in Asia. No political measure can possibly have the same efficacy in regenerating the old Asiatic East, that is to say, bring back cultivation, industry, commerce, and the arts of those celebrated countries which were once the cradle of civilization, and consolidate the power of the Porte by centralizing the scattered yet vivacious forces which it possesses,"* whilst Sir William Andrew, who worked incessantly on behalf of the scheme, reported that through the agency of the proposed railway "the quiet possession of British India would be secured and the advancing standards of the Barbarian Cossacks who would overshadow the world would recoil before those emblems of power and progress, the electric wire and the steam-engine, and his ominous tread be restrained behind the icy barrier of the Caucasus." These statements were written, of course, before the construction of the Suez Canal, but they show that both French and British were fully alive to the political value of a railway to the East.

During his first journey, Chesney took elaborate soundings

* "Memoir on the Euphrates Valley Route," by Sir W. P. Andrew, 1857, p. 225.

of the Euphrates and came to the conclusion that there were two difficulties in the way so far as the actual route was concerned. For two years he besieged the various authorities with his pet scheme, secured the interest of King William IV, Lord Stratford de Redcliffe, and other important men, and managed to get a Select Committee appointed in order that the scheme might be considered in all its aspects. As a result the British Government sent out two subsequent expeditions, of which the first, under the command of Chesney, set sail for the Bay of Antioch in 1835, transported two steamers in sections from Seleucia to Bir on the Upper Euphrates, and after strenuous labours reached the mouth of that river, having proved that the Euphrates was navigable from within a short distance of the Mediterranean coast. But unfortunately nothing was done to carry Chesney's theories into operation.

The scheme for connecting India with England was again under consideration in 1856, when Sir William Andrew took active steps to bring the question before the public. A fresh expedition was organized and the result was extremely satisfactory; but at this period the Government did not dare to encourage a scheme which was regarded with hearty dislike by Lord Palmerston's ally, Louis Napoleon. In 1871 a strong committee of the House of Commons, of which Sir Stafford Northcote was chairman, again considered the project, when several authorities spoke strongly in its favour. Amongst them, the former British Ambassador to Turkey (Lord Stratford de Redcliffe), fully aware of the importance of binding Turkey to Great Britain by economic as well as by political ties, urged the Government to take steps to provide an alternative route to India; whilst Lord Strathnairn (Sir Hugh Rose), Sir Bartle Frere, Mr. William Gifford Palgrave, Sir Henry Rawlinson, Sir William Mackinnon, Sir Richard Burton, Sir Henry Green, and Sir Donald Macleod—authorities who were fully competent to give an opinion—were also in favour of a direct railway between the Mediterranean and the Persian Gulf. Moreover the Indian Government expressed " an earnest desire that it may be found practicable to carry out the project," and Musurus Pasha, one of the leading Turkish statesmen of that period, who was then Ambassador in London, wrote on August 7, 1871, that he would like to see constructed a railway from Constantinople to Basra, and that "the Imperial Government would readily grant the same terms for making it, but as I fear this is more than can be accomplished at present, I content myself with the line from the Mediterranean to the Persian Gulf."

Three factors, in addition to the political position, militated against the success of the Euphrates Valley railway scheme. The first was the construction of the Suez Canal, which opened a short sea route to the East. De Lesseps himself had been strongly in favour of the railway. "I have personally maintained," he wrote in the *Railway Times* in 1857, " and I shall continue to maintain, that the Euphrates Valley railway will be a benefaction to countries now disinherited, and, what is more, my experience of the Arabs and of the deserts of Arabia leads me into the persuasion, in opposition to what is generally believed, that the pretended difficulties as to the maintenance and safety of the railway are prejudices as baseless as the fears respecting the silting up of the Suez Canal." The second factor was the cost of the railway, estimated at from eight to ten million pounds, and the probability that it would not be a commercial success. The third factor was the belief of many authorities that the intense heat of Mesopotamia would prevent, for a considerable portion of the year, the use of the railway for the conveyance of troops and that its strategic value would thus be considerably lessened.

The opposition to the Euphrates railway scheme was well put by Lord Curzon, who, writing some years later (in 1892), stated that "its superficial attractions, judiciously dressed up in a garb of patriotism, were such as to allure many minds," and stated that he himself had felt, "without having ever succumbed to, the fascination." The grounds upon which such a railway should be constructed and by which the policy of constructing it might be determined were fourfold : physical, political, military, and economic. " I believe," stated Lord Curzon, " that in each of these respects the scheme of a Euphrates Valley railway, if tried, will be found wanting. The temperature in these sandy wastes is excessively torrid and trying during the summer months, and I decline to believe that during half the year any general in the world would consent to pack his soldiers in third-class railway carriages for conveyance across these terrible thousand miles, at least if he anticipated using them in any other capacity than as hospital inmates at the end. Not only does it ignore the true strategical line for the defence of Asia Minor, which lies greatly to the north (within the radius of Urfa, Diarbekr, Mardin, and Mosul),* but laid as it would be across a lengthy and utterly unprotected length of country, the railway would be peculiarly exposed to attack, and would consequently provide a most unsafe line of communication in time of war. But strongest of all are the commercial and fiscal objections."†

Nevertheless, in spite of these strategical objections, it is to be regretted that this railway was not constructed, for it is probable that had it been in existence when the Germans first became active at Constantinople their subsequent policy would have been considerably modified; whilst Great Britain's position in Mesopotamia would have been assured and the painful operations that are now taking place would in all probability have been entirely unnecessary. The Bagdad railway depends for its strategic success entirely upon military power, whereas the Euphrates Valley railway, from Seleucia, Alexandretta, or whatever other Syrian port might have been selected, would have depended in the main upon sea-power for its success and defence.

The Bagdad railway, which was to be the instrument of German expansion in the East, the iron fist thrust at the heart of Asia, was commenced less than thirty years ago; for it was not until September 1888 that the Germans secured their first railway concession in the Asiatic dominions of the Sultan. But before entering upon the intricate history of the construction of this line it will be well to examine German opinion as to its significance for the Fatherland, so as to realize what grounds there have been for the feverish anxiety of the German Government that this great engineering work should be pushed to a rapid conclusion. The Germans have thoroughly realized that in the construction of economic-political-strategical lines joining East and West lay their best chance of ensuring the establishment of the German Middle-Asian Empire, bringing under Teutonic control the entire region from the Mediterranean to the Persian Gulf, and providing convenient stepping-off

* The route at first selected by the Germans for the Bagdad railway.
† "Persia and the Persian Question," by Lord Curzon, vol. i, 1892.

places from which an advance might be made on Egypt in the one direction and India in the other." *

As has been the case in Africa, where they sought to establish their predominance as a great Central African Power, and to attain this end pushed forward the construction of the Tanganyika railway, joining the Indian Ocean to the central lake system—in this respect taking a leaf out of the British book—and planning and commencing other scarcely less important routes; so in Asia Minor they endeavoured to secure their position by means of the iron fetters placed across Turkish soil. "The Germans have a great strategic interest," wrote Lieut.-Col. Hildebrant in 1902, "in the Bagdad railway, for in the case of the eventual blockade of the Suez Canal, a blockade which in consequence of political difficulties or later of military operations is not to be considered as impossible, this railway line will constitute for Germany the most direct route to the East of Africa and of Asia"†; and in the same year Dr. Rohrbach, perhaps the most active exponent of Bagdadism, wrote exultingly in the *Zeit* that "now there is no longer any doubt. The company of the Anatolian railways, which is under the direction of the German Bank of Berlin, will have the technical and financial control of the enterprise. That is to say, that the Bagdad railway is in fact a German enterprise, as has been desired, in spite of the jealousy of our adversaries at Constantinople." ‡

A little later the true inwardness of the Bagdad policy, so far as Africa and Asia are concerned, was revealed by the same writer in the following passage in his book on this subject, the opening sentences of which have already been quoted (p. 47). "England," stated Rohrbach, "can be attacked and mortally wounded by land from Europe only in one place —Egypt. The loss of Egypt would mean for England not only the end of her dominion over the Suez Canal, and of her connexions with India and the Far East, but would probably entail also the loss of her possessions in Central and East Africa. The conquest of Egypt by a Mohammedan Power, like Turkey, would also imperil England's hold over her sixty million

* Pratt, *op. cit.*, p. 331.
† *Revue internationale über die gesammten Armeen und Flotten*, March 1902.   ‡ *Zeit*, January 30, 1902.

Mohammedan subjects in India besides being to her prejudice in Afghanistan and Persia. Turkey, however, can never dream of recovering Egypt until she is mistress of a developed railway system in Asia Minor and Syria, and until, through the progress of the Anatolian railway to Bagdad, she is in a position to withstand an attack by England upon Mesopotamia. . . . The stronger Turkey becomes, the greater will be the danger for England, if, in a German-English conflict, Turkey should be on the side of Germany; and, with Egypt for a prize, it would certainly be worth the while of Turkey to run the risk of fighting with Germany against England. . . . The policy of protecting Turkey, which is now pursued by Germany, has no other object than the desire to effect an insurance against the danger of a war with England."

Elaborating the same ideas in further articles he tried to show that Egypt was indeed "the spinal cord of the British Empire." "If England should lose Egypt and the Suez Canal," Rohrbach stated, "she would have no solid outpost upon the route to the East. For on the day when she may be reduced, in order to maintain her position in Asia, to rely upon her possessions at the Cape, one will see how far the Boers are racially conscious and how little regard they have for England. There is therefore not the least exaggeration in saying that Egypt is the keystone of the British Empire. If England lose Egypt there is an end to her position as a world-power. When the German Emperor sought the friendship of the Turks, when he lent them officers for their army, when the Deutsche Bank commenced to construct a railway which one day, when it is connected with the Syrian railways, will enable the transport of Turkish troops to the Egyptian frontiers, the English thought, ' These are the first scratches of the German claws! Germany foresees that a conflict with us is about to take place, since to hold the markets of the world is for her and for us a question of life or death. And she in turn prepares, now that we have withdrawn, alas, the clutch that we had upon her throat at Heligoland, the place where she can throttle us at her ease.' The encircling policy directed by England against Germany has no other reason." * The construction of the Bagdad railway,

* "L'Evolution de l'Allemagne comme Puissance mondiale," in *La Revue Politique Internationale*, 1914, No. 7, pp. 28-29; translated from the German of Paul Rohrbach.

quite as much as the building of the German fleet, was the German reply to our cession of that tiny island in the North Sea which was in itself the key to German world-power.

Many other equally illuminating passages might be quoted to show the inner significance of the German intrigue at Constantinople and to demonstrate how German activities in all parts of the world fit piece by piece into the great design of aggressive Pan-Germanism. "May the new century not finish," wrote Dr. Hugo Grothe, "without a proper settlement of the colonization question in Mesopotamia, so that near German villages German ploughs and spades may do their work; that in the plains that adjoin the Euphrates and Tigris, and in the country lying between Aleppo, Urfa, Mardin, and Nisebin, German hands may raise cornfields such as those in the south of Russia; that German vineyards may be cultivated in the valleys of the numerous rivers which flow from the Taurus mountains similar to those in Palestine and the Caucasus, and may it help to the economical welfare of Turkey and our progressive growth."* Two other opinions on the importance for Germany of the Bagdad railway may be quoted. In the *Neue Zeit*, Herr Karl Radek wrote that "the strengthening of German imperialism, the first success of which, attained with so much effort, is the Bagdad railway; the victory of the revolutionary party in Russia; the prospect of a modern revolutionary movement in India . . . the movement towards nationalism in Egypt; the beginning of reform in Persia— *all this has raised to an extraordinary degree the political significance of the Bagdad railway question.* The Bagdad railway, being a blow at the interests of English imperialism, Turkey could only entrust its construction to the German company, because she knew that Germany's army and navy stood behind her, which makes it appear to England and Russia inadvisable to exert too sensitive a pressure upon Turkey"; whilst Professor R. Mangelsdorp, a well-known authority on German foreign policy, stated that "the political-military power which organized railway systems will confer upon Turkey is altogether in the interest of Germany."†

* Quoted by Dunn from Grothe's *Die Bagdadbahn*.
† Quoted by D. McLaren in his "An Australian in Germany," 1911, pp. 299-300, from *Die Neue Zeit* for June 2, 1911, and *Akademische Blätter* for June 1, 1911, respectively.

It will be noticed that in all these statements practically no mention is made of Russia—a highly significant omission in view of the direct Russian interests that were threatened by the German advance to Bagdad. Britain was the enemy, not Russia, which apparently opposed the success of German imperialism. Yet it was the opposition of Russia which brought about the diversion of the railway to a more southerly route than had at first been proposed, and Russian interests in Transcaucasia were perhaps on the whole more directly threatened by the German advance than were those of Great Britain at Bagdad. The construction of a line towards Bagdad by the route at first proposed by the engineer von Pressel, by way of Angora, Amasia, Sivas, Diarbekr, Mardin, and Mosul, would not only have followed the true strategical line for the defence of Asia Minor, and by means of a branch railway have brought the great fortress of Erzerum in direct communication with the Turkish capital, but it would have avoided the serious engineering difficulties connected with the crossing of the mountainous region known as the Taurus. Had such a line been in existence at the outbreak of the present war it is probable that the Russian advance on Erzerum would have been counteracted by the excellent facilities that would have existed for transporting troops to the threatened districts. To this extent, therefore, Russia checkmated German plans, and by so doing should have reaped the usual harvest of hatred and recrimination.

The construction of the Bagdad railway was in reality the eastward extension across the Bosphorus of the great system of railways that had been planned to carry German commerce towards the Adriatic and Ægean Seas. German activities in this direction were seconded by the group of international financiers whom Bismark affected to despise, but who, nevertheless, by advancing the money for the making of railways through Austria-Hungary and the Balkan Peninsula, rendered possible the realization of German designs. The strategic value of such railways was fully recognized by Moltke, who, in a letter written in 1844, declared that whilst Germany was building railways the French Chamber was only discussing them, and a little later (in 1851) a scheme was drawn up in Austria for the con-

THE BAGDAD RAILWAY 63

struction of railways from the special point of view of strategical requirements.*

Through the genius and activity of Wilhelm von Pressel, who died at Constantinople in May 1902, almost in penury, after having planned and carried out a great series of railways for the financial magnates of Vienna, Berlin, and Paris, the arms of Germany were thrust across the Balkans in the direction of Asia Minor. Von Pressel was at first employed by the brothers Pereira of Paris on the network of railways in Northern Switzerland; and later, from 1862 to 1870, he constructed on behalf of the Austrian Südbahn, patronized by the Rothschilds of Vienna and Paris, certain important lines in the Tyrol, Carinthia, Styria, Carniola, and Hungary. It was the enterprises of Baron Hirsch that led von Pressel to turn his attention to Turkey, and in 1872 he was invited by the Ottoman Government, upon the initiative of Edhem Pasha, Minister of Public Works, to give his advice upon railways in Asia Minor.†

As an enthusiastic engineer he soon realized what an important, if not paramount, part railways would play in the regeneration of the Turkish Empire, and after the construction of two lines from Haidar Pasha, opposite Constantinople, to Ismidt, he suggested the continuation of the railway through Angora to Bagdad, choosing this route because the cost of construction of a line to the south, passing through the Taurus, would be much greater, and also because ": the adoption of the southern route would have the infallible consequence of rendering Smyrna superior to Constantinople; for it is Smyrna which would thus become the head of the line throughout Anatolia. If this route be adopted this movement would become more and more accentuated and would result in the commercial ruin of Constantinople." ‡ This possibility was, however, obviated by the simple device of blocking the line from Smyrna to the interior at the point where it approached the Bagdad railway.

Previous to the commencement of the Bagdad railway only one short line had been constructed upon the proposed route

* Pratt, *op. cit.*, pp. 8–9.
† *See* his " Les Chemins de Fer en Turquie d'Asie," 1902.
‡ Quoted from his book.

—that from Haidar Pasha to Ismidt, which was finished in the year 1873. Nothing further was done until 1888, when Mr. Alfred Kaulla obtained a concession to continue the railway as far as Angora—a section which was intended to be the first portion of a great strategic-economic line running through the centre of Asia Minor to Bagdad. Although Mr. Kaulla's name alone appeared in public, he acted in reality as the mandatory of the Deutsche Bank of Berlin and of the Württembergische Vereinsbank of Stuttgart,* and thus was the agent of Germanic interests in the East. A little later (from 1893 to 1896) a further branch was constructed as far as Konia and the present Bagdad railway took its first definite direction towards the Persian Gulf.

From this time forward the most persistent endeavours were made to obtain a concession for the construction of a railway to the Persian Gulf. The first results of the Anatolian railways having been found to be satisfactory, German engineers, surveyors, and military officers were sent to Asia Minor to study the proposed routes and to prepare the way for the coming economic invasion. German attention became fixed on Anatolia, and with their usual Teutonic thoroughness Germans began to prepare the way for its coming commercial conquest. An interesting atlas of the country was published in 1898 † as well as a most important work entitled " Kleinasiens Naturschatze," the joint production of two German officers, Lieutenants Karl Kannenberg and Schaffer. From the commercial point of view Asia Minor was being studied in every direction. From the political and strategic standpoint it was being carefully examined in connexion with the larger schemes of world-policy favoured at Berlin.

It was at this period that the most striking impetus was given to German enterprise in the Near East by the dramatic visit of the Emperor William to Constantinople and Palestine. The journey, which was undoubtedly the result of long and carefully considered plans, was timed at a well-chosen moment ; for the shadow of the Boer War was stealing across the political horizon, Lord Kitchener was advancing in the Sudan, whilst

* Chéradame, p. 21.
† " Handels und Produktenkarte von Kleinasiens," by Dr. E. Friedrich, 1898.

the coming dispute between Britain and France over the valley of the Nile could be anticipated by any one with an inner knowledge of the clash of colonial interests in those regions. In another chapter the Kaiser's visit to the Sultan and his spectacular tour in the Holy Land have been described. It is only necessary here to emphasize the fact that the tactics employed by the Emperor in dealing with Abdul Hamid were entirely successful and that the greatly desired concession for the construction of a railway to the Persian Gulf was as a result soon forthcoming.

This concession, which is exhaustively analysed by Chéradame, provided for the construction of a railway from Konia, through Adana, Haran, Mossul, and Bagdad, as far as the great port of Basra, situated about sixty-seven miles up the Shatt-al-Arab from the point where the combined rivers Tigris and Euphrates fall into the Persian Gulf. It also provided for the construction of branches, one of which was to run to Aleppo and another from Zobeir (close to Basra) to a "point on the Persian Gulf to be determined upon," evidently meaning the important strategical harbour of Koweit. In addition the concessionaires obtained certain rights of navigation on the Tigris and Euphrates as well as an annual guarantee of 16,500 francs per kilometre against possible loss—12,000 francs for construction and 4500 for working when the line was opened.

The building of the Bagdad railway, politically, financially, and structurally has been a slow and laborious process. Interests had to be conciliated, the necessary funds provided, rival nations had to be jockeyed out of their privileged positions, and, above all, the support of Turkish politicians had to be bought at a price. It is not proposed to describe here the sordid financial business connected with German railway exploitation in the East. The details are exceedingly complicated, and indeed practically unknown save to those who have been personally benefited by the immense sums of money which have been squandered over the venture. Although the railway is not completed, not less than £12,000,000 can have been expended previous to the outbreak of war, since which time the construction has been carried on with feverish haste.*

* The capitalized value of each of the twelve sections of the line was estimated at 54,000,000 francs.

The primary conception of the Germans has been to risk no money without the most absolute guarantee against its loss. Herr Gwinner and his associates of the Deutsche Bank, in spite of the fact that Russia and Britain, and finally France, boycotted the bonds, have nevertheless proved themselves masters of finance in providing the funds necessary for construction. The iniquitous system of kilometric guarantees has already cost Turkey many millions of pounds. It has been computed that between 1889 and 1909 Turkey spent over ten millions sterling in thus guaranteeing the success of the Anatolian, Bagdad, and other railways, or, in other words, in securing German capitalists against the loss of their money. What other country in the world could have been forced into thus paying for money which had been offered at much better terms in other quarters?

But the German financial magnates held Turkey completely at their mercy. The Deutsche Bank, directly or indirectly connected with the greatest financial concerns of the Fatherland, such as the mines and docks of Herr Thyssen, the steamships of Herr Ballin, the engineering works of Herr von Rathenau, was able to exercise a crushing financial control over the enterprise. Although both Russia and Britain were asked to participate in the venture—that is, to lend money but not to assume their proper share of political control—they held aloof; the former because she believed it was an aggression against her influence in the Caucasus and Persia, the latter because she did not then desire the continuation of the line to the Persian Gulf. French financiers were more complacent, however, although M. Delcassé had expressly stated that his Government could not advise the participation of French capital unless guarantees were obtained that such capital should have a share in the direction, construction, and exploitation of the enterprise.*

* " When the secret history of the Bagdad railway is revealed it will become obvious that the interests of France were betrayed mainly by M. Rouvier and his syndicates. We have it on the authority of M. Chéradame that M. Rouvier, before becoming French Minister of Finance and Prime Minister, controlled a private bank which had extensive dealings with the omnipotent Deutsche Bank, and which was financially interested in the great German railway scheme. Indeed M. Rouvier, a French Minister of Finance and Prime Minister, appears as a financial agent and mandatory of the Deutsche Bank." (Sarolea, p. 272). " All the leading men whom I have

THE BAGDAD RAILWAY

The political, like the financial, history of the Bagdad railway is a maze of complications. Whilst Europe was engaged in preparing for the coming Armageddon, a diplomatic struggle of the first magnitude was proceeding over the question of the Bagdad railway. The full history of the prolonged negotiations involving the British, German, French, Russian, and Turkish Governments, if it could be written by any of the chief actors in the diplomatic drama, would form an interesting and deeply instructive study. At present little save the broad outlines of the struggle are known, or likely to be known, to the general public.

In 1903, when the Bagdad railway was for the first time under the consideration of the British Government, an outline of the German proposals was submitted to Parliament, but no agreement was come to because of the dispute regarding the final section of the line from Bagdad to the Persian Gulf. Owing to the important British interests in the head-waters of the Gulf, it was of paramount importance that Great Britain should have more than a nominal share in the control of the final section of the railway. The attitude of the British Government with respect to the terminus of the railway roused the wrath of German chauvinists. The *Frankfurter Zeitung* innocently proclaimed that the railway was a purely commercial affair. "While people in Germany have accustomed themselves to treat the Bagdad railway as an exclusively commercial affair, Englishmen are apparently unable to divest it of the political aspect with which it has been artificially endowed. English supremacy in India, control of the Persian Gulf, the pretended protectorate over the Turkish town of Koweit, all serve as a basis for demands directly concerning what is, indisputably, Turkish territory." The *Vossiche Zeitung* kindly stated that "the Wilhelmstrasse will repay Downing Street on the Persian Gulf for unfriendliness shown in the Morocco question," whilst other papers tried to work up an agitation

met in Turkey, Frenchmen or foreigners—and amongst them many consuls and members of the diplomatic body—consider M. Rouvier as the very active collaborator of German policy in Turkey; nay, the word has been used to me, as the agent of the Deutsche Bank." (Chéradame, p. 275.) These are, of course, political views which cannot be discussed here, but they throw an interesting sidelight on the division in France which existed upon the question of the Bagdad railway.

against Great Britain. The question of Koweit was in reality the crux of the whole matter and the wrath of Germany was aroused owing to the fact that she was again balked in her attempt to secure an entry into the Persian Gulf.

The subsequent history of the railway may be passed over until the year 1911, because however interesting are the events in themselves they do not specially bear upon the progress of Germany towards the East. But in that year, on March 18, two important conventions respecting the railway, which may be regarded as supplementary to that of 1903, were signed between the company and Turkey. The first related to the prolongation of the line from El Halif to Bagdad, and made the necessary financial provisions for the construction of this portion of the railway. This section was to be completed within five years from the assent of the Government to the company's plan of construction. The second convention conferred upon the company the right to build a branch line to the Mediterranean at Alexandretta, a railway of about thirty-eight miles in length but of enormous importance as a connecting-link in the route from Salonika to Asia Minor.

The position of the German company at Alexandretta was further strengthened by the arrangement for the construction of a new port, with the necessary docks and wharfage accommodation. Alexandretta, in fact, seemed destined to become a most important German commercial, if not strategical, stronghold. Further, after the signing of the two conventions, a declaration was handed by the company to the Grand Vizier regarding the conditional renunciation of its rights to construct the line from Bagdad to the Persian Gulf. This last arrangement, the precise terms of which were not made known, but which were undoubtedly in favour of Germany, was due to the opposition of Great Britain to the construction of this final section of the line by Germany. Although a compromise had apparently been arrived at, the price of this compromise was the important port of Alexandretta. In 1903, Abdul Hamid had resolutely opposed German claims to this port. By securing what was practically a lease of one of the most important harbours on the eastern sea-board of the Mediterranean, with a trade valued at three and a half millions sterling annually, the Germans would have been able to obtain a virtual monopoly of the trade passing through these important regions and South-Western Anatolia would have become a German reserve.

But the portion of the conventions that led to the greatest controversy, and to negotiations that were not finally concluded at the outbreak of the present war, was the knotty question of the control of the Bagdad–Basra section of the line and its extension to a port on the Persian Gulf. The full history of these negotiations is not known. The British Foreign Office maintained the profound and disquieting secrecy which has been characteristic of all diplomatic action since the days of Lord Palmerston, and such information as was vouchsafed from time to time may be compared with the crumbs that fell from the rich man's table. So far as Great Britain was concerned negotiations were carried on directly with the Porte and only at a later stage with Germany; but all the time it was apparent that German influence was directly behind the Turkish Foreign Office and that the Porte was only the intermediary between the two parties. Both Lord Morley and Lord Haldane took part in the business, the former going to Germany in 1911, the latter spending a "holiday" there a little later—when questions other than those connected with the Bagdad railway were fully discussed. If secrecy be the essence of diplomacy there can be no doubt that our diplomatic emissaries performed their duties with tact and discretion; for the man in the street, although aware that important negotiations were pending and important decisions were being arrived at, received no information that was likely to lead to an outburst of popular feeling in the country. His enthusiasms or dislikes, if he had any, were carefully avoided.

Germany, whilst abandoning her claims to the construction of the Bagdad–Basra section and agreeing that this portion might be built under international control, nevertheless stipulated that the share to be given to the Bagdad Railway Company should not be less than that assigned to any other country, and further that the share of the Turkish Government should not be less than forty per cent.—thus establishing a preponderance for Germano-Turkish influence. This condition was naturally unacceptable to Great Britain, for the Turkish Government having regained its liberty of action regarding the section of the railway between Bagdad and the Persian

Gulf, " His Majesty's Government now wish to arrive at a settlement which would remove all apprehension that the Bagdad railway and its terminus would create diplomatic friction between the parties interested " *—a feeling to which the German condition certainly would not conduce.

In the meantime, by the Potsdam agreement arrived at during the meeting of Tsar and Kaiser in November 1910, Russia finally decided that she did not desire to have any voice in the control of any portion of the Bagdad railway, and in return for stipulations safeguarding Russian interests agreed not to place any difficulties in the way of the scheme. The true reason for the withdrawal was, however, an arrangement whereby Germany agreed not to oppose the construction by Russia of a railway in the north of Persia if she might be permitted to build a railway from Bagdad to Khanekin, an important city on the Persian borders from which it was eventually intended to construct a line to Teheran. Had this been done a severe blow would have been struck at British trading interests in this quarter, for the Bagdad-Khanekin trade route had been developed exclusively by Englishmen, and our trade over it already amounted to more than one million sterling a year, compared with less than £100,000 as the value of the goods contributed by all other European countries.† Whatever was the nature of the agreement with Russia, her withdrawal tended to weaken British influence and eventually led to the abandonment of any British claim to participation in the construction of the Bagdad-Basra section.

For two more years the long and tedious negotiations with the Turkish Government continued in their secret courses, but matters began to move when, in February 1913, Hakki Pasha arrived in London in order to expedite the discussion between Great Britain and the Porte. A number of conventions were prepared, and on May 30 Sir Edward Grey made an important announcement as to the scope of draft agreements with the Turkish Government. The object of the Porte in thus hastening the negotiations had been twofold—to remove British objections to the proposed increase in the Turkish customs duties and to enable Germany to carry the railway as

* Speech by Lord Morley in the House of Lords, March 22, 1911.
† *Asiatic Quarterly Review*, 1911, p. 233.

far as Basra. The increase of the customs dues, which directly or indirectly would be applied to the construction of the railway, had to be vetoed unless British interests were protected by some binding agreement.

In the preparation of the new conventions the spirit of compromise came to the aid of the German financiers who were sheltering behind the skirts of the Turks. Great Britain not only recognized the suzerainty of the Porte over Koweit, which was to be an autonomous district of the Ottoman Empire, but also definitely left to Germany the construction of the section as far as Basra. In return for these concessions, the Porte (*a*) engaged not to interfere with the internal affairs of Koweit and explicitly recognized the validity of the concessions concluded between the Sheikh and the British Government; (*b*) abandoned its pretensions to suzerainty over the Peninsula of Al Katr, the Bahrein Islands, Muscat, and the territories of the Trucial Chiefs in the Persian Gulf; (*c*) and recognized the right of Great Britain to undertake in the future, as in the past, the duty of policing, buoying, and lighting the Gulf. In addition there were to be two British directors on the Railway Board as a guarantee against differential rates.

The agreement outlined by Sir Edward Grey also recognized that "the navigation of the river up to and beyond Bagdad is a substantial British interest which may be developed and consolidated." If Basra were to be the terminus of the railway, the settlement of the long-standing difficulties connected with the navigation of the Shatt-al-Arab was an urgent necessity, especially as in the Karun River, which flows into the Shatt-al-Arab, Great Britain had direct and highly important interests. The value of these interests need not be enlarged upon here, but it is satisfactory to notice in connexion with the successful German drive across Asia Minor to Basra that she failed in two important respects: (1) to secure the harbour of Koweit, (2) to obtain the control of the immensely valuable oil-fields in the delta of the Euphrates River and particularly in the neighbourhood of the Karun River. These petroliferous areas of enormous richness, where as much oil was running to waste in one day as is produced in Canada in a year, were being developed by a company on behalf of our own Government. The territories of the Anglo-Persian Oil Company formed a tempting bait for the Germans, but they were too late to secure their possession.*

The preliminary arrangement with Turkey was heralded in Germany as a triumph for German diplomacy. The *Berliner Tageblatt* on December 29, 1913, stated that " for years this undertaking has threatened to become a bone of contention between Russia, England, and Germany. The German Government has now, through its cleverness and tenacity, succeeded in removing all differences, and in bringing the line altogether into German possession." This is nothing more than a statement of fact. Without blaming our own diplomacy in the matter unduly or emphasising its want of continuity and excess of vacillation, a measure of respect cannot be withheld from German statecraft which during the whole proceedings connected with the railway, financial and diplomatic, displayed an adroitness in meeting and overcoming the opposition of Great Britain, France, and Russia that showed the Germans to be able, if not masterly, negotiators. The position was doubtless turned to their advantage in many ways by events in the larger sphere of world-politics, but nevertheless the difficulties in the way of the Germans were sufficiently pronounced to have turned aside any diplomatists but the most tenacious and persistent.

The sudden outbreak of war in August 1914 put an end to the Anglo-German negotiations. An arrangement with Germany had become necessary after the negotiations with Turkey had been concluded. The former negotiations had been strictly with the Porte as a sovereign Power, though nevertheless Germany had been consulted at every step. "Hakki Pasha," stated "Asiaticus" in the *National Review*,† " who handled all the negotiations with the Foreign Office, though nominally

---

* The dispatch of the Admiralty Oil Commission in 1913 must have been a severe blow to the Germans, for not only was it reported that the areas around the Karun River were of exceptional richness but also that oil was to be found in many portions of the Persian Gulf littoral, at Koweit, Burgan, Bahrein, Daliki, Lingeh, Kishm, and Sirim—all places which but for British foresight might have fallen into the hands of Germany. It may be noted that the pipes bringing the oil from the fields to the port of Abada and the Persian Gulf were cut by Persian tribesmen, acting under German instigation, on February 5, 1915—a poor but annoying revenge for the loss of the fields.

† March 1915.

the representative of Turkey, in reality represented Germany. He never took any step while he was in London without consulting the German Embassy, and no decision was agreed to without reference to the German Foreign Office."

Little is known about the negotiations carried on between Berlin and London subsequent to the agreement with Turkey, but on June 15, 1914, six weeks before the war, the following Reuter telegram from Berlin was published in the English Press : " The Anglo-German agreement regarding the Bagdad railway and Mesopotamia has been initialled in London by Sir Edward Grey and Prince Lichnowsky, the German Ambassador. A complete understanding has been reached on all points at issue. The agreement will not come into force until after the conclusion of the negotiations with Turkey, as on some material points the assent of the Porte will be necessary. The contents of the agreement can, therefore, not be divulged at present." On June 29 Sir Edward Grey briefly announced : " We have made various agreements with Turkey; we have made agreements also with Germany separately on the Bagdad railway and some kindred matters. We have also made agreements with Turkey about the Bagdad railway and kindred matters, and about the Persian Gulf generally." And there the matter rested until the stern arbitrament of war cut short all negotiations and left the unsigned documents to their rest in the pigeon-holes of the Foreign Office, from which it is to be hoped they will never be withdrawn.

" In tracing the development of German expansion in Asia," states Mr. Sarolea in his book on Anglo-German relations, " we shall find one additional proof of the absurdity of the German grievance that England has pursued a policy systematically hostile to Germany. We shall see that in the case of the Bagdad railway not only have the Powers of the Entente Cordiale done nothing to oppose Germany, but that French statesmen have again and again promoted German claims, and that England in her desire to conciliate her neighbours has betrayed some vital imperial interests, and has allowed Germany to assume a formidable position, threatening both Egypt and India, a position from which she is not likely to retreat, and yet from which she will have to retreat if an armed conflict is to be avoided." An examination of the Bagdad negotiations reveals the justice of this contention.

At the commencement of the Bagdad troubles Great Britain, Russia, and France had almost equal claims to participation in the enterprise, but each in turn abandoned these claims in favour of Germany, whose interests in reality bore no comparison with those of the Entente Powers. Russia, who in 1900 had been able to divert the line to the southward,* withdrew all opposition ten years later. France, by the agreement of February 15, 1914, in exchange for the recognition of a railway " sphere of action " in the north and north-west of Anatolia and in Syria, definitely withdrew from participation in the Bagdad railway,† and Great Britain, as has been seen, withdrew all opposition in 1911, and only safeguarded her special and unique position in the Persian Gulf.

The Bagdad railway, which has been a continuous menace to the peace of Europe during the last ten years, was not completed at the outbreak of the war. The line starts from the palatial railway station at Haidar Pasha on the Asiatic shore of the Bosphorus, and passing through Konia (Iconium), one of the most ancient and important cities of Asia Minor, proceeds over a level plain to Bulgurlu (reached in 1904), a few miles beyond Eregli, where commences the gradual ascent into the foothills of the Taurus Mountains. There for some years the rails remained poised over the edge of the desert because the German financiers who had pocketed considerable sums over the construction of the railway across the less difficult country were not disposed to disburse their savings by squandering money in the mountainous Taurus region. But financial difficulties were overcome and within the past two and a half years the line has been carried through the country between Eregli and Adana by a series of tunnels, bridges, and viaducts. The Baghtche Tunnel (16,028 feet long), undoubtedly the most important work in railway construction in Turkey, was almost completed at the end of 1915. The construction of this tunnel, through the Amanus Mountains, was a most

---

* It has been stated that this portion of the line, which was constructed as far as Angora, has during the war been continued to Sivas, which is on the direct route to the fortress of Erzerum.

† " L'Allemagne d'Outre-Mer," by Camille Fidel, 1915, p. 59.

notable achievement, and when other tunnels between Aleppo and Konia are finished the way towards the Egyptian frontier will be open to the passage of Turkish troops. The total length of the tunnels it has been necessary to construct in this small section is not less than 26,250 feet. At the present moment (March 1915) work on those portions of the line which were being constructed before the war began has been completed. Between Aleppo and Bagdad two sections of the railway have been completely finished and are now in use. They are the section from Mostimie (Mustimie) to Ras-al-Ain (about 186 miles), and the section from Samarra to Bagdad (about 88 miles). Between these two sections lies the stretch of line from Ras-al-Ain to Mossul and hence to Samarra, about 366 miles long. Of the total length of 1510 miles from Haidar Pasha to Bagdad 1117 miles are already in use, leaving only a comparatively small distance to be covered.*

In another chapter attention has been directed to the French railways in Syria, but it should here be stated that not only has the German company secured the concession of the Trans-Mesopotamian highway, but it also obtained control of most of the branch railways already in existence. Two of the most important, which were in the hands of the French, were bought up—the line from Smyrna to Afiun-Karahessai, the most direct trade route into the interior of Anatolia, and the railway from Adana to Mersina giving access to the Gulf of Alexandretta. The Hedjaz line, to which too little attention has been given in this country, designed ostensibly for the pilgrim traffic to Mecca but in reality a strategical railway of considerable importance intended to strengthen the Sultan's hold over the semi-independent tribes of Southern Arabia,† was commenced in the year 1900.

This railway follows the old Derb-el-Haj, or pilgrim route,

* Quoted by the *Daily Telegraph* (January 26, 1916) from the *Hamburger Fremdenblatt*.

† For many years Turkish influence in Arabia has been on the wane. In a paper by Mr. Archibald J. Dunn on " British Interests in the Persian Gulf," read before the Central Asian Society in 1907, the author stated that " it would seem that Arabia is practically lost to the Sultan, for the Arab troops have repeatedly defeated the Imperial forces under Feizi Pasha, with heavy losses." A strong movement was engineered in 1905 for the formation of an independent Arabian kingdom under a sovereign who would be the " religious Caliph " of all Moslems.

from Asia Minor to Mecca, and starting from Hamah, where it joins the railway from Aleppo, runs due south to Damascus, whence it is continued into the deserts of Arabia, passing within easy distance of Egypt.* It has been arranged that a branch built from Rayak, north of Damascus, was to have been carried to within a short distance of the Egyptian frontier,† but this, fortunately, had not been done at the outbreak of the war.‡ The full strategical importance of the narrow-gauge Hedjaz railway has only recently been appreciated. The significance of a railway connecting Aleppo with Mecca was quickly recognized by the Germans. No less an authority than von der Goltz pointed out the importance of this line. " The great distance dividing the southern provinces from the rest of the Empire," he wrote, " was not the only difficulty in holding them in control, but it made Turkey unable to concentrate her strength in case of great danger in the north. It must not be forgotten that the Osmanlie Empire in all former wars on the Danube and Balkans has only been able to utilize half her forces. Not only did the far-off Asiatic provinces not contribute men, but they, on the contrary, necessitated strong reinforcements to prevent the danger of their being tempted into rebellion. This will be quite changed when the railroads to the Persian Gulf and the centre portions of the Red Sea are made. The Empire will then be in a way rejuvenated and have renewed strength." § The Hedjaz railway, which was thus to become one of the instruments of Turkish regeneration, was started as a national and almost holy work by the Ottoman Government. All Turkish officials, whether Mohammedan or Christian, were compelled to pay one month's salary towards the cost, and all followers of the Prophet were asked to aid in the work. In this way and by other means about £3,000,000 was raised.|| It must, however, be recognized that the Hedjaz railway in its present condition is not of the same military value as the well-constructed broad-gauge railways of Europe. The line running from Aleppo to Rayak, where is

* A good account of the Hedjaz railway was contributed by Angus Hamilton to the *United Service Magazine* in 1908.
† Pratt, p. 335.
‡ The railway has since been constructed as far as Beersheba.
§ Quoted from the preface to a book by Auler Pasha, by Angus Hamilton, in his " Problems of the Middle East," 1909, pp. 274-5.
|| Hamilton, *op. cit.*, p. 276.

the junction with the railway to Beirut, is the weakest part of the system, as the gradients are steep and trains merely consist of three or four carriages each and the gauge is one metre only.* Moreover, farther south, especially when Mezerib has been passed, there are great difficulties in connexion with the supply of water and especially owing to the want of fuel. These difficulties would doubtless be overcome in time, but at present they are serious factors militating against the military value of the railway to Mecca.†

In conclusion it should be understood that the scheme which is generally known as the Bagdad railway in reality embraces three separate and distinct regions of Asiatic Turkey: Anatolia, Syria and Palestine, and Mesopotamia. These regions the Germans had marked as their own. Whilst in the earlier phases of the Bagdad idea German attention was mainly devoted to the desirability of the economic conquest of Anatolia and the settlement of German colonists along the route of the railway— a proceeding which was vetoed by the Sultan—German ideas gradually widened until they embraced the whole extent of the Sultan's territories in Asiatic Turkey. Diplomacy having long ago failed to hold in check the aggressive tendencies of modern Teutonism, nothing, save the war, would have prevented the fulfilment of these aims, which were to be accomplished through the instrumentality of rail-power in the construction of railways towards the Persian Gulf in one direction and the Red Sea in the other.

* *Times*, March 17, 1916, "The Main Lines of Turkish Communications in Asia."

† Recently portions of the Hedjaz railway to the north of Medina have been destroyed by the Arabs in order to prevent the transport of Turkish troops towards Mecca.

CHAPTER IV

GERMANY AND THE PERSIAN GULF

THE Persian Gulf, the most ancient of maritime commercial routes, whose waters were at one time crowded with the shipping of Antiquity and will again in all probability carry a not inconsiderable portion of the commerce passing between East and West, bears in some respects a close analogy to the Adriatic Sea. Not only has the possession of the Gulf become one of the main objects of Germanic policy, a desired and most desirable acquisition for any Power that intends to dominate Central Europe and to control the commercial routes to the East, but in its geographical position and in many of its topographical features it bears a striking resemblance to the western waterway. If we imagine Asia Minor and Persia to represent Austria-Hungary and the Balkans, the similarity immediately becomes apparent.

" The strategic position of Persia," states Professor Usher, " is of great significance. Her territory marches with the boundaries of Asia Minor and flanks the Bagdad railway and the rich district of the Tigris and Euphrates upon which England has long had designs. It controls the northern coast of the Persian Gulf, the coast road to India, the most important harbours, and, from a military point of view, is absolutely essential to the safety of the English in India. On the other hand the roads to the Black and Caspian Seas, the Persian Gulf, and South-Western Asia all pass through Persia, whose condition becomes, therefore, a matter of the utmost importance to England and to Russia. . . . It is obvious that Persia is of importance to England and to Russia, neither of whom is willing to allow the other exclusive possession, and neither of whom can permit that territory to fall into the hands of people unwilling to recognize their interests." *

* " Pan-Germanism," by R. G. Usher, p. 165.

The hinterland of the Persian Gulf, therefore, like the territory lying to the north and east of the Adriatic Sea, is a natural avenue of traffic from other more populous and more highly developed regions. The struggle for the possession of this maritime avenue, like the struggles for the Adriatic, has been dictated by the necessities of a people in the course of a national and expansive regeneration, and as the economic and strategical significance of the Gulf was fully revealed it became a question whether it should be controlled by Russia, with her imperative needs for a window to the south, dreamed of by the great Peter when he established the Muscovite Empire upon the Baltic ; by Germany, who was seeking a direct route to the East in order to carry her commercial forces to the gates of India ; or by Great Britain, whose long-established interests in her great eastern dependency gave her a clear right to protect that Empire against foreign attack.

If we compare the topographical features of the Adriatic and Persian Gulf, we shall be struck by two great similarities. Both form main avenues for maritime traffic, leading in a south-easterly direction to rich territories offering every inducement to commercial enterprise—the one leading to Asia Minor, Syria, and Mesopotamia ; the other conducting the merchant to India, Ceylon, and the Far East. In both cases, too, the western shores are wanting in good natural harbours, whilst the eastern coasts are indented and backed by ranges of mountains ; and in both cases the exit is controlled by a comparatively narrow passage, the Straits of Otranto and Ormuz respectively. In the north of the Gulf, with respect to their commercial and strategic importance, Basra and Koweit roughly correspond to Venice and Trieste, whilst Valona (Avlona) and Bunder Abbas, sheltering behind the island of Kishm, respectively dominate the exits of the two seas. Farther south, in the Gulf of Oman, the city of Muscat, situated around its land-locked harbour, occupies a position somewhat similar to that of Malta with respect to the sea-route from the Adriatic, and capable, in the hands of a strong Power, of commanding the whole of the trade passing through the Persian Gulf.* With these similarities there

* In this connexion the extreme heat of the stretch of coast between Muscat and the peninsula of Al Katar must be taken into account. " Beyond the unscalable heights of Musendam which stand sentinel over the entrance to the Gulf," states Mr. Lovat Fraser in his " India under Curzon and After,"

is, nevertheless, one great difference. No great navigable river system falls into the Adriatic whereas the Persian Gulf receives the waters of two of the greatest and most celebrated rivers, the Euphrates and Tigris, with their respective tributaries, which form a noble estuary at the head of the Gulf.

The importance of the Persian Gulf is, of course, intimately connected with the completion of the through routes of communication with Europe. The construction of the Bagdad railway and its continuation to Basra would at once render the Gulf a highway of the greatest importance, but the continuation of the railways of Caucasia into Persia would enormously enhance its value. At present these lines run from Poti and Batum on the Black Sea to Tiflis and thence in one direction to Baku, on the Caspian, and in the other through Alexandropol to Julfa on the Persian borders. From this point the line has recently been continued to Tabriz, whence it is suggested that it should be constructed to Kasvin, which is on the proposed route from Baku, along the Caspian, through Resht to Teheran. That city is the proposed termination of the railway to Khanekin and Bagdad, from a point on which route the line would be constructed to Mohammerah on the Shatt-al-Arab below Basra. In this connexion it will be remembered that Sir Edward Grey stated on May 30, 1913, that the British Government was supporting the application of a British syndicate to construct a railway from Mohammerah to Khoramabad, and that it was no longer the Government's intention to oppose the construction of this railway.* The last line, continued to Kermanshah, would supply the necessary communication with the Persian Gulf and in addition would traverse the rich oil regions in the hands of the Anglo-Persian Oil Company. Without entering into the intricate questions connected with the construction of the Trans-Persian railway, political, economic, and strategic, from Teheran to Karachi,† it is apparent that the building of the lines already

" is the wondrous tropical fiord of Elphinstone Inlet, nineteen miles long, probably the hottest place on earth, a majestic solitude of mountains and deep waters, where the hardiest of men cannot live the whole year round. . . . To penetrate these torrid retreats is to reach the loneliest and most desolate places in the world ; yet, if their climate were less intolerable they would shelter the whole British Fleet."

* Now under construction.

† On this question *see* the Paper read before the Central Asian Society on February 8, 1911, by Lieutenant-Colonel A. C. Yate, entitled " The

indicated would produce an enormous economic effect in the Persian Gulf, and would provide a greatly needed outlet for Russian trade in this quarter. They would, moreover, counteract the effect of the Bagdad railway by establishing alternative routes through the Black Sea or across the Caucasus.

In view of these possibilities and in consequence of our long-established interests in India, the control of the waterway leading directly to the western coasts of India has become, during recent years, one of the most important questions in world-policy. Until the plans of Germany in connexion with the Bagdad railway became fully revealed, and even until the conclusion of the agreement whereby the respective interests of Russia and Great Britain in Persia were finally defined, the chief danger to British interests seemed to lie in the expansion of Russia towards the south-east, and the possibility that this movement would ultimately threaten the stability and safety of our Indian Empire. The preservation of our privileged position in the Gulf became, therefore, a matter of supreme importance, and no British Government dared to sacrifice, either to the sentimental claims of party or to the demands of a peace-at-any-price faction, our interests in these waters. The Indian Government adopted a firm attitude on this point, and the Foreign Office, which in the past has so frequently appeared to take the line of least resistance, was emboldened to follow a policy that would have delighted the heart of Palmerston. In whatever way British interests may have been sacrificed in Persia itself, owing to the larger necessity for meeting half-way the aspirations of a Power whom it would have been folly to antagonize; in the Persian Gulf, at least, there has been very little or no weakening. This has been due, during recent years, in no small measure to the attitude of Lord Curzon, whose masterly grasp of Eastern affairs has been an asset of extreme importance to British imperialism.

The strategic significance of the Gulf has been recognized by the most diverse authorities. In 1902 the American Admiral A. T. Mahan, one of the best authorities upon the relation of sea-power to imperialism, wrote that "the control of the Persian Gulf by a foreign State of considerable naval potentiality, a

Proposed Trans-Persian Railway," and the article in *Questions Diplomatiques* for April 16, 1911, by M. Saulve, entitled "Le Transiranien."

'fleet in being' there based upon a strong military port, would reproduce the relations of Cadiz, Gibraltar, and Malta to the Mediterranean. It would flank all the routes to the farther East, to India, and to Australia, the last two actually internal to the Empire, regarded as a political system; and although at present Great Britain unquestionably could check such a fleet, so placed, by a division of her own, it might well require a detachment large enough to affect seriously the general strength of her naval position." * In the same year a German writer stated that " if the Persian Gulf becomes the permanent possession of a foreign Power, and if, moreover, the Bagdad railway is opened to the commerce of the world and to communications by new lines of transport, from the West to the East or vice versa, not only will the economic position of England be changed, but her military importance in Asia will undergo a transformation and a most unfavourable development " †; whilst the late Homer Lea expressed similar opinions. It was, therefore, a necessity to prevent any Power establishing a naval base in these regions, and to this end British policy in the East has been primarily directed, not in any dog-in-the-manger policy, but in the same spirit that would prevent the establishment of a foreign base on the banks of the Thames—the Persian Gulf being the Indian Thames and occupying in some respects towards India the same position as that river does towards London.

Great Britain has always been at cross-purposes with other nations in the Persian Gulf. For the last sixty years the waters that divide Arabia from Persia, one of the two buffer States between Europe and our Indian Empire, have been the scene of constant political intrigue on the part of four Great Powers having, or professing to have, special interests in these regions. Of these Russia has been the most formidable rival whom British diplomatists have had to keep at bay; but of late years it has been Turkey, backed by strong and generally secret German influences, and Germany herself who have attempted to advance into Persian waters.

The importance of preventing any strong military Power from acquiring a dominating influence either in Southern Persia,

---

* " Retrospect and Prospect," by A. T. Mahan, pp. 224–5.
† *Internationale Revue über die Gesammelen Armeen und Flotten*, June 1902.

Mesopotamia, or Eastern Arabia was recognized early in the last century when Great Britain, acting on the advice of Indian officials, entered into treaty relations with the rulers of the several States upon the shores of the Persian Gulf. Oman, with its capital Muscat, lying at the most important strategic point of Eastern Arabia, at an early period fell under British influence; but other States, such as the Bahrein Islands, the centre of the important Persian Gulf pearl-fisheries, and Koweit, the best harbour at the northern end of the Gulf, were also attached to the British orbit by strong political and commercial bonds. The value of Muscat is due to its position as a sally-port at the entrance to the Gulf whence all shipping passing that way could be easily attacked by a "fleet in being." For centuries before the age of steam Muscat dominated the surrounding littoral and its rulers gradually extended their influence until they controlled not only the adjacent coasts but also the greater portion of the East African littoral and erected a great maritime and trading State whose interests were centred in the Arabian and Indian Seas. Especially after the decline of the Portuguese Empire in the East did the commercial importance of Muscat, with its outpost at Zanzibar, become established.

But with the firmer control of these waters by British sea-power the importance of Oman gradually declined, and during the nineteenth century its foreign and commercial interests became almost exclusively British. The State was practically under the suzerainty of the Indian Government, and though it was not a political dependency like Aden, it nevertheless came to occupy a position which brought it within the British orbit. Although both France and Great Britain mutually pledged themselves, under the treaty of 1862, to preserve the independence of the Sultanates of Oman and of Zanzibar,* the former Power endeavoured, during the period when we were consolidating our position at Zanzibar, to establish a coaling-station at Muscat.† The French Consul, M. Ottair, succeeded

* Zanzibar became a British protectorate in 1890. See "The Germans and Africa."

† The treaty of March 10, 1862, was as follows: "H.M. the French Emperor and H.M. the Queen of Great Britain and Ireland, taking into consideration the importance of maintaining the independence of the Sultan of Muscat on the one part and the independence of the Sultan of Zanzibar on the other part, have deemed it advisable to engage reciprocally to respect the independence of these two princes." (Dubois, *op. cit.*, p. 704.)

in obtaining the support of the Sultan and the confidence of many of the local Sheikhs, and in November 1898 it was announced in the *Journal des Débats* that France had secured a coaling-station at Bunder Jisseh (Bandar Jissa), a land-locked bay, protected by a precipitous island three miles long and capable of being fortified, about five miles south-east of Muscat. Colonel Meade, the Political Resident, arrived in the Persian Gulf in February 1899, and was instructed to insist upon the revocation of the agreement, whilst Admiral Douglas, in H.M.S. *Eclipse*, was sent by Lord Curzon, who had recently become Viceroy of India, to support this demand. This action was based on a secret agreement with the Sultan, made in 1891, by which he promised not to permit any foreign Power to occupy any part of the State of Oman. The matter caused some excitement in France, and an affair that at one time seemed likely to create serious trouble was amicably settled.*

The attempt on the part of France, justified on the grounds that Great Britain already had a coaling-station at the entrance to Muscat Harbour, and that both possessed equal rights in Oman, was nevertheless an endeavour to establish a base near the Persian Gulf, and Lord Curzon's action on this occasion was fully justified by our privileged position in these waters. " I should regard," he had written in his book on Persia, " the concession of a port upon the Persian Gulf to Russia by any Power as a deliberate insult to Great Britain, as a wanton rupture of the *status quo*, and as an intentional provocation to war; and I should impeach the British Minister who was guilty of acquiescing in such a surrender as a traitor to his country." Lord Curzon's words applied, of course, equally to France and Germany. Britain claimed and exercised a paramount influence in these regions. For these reasons she withstood the then pressing danger of a Russian advance through Persia and checked the Russian diplomatic and

---

* To illustrate how history is interpreted it may be stated that Mr. Lovat Fraser writes in his book that M. Delcassé said that the threat to bombard Muscat had been due to the " incorrect and spontaneous intervention of local agents," whilst M. Dubois states that the British Government expressed its regret for " l'intervention aussi incorrecte que spontanée du vice-roi des Indes." If the meaning of M. Delcassé's words be that attributed to them by M. Dubois there is no doubt that the British Government promptly repudiated such a suggestion.

commercial moves equally with those of France, being fully aware that the presence of any other Power would inevitably lead to friction and might, in certain eventualities, become a menace to the safety of the Indian Empire.

With Russia we came to a friendly understanding in 1907, which at the time was generally understood to be at the expense of the expiring and faction-ridden Empire of the Shah. *Punch's* cartoon representing the British lion and the Russian bear mauling between them an unfortunate Persian cat, whilst the first exclaimed, "You can play with his head and I can play with his tail and we can both stroke the small of his back," fairly accurately represented the popular impression of the document which divided Persia into three spheres—the northern assigned as the political and commercial hunting-grounds of Russia, the middle district designed to serve as a buffer between the two ardent lovers, and the southern portion intended to be reserved for the activities of Great Britain. The treaty, however, served its purpose and closed the long controversy between Great Britain and Russia respecting the exploitation of Persia.

But with respect to Germany the position was very different. Teutonic intrigues were then but dimly perceived; for German agents worked in the dark and frequently sheltered behind the back of Turkey. With Russia, Germany came to some kind of understanding in 1911, when she professed to agree to a self-denying ordinance (the worth of which has since been shown) so far as political and economic concessions in Persia were concerned, in return for Russian diplomatic support on the Bagdad railway question; but so far as Great Britain was concerned there was no operative agreement, for the arrangement of 1914 was never definitely concluded.

Whilst Germany was steadily advancing her interests in Anatolia and Mesopotamia her agents in the Persian Gulf were stealthily performing their allotted tasks. German intrigues in Persian waters did not commence before the year 1896, that is, not until Teutonic interests in Turkey were being actively fostered. The aims of Germany have been ostentatiously commercial. In reality they have also been political and designed to obtain for the Fatherland a territorial footing in regions where there were no special German interests, in order to prepare the way for the establishment of a naval base. When Herr Wonckhaus, whose agent was recently discovered at Bahrein writing a detailed statement of the composition of the British forces proceeding to Basra, commenced his operations * there were practically no Germans in the Gulf. Wonckhaus started trading under the guise of a dealer in shells and mother-of-pearl. He established his depot at Lingah, not far from Bunder Abbas, at the southern end of the Gulf, a convenient spot for political intrigue with the predatory tribes of Southern Persia, and in 1901 removed to the Bahrein Islands—the political history of which during his residence gives ample grounds for reflection. Here he prospered exceedingly and within fifteen years the German agent—for there can be no doubt that Wonckhaus was acting as the representative of more highly placed individuals—opened other offices at Basra, Bushire, Mohammerah, and Ahwaz, where the houses and offices of the firm " were luxuriously furnished. Every month they used to remit large sums to the Bagdad railway. Every one wondered," states Major Murphy, " where the money came from. . . . It is not too much to say that the aims of this firm were firstly political and secondly economic, and that its representatives were all trained intelligence officers. Owing to the menacing attitude of Turkey and the certainty of her being eventually goaded into war by Germany, I had sent off one of my gun-running agents from Bushire at the beginning of September to find out what was going on in the Basra Vilayet. . . . On the plea of making inquiries about a *jihad*, which he pretended to be anxious to join, he was allowed to wander about the Turkish and Arab camps for nearly six weeks. He

* In a paper read before the Royal United Service Institution of India, Major C. C. R. Murphy revealed the operations of the industrious Wonckhaus. " Shortly after our arrival at Bahrein," he states, " some of us were sent to arrest a German named Harling, who was Wonckhaus's agent there. As we entered his office he was signing a letter, which was picked up and read. It turned out to be a report on the strength and composition of Force D, and was addressed to the German Consul at Bushire. It finished with the remark that so far only about five thousand troops had come up the Gulf, but that ten thousand more were shortly coming from India. Amongst his papers we found a copy of another report giving accurate details of General Delamain's force. This report had been written and dispatched to Bushire within four hours of our arrival at Bahrein." (*J.R.U.S.I. India*, October 1915.)

used to watch the Wonckhaus coterie travelling up and down the river in the Turkish gunboat *Marmaris* and showing the Turks where to put their guns. This was, of course, long before war had broken out." Wonckhaus, as the first of the German traders on the Gulf, deserves a niche in the Temple of Fame, and it should be recorded that his commercial work saw fruition in the year 1906, when the first vessel of the Hamburg-Amerika Line to visit Persian waters steamed up the Gulf and commenced the series of regular sailings that have since taken place. But as has been seen his political work continued until the outbreak of war.

In the year following Wonckhaus's appearance, Germany established a Vice-Consulate at Bushire, when there were exactly six Germans in the whole of the Gulf,* and since that date the intrigues of Germany in these regions have been incessant. The operations of the Germans have been marked by the underhanded and insincere, but nevertheless clever, diplomacy dear to the Teutonic mind. Turkey, far more the "mauled cat" than was the Persia of *Punch's* cartoon, was constantly drawn into the game, especially at Koweit, Bahrein, the small island of Halul, in the centre of the Gulf, and on the Karun River. The story of German intrigues on the Gulf has been well told in "*The Times* History of the War,"† and the full history would occupy too much space to be related in this volume.

In 1899, when the German Emperor was seeking concessions at Constantinople and appearing as a commercial Tannhauser at Damascus, the German cruiser *Arcona* paid a visit to the Gulf ports, made elaborate soundings, carefully surveyed all likely spots for the establishment of a harbour, and demonstrated to the natives the power of Imperial Germany. It was generally understood that the cruiser was seeking for a suitable terminus for the Bagdad railway.

But the Indian Government was now fully alive to the new danger that threatened British interests in these regions. Accordingly in January 1899 Lieut.-Col. M. J. Meade, British Resident in the Persian Gulf, who was then at Bushire, received orders to proceed at once to Koweit and to endeavour

* Lovat Fraser, *op. cit.*, p. 93.
† See "*The Times* History of the War," Part XXIX.

to get the Sheikh to agree not to cede, in any way whatever, any of his territory to a foreign Power without the knowledge and permission of the British Government. As secrecy was all-important the British Resident first went on a shooting trip to a neighbouring island and crossed over to Koweit during the night.* A Turkish corvette lay at anchor in the harbour and an attempt was made to prevent communication with the Sheikh, who, states Lieut.-Col. Meade, "wanted to be brought under our protection and to be guarded against the Turks, for whom he had, or at any rate professed to have, a great hatred." The Sheikh entered into an agreement with the British Government and later he accepted a British Resident at Koweit. The exact terms of the agreement have not been made public, but they were sufficiently indicated by Mr. Balfour's reference on April 8, 1903, to "territories of a Sheikh whom we have under our special protection and with whom we have special treaties."

The position of Koweit, with its natural harbour—a bay about twenty miles in length and ten miles in width, some distance to the south of the Shatt-al-Arab—renders it of peculiar strategic and commercial importance. For many years the Turks, who had been endeavouring to extend their influence over the Arab tribes of Eastern Arabia, had been trying to get this district within their power; but the Sheikh had stubbornly refused to acknowledge their suzerainty and had resolutely preserved his independence. The action of Colonel Meade in according to the Sheikh the protection of the British Government strengthened his position and enabled him to withstand the aggressions that were to follow.

Early in 1900, Herr Stemrich, who was then German Consul-General at Constantinople and subsequently became Minister at Teheran, came overland at the head of a mission which was making a rough survey of the proposed route of the Bagdad railway and arrived at Koweit.† Here the German mission attempted to buy twenty square miles of the coast for the terminus of the Bagdad railway, but in spite of German and

* In a letter to the *Pall Mall Gazette* on January 25, 1916, Lieut.-Col. Meade gives an account of this mission.

† This mission, in addition to Stemrich, consisted of the engineers Mackensen, von Kapp, and Habich, and was also accompanied by Major Morgen, Military Attaché at Constantinople.

Turkish pressure the Sheikh resolutely refused to part with any of his possessions, and the Germans were obliged to retire discomfited, having been outwitted by Lord Curzon, to whom must be ascribed the credit of the agreement concluded in the previous year.*

This direct rebuff to Germany led to a renewal of Turkish attempts to obtain control of Koweit. For many years the Sultan had claimed a kind of protectorate over the territory, which, according to Mr. Lovat Fraser, who has examined the available evidence, was never more than a "polite fiction," inasmuch as although the Sheikh had paid a small tribute to the Porte such payment had been intermittent and was in reality only a recognition of " that ill-defined though tangible respect which most Mussulman magnates proffer to one who, whether he be Khalifa or not, is still the greatest monarch in Islam."† Early in 1901 a Turkish corvette steamed into Koweit harbour and its commander announced to the Sheikh that he proposed to take possession of the town on behalf of his Imperial Master, but a British cruiser was fortunately in the harbour, and after a short but sharp parley the Turks withdrew, only to return later in the year with a high Turkish official, whom it was proposed to leave as the representative of the Sultan. But again a British naval officer intervened, upon his own responsibility,‡ and the Sultan's envoy was ordered to depart. Other endeavours were made to seize Koweit, or at least to secure the recognition of the Sultan's authority, but the British Government, realizing that Germany was instigating all these attempts, supported the Sheikh, and the Koweit question remained a matter for diplomatic correspondence and was only settled by the inoperative agreement of 1914.

In the meantime, however, an attempt, this time successful, was made to establish Turkish posts on Bubian, an island

---

* Colonel Meade states in his letter : " It is, however, a question whether the real author of our timely interference was not the then Viceroy of India, Lord Curzon, whose knowledge of, and interest in, all matters pertaining to Persia and the countries adjoining it were unequalled. He had not long before been at the Foreign Office, and no doubt still influenced its foreign policy not a little."

† Lovat Fraser, *op. cit.*, p. 98.

‡ Lovat Fraser.

about twenty-six miles long, which on the north side commanded the harbour of Koweit. Here, between the island and the shore, a long and deep inlet, the Khor Abdalla, seemed to offer a safe anchorage for German vessels. Owing to a piece of sharp practice on the part of the Kaiser, the British Government, after making a formal protest, failed to support the Sheikh of Koweit in his claim for protection against this new encroachment and the Turkish posts were allowed to remain.*

Other attempts were made to establish a German station in the Persian Gulf. A German syndicate asked for a monopoly of the pearl fisheries centring around the Bahrein Islands which lie near the peninsula of Al Katar in a deep bight of the Gulf. Here British interests had been safeguarded by treaties concluded with the Chief of Bahrein in the years 1820 and 1856, and particularly by the conventions of 1861 and 1880. By the convention of 1861, under which the Chief had engaged to abstain from war, piracy, and slavery by sea, on condition of British protection, it was enacted that " the British Resident engages that he will forthwith take the necessary steps for obtaining reparation for every injury proved to have been inflicted, or in course of infliction by sea, upon Bahrein or upon its dependencies in the Gulf." By that of 1880, the Chief of Bahrein agreed " to abstain from entering into negotiations or making treaties of any sort with any State or Government other than the British, without the consent of the British Government." By a further arrangement in 1892 he agreed not to sell, mortgage, or otherwise give for occupation, any part of his territory save to the British Government. Similar agreements had been made with the other petty chieftains of the Persian Gulf, who owing to these arrangements

* In " *The Times* History of the War," Part XXIX, it is stated that " the British Embassy at Constantinople was at that period exceedingly inactive, and the Home Government had passed from the ' hot ' fit to the ' cold ' fit. An incident which happened at a meeting between King Edward and the German Emperor is understood to have contributed to the change. The Emperor was eager to talk about Koweit, in which he took a deep and direct interest. King Edward was armed with certain notes on a sheet of paper. The Emperor asked if he might have the notes, and then promptly, but most improperly, recorded them as an official communication. The notes contained a questionable admission. It was thought best to condone the Emperor's sharp practice, but British policy at Koweit suffered in consequence."

were generally known as the Trucial Chiefs. Under these agreements the position of Great Britain in the Gulf seemed to be fully safeguarded, even against so-called commercial penetration, and Lord Lansdowne subsequently made the position perfectly clear when he announced in the House of Lords on May 5, 1903, that " we should regard the establishment of a fortified port in the Persian Gulf by any other Power as a very grave menace to British interests, and we should certainly resist it by all the means at our disposal." This, of course, constituted a species of Monroe Doctrine over Persian waters and was designed to prevent foreign encroachments in a region that was of great strategical importance. Nevertheless the Germans attempted to enter into direct negotiations with the Sheikh of Bahrein, but they were again warned that British interests were to be respected.

At least three other attempts were made to secure an entry into this region. German agents in Constantinople tried to persuade the Sultan to give them a lease of Halul, a small island about seventy-one miles from Ras Rakkim, the northern point of the peninsula of Al Katar, over which the Sultan had absolutely no control or even shadowy rights. Rebuffed in this direction the Germans sought to establish rights on Abu Musa, a small island at the commencement of the Great Pearl Bank and containing large deposits of iron oxide, where the firm of Wonckhaus, doubtless acting for the Hamburg-Amerika Company, acquired from some Arab traders a concession for working the mineral deposits. Here they came into open conflict with the local Sheikh, and one of their boats flying the German flag was fired upon by the Sheikh's armed retainers. This was, of course, one of those incidents desired by the German Foreign Office.

The German Press was up in arms, there was much talk about the insult to the German flag, and but for the prompt action of the British Government an international incident would have been manufactured and direct intervention by the German Government might have been decided upon. A further attempt was made in the region of the Karun River, where a Dutchman, acting as the agent of German interests, tried to obtain in the territories of the Sheikh of Mohammerah, who, under the suzerainty of the Persian Government, controls the country eastward of the river as far as the Hindiyan district and northward to thirty miles above Ahwaz,* a concession for an irrigation scheme.

This important port is visited by vessels of various steamship lines, including the British India, Hamburg-Amerika, and Ellerman and Bucknall Companies. The German authorities applied to the Persian Government, but the Sheikh of Mohammerah, in whom the rights were really vested, made it clear that he was not disposed to allow his sovereignty to be overruled by the Persian authorities.

The handling of these incidents, small in themselves, yet of importance as showing the persistent endeavours of Germany to obtain a foothold in the Gulf, demonstrate the watchfulness of the British Foreign Office, or more probably the sensitiveness of the Indian authorities to any encroachments in the Persian Gulf. German intrigues, in the guise of commercial adventures, could not be tolerated, and up to the outbreak of hostilities were successfully resisted.

If we examine briefly the history of this ancient highway we shall see how entirely just was the British claim for dominance in these waters. Of the four Powers who have struggled to obtain, or to retain, influence in these regions, Great Britain alone, by reason of her close and intimate relations with the Trucial Chiefs and her long work in suppressing the slave trade and in policing the Gulf, has any claim to a privileged position. Since the downfall of the Portuguese power and the decline of the barren little island of Ormuz, which as Purchas relates is a place " which nature hath made barren ; industry plentiful," from its former splendour as the key to Portugal's empire in these regions, to the miserable little village of about three hundred mat huts which it is to-day, Great Britain has continuously strengthened her position. " If all the world were but a ring, Ormuz the diamond should bring," sang Sir Thomas Herbert in the heyday of Portuguese power ; but since that date and throughout the whole of the seventeenth and eighteenth centuries, with the exception of the short-lived incursion of the Dutch and the period of French expansion in the East, British ships and British sailors remained supreme in Persian waters ; only threatened by the navy of Oman and the aggressions of Arab pirates. Turkey had very little influence

* " Persian Gulf Pilot," p. 295.

over the eastern shores of Arabia ; Russia did not succeed in establishing her influence in Persia until comparatively recent times ; France had no real interests to be safeguarded ; and Germany, the parvenu, only appeared on the scenes as an intruder without any other claims to recognition except such as she could secure by intrigue or by downright bluff.

Although it would be interesting to trace the devious course of German diplomacy in Persia the time has not arrived to relate the full story of Teutonic intrigue in the Empire of the Shah. As in Turkey, so in Persia, German agents have been busy in laying the foundations of *Weltpolitik*, encouraged in this course by the fact that Persia, like Asia Minor, is a commercial and strategical route of supreme importance. But owing to the enormous preponderance of Russian influence in Northern Persia the task of German agents has been far more difficult than was the case in Anatolia, and, moreover, has had to be carried on with much more secrecy.

Germany attempted to secure influence in Persia in three directions : economic, educational, and political. In 1907 the Director of the German Eastern Bank obtained an important concession for the opening of a bank in Teheran, with branches at Tabriz and other important centres ; and other valuable concessions were also granted to the same firm but were afterwards annulled on the united protests of Russia and Britain. German activities in this direction were mainly directed towards securing financial control by means of loans for the establishment of German industries. Germany also wished to lend money to the Persian Government. Such operations were of course legitimate, but they were accompanied by political intrigues specially aimed at Great Britain and Russia. In 1907 the German Ambassador, alone of all the representatives of the disinterested nationalities, took part in the political crisis, and although he was recalled, his successor displayed considerable political activity in matters entirely apart from his duties.[*]
In October 1907, for instance, an important German school, directly supported by the German Government, was opened in Teheran. This school, the most important educational institute in the capital and the most fruitful source of German influence, was subsidized by the German authorities to the

[*] *Novoe Vremya*, November 5, 1914.

extent of from £2000 to £2500 annually. The constant disorder in Persia, due in some measure to German intrigues, seemed to offer an excellent opportunity for the furtherance of Teutonic interests; and the appointment of an armed police force, under Swedish officers, facilitated the work of the secret agents of Germany. There can be no doubt that by indirect means the Germans secured the appointment of officials well disposed towards Teutonic aims. How insidiously they worked and how industriously they prepared their plans was revealed on the outbreak of war, when many of these Swedish officers threw in their lot with the Germans and took part in the attempt to bring Persia into the war on the side of the Central Powers. Lord Crewe, in a statement in the House of Lords on December 8, 1915, said that "German intrigue had been busy with the force of gendarmerie which had been raised originally under Swedish officers," and he proceeded to make it clear that whilst all were not implicated in the charge of unneutrality yet "some of the other Swedes have not been to the same extent under the control of their own Government," and had assisted the Germans in Persia.

The full extent of the German conspiracy in Persia has yet to be revealed. It is in reality a repetition of the attempt of Napoleon in the early years of the last century to secure the adhesion of Persia to the French cause, but far more formidable, far better organized, and of far greater extent. In every direction Persia had been traversed by German secret agents who tried to persuade the inhabitants that with German aid they could easily overthrow the unnatural yoke imposed upon them by Great Britain and Russia, and thus secure the complete independence of their country from foreign control. Long prior to the outbreak of war a formidable anti-foreign agitation was in full swing. Through the agency of their Consuls established at Benner, Bushire, Azerbaijan, Ispahan, and Resht, all of whom were trained political agents, the German Government controlled the threads of a great Teutonic conspiracy. By means of spies who adopted the costume of the country and posed as converts to the national religion, the German Government got into touch with the disaffected, and either by means of direct bribes or vague promises enlisted them in the Teutonic cause. One of these agents, a certain Dr. Pugin, who went to Ispahan ostensibly as a dealer in carpets and aniline dyes, adopted the name of Ahmed Beg and exhorted the ignorant or fanatical Persians to show their sympathy for the Moslem Kaiser, who was as ready, he told them, as they were themselves to recite the Kalima according to the formula prescribed by the Shiahs. This statement was reiterated both in public addresses and in sufficiently inflammatory pamphlets.* Such action was only part of a great conspiracy carried on in a similar manner in India, Afghanistan, Arabia, Egypt, the Sudan, and the Mohammedan countries of Northern Africa.

The conspiracy in Persia, which aimed at securing the person of the young Shah, has been thoroughly exposed in many quarters. On November 27, 1915, the *Novoe Vremya* published the following telegram, which demonstrates how thoroughly the Germans had prepared their plans:

" The Chief of the Persian gendarmerie, Colonel Edval, on November 15, when the Shah was hesitating at the eleventh hour, was energetically persuading him to leave the capital with Prince Reuss† and the Turks. He did not attempt to conceal his participation in the conspiracy so sure was he of the success of it and of his immunity from penalty. Another officer of the gendarmerie, Captain Oenset, furnished a German called Schonemann with machine-guns for his attacks on our Consul, and the German Consul of Kengavar is now leading the German bands which attacked the Persian Cossacks in Kurdistan. A third officer captured the British Consul at Shiraz. The fourth, Major Golstrom, initiated the massacre at Hamadan. With the assistance of the gendarmerie, the Germans erected at Burugirg, near the line which is called our sphere of influence, a large munition factory. . . . This is not all. But it is sufficient to show how far the Shah's Government has gone. With its cognizance and even assistance the Germans are preparing in Persia a massacre. With its cognizance and assistance the German-Turkish agitators have penetrated into Afghanistan and India, calling upon the Moslems to open war on Russia and England. To crown all, they have placed at the disposal of the enemy the Teheran arsenal with its stores of Russian

* *Standard*, December 4, 1915.
† This royal bandit is Henry XXXI of Reuss, who was formerly German Consul-General in Calcutta.

munitions and its main military force—the gendarmerie corps." *
But, as we know, the Shah drew back at the last moment and in spite of the formidable conspiracy with which he was threatened refused to countenance the German plans. The news of the advance of Russian troops in the direction of the capital produced a profound effect and the Germans, Austrians, and Turks sought refuge in flight. The subsequent history of events in Persia is as dramatic and interesting as any of the proceedings in the main theatres of the war, but does not come within the scope of this volume. It is sufficient to state that the disappointed conspirators were driven back upon Hamadan and Kermanshah and that the armed levies who proposed to capture Persia were decisively defeated.

Whilst it is certain that no part of Persia was free from German activities, both before and during the war,† German agents were equally active in every Mohammedan country under the control of the French, Italian, or British Governments. Their object, as is well known, was to stir up a Holy War; but in this they have hitherto signally failed. No rumour was too base and no lie too incredible with which to work upon the feelings of the more fanatical and ignorant sections of the Mohammedan population. On the one hand the Germans spread rumours of the forthcoming march by Turks and Germans upon India, with the idea of fomenting disturbances in Persia and Afghanistan. On the other hand they let it be known all over Syria and Anatolia, Algeria and Tunis, Eritria and Tripolitania, that Egypt would be handed back to the Ottoman Sultan, and that the Turkish Empire would again become supreme over Northern Africa.

German activities in Egypt had long been connected with the Pan-Islamic movement, which of all the various "Pan" propaganda of the last few years, only excepting Pan-Germanism, was the most insidious and the most dangerous. This movement, which received the august approval of the German Emperor

* Quoted from the *Times*, December 11, 1915.
† Sir Thomas Jackson, speaking at the meeting of the Imperial Bank of Persia on December 13, 1915, stated that their activities in Persia were directed by the German Consuls, and that "it would hardly be an exaggeration to say that Southern Persia was still largely under German domination and control," and further, that "no part of the country had been free from their activities."

during his visit to Damascus, was designed to unite Mohammedans of all sects in one great and all-embracing effort to throw off foreign control, and was mainly directed against Great Britain and France. Its ramifications spread into every country where Mohammedanism was the prevailing creed, and it was especially active in Egypt, where, but for the strong governance of Lord Kitchener, it might have succeeded in undermining the basis of British power. In Egypt it was closely connected with the activities of the Nationalistic party.

The Pan-Islamic agents, generously paid by the Turkish Government and secretly supported by the Germans, overran Arabia, India, and Afghanistan; and the holy cities of Mecca and Kerbala, whither tens of thousands of Mohammedan pilgrims journeyed every year, were centres of activity. German agents, such as the notorious Karl Neufeld, who was released by Lord Kitchener after years of imprisonment at Omdurman under the brutal Khalifa, worked energetically in the German cause and directed the politico-religious movement which was to end in the overthrow of Great Britain. In Egypt the so-called Patriotic party, guided by the Pan-Islamic newspaper *El Lewa*, became most active after the success of the revolution at Constantinople, and openly asked for the return of Egypt to Turkey and the abandonment of the British occupation; but in combating the claims of the Arabs to the restoration of the Khalifate, they brought about a split in their own party, and this action, combined with the vigorous attitude of the British administration, resulted in its downfall. The President, Muhamed Ferid Beg, fled to France, and there, in the columns of one French paper and of several organs of the Arabian Press, " published a series of articles in which the participation of Germany in the matter of Pan-Islamic propaganda was set forth."* Some of the members of the party transferred their attention to Afghanistan, but the Amir, who saw the drift of the Turco-German intrigues, refused to participate in any movement that would jeopardize his own position.

In this necessarily brief and rapid survey no attention has been given to German propaganda in India, where the tentacles of Teutonism have spread in every direction. Not the least active exponents of Pan-Germanism were the German mission-

* *Russki Invalid*, December 6, 1914.

aries, and although it would be unfair to overlook the great work many of these missionaries have carried on, particularly those attached to the Basel Evangelical Missionary Society and those of the Grossner and Leipzig Missions, it would be more foolish to believe that German missionaries are incapable of fomenting political agitation.* With the occupation of Basra by the Anglo-Indian troops, an event which is comparable in importance with the capitulation of Kiao-Chau, the first step was taken to defeat the schemes of the Pan-German party and to eradicate the deeply rooted evils that had so long been troubling the Mohammedan world.

* *See* on this subject an article in the *Nineteenth Century* for August 1915 on " German Missionaries in India."

CHAPTER V

THE GERMANS IN PALESTINE

THE year 1898 marks a definite step in the movement for the Germanization of the East, for it was in that year that the German Emperor entered upon the Oriental stage and definitely proclaimed his intention of becoming the Protector of Islam. With appropriate solemnity and in the full glare of publicity the Western Kaiser, surrounded with all the pomp and circumstance of an Eastern monarch, spoke to the multitudes of the Faithful—Mohammedans, Roman Catholics, and Protestants—almost at the same time and with the same voice, and dexterously showed to an amused and too tolerant world the eclectic nature of his religion, all-embracing and all-tolerant. Like some ancient Crusader he advanced to the sacred precincts of the Holy City of the Christians, solemnly blessed the hallowed ground, planted the sword of Teutonism firmly in the soil of the Holy Land, and grasped in friendship the dripping hands of Abdul Hamid—stained with the blood of thousands of his Christian subjects who had just been butchered in Armenia.

It was a period when Christian humanity was horrified with the atrocities committed by order of the Sultan; when Great Britain, at length awake to the horror of the situation that confronted the Christian Powers of Europe, was recoiling from the evil that then reigned at Constantinople and was endeavouring to secure the cessation of the gross inhumanities that characterized Turkish rule; and when the so-called Concert of Europe, ineffectual, unreal, and practically non-existent, was being still further weakened by dissensions between the Powers. The shadow of Fashoda and of the sharp and short conflict between France and Great Britain concerning the valley of the Nile; of the coming struggle in South Africa; and of the ominous happenings in the Far East; were already spreading over the European horizon, threatening alike the permanence of the Concert and the continuance of a precarious peace; when with dramatic suddenness the Emperor William, proclaiming the eternal friendship of Turk and Teuton, threw the good German sword into the Oriental balance. The hands of Germany were already stretching forward to grasp the coveted lands of the Middle East, and the Kaiser, interpreting aright the aspirations of his countrymen, was preparing the way that was to lead to the Persian Gulf and was opening the gateway of the Orient to Teutonic commercialism.

Yet this sudden coming of the German Emperor—this imperious and impetuous knocking upon the western portals of Asia—was in reality no isolated or unexpected event; for Germans had been industriously working upon the soil of Palestine for many years, and preparing silently and effectively the stage trappings for the advent of their sovereign. The story of the German colonies in the Holy Land is but a small incident in the larger history of Germanic expansion; for those outposts of Teutonism, founded by religious enthusiasts, working, perhaps unwittingly, on behalf of their Fatherland, had hitherto been neglected in the political world and were but weak and feeble communities though containing the seeds of future expansion. Yet, although comparatively unknown in Germany, these small colonies had not escaped the attention of enthusiastic Pan-Germans,* who saw in them yet another evidence of the virility of a growing nation forced to send its sons to distant lands, to live and struggle and build under a foreign flag.

The colonies of the Templars in Palestine were founded by an idealist who dreamed visions and formed plans for re-establishing the Society of the Knights Templars at Jerusalem and re-erecting upon a modern basis the departed glories of that great Order. The project of founding colonies of Templars in Palestine was first conceived in the year 1864 by Christoph H. Hoffmann, who, having formed a committee to aid in their establishment, was able four years later to send a commission

* The German colonies in Palestine are shown in the Pan-German Atlas of Dr. Paul Langhans, issued at Gotha in 1893. The map shows four settlements then in existence—at Jaffa, Sarona, Rephaim, and Haifa; and also that German churches were established at these places and at Bethlehem, Beirut, and Smyrna.

to study the ground and to report upon the most favourable situations for founding agricultural settlements in Palestine. Although the Prussian Government were opposed to the scheme, fearing complications both with France and with the Turkish authorities, Hoffmann persevered with his plans, and in 1869, with his wife and a small number of adherents, left Southern Germany and landed at Haifa, where he founded a small colony which was destined to become the centre of German ambitions in Palestine. His followers, pious folk of unorthodox views, rejected the accepted dogmas of the Trinity and the Divinity of Christ. Basing their creed on the prophecies of the Old Testament, they determined to found in the Promised Land an ideal community which would serve as a centre for the regeneration of Christendom. Gradually, however, other views and ideas prevailed, and the somewhat primitive and idealistic aims of the colonists were modified; for as other Germans settled within the new communities, the plans of the original settlers, who were mainly agriculturists and tillers of the soil, were broadened by the leaven of Pan-Germanism and by the inculcation of patriotism; whilst many of the colonists subsequently reverted to Lutheranism. Their numbers were at no time large, but the Templars bought land, built houses, established businesses, and, wherever they settled, were able to exert considerable influence. In 1878, the Sultan becoming alarmed at this influx of Europeans, refused to sell any more land; but the mischief had already been done, for the little communities were firmly established and were even at that time acting as sentinels of Teutonism in the midst of a sea of Mohammedans.

The German colonies in Palestine, which formed so convenient a tool for the Emperor William during his visit to that country, were at Haifa,* Jaffa, Sarona, and Jerusalem, and although their population was small—certainly not more than two thousand in the year of the Kaiser's visit—they formed excellent centres for the propagation of *Deutschthum* in a country that was destined, if the desire of Moltke were ever fulfilled, to become a principality under the control of a

* The course of German intrigue at Haifa is well illustrated in the case of the Jewish University there. The German members of the Board made a stiff fight to have German declared the official language, but were outvoted.

German ruler and one of the chief bucklers of Teutonism in the East.

The smallness and apparent insignificance of the German colonies were their best protection. Yet although their founders were probably unaware of it, they nevertheless fitted into their allotted places in German world-policy and became of great service to the Fatherland. " When I was transferred from Bagdad to Jerusalem," wrote Canon Parfit,* " it was a German tourist agent that landed me at Jaffa, took me to the famous German hotel at Hardegg in the flourishing German colony, escorted me to the train which landed me in the Holy City, as every pilgrim knows, by the side of another well-ordered German colony that has spread like a modern garden suburb along the valley of Ephraim."

" Whilst living for a few years at Jerusalem," continued Canon Parfit, " I watched the erection of three remarkable buildings ; the magnificent German Roman Catholic church on Mount Zion, with the highest and noblest tower in Jerusalem, that dominates the whole city ; the massive German hospice near the Damascus Gate, which every one declared to be ridiculously like a fortress ; and the beautiful mansion or sanatorium on the heights by the Mount of Olives, with another huge tower that commands the Jordan Valley, *and is furnished with a wireless installation* which was tested by Prince Eitel when, with becoming pomp, he opened this princely palace a few years ago. It is rumoured that this wireless installation has been of inestimable value to the Germans since the outbreak of war."

Although ostensibly erected in the cause of religion and philanthropy these extraordinary buildings were certainly intended to further the political and military aims of the Fatherland. The Augusta Victoria Stiftung on the Mount of Olives, supposed to be a rest-house for German missionaries, was supplied with a powerful searchlight dominating the whole countryside,† whilst it was also probably the repository for a store of arms and ammunition likely to be of use in the event of hostilities. A writer in the *Near East*—a newspaper not usually given to sensational reports—stated on September 11,

* *Evening News*, January 13, 1916.
† *Near East*, September 11, 1914.

1914, that "three years ago some heavy cases, described as furniture for the Stiftung, were landed at Haifa and brought in mule-carts through the country. This surprised every one, for, by one of the innumerable Turkish concessions, everything for the Stiftung was cleared at the Jaffa Customs duty free, as the Stiftung was a philanthropic institution; why, then, should these cases of furniture be suddenly brought from Haifa, at such cost and difficulty, during the rains, when roads between Haifa and Jerusalem practically do not exist? The cases reached Jerusalem, and were taken up to the Stiftung at night, and their extraordinary weight amazed the carters. One of the carts broke down, the cases fell heavily to the ground, and one of them breaking a little disclosed the iron muzzle of a small cannon." *

The tempestuous visit of the German Emperor to Palestine was the outcome of a long-cherished plan for facilitating the entry of Germany upon the Eastern sphere. The Emperor William, determining to succeed where Napoleon had failed, had realized that if Germany were to take her position as an Eastern Power, it would be necessary to conciliate, not to fight, the Turks. For many years the Sultan had stood alone and friendless in the face of an outraged Europe, deriving what comfort he could from the commercial embraces of the Germans, who were determined to secure advantages which other nations hesitated to take. The orientation of German policy became a fixed resolve of the Kaiser, and nothing could better serve his political purposes than the hostility manifested by the non-German Powers towards the crowned assassin who then reigned at Constantinople.

The tortuous avenues of diplomatic policy having been successfully traversed by the Kaiser's agents, who prepared the way by deftly flattering the Turkish authorities and by more substantial but probably more pleasing methods, finally announced to the Sultan that the long-expected visit of the German Emperor was to take place. The journey had been planned four years earlier, or at least the first intimation of the Kaiser's desire had then been made known, for in conversation with Mr. John M. Cook upon Mount Vesuvius the Emperor

* A similar incident happened at one of the Indian ports some years previous to the war.

had stated that he hoped to make the journey under his guidance.*

The Emperor first visited Constantinople (October 18, 1898), where he was received with enthusiasm by the German community. Accompanied by Prince von Bülow, he exercised his undoubted powers of fascination over the Sultan and secured the concessions which were to render possible the building of the Bagdad railway. The extension of German railways into Asia Minor, so successfully negotiated on this occasion, was the main purpose of the Emperor's visit. " It is daily becoming more evident," wrote *The Times* correspondent, " that, with the development of railway connexions, the great overland highways to the East will gradually supplant the maritime routes and the ancient land of Nineveh and Babylon, of Tyre and Palmyra, which forms the meeting-point of East and West, the link between three continents, will regain much of its ancient importance. It is in accordance with the far-seeing character of German policy to have recognized this truth." †

But the secret negotiations at the Turkish capital required an imperial and dramatic background, and this was supplied during the subsequent visit to Palestine, where elaborate preparations had been made for the Emperor's reception. Both Germans and Turks realized that this was no ordinary visit of ceremony, but an event which marked a new and decisive episode in the troubled history of the Near East. The romantic and impulsive Kaiser of the Germans, the modern representative of the temporal power of the Holy Roman Empire, the Protestant sovereign of a reunited people, in following in the footsteps of Barbarossa and Frederick II, was entering upon a new crusade—a crusade of commercialism backed by the military power of the German Emperor. The visit was a direct challenge to Russia and to France, and indirectly—but more potently— to Great Britain. In Russia the proceedings of the Emperor were watched with undisguised hostility, and the Russian Press denounced the growth of German influence in Palestine and the implied claim of the Kaiser to dispute the joint protectorate of Russia and France over the Christians resident

* " With the Kaiser in the East," by Sir William Treloar, 1915.
† *Times*, October 18, 1898.

in Turkey.* France feared for her influence in Syria—Russia foresaw the inevitable tendency of the new German aggression.

Nothwithstanding the evident hostility of the Russians, openly manifested during the Kaiser's stay at Constantinople, when the Russian Embassy, alone amongst those at Pera, refrained from hoisting its standard, and the more courtly but none the less sincere enmity of the French, the Kaiser carried out his original plans.

On the morning of October 31, the anniversary of the day on which Luther had nailed up his memorable theses at Wittenberg, after staying the night on German soil in the German colony at Jerusalem, the Emperor William proceeded to perform the first of his ecclesiastical functions. Surrounded by a host of divines, the Kaiser, standing in the Protestant church, the woodwork of which had been brought from the city of Luther, figured as the secular head of the Reformed Faith in Germany; whilst on the afternoon of the same day he was the leading personage in a ceremony which was evidently designed to represent him as the patron and protector of German Catholicism. Here in the new Roman Catholic church, built upon land presented to his father the Emperor Frederick by the Sultan, the Kaiser formally transferred the ground to the German Catholic community. "Every detail of that ceremonial was arranged with a view to effect—the hoisting of the Imperial Standard on Mount Zion, the Kaiser standing by with drawn sword, the salute rendered by some two hundred German soldiers and sailors, all fully armed and accoutred, the presence of the Latin Patriarch, the absence of a Turkish escort." † The site upon which the Kaiser took his stand had long been venerated as holy ground, for it lay close to the Cœnaculum, or scene of the Holy Supper, and is supposed to include the place where the Virgin Mary's house had stood. Here the Kaiser intimated as plainly as possible that it was his intention to protect the German Christians of Turkey.

A few days later (November 8), at Damascus, the head of Christian Germany, who but a week before had preached from

* The *Novosti* suggested that France and Russia should co-operate in order to maintain their respective rights, and declared that the Dual Alliance would not regard with indifference the creation of a new German political centre in Turkey.

† *Times*, November 23, 1898.

the altar-steps of a Protestant church and had raised his banner on Mount Zion as the Protector of German Catholicism, publicly proclaimed his undying friendship for the Kalif of Islam : " Let His Majesty the Sultan, as well as the three hundred millions of Mohammedans who venerate him as their Kalif, be assured that the German Emperor will always remain their friend." The Kaiser's words were instantly taken down by Tewfik Pasha, the Turkish Ambassador at Berlin, and telegraphed to the Sultan, whilst next day, translated into Turkish and Arabic, and printed in letters of gold, the message was circulated among the population of Damascus.

With these words the Emperor William proclaimed his world-policy and uttered a direct challenge to Great Britain as the chief Mohammedan Power. " The journey," stated the *Berliner Tageblatt*, " has been a triumph of German policy, which for the next ten years will be paramount in the Levant."

The triumphal progress of William II was indeed to set the clock of Europe for a decade. No such scene had been witnessed since our own flamboyant Henry VIII embraced the equally flamboyant Francis I with such theatrical and spectacular display on the Field of the Cloth of Gold. Under the auspices of Cook, the modern representative of the organizers of the meeting on the plain of Ardres, the German Emperor proclaimed a new policy and a new ideal, which was received with delight by his exiled countrymen in Syria and by the militant Pan-Germans to whom the Kaiser in reality spoke. Here at length in the ancient city of Damascus within easy reach of the French community at Beirut, the Emperor announced the world-policy of Germany amidst the plaudits of those who were present. The testimony of the German pastor Naumann may be quoted to show with what delight this sentimental protectorate over the Mohammedan world was received in German circles. " All weakening of the national German energy," he wrote in the following year, " by peace societies or by other similar efforts, serves the redoubtable and growing power of those who to-day dominate the world from the Cape to Cairo, from Ceylon to the Arctic Ocean. . . . Let us have no friendship with England, but let us follow a national policy. That is the cause which determined our attitude in the Eastern question. For that profound reason we must be politically indifferent to the sufferings of the Christian peoples in the Ottoman Empire. If Turkey falls asunder to-day it will become the plaything of the Great Powers. And we, as so frequently in the past, should be left in the lurch. We must prevent that catastrophe. Turkey must receive the constitution she needs in order to be able to keep afloat yet a little while longer. Bismark has counselled us to separate our internal policy from our foreign politics. As Christians we welcome the expansion of the Faith, but our politics have no occasion to be concerned with Christian Missions. The truth is, as it has always been, that we must seek for the greatest and the most important moral work. When we have made our choice we must never turn back. William II has made his choice. He is the friend of the Padishah because his faith is in a greater Germany." * The regeneration of Turkey was to be the greatest task of all because it served the political needs of the Fatherland. "We shall undertake a kind of friendly protectorate and upon all the coasts of the Mediterranean the Germans will become established. This ancient sea will witness many things in the future. We have between our hands a portion of the future life of Germany."

This then was to be the future of Syria and Asia Minor —a moral fief of the German Empire. The Kaiser's eloquent passages at Damascus—his grandiloquent message to the Mohammedan world—were intended to prepare the way for German expansion in the East. The moment was well chosen. Already France and Great Britain were in measurable distance of war over the Fashoda affair—which in reality caused the Emperor to shorten his tour, which was to have extended to Egypt and the banks of the Nile, and to hasten back to Berlin— and the theatrical display at Jerusalem and Damascus was generally overlooked in the immediate Franco-British tempest which then occupied the minds of European statesmen.

But German expansion in Syria could only be at the expense of other nations with long-established interests in Turkish Asia. For many centuries France had exercised a form of protectorate over the Christians of Syria, which, had Great Britain and France been able to settle their differences, might have been transformed into actual political control. It was

* Friedrich Naumann's "Asia," pp. 145-8

to fight this Gallic influence that the Kaiser raised his threatening sword. The golden message of Damascus was immediately directed against the time-honoured prestige of France in Syria, and was intended to convey to the Mohammedan world an assurance that its interests would be protected against further encroachment by the predatory Christian Powers.

The question of the protection of the Christians in Syria and Asia Minor had always been a bone of contention between the Great Powers. On the one side Russia, by the Treaty of Kutchuck Kamardji in 1774, claimed the general right of making representations on behalf of the Greek Church in the Ottoman Empire, although that right in reality was limited under the treaty to one specified church in Constantinople. This claim led, among other causes, to the Crimean War. On the other side France, in virtue of ancient arrangements that had been made long before the Turks had captured Constantinople, claimed a general right of protection over the Christians in Syria—a claim that had been subsequently recognized by the Porte. This claim and the exercise of this direct influence originated during the reign of Louis IX, who in return for the services rendered by the Syrian Christians during his expedition against Egypt granted them a charter in the year 1250, in which he gave a general promise of protection against their enemies. The exceptional privileges of the protection of the Christians enjoyed by France were not confined to the Lebanon. They were exercised throughout the whole of the Sultan's dominions, both in Europe and Asia. Apart from the ancient compact of the thirteenth century they may be said to have commenced with the treaty negotiated by Jean de la Forest, Chancellor of the Order of Saint John of Jerusalem, in the name of Francis I. This treaty was signed by Sultan Soliman and the French monarch in 1535. The Maronites of Lebanon, one of the most fertile regions of Palestine, had been able to maintain their religion in spite of the Moslem invasion, and had from time to time claimed the protection of the chief Christian Power of Europe. Thus in 1651 Louis XIV renewed the engagement of his ancestor, and in 1735 it was again recognized by his successor Louis XV, since which date it has never been abrogated. Five years later, in 1740, the capitulation with France guaranteed to that Power the protection of all persons "professing the Frankish religion" to whatever nationality they might belong.* The privilege then recognized by the Sultan was never seriously disputed. Even the Berlin Congress, in its desire to maintain as much of the *status quo* as possible, did not rescind the ancient convention but declared that "the rights possessed by France are expressly reserved, and it is well understood that no alterations can be made in the *status quo* of the Holy Places," but at the same time confirmed the rights acquired by various Powers since that date under different capitulations with Turkey.† Moreover, when in 1860, owing to the disturbance between the fanatical Druses, an heretical Moslem sect, and the Maronites, Napoleon III found it necessary to intervene on behalf of the French protégés, this right of intervention was recognized by the European Powers, who in a convention signed on August 3 in that year allowed the disembarkation of a French force of six thousand men at Beirut.

Subsequently an international commission summoned to that city elaborated a kind of constitution for Lebanon, which was separated from the Turkish pashalik of Syria and put under a Christian governor, whilst Austria, Russia, England, and France constituted themselves "guardians" of the small province.‡ This was a notable and assured triumph for France because by taking this action the European Powers recognized the peculiar and privileged position of France in this portion of Syria. It is clear, therefore, that although French influence in Syria was not acknowledged to be exclusive, it was nevertheless held to be sufficiently established for her to assume the leading rôle in the execution of the Lebanon reforms.

* "The protection of the Christians of all nationalities in the Levant was never conferred specifically on France by any treaty. In the first centuries it was assumed because the Western Powers had not Consuls in all parts of the Ottoman Empire. However, the French invoke a phrase in the 1740 treaty, placing "on the same footing the bishop depending on France and the other priests, monks, and nuns who profess the French religion, of whatever nature or kind they may be." ("French Claims in Syria," by T. F. Farman, *Contemporary Review*, September 1915.)

† Austria claimed the right of protection over the Christians in Macedonia and Albania in virtue of arrangements with the Porte in the years 1699 and 1718.

‡ See "L'Influence française en Syrie," by Paul Roederer, in *Le Mois Colonial*, Avril 1906.

Apart entirely from the religious question, France exercised a very real and tangible influence throughout Syria. This influence, already considerable in the sixteenth century, when the French had established important commercial enterprises at Sidon, then the most important city of the Syrian littoral, where they carried on a large trade under the protection of the French flag, although suffering an almost total eclipse when Bonaparte reversed the traditional policy of France and attacked Turkey, had been steadily growing during the latter half of the nineteenth century. In 1842, when France was expanding along the Mediterranean, French Jesuits established a university at Ghazir, which soon became celebrated throughout Turkey and Egypt and attracted large numbers of students, who naturally fell under French influence. This university was removed to Beirut in 1876. Here, through the aid of Jules Ferry and Léon Gambetta, a faculty of medicine was established, and the University of St. Joseph at Beirut acquired a strong position as a centre of French culture as well as a rallying-point for French political propaganda.*

In other ways, too, the French had been able to obtain a position in Syria in many respects analogous to that in Egypt previous to the British occupation, and Beirut, from a comparatively small seaport, became through French enterprise an important and thriving city. Commercially France held a strong position, although of recent years this position had been seriously threatened by the constant advances of German and British trade in Syria and Palestine. But though other nations were not slow in endeavouring to secure advantages from the situation created by French energy, the fact should nevertheless be recognized that it was largely owing to such enterprise that " this reaping in others' fields " became possible. In 1859, for example, one of the few good roadways in Asiatic Turkey was constructed by the French between Beirut and Damascus, which opened up the country and enabled the products of the interior to be shipped to French ports. This roadway was largely superseded by the construction by a French company of a railway between those two cities in 1892, when at the same time extensive jetties, quays, and warehouses

* When the University was closed, immediately after the Porte had declared war against the Allies, it contained about one thousand pupils.

were built for the ever-increasing trade. Moreover the construction of railways from Beirut to Homs, Hamah, and Aleppo, and the building of other lines, particularly from Smyrna, was a clear sign of the vitality and resource of France in Syria and Asia Minor. It was doubtless these railways that the Kaiser coveted when he first made his proposals to the Sultan for the building of the Bagdad railway—one branch of which was to run to the Persian Gulf, whilst the other was to be joined with the Mecca line in order to reach the southern extremity of the Red Sea.

But it was perhaps in the purely intellectual sphere that French influence in Syria was greatest. The French language was largely spoken by the more educated classes—Mohammedans and Christians alike. It was the language of the cultured, and as such was the tongue of those who wished to be in the fashion and to demonstrate the superiority of their education.* The spread of French culture had been brought about mainly through the influence of schools established under French direction.* "Lebanon and Beirut contain," stated a writer in *Le Mois Colonial*, "proportionately to the number of the inhabitants, more schools in which the French tongue is the principal and obligatory language than there are in Paris itself. There is not a *salon* in this little country where French is not spoken. Imagine a Frenchman who has landed at Beirut with but a vague idea of the country—what will be his astonishment and his joy when instead of seeing the uncultured country of his dreams he finds himself almost at home; for in whatever hotel, restaurant, café, or shop he may enter, he will hear French spoken. I will go further. Let us suppose that this Frenchman is not well educated. What will be his amazement when he hears his maternal language spoken by the natives more correctly than he himself speaks it." † Allowing for a little natural and perhaps pardonable

---

* "Syria, which has been under French influence since the Crusades," wrote M. Georges Poignant in an article entitled "Les Intérêts français en Syrie" in *Questions Diplomatiques* in 1913, "has become ours by reason of the material and moral work which France has accomplished there during the nineteenth century. This admirable work, the most remarkable example that exists of 'peaceful penetration,' has given us rights that we cannot allow to be limited in any way."

† *Le Mois Colonial*, 1911, vol. ix, p. 156.

exaggeration, the fact remains that French education had obtained a strong hold in Western Syria. "When one travels in Syria," states another writer, "one might almost believe oneself to be in a French dependency. There are 130,000 children in Syria receiving instruction from our religious teachers. Nearly 40,000 are taught in French.* Upon all the railways French is spoken. A Frenchman could actually traverse all these regions and be sure not only of being well received, but also of being able everywhere to make himself understood. The Germans perfectly understood the prestige of our language —so much so that it is the administrative language of the Bagdad railway itself." † The position of France in Syria is such that the French Republic has every right, moral, political, and religious, to claim and exercise a protectorate over this portion of the Sultan's Dominions, in view of the attitude adopted by Turkey towards the Allies. These French claims have been ably expressed by M. Charles Vincent. "When we speak of the creation of a French protectorate in Syria," he writes, "we do not mean a sanctionless authority, limited by revocable conventions, or a fragmentary possession. It is the whole of Syria which should fall to France, from the Taurus Mountains to Mesopotamia and Egypt, the Syria of the Gulf of Adana—that is to say, the port of Alexandretta as well as those of Beirut and Jaffa—the Syria of the Lebanon . . . and the Syria of Damascus, that city of 400,000 inhabitants, where, during the last half century, Islam has been in daily contact with the missionaries of the French Catholic Schools. Syria has proclaimed herself our daughter by adoption. . . . No logical denial and no economic quibble could be raised against the secular right of France to the

---

* In a report, " Sur le Nombre des Français à l'Etranger et sur les Institutions qui leur viennent en Aide," contained in the *Bulletin de la Statistique générale de la France*, 1915, vol. iv, pp. 121-200, interesting particulars are given regarding the French in Syria. The total number of French in Asiatic Turkey is given as 4600 (though it is stated that these figures are probably much larger), of whom more than half are in Syria and Palestine, particularly at Beirut, Damascus, Jaffa, Jerusalem, and Smyrna. The number of scholars in the French schools is given as more than fifty thousand. In the Consular district of Beirut there are more than two hundred schools, with about thirty thousand pupils.

† M. Eugène Gallois in "La Revue des Questions Coloniales," 1914, p. 206.

protectorate not only of the Holy Land but of the whole of Syria." *

Such being the position in Syria it is not to be wondered at that the incursion of the German Emperor aroused deep resentment in France, where doubtless, but for the strained relations with Great Britain, his bombastic claim to be the friend of Mohammedans and Christians alike might have called for strong representations on the part of the French Government. Unfortunately for France, however, it was also feared that Great Britian had certain ulterior aims in Syria. The statement of Lord Beaconsfield that "France had only sentimental interests in Syria" was not forgotten, and although this country was fully occupied in the Sudan, the fact that Cyprus—the strategic sentinel of the Syrian coast—had been seized by Great Britain could not be overlooked. The position, therefore, so far as France, with her apparently waning influence, was concerned, was difficult. In spite of the spread of French culture in Syria her influence as a political Power was undoubtedly decreasing. Every German who arrived in the country became a silent worker against the Republic.† Even the Zionists, the Jewish settlers mainly from Germany and Russia, who furnished the larger part of a considerable Israelitish immigration, were working against France. "William II, always a clever politician," stated *Le Mois Colonial* in 1910, " has been able to use a two-handled weapon. On the one hand, in favouring the exodus of the Jews towards the Holy Land he is able to rid Germany of a people who in general are extremely unpopular and are often badly treated ; whilst on the other hand, as these Jews retain the status of Germans, a nationality of which they are proud, and are assured of the protection and help of their Emperor, they constitute a powerful agent in his policy of

* *Revue Hebdomadaire*, March 1915. In this respect we may bear in mind the French song, "Partant pour la Syrie."

† The present President of the Republic, M. Raymond Poincaré, then Foreign Minister, strongly asserted the claims of France in Syria in a speech in the Senate on December 31, 1912. " I have no need to emphasize the fact," he stated, " that in Lebanon and Syria especially we have traditional interests, and that we intend to have those interests respected. We are resolved to maintain the integrity of the Turkish Empire in Asia, but we shall not abandon there any of our traditions ; we shall not repudiate any of the sympathies that we have acquired ; we shall not give up any of our interests."

peaceful penetration."* It is then pointed out as a peculiar fact that many of the Russian Jews speak a German dialect and soon become merged in the German Jewish community.†

The entry of Germanism into Palestine had become an accomplished fact. The Kaiser's appeal to his exiled compatriots and his dramatic communication to the three hundred millions of Mohammedans were but the first outward manifestation of a definitely settled policy, and France, in common with Great Britain and Russia, could only watch and wait.

* *Le Mois Colonial*, 1910, p. 279.

† In an amusing article entitled " The Russian Battle of Dorking " (*United Service Magazine*, June 1902), describing how a Russian Rip Van Winkle awoke to find Moscow in the possession of the Germans and the greater part of Russia to have become Germanized, attention is also called to German progress in the Near East. When the writer awoke after a long sleep it was to find a German-Austrian prince ruling over Crete, and German princes in Macedonia, Albania, and Armenia, whilst the Holy Land had been placed under the control of a German general. " The Germans, and under their ægis the Jews, also proceeded to carry out vigorously the colonization of the Holy Land ; the former seized upon the agricultural pursuits, while the latter carried on the petty trade."

CHAPTER VI

THE RUSSO-TURKISH WAR

IT is now generally conceded that the Crimean War of 1854-6 was a stupid blunder on the part of British statesmen. The attempt that was then made to re-establish the tottering Turkish Empire and to check the Russian advance was a fatal error in policy, repeated again in 1878, of which the effects to-day are only too apparent. Had the European countries whose interests were centred in the Ottoman Empire come to a satisfactory arrangement among themselves and agreed to the establishment of a British Protectorate over Asia Minor and a French Protectorate over Syria, with ample compensations for Russia in the Balkans and Caucasus, or even had the policy initiated by Beaconsfield in 1878 been continued by successive Governments, all might possibly have been well; but British policy was uncertain and wavering, distrust of Russia was the prevailing prepossession of both political parties, and our subsequent virtual abdication of influence at Constantinople under Gladstone gave a fatal direction to the course of events. Few people to-day know why the Crimean War was fought and fewer still realize what were its unfortunate results.

It is not possible here, and would indeed lead us far from the main purpose of this book, to deal with the historical causes, or to describe the events, of that war. Ostensibly fought by Russia about the guardianship of the Holy Places, the cause of it lay far deeper in the increasing pressure exercised by Russia upon the moribund Ottoman Power and the fear felt by Great Britain, France, and the Mediterranean countries that Russian influence would soon be paramount throughout the Near East. The unfortunate Christians who were to be delivered from their long anguish of misgovernment were eventually sacrificed to the greed of the Christian Powers, and the mockery of a war fought for their liberation from the Turkish yoke by Russia on the one side, and for the reform of the conditions under which they lived by Great Britain, France, and Sardinia on the other, in close alliance with the unspeakable Turk, is ample justification for the opinions of those who believe that neither religion, sentiment, nor even duty have been sufficient guides for diplomatic action when other interests intervene.

As the Ottoman Power decayed and Turkey became more and more unfit to rule the Christian peoples of the Levant, Russia, continuously advancing into the lands vacated by the retreating Turks, more and more adopted the attitude of protector of the unfortunate races who were still subject to the Sultan. And with this advance the Christian Powers of Western Europe became convinced that their political interests could only be served by re-erecting the shattered edifice of Turkish control, with due safeguards, worthless and imaginary as they proved, for the welfare of the threatened populations of Turkey and Asia Minor. The fear of Russia outweighed all other considerations. When the Emperor Nicholas wrote of Turkey as " a sick man dying " it was believed that he was prepared to rob the decaying Empire solely for his own benefit, and every intention that was manifested by the Russians for ameliorating the condition of men of their own race and creed was looked upon as a deep political plot to secure the hegemony of the Turkish Empire. It may have been. But in any case European diplomacy need not have hesitated to share in the spoils, seeing that never before had it neglected to take an adequate *quid pro quo* for its services.

The intentions of the Emperor Nicholas were made abundantly clear to British statesmen. They included the formation of the territories of Serbia and Bulgaria into principalities under Russian suzerainty, in return for which Great Britain would be permitted to occupy Egypt and Crete; whilst Constantinople itself, the key to the situation, was to be held by none of the Great Powers. But the intentions of the Russian Emperor, universally mistrusted by the Western Powers, merely served to arouse in Great Britain a feeling of deep resentment against Russian aggression; and Lord Palmerston, in spite of the opposition of Lord Aberdeen, but backed by the support of Sir Stratford Canning (Lord Stratford de Redcliffe), then representing Great Britain at Constantinople, fell under the influence of Napoleon III, who was anxious to consolidate his position by a successful European war. Great Britain "drifted into the war," whilst Prussia and Austria, only concerned in the limitation of Russian ambitions, stood aside in order that others might do work, the results of which, in the event of the success of the incongruous Allies, could only be most satisfactory for themselves.

The results of the Crimean War were disastrous for Russia, but they were perhaps on the whole more unfortunate for Great Britain, who became deeply pledged to a course of action in which continuity of policy, impossible apparently in a democracy, was the main factor for success. By the Peace of Paris, signed on March 20, 1856, Russia was thrust back and her naval power on the Black Sea eliminated. The Moldavian frontier was redressed to render it more easily defensible against a Russian advance, and the Black Sea was interdicted both to the Russian fleet and the navies of any other Power; whilst Turkey was permitted another breathing-space, the signatories promising " to respect the independence and territorial integrity of the Ottoman Empire." Europe took upon herself the responsibility claimed by the Tsar of securing religious toleration for the Sultan's dominions, and like a committee managing a patriotic society eventually broke up into hostile groups, inefficient and unable to secure redress for the evils that characterized Ottoman rule. The sick man of Turkey was to be cured by the drugs in the Western political pharmacopœia, but unfortunately the doctors were quacks, whose lack of knowledge was only excelled by their desire to secure adequate payment for their services.

" The war of 1854," wrote Froude during the Russo-Turkish War of 1877, " was a step in what I considered then, and consider now, to have been the wrong course—a course leading direct, if persisted in, to most deplorable issues. The war had been made inevitable from the indignation of the Liberal party throughout Europe at Russia's interference in Hungary.* Professedly a war in the defence of Turkey, it was fought really for European liberty. European liberty is no longer in danger,

* *I.e.* when Gortschakov lent his aid for putting down the Magyar revolt.

nor has the behaviour of Turkey since the peace been of the kind to give her claim to our interests for her own sake. . . . The Turk was to rise out of the war regenerate and a " new creature." He was to be the advance guard of enlightenment, the bulwark of Europe against Barbarism. There was no measure to the hopes which English people indulged in in those days of delight and excitement. But the facts have gone the natural way. The Turk has gone back not forward. . . . Unhappily England could not agree with the other Powers on the nature of the remedy required. Russia has been obliged to take active measures and at once the Crimean ashes have again been blown into a flame ; there is a cry that Russia has sinister aims of her own, that English interests are in danger, and that we must rush to the support of our ancient friend and ally." *

Although we may justly question whether the Crimean War was fought in the interests of European liberty, Froude on this occasion sums up correctly the tendency of British policy, and a brief examination of succeeding events strengthens the view that on this as on other occasions Great Britain failed to appreciate the new course of events in Europe, and by constantly opposing Russia worked to the infinite advantage of Austria and Germany.

The diplomatic history of the years following the Crimean War shows how futile was the settlement arrived at by the Paris Congress. It is a record of the progressive undoing of the settlement, due partly to the unsoundness of the arrangement, but more especially to the political conditions prevailing in Great Britain. It is not the aim of this book to point out how the party system reacted unfavourably upon our position in the East and resulted in an uncertain and wavering policy which is best exemplified in the conflict between Disraeli and Gladstone during the seventies. The former, a statesman of clear vision, if properly supported, might have negotiated a satisfactory settlement of the Eastern question ; but his position was unfortunately weakened by criticism and opposition within the Cabinet, so that the plans he suggested were never carried to their proper conclusion, and far-sighted measures, offering some chance of permanence, were not efficiently

* Quotation from *Journal of the United Service Institution of India*, 1915, p. 450-1.

supported. In foreign politics as in other things continuity of policy is indispensable. Unfortunately the only connecting-link between the action of Disraeli and Gladstone was hostility towards Russia. Whilst the former was ready to welcome a strengthened Turkey, doubtless with the ultimate aim of establishing a British "sphere of influence" in Asia Minor, the latter was hostile to Turkey, Russia, and Austria alike, but was never prepared to justify his hostility by vigorous action, and after protesting, generally and weakly gave way. The difference lay between the aims of a statesman and those of a politician. "As a matter of humanity," stated Gladstone in 1877, "I wish with all my soul that the Sultan were driven bag and baggage into the heart of Asia"; whilst three years later, in connexion with Austria, he stated that "it was impossible to put one's finger on one point of the map where Austrian influence had been exerted for good," * and " Austria has ever been the unflinching foe of freedom in every country of Europe. Austria trampled Italy under foot, Austria resisted the unity of Germany." There is no cause for wonder that under these circumstances British policy was so weak and changeable and that Germany eventually benefited from the vacillation of British Cabinets.

In Turkey itself events rapidly went from bad to worse, and whilst the Powers quarrelled amongst themselves there seemed little likelihood of the Sultan initiating the reforms that had been promised. In the Balkan Peninsula all warnings of events had been lost on the Turk, who, remembering Palmerston's refusal in 1862 to act on Brunnow's suggestion of aiding the insurgent Christians, counted upon the continuance of our traditional policy of hostility to Muscovite expansion and our unwillingness to take an active part in the dismember-ment of the Ottoman Empire. Neither the activity of France in Syria in 1860, nor the formation of the Danubian principality of Rumania in the following year, nor the activity of the Serbs, nor even the revolt in Bosnia-Herzegovina in 1875, were sufficient to arouse the Sultan to the danger of his position; and it was only when Russia, convinced that the time had arrived for action, prepared to compel the acceptance of the reforms suggested by the European " Concert " that he prepared

* Speech on May 17, 1880.

to meet the threatened danger. Even at the last moment he believed that the coercive proposals of Austria, Prussia, and Russia could be evaded so long as the British Government continued to assert that the Porte had not had sufficient opportunity to execute the latest reform. With the acceptance of the programme of administrative reforms embodied in the celebrated Andrassy Note, prepared by the Austrian Chancellor, Count Andrassy, in concert with Bismark and Gortschakov, by Great Britain, the Sultan's position became hopeless; but the acceptance came too late to prevent the war, for though the Sultan signified his consent to the programme of reforms on February 11, 1876, the warlike people of the Balkans were already in active revolt.

The Andrassy Note, which met with a chilling reception from the British Government, embodied proposals for the improvement of the lot of the peasantry, complete religious liberty, the abolition of the farming of the taxes, and other reforms to be applied to the revolting districts; but the Sultan's promises of reform were universally distrusted by his insurgent subjects, and when further demands were made in the "Berlin Memorandum," drawn up by the three Imperial Chancellors and issued on May 13, events had so far progressed owing to the massacres at Salonika, the frightful atrocities committed by the Bashi-Bazouks, and the confusion existing at Constantinople due to the dethronement and subsequent murder of the Sultan, that peace was impossible. War, moreover, was rendered doubly certain through the action of the Beaconsfield Ministry in refusing its assent to the Berlin Memorandum (already accepted by France and Italy) and making no alternative proposals. Turkey was further encouraged by the fact that on May 24 the British fleet was ordered to the Dardanelles.

Under these circumstances commenced the Russo-Turkish War which was to have such decisive results for the whole of Europe. The question that faced the Great Powers and really affected the policies of the European Governments was not so much the future independence of the Balkan States, but whether the conflict could be localized and a general conflagration prevented. The position of Great Britain had been made clear in a communication presented to the Russian

Government, through the Russian Ambassador in London, Count Shouvalov, in which Lord Derby, then responsible for Foreign Affairs, summarized British interests in the Levant. On her side Russia agreed to limit the area of hostilities in the evident hope that by these concessions the neutrality at least of Great Britain could be secured. Both Egypt and the Suez Canal were ruled out of the area of operations, although these formed part of the Ottoman Dominions, and the Tsar, as at the time of the Crimean War, expressly stated that the conquest and occupation of Constantinople formed no part of his plans, since the future of the Turkish capital was a question of common interest that could only be settled by an understanding amongst the Great Powers.*

Nevertheless it seemed possible that as the object of the war could not be considered attained until the Christians of Turkey were "placed in a position in which their lives and liberties are adequately protected against the intolerable abuses of the Turkish administration," a temporary occupation of Constantinople would be necessary; and on this question a conflict of interests, if not actual hostilities, between Great Britain and Russia, seemed only too probable. "It is not towards conquest that we march," stated the Grand Duke Nicholas, in command of the Russian Army, "but to defend our insulted and oppressed brethren, and to defend the faith of Christ." The ostensible objects of the new crusade were thus clearly defined, but in a Note addressed to the Powers on April 7, Prince Gortschakov spoke also of the interests of Russia— a term which caused great uneasiness to the British Government. What were these interests and how did they clash with those of Great Britain and Austria?

Before considering the results of the war, the general position in the Balkan Peninsula must be understood. Russia entered upon the war under most disadvantageous conditions. She could attack in four directions, but two of these were closed to her by the operations of European diplomacy. On the Black Sea, owing to the stipulations of the Declaration of Paris, she had no superiority of strength and was therefore unable to use sea-power as an efficient weapon of offence, whilst the way through Serbia was closed owing to the attitude

* Hertslet's "Map of Europe," vol. iv, p. 2625.

of Austria, who was unwilling to allow Russian troops to advance over the Austrian highway to Salonika. There remained, therefore, the passage through Rumania, a principality still subject to Ottoman suzerainty, and the roads through Caucasia into Asia Minor.

Rumania in this matter was placed in a particularly unenviable position, similar to that occupied by her at the present day. This little country, occupying the delta of the Danube, was placed between the upper and nether millstone and liable to be severely handled by whichever of the Powers happened to emerge victorious if her statesmen failed to adopt the right attitude at the right moment. It is not surprising, therefore, that Prince Charles hesitated to commit his small State to a definite policy, particularly as Bismark, when appealed to, had adopted a cryptic attitude and had advised that "every one should do what he considered best for himself." But in reality the German Chancellor went as far as he was able by sending more effective counsels through the German Crown Prince and advising the German Sovereign of Rumania "not to offer serious opposition to Russia, to speak of a duty towards the Porte, to dwell upon his conventional obligations, and then to yield to pressure."* The opposition offered by John Bratiano, the Rumanian representative, during his interview with Gortschakov was rather a matter of form than a direct challenge to Russia, for in reality Rumania had no choice in the matter and was forced to accede to the demand for a free passage for the Russian army. The co-operation of Rumania was secured in a convention signed on April 16, in which friendly treatment was promised for the Muscovite troops, although the active intervention of Rumania was still subject to the course of events. In return for this concession the Tsar promised to "maintain and defend the actual integrity of Rumania," a promise which, as will be seen later, was not fulfilled when Russia demanded and seized the province of Bessarabia and thus earned the hostility of the Rumanian people. Rumania's attitude was further defined when on June 3 Prince Charles, her Hohenzollern Sovereign, repudiated Turkish suzerainty over his principality.

The way thus being opened for the passage of the Russian

* Hanotaux, "Contemporary France," vol. iv, p. 310.

troops across the Danube and through the difficult passes of the Middle Balkans, the attitude of the other Balkan States remained to be considered. Would they efficiently co-operate with Russia or leave to that country the self-imposed task of liberating them from the Turkish yoke ? Greece, who had much to gain by active intervention, did not rise to the occasion. As the direct heir of the " sick man " at Constantinople, she represented the cause of Hellenism in the East, and it might have been expected that she would lend her active aid to the Russian invasion. Unfortunately, however, although she was narrowed in her situation on the continent, and desired to enlarge her borders and to advance upon Salonika, to reign over the Archipelago where Hellenic life survived under Turkish domination, and to take her place as the leading naval Power of the Balkans, she had to consider the wishes of Austria as well as the interests of her countrymen who were scattered along the Levantine littoral and liable to be overwhelmed by the Turkish power. Neither Austria nor Russia was sympathetic, and the attitude of Great Britain was at least cryptic, if not entirely unsatisfactory. Moreover, weakened internally by deplorable administration, badly organized, and lacking both the necessary means and the necessary army, she hesitated to sacrifice the Greek colonies beyond the limits of her borders to Turkish retribution and to possible disaster. The Greeks remained neutral, therefore, until it was too late to take effective action.

In the Mid-Balkans there was Bulgaria, inhabited by a race who had been so throughly crushed for centuries that it seemed hardly possible to realize that this was a Christian people, so terrible was the yoke imposed by their Mohammedan masters. The "Bulgarian atrocities," in which the British Government had affected to disbelieve until the resounding voice of Gladstone had proclaimed them to an unwilling world and until they had been thoroughly exposed by Mr. Walter Baring,* who reported that " the numbers given of fifteen to twenty thousand victims and more than a hundred villages destroyed do not appear to be exaggerated," were one of the direct causes of the war—but no help could be expected from a

* Brother of Lord Cromer. Mr. Baring was then a member of the staff of the British Embassy at Constantinople.

people thus situated, " a peaceful and hard-working race, who for five centuries past have tilled their soil to the almost exclusive profit of their oppressors " *; for slaves under the lash, and such were the Bulgarians, could not co-operate effectively in military operations.

There remained the Serbians, who, under the guidance of their prince, Milan Obrenovitch, impetuous, rash, headstrong, and lacking in political foresight, had impulsively thrown themselves upon the Turks on behalf of the insurgents in Bosnia-Herzegovina; and the Montenegrins. The former, sullen and defeated, nourishing their ambition of dominating the way to Salonika and of re-erecting the former Serbian Empire, had been sacrificed to the ambitions of Austria, who feared the extension of Russian influence in this direction, and were unable to offer the assistance that might have been forthcoming but for their precipitate action in prematurely attacking the Turks. The latter, " the Benjamin of the family," occupying a strong position amid the mountains, threatening the Austrian road to the Ægean, and dominating the way to the Adriatic, were unable to give effective assistance. Russia, therefore, had to depend entirely upon herself, with the possible help of Rumania should the latter State become convinced that only her aid would prevent the return of the Turks to the Danube.

The events of the War of Liberation need be described but briefly. Russia and Turkey were not unequally matched. The collapse of the Ottoman power, which was universally expected in Western Europe, was not so imminent as appeared, and the Turks in manifesting their old military spirit and rallying to the support of their threatened sovereign were able to meet the Russians upon almost equal terms. Favoured by strong strategical positions and defended by the famous quadrilateral —the great fortresses of Rustchuk, Shumla, Varna, and Silistria, with the further strong positions at Plevna, Sofia, and Tirnova—they were able to oppose an effective barrier to the advance of the Russian army, whilst the Balkan mountains had to be crossed before the final blow could be delivered against Adrianople or Constantinople. Two of the fortresses —Shumla and Rustchuk—were connected by rail with the port

* " Manifesto of the Bulgarian Nation," August 14, 1876.

of Varna, where the Turks could land their troops, whilst only two or three passes could be attempted by artillery. The Russian offensive therefore could be strongly held and Turkey, if she were only able to muster, arm, and clothe her troops, was in a position to offer a strong resistance to the advance of the Russian forces. The Turks, as born fighters, were able to sustain existence on what for any other people would be considered inadequate supplies, and they were able, moreover, to demand and take whatever they required from the peasantry over whom they ruled. Yet in London and Paris it was fondly believed that the Russians had but to march to conquer, and it was thought that the ragged legions of the Sultan would melt away before the Russian rising sun. Already in imagination Constantinople was securely held by the Russian hosts.

The two campaigns, in Asia Minor and European Turkey, commenced simultaneously. War had been declared on April 12, 1877; but owing to inadequate preparations the Russians did not reach the slopes of the Balkans before July, having marched thus far owing to the inertia or strategy, for we know not which, of the Turks, who made no attempt to stay their onward rush. But the facility of the Russian advance added to the danger of the situation; for the Turks now concentrated their forces, and threatening the rear of the Russians advanced under Osman Pasha and halted upon the heights around Plevna, where the Turkish commander entrenched his troops and took up a strong position from which he was able to threaten the advance forces of the Russians under Gourka. With Osman in this position it was no longer a question of advancing upon Adrianople and Constantinople, through the passes of the Balkans, but the vital question of defeating the rapidly concentrating Turkish forces.

The Turks, confident in the belief that they were under excellent command, and fired by the message of the Sultan that they were entering upon "a Holy War against the enemies of the Faith," and that "the swords of the believers will open the gates of Paradise," rose to the occasion, defeated the army of the Grand Duke with great loss, and firmly established themselves in positions threatening the Russian communications and rendering impossible any advance southwards. At the same time, in Asia Minor, the Turks who had retired upon Erzerum took the initiative, relieved Kars, and severely defeated the Russians.

The unexpected rivival of Turkish power was received with joy in Vienna and Budapest, whilst in London, where it was now thought that the Turkish arms would be victorious, Beaconsfield prepared to dictate the terms of peace, confident in the belief that British policy was about to triumph at the expense of Russia. But at this juncture, when the future stability of Turkey seemed assured, occurred one of those dramatic changes that upset the plans of the most astute, and render abortive the careful preparations of diplomacy. Rumania, afraid of the ultimate result to herself of a Russian defeat, and doubtless aware that her position in that event would be seriously complicated, decided to take an active part in the war. " How terrible would be our position," stated Charles of Hohenzollern, " if the Turkish troops were allowed to take the offensive and bring the scene of war across our frontiers. We are obliged to co-operate with the Imperial forces of Russia in order to hasten the end at all costs."

The intervention of Rumania was decisive. Prince Charles, having been invested with the supreme command of the allied troops before Plevna, a general assault was ordered for September 11 by the Russians and Rumanians; but again, as on previous occasions, the Turkish arms prevailed, and it became necessary to invest the Turkish positions. Had Osman been adequately supported from headquarters the result might have been different, but he was unable to break the iron cordon by which he was surrounded; and on December 10, 1877, he surrendered with forty thousand men, owing to lack of food and ammunition and the inertia of the Turks, who, under adequate generalship, might have relieved the situation. The defence of Plevna " affords the most brilliant example in modern warfare of the power of a force strongly entrenched in a favourable position to ' contain,' that is, to hold or hold back, a greater force of the enemy." *

With the fall of Plevna there was nothing to stop the onward march of the Russian troops. They crossed the

* " Development of the European Nations," by J. Holland Rose, 1914, p. 218.

mountains and Turkey was at the complete mercy of the Russians. The position of the latter was rendered doubly secure owing to the victory of the Montenegrins in the west, and of the Serbians, who, after the battle of Pirot, took possession of Nish; whilst the Greeks, who had awaited the course of events, now entered Thessaly. In Asia Minor the Turks were driven from Kars and the fall of Ezerum was but a question of time. The Turkish Empire seemed about to collapse before the assaults of its enemies, and it appeared as though the cross would again be erected over the Mosque of Saint Sofia. After the fall of Adrianople, on January 20, 1878, the Russians were in a position to dictate terms of peace, and eleven days later the preliminary terms were arranged at Adrianople, whilst the actual treaty was signed on March 3 at San Stefano, a small village in the vicinity of Constantinople. The whole of the Balkans seemed to have become a Russian fief.

In the Chancelleries of Europe the perturbation was great. The fruits of victory must at all hazards be snatched from Muscovite hands. A permanent peace could only be secured by diplomatic action. At once Russia found herself confronted by a formidable, yet incongruous, combination. The British Cabinet, although convinced that Russia must be checked, was apparently hopelessly divided. There were those who desired peace at any price. There were those who wanted immediate war with Russia. There were those who desired to see the cross on Saint Sofia and those who thought that Russia might be permitted to take Constantinople and to hold the Turkish capital temporarily, whilst there were " the Prime Minister and the Chancellor of the Exchequer (Northcote) who desired to see something done, but don't know exactly what." * Into this diplomatic turmoil stepped Bismarck, the silent watcher, and threading the mazy avenues of the political wilderness, imposed his will upon the Powers, as the " honest broker " of Europe—in the interests of Germany—apparently the least concerned of the Great Powers.

* " Life of Sir Stafford Northcote," p. 106.

CHAPTER VII

THE BERLIN CONGRESS

The Congress at Berlin, which was to settle the future of the Turkish Empire as well as to formulate, if not in words at least in practice, the main lines of European policy, marks one of those dramatic pauses in the history of the world when statesmen meet face to face in the council chamber as the representatives of seemingly irreconcilable national policies. The deep undercurrent of mistrust and mutual recrimination that divided Europe into three hostile groups, each determined to secure, or to prevent others from securing, the plums out of the diplomatic pie, was not always apparent to the onlooker. The tumultuous and swelling currents that met beneath the surface only occasionally rippled the seemingly placid diplomatic waters—although there were tense moments when it appeared as though the pent-up forces would burst upward and carry away the amiable diplomatists who were so frigidly or so effusively, as the case might be, polite to each other. Such moments occurred when the Russian Chancellor cast down his papers and spectacles; when Gortschakov and Disraeli were finally settling the Russian frontiers of Asiatic Turkey; or when the "honest broker" who presided over the destinies of the Congress exercised his bitter, but polite, irony at the expense of one or other of the Great Powers. Since it had been written in the Book of Destiny that some of the main questions before the Congress were to be settled behind the scenes, and sometimes behind the backs of the interested parties, whilst others were not to be discussed at all, the Assembly was frequently fore-ordained to meet and consider plans that had already been settled by secret combinations, and nothing remained for discomfited parties but to acquiesce in such esoteric arrangements with the best grace possible.

The old gentlemen of the Congress, amongst whom were the foremost and keenest diplomatists of the period, appeared to be engaged in some pleasing and fascinating game requiring some degree of skill and a considerable amount of sang-froid, but nevertheless apparently little calculated to ruffle the temper or to try the nerves. The intervals that were not spent in the Council Chamber seemed to be passed in social engagements and in a round of entertainments which apparently left little time for the serious work in hand. Visits to the country house of the Crown Prince, to official receptions, mingled with informal supper-parties and more formal balls, supplied plenty of relaxation; whilst on one occasion the Congress spent what was perhaps the most exciting hour of the whole proceedings upon a small yacht, which, owing to a sudden squall, seemed likely to upset and put an end to European diplomacy.*

But, as we know, the seemingly aimless proceedings of the plenipotentiaries were watched with intense interest by those whose business it is to follow the movements of the august. Every visit was duly noted and its precise significance analysed. That prince of journalists, De Blowitz,† angled cleverly in the dark waters, collecting and materializing information for the tingling ears of the outside public; whilst others, only less successful, kept the Press of Europe constantly supplied with the crumbs that fell from the diplomatic table. Inside the closed doors of the Congress during those fateful days of 1878 old gentlemen chatted pleasantly, looked at maps of Europe and Asia, toyed with the possessions of the Sultan, rearranged frontiers, struck diplomatic balances, regardless of the interests of inarticulate nations and of the smaller Powers, such as Rumania and Serbia and Montenegro, who were not admitted into the inner precincts but were forced to wait outside; always thought of " their high civilizing

---

* Prince Hohenlohe relates this little anecdote, together with another amusing incident, at the residence of the Crown Prince, which will not be related in these pages.

† So successful was De Blowitz in gathering news that he was generally credited with having at his command some mysterious means of obtaining information. On one occasion before the commencement of proceedings Bismarck is reported to have solemnly looked under the table, and when asked what he was doing, to have replied, " I am looking for Blowitz."

mission," of which they were reminded from time to time by Bismarck, but quickly and conveniently forgot when the time arrived for action; erected buffer States between the predatory Empires of Russia and Austria-Hungary, and settled a dozen questions of the utmost moment. Outside in the corridors of Europe, excited crowds awaited the decisions of the Congress, standing in fear and trembling lest the fragile diplomatic swords in the hands of the plenipotentiaries should snap during the secret encounters and plunge the whole of Europe into a devastating and terrible war.

The chief fact which strikes the unprejudiced outside observer in all these diplomatic proceedings is the apparently aimless fashion in which two or three individuals meet together and discuss and settle the destinies of millions of their fellow-creatures and by a series of concessions and undertakings rearrange the map of Europe. Never was this process more apparent than during the Congress of Berlin, when Germany first assumed her position as the arbitrator of European policy. Armed with full powers over the future of enormous territories, the plenipotentiaries shuffled and reshuffled the " cards of Providence "—sometimes, if the testimony of some of their number is to be believed, without any appreciation or real knowledge of the situation. Yet the permanent officials behind the scenes, the real masters of the Congress, who suggested and directed the policy of their chiefs and studied the true underlying factors of the political situation, would probably be able to show that the plenipotentiaries were in reality less simple than they affected to appear. The incident of the map of Asia Minor related by Count Shouvalov, if it be accepted as true, would indicate that both Lord Beaconsfield and Prince Gortschakov, the two protagonists of the duel, were unacquainted with the *terrain* of their diplomatic battles. According to Shouvalov, Lord Salisbury said, " My dear Count, Lord Beaconsfield cannot negotiate, he has never seen a map of Asia Minor." Certainly the incident, if true, throws a flood of light upon diplomatic methods, but it is to be feared that some exaggeration has crept into the anecdote. This is what Count Shouvalov narrates in his Memoirs. " This last Assembly," he writes, " devoted to the Asiatic question, was a serious occasion. On its result hung the issues of peace and war. The President suggested that the two negotiators, Lord Beaconsfield and Prince Gortschakov, should sit side by side to point out the tenure of their agreements. The two gentlemen therefore took their places, each one spreading before him a map traced for the occasion. We others stood in a group behind them. I at once foresaw the trouble and confusion that would ensue. Gortschakov's map had one line only, that of San Stefano, and the Prince declared emphatically that ' my lord ' had accepted it. Beaconsfield, however, replied to the Prince's declaration by a laconic ' No, no,' and pointed out on his own map the line to which he had consented. Now, to my great astonishment, this line, in all its sinuosities, was precisely the one that we had the right to accept as the extreme limit of our agreement. The contradiction between the plenipotentiaries tended to embitter the discussion. Each stood obstinately by his own line, when Prince Gortschakov got up, seized my hand and said to me, ' There is some treachery; they have had the map of our Etat Major.' I learned afterwards that on the previous day Gortschakov had asked for a map of Asia Minor. He was given the confidential map of the two lines. He showed it to Lord Beaconsfield, lending it to him for a few hours so that Lord Salisbury could see it. The Englishmen, noticing a line that threw back the frontier of San Stefano, had adopted it for their own map. This was the explanation of the imagined treachery." [*] Incidents of this nature, if of frequent occurrence, naturally tend to shake the confidence of the uninitiated in the wisdom of European diplomatists.

The Congress of Berlin, which first met on June 13, 1878, was called upon to settle the situation that had arisen as the result of the Treaty of San Stefano, the preliminary treaty of peace which had been agreed upon between Russia and Turkey—a settlement which the other Powers of Europe declined to recognize. They refused to acknowledge the right of Russia to settle the various important questions connected with the rearrangement of the Balkans and the rectification of the Asiatic frontiers, because two of them at least—Germany and Austria-Hungary—feared the extension of Russian influence

[*] Quoted by Hanotaux from "The Souvenirs of Count P. Shouwaloff," vol. iv, pp. 354–5.

in the Near East; whilst three others—Great Britain, Italy, and France—feared in addition the possibility of Russia becoming a Mediterranean Power. The various matters connected with the affairs of Montenegro, Serbia, Bulgaria, Bosnia, and Herzegovina, as well as the settlement of the pecuniary and territorial claims of Russia against Turkey, including the position of Rumania, were the joint concern of all the Great Powers. Germany, as seemingly the least directly affected, though in reality having a vital future, yet unappreciated, interest in these regions, undertook the rôle of mediator. Bismarck, the man of destiny, who had long awaited and had long prepared for this opportunity, assumed his natural position as President of the Congress and held the heavily weighted scales of justice. In February 1878, after having counselled that the British Fleet should retreat from the position it had taken up as a counterbalance to the Russian army then menacing Constantinople, he took the initiative in the Reichstag (on February 19) and " performed one of the most considerable acts in modern history " when he posed as the moderator and in a masterly survey of the European situation stated that " what will entail a change in the stipulations of 1856 will doubtless need the sanction of the Powers that signed them." In this direct but simple phrase the German Chancellor showed that he was prepared to bid for the support of Austria-Hungary at the expense of Russia, and gave an indication of the future course of German diplomacy, which was even then preparing the way of expansion towards the Adriatic and Ægean Seas. Russia had advanced as far as Germany would permit—and much farther than was thought expedient by those who directed the foreign policy of Great Britain.

Bismarck's declaration marked the commencement of a new era in Teutonic policy. "Here in the Reichstag," states Hanotaux, "originated the tendency that the world's business was long to take, even to the defeat of Russia at Mukden, and the distant concurrence of Germany and England. . . . The future of Russia, France, and England, the future of all the Powers, depended on the direction taken by Germany at these cross-roads of fate," and although few then perceived the wide avenues that were being opened to Teutonic influence, Bismarck certainly, and other German politicians, knew that the way was being prepared for the German advance. The main question at issue was not the conflict of interests between Great Britain and Russia, nor the question of what was to become of the Turkish capital, nor even the future of the Christian races of Turkey, but the future of Slav and Teuton. " The main point of this Eastern problem," stated Herr Windthorst, " lies in the question which of the two elements—Germanic on the one hand, Slav on the other—is to dominate the world ? *We* must embrace the German interest in its universality."

It is not necessary to discuss in detail the events preceding the Congress, nor even the deliberations and the results arrived at by that historical assembly. Only as it affected Teutonic destinies need it be dealt with in these pages, for it became the instrument of German ambitions and set a barrier across the advancing tide of Slavdom. The part played by Great Britain directly facilitated the growth of German influence ; for the bolstering up of the Turkish Empire enabled Germany to prepare and mature her future advance. British policy in connexion with Russian expansion has been discussed briefly in the previous chapter, but it may now justly be questioned whether our attitude of unbending hostility towards Russian aims and our constant and unwavering distrust of every Russian move were entirely justified, and it may be asked whether we should not have furthered the interests of the British Empire to greater advantage had we arrived at an understanding with Russian statesmen. Unfortunately, Germanic influences at the British Court and the inability of diplomatists to gauge correctly the trend of German policy or to foresee the marvellous growth of the German Empire blinded the British public as to the true position of affairs and rendered them incapable of judging whether Teuton or Slav were the real enemy. By supporting the tottering Ottoman Power, British statesmen not only played into the hands of Germany, but they forsook those whom sentiment as well as interest should have protected. The Christians of Asiatic Turkey were sacrificed to unsound political theories, and the subsequent Armenian and other massacres from that date till now are directly attributable to the unfortunate course of British policy.

British interests in the East were defined in a dispatch sent by Lord Derby to Count Shouvalov on May 6, 1877, when it was pointed out that these fell under five main headings, directly concerned with the Suez Canal, Egypt, Constantinople, the Bosphorus and Dardanelles, and the Persian Gulf. The first of these was undoubtedly connected with "the necessity of keeping open, uninjured and uninterrupted," the communications between Europe and the East, and for this reason Russia was warned that any attempt to interfere with the Canal or its approaches would be regarded as a "menace to India and as a grave injury to the commerce of the world," and would be looked upon as inconsistent with the maintenance of neutrality by Great Britain. This was, of course, subsequent to Disraeli's masterly stroke of policy with regard to the Suez Canal shares,* and expressed the firm determination of the British Government to maintain, even at the expense of war, its privileged position with regard to this international waterway. Further, the British Government declared that the mercantile and commercial interests of European nations were so largely involved in Egypt that any attack on that country would not be regarded with unconcern by Great Britain. For this reason all questions connected with the Egyptian sphere were deliberately ruled out of the Berlin discussions, although the troops of the Khedive had valiantly fought at Plevna for the Turks—and in this action the British Government were directly supported by France, because the question of Egypt was one to be settled between those two Powers alone.

The third question discussed in the Berlin Note was the future of Constantinople. The British Government were not prepared "to witness with indifference the passing into other hands than those of its present possessors of a capital holding

* At the end of November 1875, Disraeli, having learned from Lord Derby, then Foreign Minister, that the Khedive's Suez Canal shares had been secretly offered to, and refused by, the French Government, entered into negotiations with Ismail and purchased the shares for the sum of £4,500,000, a stroke of policy that is now universally acknowledged to have been thoroughly justified on all grounds, financial, political, military, and economic. Disraeli's foresight was not, however, recognized in all quarters. Both Gladstone and Granville disapproved of the purchase, as they subsequently objected to the retention of Egypt. The policy of "scuttle" applied with peculiar force to certain Liberal patriots.

so peculiar and commanding a position." Further, the Ministry objected to any alteration in the status of the Bosphorus and Dardanelles, and definitely expressed their intention of protecting their interests in the Persian Gulf against any interference in that quarter.

British interests having thus been defined previous to the Russo-Turkish War, Austria-Hungary, in a dispatch from Count Beust, expressed her desire to share in the definitive regulation of the conditions of peace, and invited the Great Powers (February 5, 1878) to take part in a Conference at Vienna (and subsequently at Baden), but after Bismarck's speech in the Reichstag, acting on German inspiration, suggested that the proposed Conference should be a Congress attended by the Prime Ministers of Europe and that the place of meeting should be Berlin (March 7). "My Government," wrote Count Beust, "is of opinion that a Congress of the Powers would have the greatest chance of arriving at practical results if this Congress were to meet in Berlin." By so doing he indicated to the world at large that Bismarck's influence was supreme and that the main lines of policy had already been settled by the Austro-Hungarian and German Governments. On one point the two Teutonic Governments preserved identical aims, for the independence of the delta of the Danube—one of those Germanic outlets which Moltke had desired many years before—was a principle that could not be ignored. The agreement between Germany and Austria on this point was therefore complete, and the Duc Decazes, French Minister of Foreign Affairs, was informed by a correspondent at Vienna (June 1877) that "should Russia deceive us in this, or ignore this principle, we shall fight her; this is definitely settled, our military position assures us the advantage"; and further, that "*Prussia will side with us*," and that the Austrians were sure of Prussia's attitude. Herein, stated the writer, "lay the secret of Count Andrassy's calmness of demeanour in confronting the question of the East." *

The understanding between Austria-Hungary and Germany, therefore, was sufficiently defined to enable the two countries to control the results of the Congress, and it only remained for Great Britain to make what terms she could with the

* Hanotaux, vol. iv, pp. 311–12.

former country so as to meet Russia with an undivided front. For this purpose the British Ministry let it be known that they were prepared to support Austria-Hungary in Bosnia-Herzegovina, and at a preliminary negotiation at the Congress the recognition of this step by Germany, so agreeable in itself to Bismarck, was obtained; whilst both countries signified that they were prepared to support Great Britain's policy with regard to the erection of a buffer State between Bulgaria and Turkey and the settlement of the question of the Dardanelles. Thus, previous to the actual meeting of the Congress, the position of the United Kingdom had been greatly strengthened, and through the vigorous diplomacy of the British Cabinet she was enabled to take a strong line throughout the proceedings.

Lord Beaconsfield's position was, in fact, made doubly secure by two successful acts of diplomacy that vitally affected British policy. For some time the British Foreign Office had been secretly negotiating with the Porte, which was prepared to make considerable sacrifices in order to secure British support. On June 4, nine days before the diplomatists assembled at Berlin, the secret Cyprus Convention was concluded, by which it was agreed that if Russia retained the three districts in Asia Minor which she had definitely decided to keep at all hazards, viz. Batum, Kars, and Ardahan, Great Britain should hold the island of Cyprus, which occupied a most important strategic position in the Mediterranean and in some respects was a veritable key to Asia Minor.* On her part, Great Britain agreed to take up arms on behalf of Turkey should there be further Russian aggressions, and at the same time pressed for better protection for the Christians in Asia Minor—an arrangement which was subsequently shamefully neglected by the British Government. "The story of the misgovernment and massacre of the Armenian Christians is one that will ever redound to the disgrace of all the signatories of the Treaty of Berlin; it is doubly disgraceful to the Power which framed the Cyprus Convention." † At the same time,

* At that time it was considered probable that the Euphrates Valley railway might be constructed from Alexandretta or some neighbouring port, in which case Cyprus would have been of enormous strategic importance.

† "Development of the European Nations," by J. Holland Rose, p. 244. It may here be mentioned that the fruits of the Berlin Congress which were to be gathered in Asia Minor were deliberately sacrificed by the

by direct negotiations with Russia, Great Britain undertook not to oppose Russian schemes with regard to Bessarabia in return for the Russian acceptance of the Eastern Rumelia arrangement.

The news as to the Anglo-Russian agreement leaked out previous to the meeting of the Congress, and was vigorously denied from the Ministerial bench in Parliament, but the Anglo-Turkish Agreement and the cession of Cyprus were not generally known, for even the Turkish plenipotentiaries were kept in ignorance of this important event for upwards of a month during the most critical proceedings of the Congress. It has been asserted, however, by Karatheodory Pasha, one of the Turkish delegates, that the Cyprus Convention was known both to Austria and Germany. " The Anglo-Turkish agreement," he says, " which had just been divulged, contributed to excite the envy of the Austrians. They had early gained knowledge of the arrangement secretly concluded between England and Turkey; there is no room for doubt that M. von Bismarck had been admitted into the secret, as Count Andrassy would not have ventured to keep him uninformed on such an important matter, and while the English in possession of Cyprus found it quite natural to support the Austrians in their occupation of Bosnia, the latter, on their side, redoubled their efforts towards not leaving the Congress with less profit than did England." * In any case, when the secret became known the excitement was intense, especially in France,† who felt herself betrayed by

succeeding Gladstonian Ministry. The excellent system established by Lord Beaconsfield, who sent British Consuls to Asia Minor to report upon the Turkish reforms in the Christian districts and to watch over the interests of the persecuted Armenians and Greeks, was abandoned by Gladstone in 1882. The Liberal Premier wished, in spite of solemn undertakings on the part of the former Government, to limit British responsibilities in the Levant, and in the year 1882 withdrew the Consuls and abandoned the Christians to their fate. This deliberate betrayal of those who had a right to look for British protection on the part of one who wished to clear the Turks out of Europe " bag and baggage," and the consequent diminution of British prestige in the Near East, is the most serious blot upon Gladstonian foreign policy and marks it as both insincere and treacherous. Gladstone's action prepared the way for Germany, who was not slow to take advantage of the changed position of affairs. To-day we are reaping the fruits of this betrayal.

* Hanotaux, vol. iv, p. 375.
† The Agreement was communicated to M. Waddington on July 7.

an action which threatened her position both in the Mediterranean and Egypt. Lord Salisbury, however, invited France to look for compensation in Tunis, and the crisis was successfully passed. In London the position was well understood, and the action of the British Cabinet was generally warmly applauded—in spite of the fact that Lord Derby stated that one of the reasons for his retirement had been connected with this very question.* Beaconsfield himself thoroughly enjoyed the situation in spite of, and perhaps because of, the angry criticisms of his opponents. On the night when the Cyprus Convention became known he attended a brilliant reception and was the cynosure of all eyes. Unconcerned and inscrutable, he made the round of the assembly, and at length, stopping before Princess Radziwill, was met by the question, " What are you thinking of ? " " I am not thinking at all," he replied ; " I am enjoying myself." †

With the way thus thoroughly prepared by secret negotiations and the question of "reservations" with regard to the scope of the proceedings settled, the Congress met at Berlin whilst the outside world hung on the issue of peace or war. The personalities of the Congress were men of character who have left a deep mark upon European history. In the first place there was the German Chancellor, Bismarck, who with admirable decision and with remarkable insight into character presided over the meetings and was able, tactfully and decisively, to exercise his powers of moderator whenever the proceedings were disturbed or personal dislikes became too pronounced. Throughout the proceedings he steered the Congress into Teutonic waters and laid the foundations for the future Triple Alliance. In supporting Austria-Hungary he did not overlook the fact that once the Dual Monarchy was engaged in the Balkans it would not only be almost impossible to withdraw from the occupied provinces, but it would eventually become necessary for the Empire to expand towards the south and east and, it was to be hoped, in the not distant future, to reach the coveted port of Salonika,

* Lord Derby had resigned at the end of March on account of a proposal of the Ministry to send an expedition from India to seize Cyprus and one of the Syrian ports.
† Princess Radziwill's " My Recollections," p. 91.

owing to the influence which Dualism had conferred upon Hungary and the necessity for constantly balancing the two forces within the Empire. In supporting both Great Britain and Austria-Hungary the " honest broker " knew that he was changing the traditional Russo-Prussian policy ; but he realized that it would not be possible to breathe new life into the dry bones of the Alliance of the three Emperors, and that if he did not support Austria that country would sooner or later gravitate towards France and possibly, in spite of acute differences, towards Russia as well. In introducing a new power amongst the Balkan Slavs, Bismarck opened a fresh period of rivalry between Austria and Russia and created a cause of conflict which would oblige the former country to act in strict accordance with Germany's views. Thus the ruler of the Congress, looking down from his tribune, gathered the threads into his own hands and directed European policy with a keen eye to the main chance. Of the other German representatives, von Bülow, who acted as secretary to the Congress, and Prince von Hohenlohe, the amiable Ambassador at Paris, both subsequently Chancellors of the Empire, and the elder von Bülow, then Foreign Secretary, were entirely subservient to Bismarck and merely shared in his undoubted prestige.

For Austria-Hungary there appeared Count Andrassy, Minister for Foreign Affairs, who was accompanied by Count Karolyi and others. Lord Beaconsfield, the dark horse of the Congress, whose advent in Berlin had been awaited with the greatest curiosity, was ably seconded by Lord Salisbury, whilst Mr. Balfour acted as the latter's secretary. Russia was represented by the old Chancellor, Prince Gortschakov, then in his eightieth year, who until the rise of Bismarck may be considered as the most powerful Foreign Minister in Europe, at one time the friend of Germany and the enemy of France, but now forced to dance to the Bismarckian piping. The Russian Chancellor was accompanied by Count Shouvalov, then Ambassador in London, and by Baron d'Oubril, the Russian Ambassador in Berlin. Count Corti, Foreign Secretary, represented Italy ; whilst France was represented by M. Waddington, whose well-known British leanings made his position doubly difficult when the contents of the secret Anglo-

Turkish agreement were divulged, and by M. de Saint-Vallier. The Turkish delegates, who were there to acquiesce in the partition of their country, counted not at all in the deliberations; whilst the Rumanian representatives, Messrs. Bratiano and Kogalniceano, although delegates from the State that had saved Russia from disaster before Plevna, were merely allowed to speak before the Congress.*

Prince von Hohenlohe has left a little sketch of the opening of the Congress. " Before the assembly we went to the buffet, where we drank port wine and ate biscuits," he writes. " By degrees the plenipotentiaries arrived: Count Corti, a very ugly little man with a Japanese type of face, and Count Launay (the other Italian representative); then came the Turk, a man still young but insignificant; Count Shouvalov and old Gortschakov, who was very feeble; then followed the English and the French, Waddington in a grand uniform. The first meeting of Gortschakov and Lord Beaconsfield was interesting; it was an historic moment." Such was the personnel of the Congress, of whom the three chief figures were Bismarck, whose *mot*, " Le Congrès c'est moi," correctly represented the position; Beaconsfield, the Jewish statesman, the parvenu but most brilliant figure in the assembly; and poor old Gortschakov, tottering to his grave, who was constantly confined to his rooms by feigned or real indisposition. Towards the last Prince Bismarck showed but slight courtesy, for in " The Souvenirs of Caratheodory Pasha," quoted by Hanotaux, the Turkish representative states that " apart from personal civilities on the part of Prince Bismarck, we can hardly remember a single occasion on which the German Chancellor showed, by word or deed, any special political deference towards the Chancellor of Russia. The latter, however, as

---

* The position of the Rumanian delegates was indeed a pitiable one. Russia had strongly opposed even the suggestion that they should be allowed to put their case before the Congress, almost treating Rumania as a Russian " sphere " and thus forcing Rumania within the Austro-German orbit; and the consent of the Congress that they should be allowed to present their Memoir was only secured after Lord Salisbury had ironically remarked that " having heard the representatives of Greece, which was claiming foreign provinces, it would be but fair to listen also to the representative of a country which claimed only what was its own." Great Britain had expressed " profound regret " at the Russian demand for Bessarabia, but undertook not to dispute it.

the Nestor of the great European diplomatists, would have been extremely appreciative of a little incense from Prince Bismarck in the presence of the members of the Congress." Bismarck conveniently forgot that Gortschakov's action in 1870 had enabled him to secure the German triumph, and the old Chancellor, piqued at this ingratitude, kept in bed as often as possible. On the first occasion on which the Russian Chancellor was to speak before the Congress, Bismarck gave the Turkish plenipotentiary the priority, and Prince Gortschakov "tossed down his spectacles and papers in so much annoyance that they fell on the other side of the table."

The results of the Congress were definitely favourable to Germany at the expense mainly of Russia. The three Imperial Powers, Russia, Germany, and Great Britain, had stood face to face upon the routes to the East, whilst Austria-Hungary had stepped in to claim ample compensations in view of the changed balance of power; the Mediterranean Powers, France and Italy, had played a waiting game, being quite unable to press their claims before the Congress, the former merely contenting herself with promises of influence elsewhere, the latter forced to look on at the growth of Austrian influence in the Adriatic; whilst the smaller countries, Bulgaria, Rumania, Serbia, Montenegro, and Greece, stood in the ante-chamber awaiting whatever fortune their splendid and illustrious masters should allot to them. The bargaining across the council chamber and behind the scenes took small account of nationality, and the boundaries that were finally devised were such that the Balkan question remained an open sore and a perpetual menace to the peace of Europe. Bismarck arranged everything in the best interests of Germany. Macedonia, liberated by the Russian arms, was given back to Turkey, and the lot of the Christian inhabitants was rendered worse, if that were possible, than it had been before the Russo-Turkish War. For another thirty-five years this unfortunate province remained the chief centre of unrest in the Near East—a state of affairs by which Germany alone profited, because in frustrating, directly or indirectly, every scheme of reform she managed to pose as the only friend of Turkey and to prepare the way for the future Austro-German advance to the Ægean. The hopes of Greece, who had looked for a northern extension of territory and the occupation of a considerable portion of Central Macedonia, were frustrated, whilst the desire of the Serbians to be united with their kinsfolk in Macedonia and in Bosnia was equally doomed to disappointment.

In the rejection of the Greater Bulgaria, which had been provided for in the Treaty of San Stefano, Russia, who looked for a great extension of her power along the shores of the Black Sea and towards the coasts of the Adriatic, received a severe set-back which robbed her of the chief fruits of her victory so far as Europe was concerned. The great State, under Russian patronage, that was to have dominated the Central Balkans, was reduced to a country of a little more than a third of its proposed size, whilst the suggested Russian military occupation and supervision of the new administration was reduced from a proposed period of two years to one of nine months only. The erection of the semi-independent State of Eastern Rumelia, which was to remain under the direct political and military control of the Sultan, created an impossible position which was destined to be changed seven years later when the province elected to join Bulgaria. The Bulgaria of the Russian conception was thus divided into three parts : the newly created State, which was to be ruled by a prince agreeable to Russia and the other Powers ; the detached province interposed on the highway to Constantinople ; and an unredeemed Bulgaria, which was subsequently to cause so much trouble. Russian influence was checkmated, and was subsequently further diminished by the unpolitic attitude of Russian statesmen and the unexpected opposition of Prince Alexander of Battenburg, who had been appointed Prince of Bulgaria.

In the other Christian States of the Balkans further changes of the greatest importance were brought about. The little State of Montenegro, sheltering amid the secure fastnesses of its mountains, did not receive the increase of territory that had been expected, although it was granted access to the sea at Antivari. The fate of both Montenegro and Serbia had indeed already been settled when the Emperors Alexander and Francis Joseph, accompanied respectively by Prince Gortschakov and Count Andrassy, had met at Reichstadt previous to the war, in June 1876, and had agreed that Austria should take Bosnia-Herzegovina in return for Austrian neutrality during the coming hostilities. The extension of their territory had thus been hindered, and the results now achieved scarcely warranted the outlay in lives and treasure on the part of the two countries. Serbia, it is true, was permitted to expand at the expense of the Greater Bulgaria, and gained complete independence, but Austria-Hungary, by acquiring rights of military occupation over the district of Novi-Bazar—a country of great strategic importance on the highway to Salonika—thrust a Germanic wedge between Montenegro and Serbia, and prepared the way for the future German advance to the Ægean. By acquiring this territory, which is mountainous and barren, Austria's motive was undoubtedly to advance step by step upon Macedonia and Salonika, and although these rights were subsequently abandoned when Austria finally annexed Bosnia-Herzegovina in 1908, that abandonment did not necessarily mean that Austria-Hungary as an empire had given up all intentions to advance upon Salonika whenever a favourable opportunity should occur—though possibly the advance was intended to have been by the easier route through Serbia.

To the east, Rumania also gained complete independence, but in spite of the greatness of her services to Russia during the war she was now treated with ingratitude; for the Russian Government appropriated her Bessarabian districts by force, and in return merely granted unimportant extensions of territory in other directions. Russia's motives in this action were swayed by the desire that her frontiers should reach the delta of the Danube, but her attitude was stupid and short-sighted, because by administering territory that was occupied by a Rumanian population she threw away the advantage which would have resulted from having a united Rumania, outside Austria-Hungary, bent upon assimilating the Rumanian peoples within that Empire. By creating a feeling of resentment in a State that had always facilitated Russia's advance she erected a powerful buffer between herself and the Balkans.

To the south, Greece, who had recalled her troops from Thessaly on the distinct understanding that her claims would be favourably considered, received no encouragement from any of the Great Powers. Lord Salisbury, it is true, not forgetful of British sympathy with Hellenic ideals, uttered a few platitudes in favour of the British protégé; and M. Waddington, on behalf of the French Government, whilst opposing Greek claims to Crete and the northern shores of the Ægean, proposed that she should occupy practically the whole of Thessaly and the Epirus. But no other encouragement was given to these suggestions, and Greece, in common with Bulgaria, although she was promised an extension of her frontiers in Thessaly and Epirus, was also informed that " States, like individuals, which have a future are in a position to be able to wait."

As regards Russia and Turkey, matters were arranged at the dictation of Great Britain, in accordance with the desires of Germany, for it was in Asia Minor that the position was most dangerous. British policy was primarily concerned with preventing the partition of the Sultan's dominions in Asia in order that the Black Sea should not become a Russian lake. For this reason the strongest opposition had been offered to the retention of Batum, but, as has been shown, compensations were sought by Great Britain elsewhere when it had been found that Russian opinion was strongly set upon the occupation of that port. Public opinion in Great Britain was as strongly opposed to any concession, and it was only the personal ascendancy of Beaconsfield that enabled a settlement to be concluded. Batum, Ardahan, and Kars were rightly considered as positions of great strategic importance; the two former constituting for Russia a high road into Asia Minor and a pressure upon the Mohammedan Powers, whilst the latter, long a bulwark of the Ottoman power in Asia, was a most important fortress. By retaining the Bayazid district, which commanded the caravan routes between Erzerum and Persia, British opinion was somewhat mollified, because one of the direct routes to India was thus saved from the advancing Muscovite power. The fate of Batum was, however, so far as the rest of the Powers were concerned, a matter of indifference, for they were not so directly interested in the question of maritime equilibrium. Nor did they share the British anxiety with regard to the Bosphorus and the Dardanelles, with the possible exception of France. Nevertheless, although Russia desired that the Straits should remain open in time of war as in time of peace, former stipulations on this subject were not abrogated, and the position remained what it was before the war—obscure. That is, Turkey still dominated the position, subject to whatever pressure might be exerted upon her by the interested Powers.

The results of the Congress were definitely unfavourable to Russia and Italy, definitely favourable to Austria-Hungary and Germany; whilst Great Britain, in undertaking certain obligations which she did not adequately perform, had the satisfaction of seeing her supposed rival, Russia, thwarted at the precise moment when, by more skilful manœuvring, she might have obtained a stronger position in the Near East. Beaconsfield returned to London on July 16 with his now celebrated message of " Peace with honour," * and was received with enthusiasm on his way from Charing Cross to Downing Street, and Prince Bismarck departed quietly to take the waters at Kissingen, secure in his belief that the future lay with Germany and grimly satisfied that the European diplomatists had opened the route to the East—the pathway which he affected to despise, but which ere long was to be traversed by Teutonic adventurers on their way to Bagdad and the Persian Gulf. The tacit agreement of the Powers to the continental hegemony of Germany was as incense in his nostrils, for he knew that in buying Austria-Hungary he had prepared the way for greater deals in the not distant future. " Prussia," states Hanotaux, " wished to receive the commission money due for her work as ' honest agent ' ; she cherished the vast hope of a Germanic invasion of the East through a definite movement to the Danube, through her old antagonist Austria-Hungary " † ; and, in particular, she realized that in alienating Russia she had definitely arrived at the parting of the ways and might by skilful diplomacy eventually succeed in acquiring the heritage of the Cæsars in Asia Minor. Between the wavering and uncertain policies of Great Britain and

* Lord Beaconsfield, in his speech on July 27, 1878, stated that " one of the results of my attending the Congress of Berlin has been to prove, what I always suspected to be an absolute fact, that neither the Crimean War nor this horrible, devastating war which has just terminated would have taken place if England had spoken with the necessary firmness."

† Hanotaux, vol. iv, p. 345.

Russia came Germany and took her spoils. "Here lies the whole history of the Congress"; and its main result, so far as Great Britain was concerned, was to continue and increase the hostility between this country and Russia, to divert the sphere of Russian activity from the Bosphorus to the frontiers of Afghanistan and India, to prevent the possibility of an understanding between the two countries, and to create a quarter of a century of bitterness and disagreement, which it was the interest of Germany to increase in every way possible.

The juridical fictions that were adopted by the Congress of Berlin, by which diplomatists sought to cover or to explain away the real scope of their actions and to persuade a too credulous world that the "rights" of other Powers were duly respected even whilst a loaded pistol was being levelled at their heads, have led to endless friction, especially with regard to Bosnia-Herzegovina, Bulgaria, and Macedonia, and have created a position that cannot be better described than in the speech of Signor Tittoni, who was Italian Foreign Secretary from 1903 to 1909 and presided over the Foreign Office during the critical period when Bosnia-Herzegovina was finally annexed by Austria-Hungary. Speaking on June 4, 1908, Signor Tittoni said: "I have been reproached for the expression I used, of 'subtle discriminations' by which diplomacy has created a fictitious juridical status which is in contrast with the *de facto* situation. Well, I maintain this phrase. I do not judge the substance of the work done by diplomacy at the Berlin Congress, but, whatever the substance, it is certain that the form adopted was doubtful, hypocritical, and full of snares for that very peace which the Congress aimed at preserving. With that form it postponed the difficulties and did not solve them: the unconditional occupation for an indefinite term, the *de facto* possession of territories by some Powers that leaves to others a bare sovereignty which consists of nothing, are forms which lend themselves to every interpretation and usurpation and create dangerous and agitated situations which one day or other must be solved, as Bosnia, Bulgaria, and Crete have shown. And I hold that if in the future diplomacy will be more sincere and will repudiate these ' subtle discriminations,' it will be so much gained for the cause of civilization and peace." The Berlin Congress, in fact, resulted in a compromise by which each Power endeavoured to cover its actions by empty forms and stupid discriminations. None were entirely honest, and least of all the " honest broker " who fought so hard to preserve the peace of Europe.

CHAPTER VIII

GERMANY, TURKEY, AND THE BALKAN WARS

THE extraordinary development of German influence in Turkey during the last quarter of a century is perhaps the most remarkable instance of the virility, force, insight, and power of application of the German Government presented in any part of the world—because in the Ottoman Empire the position at first was certainly unfavourable for the prosecution of the Germanic ideal. In no portion of the world were the interests of other Powers so deeply or so closely interwoven into the economic and political fabric of the State; and in no part of the globe did there seem so little possibility of German aggression.

Owing to the long and close historical association between Turkey and the two chief Western Powers, France and Britain, and to the clearly defined economic and political interests acquired by Russia during her long struggle on behalf of the Slav cause, there seemed small likelihood of the Germans acquiring any special influence in the Ottoman Empire. Germany was an outsider whose presence was neither desired nor seemed desirable. Her satellite, Austria-Hungary, whose geographical position as the nearest Christian Power gave her certain rights over the Christians in Albania and Macedonia, had offended perhaps more deeply even than Russia by securing the control of two of Turkey's richest provinces, Bosnia and Herzegovina, and her merchants and bankers had small influence at Constantinople.

Yet, in spite of the apparently unfavourable *terrain* for Germanic enterprise, the antagonism that existed between Great Britain on the one side and Russia and France on the other, fed by the apparently divergent and almost irreconcilable interests of the three nations, paved the way for the advance of the Germanic Powers and opened the economic and political door to the East, which has never since been shut to the German intruder. At the close of the Berlin Congress nothing seemed more unlikely than that Prussia, although growing by leaps and bounds within the new German Empire, would aspire, or would be in a position to attempt such an operation, to control the policy of the Ottoman Empire.

Without access to the secret archives of the German Government it is impossible to determine when this deliberate policy of peaceful penetration, since so persistently and successfully pursued, was first formulated and first became the set policy of the Germanic Powers. Still less is it possible to decide what were the secret and cherished plans conceived in the fertile brain of Bismarck with respect to the Germanization of the Near East. All that is known for certain is that although Germans had always been attracted by the Ottoman magnet, they had also recognized the immense difficulties that lay in the way of a successful and aggressive policy in the Balkans. The attitude of Bismarck had been clearly and openly defined. In his oft-quoted words, " The Eastern question is not worth the bones of a Pomeranian grenadier," he had picturesquely expressed Germany's aloofness from all Oriental interests and had led the world to believe that Turkey would be left to work out her own salvation under the not disinterested guidance of the other European Powers.

Yet it may indeed be questioned whether this attitude of a statesman of such acute perception, who was able to appreciate the drift of European policy and the future course of events with such remarkable and forceful insight, were not, as a matter of fact, an assumed position intended to reassure those individuals who realized that sooner or later Germany's policy would undergo a profound change and development, and that the dreams of certain German statesmen and thinkers with respect to the control of the Eastern routes would some day be capable of translation into vigorous action. How far Austria-Hungary was intended to further the ultimate aims of the northern Empire it would be difficult to say, but it can scarcely be questioned, after the events of 1866, that after the predominance of Prussia had been assured it became the deliberate intention of German statesmen to use the Dual Monarchy for the furtherance of German schemes.

Bismarck, as we learn from the illuminating memoirs of his indiscreet Boswell, Dr. Busch, was entirely in favour of an Austrian advance in the territories of the Sultan. He informed the latter that Turkey would have to make up her mind to part with territory to Austria, and he further unburdened himself upon the same subject in January 1881, in a talk with the British Ambassador, Lord Odo Russell. " His solution of the problem," wrote the Ambassador to Lord Granville, " when the Turkish Government collapses would be the peaceful division of influence in the Balkan Peninsula between Austria and Russia ; the former to extend to the Ægean, the latter to the Straits, and Germany—that is himself —to mediate between them. The intervention of England as the leader of the Concert of the Powers stands in the way of his wishes and of the plans he has made for his neighbours, whom he looks upon as the Sultan's natural heirs. England's interests are in Egypt and Asia, as those of France are in Syria and Tunis ; and neither England nor France, he thinks, should busy themselves about the Sultan's European dominions, which do not concern them as they do Germany's neighbours, Austria and Russia." *

As we know, the German Chancellor was particularly fond of playing the part of mediator—but always with some ulterior, if not always apparent, aim. In this case, as we now fully realize, the aim was to weaken Britain and at the same time to please Russia by apparently favouring her plans. The ultimate idea, however, was the extension of Germanic interests on the road to the East.

" I should indeed like to be German Chancellor for a day," Lord Odo Russell had written a few weeks previously, in a vain attempt to rouse the British Government to a sense of the importance of British interests at Constantinople, " not to scold, but to entreat of you on both knees to leave Smyrna to her figs and sail instead straight to Stamboul and take the Sultan by the Golden Horn, and put an end to this very dangerous and humiliating conflict with the Porte, which

---

* Letter from Lord Odo Russell to Granville, January 26, 1881 ; Granville's " Life," vol. ii, p. 225.

threatens the peace of Europe and the moral influence of England if we do not strike at the root of the evil rapidly and successfully. Once our Fleet is in the Sea of Marmora all danger of a conflict ceases, and the Concert can join us and work out the problems of reforms in peace and security. ... I therefore hope that if Austria, Germany, and France decline to go to Smyrna, you will think it sufficient excuse for proposing the Dardanelles instead, and going there with or without allies. Once we have taken up our position the Powers will follow one by one, because our presence at Constantinople will be guarantee that the Turkish Empire will be made to last as long as, and probably even longer than, it can. I feel so strongly on this question that I cannot help writing strongly because I want *our* policy to be a success and a triumph ; and I fully believe that the key to success is to be found in Constantinople."* Great Britain's policy was not a success and Germany stepped in and reaped the harvest.

The first open intervention of Prussia in the affairs of the East occurred when the Ottoman army was reorganized upon Prussian models in the middle of the nineteenth century. It is characteristic of a military people that the earliest manifestations of the process of peaceful penetration should have been accompanied by the rattling of the sword in its scabbard, or, in other words, by the introduction of military reforms designed to make the Ottoman army a more efficient weapon against the growing Slav power. The Turks from the earliest ages have been a military nation. Their predominance in the Near East was secured by their military prowess, and although, when their work of conquest was once completed, their armed forces became less and less efficient by a continuous process of decay, owing to lack of organization and deeply seated political evils, the Turks nevertheless retained their old military ardour and never completely lost the aggressive spirit which in the past had made them masters of vast stretches of alien territory.

Although from the commencement of the nineteenth century attempts had been made to organize certain troops upon a European model, the movement for reorganization and

* Letter to Lord Granville, October 9, 1880 ; Granville's "Life," vol. ii, pp. 217-18,

reform made little progress, owing partly to the opposition of the Corps of Janissaries, which vigorously maintained its ancient privileges and opposed all attempts at internal reorganization. But the tragic destruction of this famous corps in the year 1826 removed one of the principal objects to reorganization, and a few years later, in 1843, the first serious attempt was made to put the military forces of the Empire upon a stronger and better footing. The reorganization coincided with the visit of Moltke, then a young officer, and his companions to Constantinople and Asia Minor, and was the first-fruits of the new policy initiated by the then Sultan Abdul Mejid. Inspired principally by Prussian models, the regulations of 1843 gave the Ottoman Empire an army possessing characteristics which were later adopted by all European States, but which at that period were only to be found in the military organization of Prussia—such, for instance, as service with the colours for a comparatively short period (five years), the formation of reserves and troops of the second line, regional recruiting, and above all, in time of peace, the organization of troops in brigades, divisions, and armies provided with a more or less efficient staff and their different services.*

But under successive Sultans, and particularly under Abdul Hamid, who lived in mortal terror of the army and feared a military revolution above all the evils that threatened the stability of his Empire, the organization became lax and a progressive deterioration took place. In the year 1882, however, the Germans, then beginning to take advantage of the weak and unfortunate policy pursued by Great Britain and to exploit the discords that existed between the Powers charged with carrying out the terms of the Treaty of Berlin, made their first decisive step in Turkey by complying with the inspired request for a military mission charged with the task of reorganizing the Ottoman artillery, and since that date a certain number of military officers have always been employed by the Turkish authorities as army instructors and military professors. They had at their head the late Field-Marshal von der Goltz, then a lieutenant-colonel in the Prussian army, who arrived in Turkey in the year 1883. With the

* On this point *see* an article in *Questions Diplomatiques*, 1912, entitled " La Réforme Militaire Ottomane."

coming of von der Goltz Germany played her first cards as a military Power in the Near East. Von der Goltz took up the work already commenced by the French military mission between the Crimean War and the year 1870.

"The German military mission," states Chéradame, "above all during its first years, was far from having all the influence that has been attributed to it. Amongst the dozen officers of which it was composed there were eleven men of but mediocre attainments, incapable of exercising any serious influence; the twelfth man was, it is true, of the greatest value. It is he who has certainly prepared the way for Germany in Turkey, and who, in obtaining the reform of the military schools and the artillery, brought into the Turkish army the Prussian military principles." The German military mission had been under consideration for some time before it became an accomplished fact. Considerable opposition had been manifested by the Crown Prince Frederick, who feared the premature extension of German interests in quarters where there seemed little prospect of ultimate success. These doubts, however, were brushed aside by Bismarck, who clearly foresaw the drift of affairs in Turkey and the possibility of Germany stepping in whilst others quarrelled about the division of the Turkish plunder. "As to the doubts of your Imperial and Royal Highness," wrote Prince Hohenlohe to the Crown Prince, "with regard to the sending of officers and Civil servants to Turkey, the Chancellor has come to the decision that he cannot share them. He considers the measures in various respects advantageous. For one thing, the duties there discharged are very instructive to those employed, and will give them the opportunity of showing their capacity, and, secondly, it will furnish us *with a number of reliable informants whom he could obtain in no other way* [the italics are not in the original]. Moreover, the influence which we should thus acquire in Turkish territory is not to be underrated," and, he added, with characteristic Prussian insensibility to the rights of others, "the consequences the arrangement may have for the Turks and its acceptability to the European Powers need not concern us."

"It is not our policy," said the Chancellor, "to further either European or Turkish interests. A European interest is, to his mind, a fiction useful to all who want to use others and can find persons who believe in the phrase. It might be useful to us to have the Turks as friends in so far as this might be to our advantage. The Turkish artillery had been trained by Prussian officers at a time when we were living on terms of the utmost cordiality with Russia, and we had thus acquired influence and useful connexions in Turkey. If Chauvinism, Pan-Slavism, and anti-German elements in Russia should attack us, the attitude and the military efficiency of Turkey would not be indifferent to us. She could never be dangerous to *us*, but under certain circumstances her enemies might be ours." * Bismarck's cynical use of Ottoman tools and his clear-sighted policy with regard to Turkey are illuminatingly shown in this letter, which reveals the real purpose of the German military mission. Nothing could be more definite than the statement of the Chancellor that Turkey might be useful in the event of a conflict with Russia.

The man who was placed in charge of this mission has since attained eminence in the German army. Although his military reputation seemed to be buried when the Turks were defeated by the Balkan League and the value of the elaborate training and years of careful preparation was openly questioned at that time, the eclipse was only temporary, and the aged Field-Marshal again became one of the most popular and respected figures in the German military clique and now is one of the most eminent in the Prussian Valhalla of departed geniuses. During the time that he was in Turkey, from 1883 to 1895, by dint of herculean labours and enormous patience, he imposed on Turkey an organization worthy of the name of an army, rearmed the infantry and artillery, organized a cohesive staff and inspection system, reformed the military schools, and transformed the heterogeneous mob of raw and disjointed troops into an efficient fighting machine. That he did not accomplish more was due entirely to the opposition of Abdul Hamid and his army of spies, who opposed the military reforms and finally succeeded in checkmating the best endeavours of the German commander by allowing the machine which he had created to become inefficient owing

* Letter from Prince Hohenlohe to the Crown Prince, July 16, 1880. Hohenlohe, vol. ii, p. 268.

to the want of the necessary stores, weapons, and ammunition.

But there is another and more unsavoury side to the German penetration of Turkey. Von der Goltz was a man of genius inspired by a high military ideal. Those who carried on the economic battles of the Fatherland were of a lower type: financial adventurers who gathered in the German orbit, and cosmopolitan intriguers who rallied to the German flag because they realized that the policy of the Empire also included a vigorous and sustained effort to capture the control of the Turkish markets. The operations of these financiers were not viewed with particular favour by Bismarck. "Bucher sent me an article from the *Deutscher Tageblatt*, entitled 'Hirsch-Bleichröder-Rothschild and Germany in Constantinople.' It disclosed the financial intrigues of this group of bankers, 'choice members of the Chosen People,' who exploit Turkey under the pretence that they are protected by the German Government in the person of its representatives. It energetically protests against this trio."* But in spite of the unsavouriness of the methods, and perhaps because of them, German enterprise in Turkey soon acquired a firm footing. In the early eighties German industry obtained its first foothold —mainly in the supply of munitions, artillery, and small arms. The shipbuilding company "Germania," opposite Kiel, supplied torpedoes for the Turkish navy. Krupp of Essen shared with Armstrong's the heavy artillery. Ludwig Loewe and Co., of Berlin, supplied small arms.† And in 1884 German capital was employed in financing, through the instrumentality of the Austrian Credit-Anstalt and the Berlin firm of Bleichröder, the Turkish Tobacco Régie. This event was the beginning of German financial influence. The growth of the economic octopus was greatly strengthened when in 1888 the celebrated Deutsche Bank entered into financial relations with the Ottoman Empire. Although it cannot be said that, prior to the outbreak of the present war, the financial obligations of Turkey to Germany were excessive in view of the enormous preponderance of French and British financial interests in the Ottoman debt, it is

* Busch's "Bismarck: Some Secret Pages of his History," vol. iii, p. 63.
† *See* an article in *The Times*, October 28, 1898, on "German Enterprise in Turkey."

nevertheless true that during recent years she has experienced far less difficulty in negotiating loans with German houses. With the drying up of the Western financial well, Turkey has naturally and almost inevitably turned to Germany for financial assistance. Such aid has always been readily tendered in the well-founded hope that German monetary assistance would pave the way for the ultimate political control which soon became the aim of all German statesmen.

No process of penetration could be more successful than that exercised by means of the subtle, hidden, and insidious operations of the financial groups who held Germany in a vice and dictated, in common with the military clique, the national policy in the Near East. As in the past, one of the strongest factors operating in favour of Great Britain and France had been the fact that between them they controlled nearly three-fourths of the Ottoman debt, France alone accounting for almost sixty per cent.; so in the present, the economic and financial progress of Germany in Turkey, exercised in a thousand secret and none too creditable directions, enabled German influence to make rapid headway at Constantinople. In the year before mentioned, the Deutsche Bank, acting in conjunction with the Berliner Handelsgesselschaft, had brought out a loan of thirty million marks. But a still more important financial step was engineered in the following year when, in conjunction with the Vienna Bank, the Deutsche Bank took over the Société du Chemin de Fer Ottoman d'Anatolie and entered upon the long series of railway enterprises in Asia Minor which finally established German economic predominance in that portion of the Turkish Empire. The main line from Ishmid to Angora, which was begun on June 13, 1889, and completed on December 13, 1892, was the first of these important enterprises, and was followed by the construction, through the agency of the Deutsche Bank, of the supplementary Anatolian line from Eskishehr to Konia, August 31, 1893, to July 29, 1896.

The establishment of this new banking connexion with the East, with its thousand and one ramifications in every avenue of Turkish economic activity, was far more important to German policy than the direct participation of German capital in Ottoman loans. German bankers and financial

GERMANY, TURKEY, AND THE BALKAN WARS 157

magnates were followed everywhere by the agents of manufacturers and merchants, and German goods soon became as well known in the Sultan's dominions as the manufactures of France and Great Britain.

The success of this economic invasion was due, it must be admitted, to the superior training and trade tactics of the Germans. Our long immunity from any serious economic opposition caused us to neglect the cultivation of so important a market, so that whilst our imports to Turkey were valued at £10,284,000 in the year 1898, when German influence first became seriously felt, they were only £9,729,690 in the year 1911, immediately before the First Balkan War, compared with German imports valued at £436,000 and £5,365,000 in the two periods respectively. This enormous increase within a decade was brought about entirely by the energy and ability shown by German merchants in their dealings with the Turks and the backing they received from their own consular officials. As *The Times* correspondent wrote on October 28, 1898: "The German export trade owes its success to the stolid, steady perseverance of German industrialists who imitate the methods of the German General Staff, and it may be added of our own admirable Sirdar (Lord Kitchener), in neglecting no detail, however trivial, in their plan of campaign. Putting their pride in their pockets, they accommodate their system to the task in hand." It must be remembered that this was written when German trade with Turkey was less than a tenth of what it is now.

The culminating and most dramatic point in German policy in Turkey was the visit of the Kaiser in the year 1898, described in a former chapter. This journey, undertaken with definite and clearly formulated designs, set the seal upon German policy in the East. It is not necessary here to follow in any detail domestic events within the Ottoman Empire, except in so far as they are connected with the main topic of this book—the *Drang nach Osten*. But in order to appreciate correctly the peculiar and dominating position attained by Germany at Constantinople it is necessary to have some idea of the events that have facilitated this rapid growth of influence. Although, four years after the Kaiser's visit, Prince von Bülow stated emphatically that "Germany does not practise in the East any active policy," * this statement, equally untrue as applied to the Near, Middle, or Far East, was fully contradicted in his own book, " Imperial Germany." " We have carefully cultivated good relations with Turkey and Islam," writes von Bülow, " especially since the journey to the East undertaken by our Emperor and Empress. Those relations are not of a sentimental nature, for the continued existence of Turkey serves our interest from the industrial, military, and political points of view. Industrially and financially, Turkey offered us a rich and fertile field of activity. . . . In the undesired, but possible, event of a general European war, the military strength of Turkey might have been exerted in our favour. For our Austrian Ally, Turkey was the most convenient neighbour possible. The introduction of our last Army Bill, which had its origin in the change of situation effected by the Balkan War, shows that Turkey's collapse was a blow to us." How the collapse of Turkey affected Germany's interests will be shown in the following pages.

German policy had in many ways become closely woven into the fabric of the Turkish national life. From economic to political control was but a short step. The favoured position of the Germans soon produced a strong philo-German party at Constantinople, which finally overthrew and cast out the last stubborn opponents, destroyed the old constitution, and swept away Abdul Hamid and his hateful régime, only to erect in its place a system yet more hateful because in posing as the friend of freedom it did not scruple to use the weapons of autocracy. The growth of this party was rendered possible by the sympathetic attitude of the Germans, who used what tools they could in the fight for supremacy. Already in 1903 Chéradame wrote that " favoured in a thousand ways the Germans in Turkey are rapidly increasing. Their colony at Constantinople has its clubs, its journals, its schools. From the Turkish point of view this exceptional position which the Sultan has given to the Germans in his Empire presents evidently serious dangers. The more they occupy Turkish territory the more the Germans experience a desire to possess it by a definite agreement. Their tendency is more and more to regard the Ottoman country as their personal property." †

* March 19, 1903.   † Chéradame's " La Question d'Orient," pp. 12–13.

Contemporaneously with the growth of German influence occurred a renaissance of nationalism in Turkey. Generations of misgovernment had not entirely obliterated the desire for adequate political reforms within the Ottoman Empire. Although the revolution, which was eventually to degenerate into a military despotism of the worst nature, was at first welcomed by the parliamentary sentimentalists of Western Europe, who perceive a panacea for all political and social evils in democratic constitutionalism, it soon became apparent that in attempting to set up a Turkish constitution modelled upon Western parliamentarism, the rank and file of the Young Turks had merely grasped the shadow of constitutional forms whilst their leaders had seized the more real and terrible instruments of power. Whatever were the demerits of Abdul Hamid there was one thing in his favour. He was too deeply versed in politics to permit the Germans to control the political destinies of his Empire. Although, as the friend of the Emperor William, he was willing enough to subscribe to German economic plans, he nevertheless checked and kept at bay all movements for securing control of the Turkish army and for the introduction, under subtle parliamentary forms, of new methods of government. Whatever may have been the secret motives that dictated the action of the Sultan—whether he feared that his own authority would be lessened and that the difficult rôle of Monarch would become even more difficult when masters became multiplied at Constantinople, or whether he mistrusted an army controlled by foreign interests—it is certain that Abdul Hamid had become decidedly less acceptable to the Germans during the last few years of his reign than in the palmy days when the Kaiser visited Constantinople. "There is reason to believe," states a particularly well-informed writer, Mr. Henry Wickham Steed, "that even before the Turkish Revolution of 1908 Germany had begun to withdraw her support from Abdul Hamid, who, despite his crimes, was the most considerable Ottoman statesman of the last generation. Abdul Hamid foresaw the Anglo-German conflict, and had sufficient respect for the resources of the British Empire to believe that Germany might get the worst of the struggle. During the last two years of his reign he began almost imperceptibly to edge away from Germany—and Germany from him." * A change of régime was not distasteful to the Germans, and there were willing tools at hand who in the event of a crisis in Turkey would be prepared to sell their souls at the bidding of the Kaiser.

The events that precipitated the overthrow of Abdul Hamid need not be dealt with here. The Young Turks, long prior to the dramatic proceedings of 1908, had been preparing for the overthrow of the old régime. Although their central organization in Paris and their main objects were well known in Europe, they were generally regarded as a body of academic enthusiasts, devoted to theoretical politics rather than to practical administration, more noisy than dangerous, who expended their scanty funds in the publication of seditious literature at Paris and Geneva, in order to introduce parliamentary methods into a country only fit to be ruled by the sword. Such certainly was the Young Turk party during its earlier career; but a decided change came over the propaganda, realized at Yildiz Kiosk and perhaps at Berlin, but generally unnoticed elsewhere.

When the political enthusiasts at Paris and Geneva began to work in conjunction with military officers and to carry on an active propaganda in the Turkish army, the position of the Sultan became more precarious, because the Ottoman throne was mainly dependent upon the military clique for its support. Young officers, such as Enver Bey, who directed the propaganda in Albania and Macedonia, had been drawn into the vortex, partly through altruistic motives and a real belief in the necessity for reform, but more probably by the promptings of inordinate ambition. Enver Pasha, if the account given in "The Near East from Within" is not to be regarded as apocryphal, when an attaché at Berlin was contemplating the overthrow of the Sultan and had already been recognized by the Emperor William as a likely instrument of German policy in the Near East. "I have had serious reason to believe," says the anonymous writer of that book, "that Enver Bey discussed these matters with the German Emperor, with whom he had been in favour from his first arrival at Berlin. William II, who had failed in his efforts

* "The Quintessence of Austria," by H. W. Steed, *Edinburgh Review*, October 1915, p. 238.

GERMANY, TURKEY, AND THE BALKAN WARS

to make Abdul Hamid a will-less satellite of the German Empire, at once saw the possibilities that could arise out of a quiet but nevertheless palpable encouragement of the ambitious young officer, who, whilst studying the discipline of the Prussian army, was at the same time profiting by all that he saw, and was preparing himself for the part which his ambition and consciousness of ability persuaded him he could take in the conduct of the affairs of his own country. When Enver Bey left Berlin, it was with a cordial letter of recommendation from the Emperor to Baron Marschall von Bieberstein, who in his turn was not slow to recognize Enver Bey's remarkable individuality and to make a close friend of him. The intimacy lasted until the Baron left Constantinople some long time after the accession of Mehmed Rechad." *

Whatever may have been the influences exerted at Berlin prior to the deposition of Abdul Hamid there is no doubt whatever that after that event the present Turkish Minister of War, the practical dictator of modern Turkey, was soon completely within the German pocket. Although a Turk of Polish descent, his sympathies were entirely Prussian.

The events that immediately precipitated the raising of the standard of revolt at Resna, on the Monastir–Ochrida Road, on July 22, 1908, and the proclamation of the Constitution at Salonika by Enver Pasha on the following day do not come within the scope of this book. It should be stated, however, that the plans of the Young Turks were hastened owing to the Macedonian reforms agreed upon at Reval in June 1908, and the determination of Sir Edward Grey to have these reforms carried out at once. They realized that only by a vigorous counter-move could Macedonia be saved to the Turkish Empire.

The triumph of Young Turkey, secured through the swift mobilization of the Macedonian troops under Mahmud Shevket Pasha, and the rapid and amazing march upon Constantinople, was welcomed throughout Europe as the victory of Western ideas over fanaticism and reaction, particularly because the revolution was signalized by a proclamation of "the perfect equality of races and creeds." A new era seemed to have dawned. The banner of reform had been raised within, and

* "The Near East from Within," pp. 54-55.

not without, the Ottoman Empire, and the hateful Hamidian system had been swept away. But the revolution of 1908, which prepared the way for the present war, in spite of its avowed political objects and although effected with little bloodshed, was in reality a military movement. The Salonika Committee soon assumed a position that was in direct variance with the noble principles that had been avowed by the leaders of the movement. The counter-revolution in Constantinople which began with the revolt of the Grand Vizier, Kiamil Pasha, against the galling authority exercised by the military leaders at Salonika, ushered in a period of political instability which was not ended by the deposition of Abdul Hamid by the National Assembly at San Stefano in April 1909. The subsequent history of Turkey has been characterized by a long and bitter struggle between the rival leaders for supreme power.

The chaos that was characteristic of Turkish political life presented an excellent opportunity for the Germanic Powers, and more especially for Austria-Hungary, to carry out certain designs that had been thwarted by the ex-Sultan. The Emperor Francis Joseph, acceding to the wishes of the Archduke Ferdinand, was the first to take advantage of the disorder into which Turkey had been plunged by the Revolution. The position of affairs at Constantinople was such that there was no possibility of successfully withstanding any aggressive move engineered from the north; and in the provinces the activities of the Young Turks who, in spite of their declarations of racial equality, were bent upon Ottomanizing the Christians of Macedonia and in unifying the system of government in the former province and in Albania, led to a state of anarchy in those two districts. The Anglo-Russian scheme for reforms in Macedonia, elaborated during the visit of King Edward to Reval a few months before the rising at Salonika, was no sooner announced than the Powers, affecting to believe that under the new régime all would go well in Macedonia, withdrew their officials and sacrificed at a stroke the whole position acquired at the cost of a naval demonstration and five years of laborious diplomacy. The Concert of Europe, which had become the jest of diplomatists and a mockery to the Christians of Turkey, was definitely broken upon the altar of sentimentalism. "The consequences of this blunder were soon evident," stated a writer in the *Quarterly Review*. "Allowed a free hand in Macedonia, the Young Turks, who had been fêted in London and Paris as the harbingers of civilization, proceeded to stretch the races of that country on a Procrustean bed. Bulgarians, Greeks, Vlachs, Serbs, Albanians—all alike were expected to renounce their nationality and to become "good Ottomans." In order to facilitate their conversion a general disarmament was decreed; and was carried out with the utmost barbarity. A conspiracy of silence was maintained in the European Press; and the world knew little of the horrors of 1910 and 1911." * Albania, which had hitherto enjoyed certain privileges and was not taxed so highly as other portions of the Empire, was soon in a state of extreme unrest, culminating in the rising of 1909, when Austria is stated to have supplied the insurgents with money and ammunition, in the well-founded hope that the province might be detached from the Ottoman Empire in order to form another of the Austrian avenues to the East. Proofs of this fact, states Mr. S. Verdad, " came to the knowledge of the Turkish Government and were supplied to me by a highly placed member of the Young Turk Committee, but it was felt that if they were made public in a detached form it would have led to a rather grave diplomatic situation." †

While these events were simmering on the Turkish hob and the military-politicians were quarrelling in the Sultan's Council Chamber, Count Aehrenthal, acting as the representative of the party of expansion in Austria, was planning the great diplomatic coup which renders the year 1908 the turning-point in recent European history.

The apologists of Austria's policy in annexing a country that had to all intents and purposes been Austrian territory since the Treaty of Berlin had enacted that "the Provinces of Bosnia-Herzegovina shall be occupied and administered by Austria-Hungary," contend that no stipulation to respect and maintain the independence and territorial integrity of the Ottoman Empire had been violated by this action. By sweeping aside the legal and diplomatic fiction under which

* *Quarterly Review*, 1915, No. 443, p. 426.
† "Foreign Affairs for English Readers," by S. Verdad, 1911, p. 106.

Bosnia-Herzegovina was still considered as Turkish territory, although occupied, administered, and governed by Austria-Hungary, Count Aehrenthal merely, it is stated, changed a theoretical dependency of the Sultan into an actual dependency of the Austrian Kaiser. The position of affairs was in some respects analogous to that existing in Egypt, where Great Britain had recognized the peculiar status of the Khedive as a vassal of the Sultan whilst acting independently, although in his name, in every important attribute of government. From this point of view Austria's precipitate action in definitely repudiating the shadowy claims of the Sultan may perhaps be justified, because the question as between Austria-Hungary and Turkey was merely the rude application of the Germanic doctrine that Might is Right. Purists might bewail the unkind blow to Ottoman susceptibilities; sentimentalists might deplore the rape of another portion of the Sultan's dominions; international lawyers, keen for the letter and not for the spirit of treaties, might regret the savage blow at an impotent foe. But there was in reality something far more important involved in Austria's sudden move than mere theorizing or sentimentalism; for Austria was holding Bosnia-Herzegovina as the mandatory of the European Powers who had been parties to the Treaty of Berlin, and she had no right to go beyond the terms of that agreement without their consent.

How far Austria ran counter to the wishes of Germany in thus forcing the question to a premature decision is not definitely known, but that her action was another blow at the sanctity of treaty rights, so frequently and openly violated, is not open to question. The breach of faith was flagrant and, as we know, nearly precipitated the European crisis for which Germany was not then prepared. Russia, weakened by her Far-Eastern adventures, was unwilling to push matters to extremities, and Austria's action was regarded as *un fait accompli*.

Our own policy with regard to the Bosnian affair was regulated by the fact that British statesmen had not realized that we had any definite interests in the Balkan Peninsula, and resolutely refused to recognize facts that should have been only too apparent to any statesmen who had made a study of the question. British diplomatic history with regard to the Balkans certainly cannot be termed a brilliant record. It has rather been a succession of dismal failures, rendered more dismal owing to the unfortunate sentimentalism by which they have been accompanied. At no period of our history has this been more evident than during the last seven years. German aims were neither appreciated nor understood, for diplomatists were not ready to acknowledge the turpitude and treachery involved in Germanic policy, and the British Government being almost entirely concerned with domestic politics gave little attention to foreign problems that were imperiously demanding solution. The Ministry seemed to be guided by the opinion that the man in the street, being completely in the dark as to the course of events in any country but his own, would fail at the decisive moment to rally to the support of the Government if they undertook a policy that seemed to have no direct concern with British interests. This was subsequently made clear by Sir Edward Grey in the House of Commons during the memorable debate on August 3, 1914, when the Foreign Secretary revealed the fact that the British Government definitely decided at the time of the Bosnian crisis that it had no concern with a purely Balkan affair. M. Isvolski, the Russian Foreign Minister, who was in England at the time, naturally asked whether Great Britain was prepared to support Russia. " I told him definitely then," stated Sir Edward Grey, " that this being a Balkan crisis, a Balkan affair, I did not consider that public opinion in this country would justify us in promising to give anything more than diplomatic support."

Our attitude at this period was a deplorable mistake and no one realized this more than the late King Edward. There can be little doubt that but for the ignorance then prevailing amongst the British public with respect to Balkan affairs the British Government might have proceeded differently, but they feared that they might act without the support of the omnipotent voter, whose ignorance was in no small measure due to the action of successive Governments in treating foreign affairs as beyond the scope of the collective intelligence. The views of the British Government may be contrasted with the attitude of one who will long be remembered as one of the greatest of British statesmen, whose clear and discerning intellect grasped the inner meaning of every German advance, who was neither influenced by the prevailing sentimentalism of modern politicians nor obliged to be subservient to the undiscerning criticisms of the ten-pound householder. What King Edward thought of the Bosnian annexation and of its probable effect may be gathered from an illuminating passage in Lord Redesdale's " Memoirs." " It was the 8th of October and the King received the news at Balmoral," writes Lord Redesdale, " and no one who was there can forget how terribly he was upset. Never did I see him so moved. . . . The King was indignant, for nobody knew better than he the danger of tampering with the provisions of the Treaty of Berlin, and he saw that to make any change in the Turkish Provinces was to light a fuse which sooner or later was bound to fire a powder magazine. . . . His forecast of the danger, which he communicated to me at the time, showed him to be possessed of the prevision which marks the statesman. Every word that he uttered that day has come true." If only King Edward could have been his own Foreign Secretary and could have acted independently of the British Ministry and with no eye to the next election, the subsequent disasters to our policy, or want of policy, in the Balkans would in all probability have been avoided.

In thus consolidating her position on the Adriatic and definitely cutting off Serbia from the sea, Austria's action produced incalculable results in European politics. " From the political point of view," stated M. Milenko R. Vesnitch, " the consequence has been the definite rupture of the Austro-Russian understanding as well as a sensible tension in Austro-Italian relations, not to mention the profound consternation which has been produced in all the Serbian race, and more particularly in Serbia and Montenegro. In this action Europe has witnessed a grievous and dangerous precedent calculated to shake all confidence in the value of solemn international relations." * That these results were fully realized in Austria at the time of the annexation is demonstrated by the following statement in a Pan-German paper published at Vienna on November 5, 1908. " Austria-Hungary may face the future with quietude," it was stated, " for Russia and England

* " L'Annexation de la Bosnia-Herzegovine et le Droit international."

have not the necessary power to pronounce the definite word. . . . And as regards Italy, she can only for the moment, willy-nilly, resign herself to the inevitable in spite of the unhappiness she is suffering because of the deception of her aspirations upon the eastern coasts of the Adriatic." The writer then frankly states that a conflict with Serbia is inevitable and also that Italy was directly aiding the Serbians in their opposition to Austria. "We can only put away our arms," he continues, "when the apple of discord has disappeared "—presumably down the Austrian throat—" that is to say, *not before we have secured the complete hegemony of the Balkans* . . . and this ideal once realized there must be expansion towards the East, where we shall appropriate all the congenerous peoples of Russia and shall then become the great Austrian Federation." *

The ultimate aims of Austria in the Bosnian annexation were thus sufficiently revealed by her indiscreet friends, who realized better than people in England what were the direct consequences of this sudden attack upon Turkish rights.

The immediate consequences were sevenfold and may be summarized as follows. In the first place, Russia was definitely shown that Austria-Hungary was, and would remain, her enemy, since she had pledged herself to a policy of expansion in the Balkan Peninsula of which the annexation of Bosnia was only the preliminary step. Secondly, Italy was alienated, since she saw that Austria was determined to establish herself firmly along the Adriatic coasts and was working to secure the control of Albania also at the first favourable opportunity. The seed of the dissolution of the Triple Alliance that had already been sown was thus warmed towards its later maturity. Thirdly, Rumania was repelled from the Triple Alliance because the Rumanians recognized clearly, perhaps for the first time, that the enemy they had chiefly to fear was not Russia but Austria, who seemed bent upon absorbing the Slav Kingdoms of the Balkans. Fourthly, the Southern Slav movement was fanned into a flame owing to the apparently definite imprisonment of Serbia and Montenegro within the frontiers already assigned to them and the probability that it was Austria's intention to attract them forcibly within the

* Quoted by Pontcray, p. 214.

Austro-Hungarian orbit. Fifthly, Greece was encouraged to press for a solution of the Cretan question: an event which caused great excitement within the Hellenic kingdom, and, but for the wise policy of Venizelos, would have precipitated another war between Turkey and Greece and possibly have forced prematurely the coming Balkan crisis. Sixthly, Bulgaria, who had slowly been gravitating towards Austria, took a leaf out of the book of her political mentor and seized the opportunity of proclaiming her own absolute independence.*
And seventhly, Italy was emboldened to adopt a yet more

* It should here be stated that the Sultan was by no means disposed to surrender without some adequate *quid pro quo* the shadowy rights of sovereignty that he still claimed over Bosnia-Herzegovina and over Bulgaria. He appealed to the Great Powers, who had always seemed about to consume the *membra disjecta* of the Ottoman Empire, against this breach of their solemn engagements in the Berlin Treaty. Serbia also appealed to the Powers, and particularly to Russia, in order to secure some compensation for herself. Russia took up the Serbian cause, but Germany, in spite of the awkward position in which she was herself placed with regard to Turkey, her protégée, supported her ally and the Kaiser by rattling the sword and delivering what in reality amounted to an ultimatum to Russia, who was unprepared for war, secured what was regarded as a German triumph over the forces of the Entente. The Kaiser's direct affront to Russia at that date welded the Triple Entente together and demonstrated the necessity for vigorous preparation for future eventualities—a lesson which, unfortunately, was almost unheeded in this country. How critical was the position of affairs at the time of the Bosnian crisis is well known. Mr. Verdad states that Russia was relying upon the intervention of Great Britain and was " badly left " by Sir Edward Grey. " As the natural protectoress of the Slav races," he writes, " Russia sent in a more than usually indignant protest, principally because Sir Edward Grey had stated in a private diplomatic communication that, in the event of hostilities actually breaking out, Russia might rely upon the support of the British Navy. When this information became known in Vienna, whence it was at once communicated to Berlin, the Kaiser promptly made arrangements for mobilizing an army corps, and the German Ambassador at St. Petersburg intimated to the Russian Government that any hostile action taken against Austria, the ally of Germany, would at once be followed by a German invasion of Russia. It is evident to me from documents which I was recently able to consult at Vienna and St. Petersburg that this was merely another example of that German bluff which became so conspicuous in international politics during recent years. Unfortunately, however, Sir Edward Grey thought otherwise, and in view of the disaster to the Liberal Party which a continental war would necessarily have involved at that time, British support was instantly withdrawn from Russia and indirectly from Serbia. The withdrawal of this aid . . . led to a feeling of bitterness against England in Russia and Serbia, who felt themselves betrayed and handed over to the Triple Alliance." (Verdad's " Foreign Affairs," pp. 112–13.) The soundness of Mr. Verdad's conclusions may be deduced from Sir Edward Grey's statement in the House of Commons already quoted.

drastic policy and proceeded to occupy Tripoli—a country which she had long coveted. The most unfortunate effect of Aehrenthal's blunder from the German point of view was that the Allies no longer worked in complete accord and that the Kaiser was given infinite trouble with his ill-assorted team. The most sinister result from the European point of view was that, in conjunction with other contributory causes, it hastened the formation of the famous Balkan League and led more or less directly to the present war. The most damning result from the moral outlook was that the sanctity of treaties could no longer be depended upon and that International Law lost not only its moral sanction but such support as it had received in the Chancelleries of Europe.

The effect of the Bosnian policy upon Italy was soon apparent. If Austria were able to secure so easy a triumph over Turkey and so easily to break the diplomatic bonds that had been fashioned by the Great Powers, there seemed no reason why Italy should not take active steps to secure compensations for herself at the expense of the unfortunate Turk. For many years the Italians had been looking towards Tripoli and Cyrenaica as a suitable territory for a new colony, but had hitherto been deterred from taking active steps by the opposition of France and Great Britain. She had long regarded the activities of France in Tunis with envy, for she looked upon herself as the natural heir of the former Roman territories in Northern Africa. The occupation of Tunis by France had been a severe blow to Italian aspirations and had brought about—an event which Bismark had foreseen—a long period of estrangement between the two Latin races. But the internal state of Turkey and the diplomatic conflict between France and Germany which was then raging presented a favourable opportunity for the realization of Italian aims, and on September 28, 1911, during the most critical period of the Morocco negotiations, when the fate of Europe was hanging in the balance, the Giolitti Cabinet sent an ultimatum to Turkey stating that with a view to the " guardianship of its dignity and interests " the Italian Government had decided to proceed to the military occupation of Tripoli and Cyrenaica, and demanding a reply within twenty-four hours. On the following day, in spite of a conciliatory answer from the

Ottoman Government, the Italian Ministry declared war and initiated the campaign for the conquest of the two Turkish Provinces in Africa.

The Turco-Italian War, primarily a war of conquest on the part of Italy, was viewed with dismay in Germany, for that country was at once placed in a most awkward position with respect to her southern ally. It was not easy for German diplomatists to persuade the Porte that a member of the Triple Alliance could have gone to such lengths as the actual conquest of a Turkish province without the tacit agreement of her two partners, or that the leading member of the alliance had been unable to restrain the junior partner from pursuing her campaign against the Ottomans. To those who realized the critical state of European politics the real facts were sufficiently apparent. The price of Italy's lukewarm adherence to the Germanic alliance was the occupation of Tripoli, and Germany in this case had been unable to withstand the Italian demand for freedom of action. Germany could not afford to adopt an irreconcilable attitude, and she was on this occasion forced to acquiesce in the unwelcome action of her Italian ally—even at the expense of so serious a blow to German plans for the political and economic assimilation of the Sultan's dominions.

Italy's action was a serious blow to Germany's prestige in the Near East. It weakened her hold over the Ottoman Government, demonstrated that there was a decided rift in the Teutonic lute, showed Turkey that she could not rely upon the boasted protection of the German Government, and directly created a new factor in the Mediterranean naval situation because "Germany foresaw that by annexing a vast territory in Northern Africa, not to speak of the Turkish islands in the Mediterranean, Italy was placing herself for a long time to come at the mercy of the superior naval power of Great Britain and France."[*] The last factor has generally been overlooked in considering Italy's position as a Mediterranean Power, but it certainly had a decided, though not pronounced, influence in determining Italy's attitude towards the Triple Entente. In the Fatherland itself the action of

[*] "The Origins of the Present War," by Sir Valentine Chirol, *Quarterly Review*, 1914, No. 441, p. 439.

the Giolitti Cabinet was regarded with particular dislike, for in the words of that most able student of European politics, Dr. Dillon, " Germany was being hoist with her own petard, and she disliked it." She would gladly herself, states Dr. Dillon, have leased or occupied Tobruk,* if circumstances had been propitious. It was gall and wormwood to her to let Turkey be mutilated and humbled by Italy, whose aggression would damage the Triple Alliance in the estimation of the world and compromise each of the three partners in the eyes of the Young Turks. Moreover, Germany had doubtless been representing to the Porte that her conversations with France over the Morocco affair afforded an excellent opportunity for a Franco-Turkish settlement also, which the strong German Government would be prepared to facilitate on the most favourable terms. The price of German good offices might have been Tobruk or some other Tripolitan harbour which might have been considered suitable as a site for a German coaling station in the Mediterranean; but Italy, distrusting her Teutonic partner, necessarily hastened her own action in view of this threatening possibility of the near future. Whether Germany in view of the delicate state of the Triple Alliance would have dared to adopt such a course—however desirable it may have appeared to Pan-Germans—is of course open to serious doubt, but in any case Italy recognized the possibility and acted accordingly.

These events almost naturally preceded the definite formation of the Balkan League. The two staggering blows at Turkey delivered by Germany's two allies demonstrated to the Young Turks, the Fatherland's chosen protégés, that Germany was unable to protect their interests. A further and far greater upheaval was to follow, which for the time being was almost to destroy the long and carefully planned work of the Teutonic diplomatists at Constantinople. The course of events within the capital was such that it was necessary to keep the city under what practically amounted to martial law, and the state of anarchy existing in more than one district in Turkey and the shadow of the coming conflict with Italy compelled the retention of large numbers of troops ready for active service. Yet, as has always been the case

* A port in Cyrenaica.

in Turkey, the most serious factor to be reckoned with was the want of money. In view of the evident necessity of strengthening the Turkish navy it was essential that money should be raised, and application was accordingly made to France, that apparently inexhaustible well from which the Turks have drawn so many millions of gold. But on this occasion the French Foreign Minister, M. Pichon, realizing the enormous indebtedness of Turkey to France and the fact that French money was in reality being employed to buy German guns and ammunition—and in this instance to purchase German ships—bluntly informed Djavid Pasha, the Turkish Minister of Finance, that the French Government objected to these proceedings and would only guarantee the loan in return for definite concessions by the Turkish authorities, one of which was that the budgets of Turkey should be administered under the supervision of an adviser of French nationality.*

To this stipulation, supported as it was by the British and Russian Governments, the Young Turks strongly objected, and, after trying private sources in France, the Grand Vizier, Hakki Pasha, turned to Germany for financial assistance. A large loan was guaranteed by the German Government—at a higher rate of interest than that offered by France—and further financial shackles were fastened around the Young Turks, fetters which bound them both in interest and sentiment to the German Government. This financial factor was one of the means employed by the Germans—a perfectly legitimate means of course—for establishing their influence at Constantinople after the deposition of Abdul Hamid.

Shortly after the floating of the loan the Turkish heir apparent was induced to pay a visit to the German capital —an event that was eagerly seized upon by the German Press as a proof of the excellent relations existing with Turkey. " These relations," stated the *Berliner Tageblatt* on August 30, 1911, " respond to-day to the sincere desire of the Turkish people, who now know who are their true friends. For a long time there was great distrust of Germany and it was believed that the German Government was not well disposed towards the new régime. The force of logic has changed that idea." The force of logic may be interpreted as the

* *See* Verdad's " Foreign Affairs," p. 108.

want of money and the fact that Germany's Turkish satellites were busily employed at Constantinople. The logic of events had also led to the partial resumption of the German military mission in the year 1910, when von der Goltz visited the scenes of his former labours. This event must not be confounded, however, with the official resumption of the mission under General Liman von Sanders after the Second Balkan War, when that officer was specially charged to redeem the lost prestige of German military teaching. Von der Goltz's visit on this occasion was of a temporary character. It was, however, another proof of the growing influence of Germany, which had suffered a temporary eclipse during the last years of Abdul Hamid. This renewed influence was largely due to the unceasing endeavours of Baron Marschall von Bieberstein, who, after having been Secretary of Foreign Affairs, took up his ambassadorial duties in the Turkish capital in October 1897—two months after the signing of the Franco-Russian Agreement. The appointment of so distinguished a diplomatist was in itself an earnest of Germany's intentions with regard to Turkey. Marschall directed German affairs at Constantinople almost until the outbreak of the First Balkan War.

That event, one of the most momentous in the annals of modern Europe, was brought about by a variety of causes, not the least of which was the state of anarchy in Macedonia. As the revolution had undoubtedly been influenced by the attempts of the European Concert to introduce reforms in that province, so the formation of the Balkan League was finally brought about owing to the vigorous and peculiar " reforms " that the Committee of Union and Progress, acting through their ministerial agents at Constantinople, permitted to be carried on in Macedonia. The process of Ottomanization led to a combination of the Christian Balkan States—an event that was not regarded with particular favour either in Germany or Austria.

Attention has already been directed to the massacres in Macedonia and elsewhere prior to the outbreak of the Balkan War. Although our sympathies are naturally with the Balkan Powers in their struggle against Turkey, it is impossible to hold the Young Turks entirely to blame for the orgy of massacre and bloodshed that ushered in their reign at Constantinople. A critical examination of Balkan history reveals the fact that the welter of blood which disgraced the last few years in the Ottoman Empire was not entirely due to the political methods of the predominant party in Turkey. The so-called Christian Powers of Europe, constantly expressing high and noble sentiments and as constantly failing to act upon their own suggestions in favour of drastic reforms, cannot be held blameless for the state of affairs in Macedonia; nor can the Balkan States themselves be exonerated from blame. A strong, vigorous, and consistent policy on the part of the European Concert not only would have stopped the massacres themselves, but also would have prevented the subsequent war; but little could be expected from diplomatists, swayed by secret motives which did not correspond with their expressed desires, influenced by political aims, frequently widely divergent and mutually irreconcilable, and working silently on behalf of esoteric instructions received from the European Chancelleries. When the house of Europe was itself in flames, there was small hope that the Augean stables in the Balkans would be saved from the raging conflagration—and there was consequently no one to apply the necessary remedies, in order to quench the fires of revolt and anarchy.

Writers who know the inner history of the Balkan kingdoms have not hesitated to state that the Macedonian disturbances were deliberately fostered by the Bulgarians, in the hope that they would be able to intervene in Macedonia, and thus to accomplish their national policy of the Greater Bulgaria, originally set up by the Treaty of San Stefano. The state of affairs into which the European provinces of Turkey had drifted was enough to make the Gods weep. Describing the policy of the Bulgarians, a writer whose authority cannot be questioned states that "the policy carried on by this body was one of the most diabolical that had yet been invented throughout the blood-stained history of the Balkan problem. A group of enthusiasts had noticed how easily sympathy was aroused once " massacres " were mentioned, and they at once set to work to encourage massacre. . . . The most effective way of doing this was to put bombs in the midst of a Mohammedan crowd in some remote village—on a market day for preference. The bomb would explode and kill three or four persons; it was whispered that this was the work of the

Bulgarians, and the immense crowd would see red and massacre every Bulgarian on whom it could lay hands. It was then easy enough to say that the bomb was the work of the Young Turks, while there could be no dispute as to who had committed the subsequent massacres."* " Nobody with first-hand knowledge of the Macedonian troubles has ever questioned these facts," writes Mr. E. N. Bennett, the well-known war correspondent, in the *Edinburgh Review*.† " So sincere an admirer of the Bulgarians as Lieut. Wagner ‡ admits them without hesitation ; and it is notorious that the Kotchana massacre, which stirred the Bulgarians to frenzy, was brought about by the same infamous use of Bulgarian bombs. The Komitidji bands stopped at nothing to keep the Macedonian agitation open. . . . The bands were not only subsidized from Sofia, Athens, and Belgrade, but actually organized by well-known officers and professors like Panitza, Nikolaieff, and Matoff."

One need not be an apologist for the Turks, as was Mr. Bennett, to realize that there is some truth in these statements, or to recognize that the position of affairs in Macedonia was not unwelcome to the secret rulers of the Balkan States, who industriously prepared the way for the coming intervention. Though the Bulgarian sovereign may perhaps be exonerated from active participation in these crimes, it must be remembered that the part he played, encouraged by the bitter rivalries of the European Powers, does not exonerate him from grave suspicion. His hands were tied by secret influences, but his own dynastic interests and the racial welfare of his subjects were directly involved in the possibility of establishing a good case for intervention. Certainly the control exercised by King Ferdinand was sufficient to have enabled him to withstand the influences that were pushing him towards war had he so desired.

One of the most acute observers of Balkan politics, Dr. Dillon, has stated that " the influence for evil which a sovereign of German extraction would wield in a ' constitutional ' country has constantly been misjudged. British statesmen,

* " The Balkan War Drama," by a Special Correspondent, 1913.
† *See* his article " The Turkish Point of View," *Edinburgh Review*, April 1913.
‡ Author of " With the Victorious Bulgarians."

in a lordly way, ridiculed the idea that it mattered in the least whether the king or the prince of a Balkan country was a German or a member of any other nationality. ' In these days of democracy,' one of them remarked to me, ' the nationality of the sovereign has no more importance than his Christian name or his height. Dynastic influences have long since been displaced by the legitimate sway of parliaments.' And Germany dumped her over-production of princes and princesses in all monarchical countries of the world, especially in ' constitutional ' realms. Yet it was precisely in those ' constitutional ' countries that the sovereigns behaved as autocrats, leading their people wheresoever they listed. In ' constitutional ' Rumania, King Carol, an honest and patriotic king, concluded a secret military convention with Austria, and therefore, of course, with Germany, in the year 1880, which he renewed in 1913. On both occasions only his own signature was attached to the instrument ; which was, however, countersigned by the actual Premier," * and the autocratic action of other sovereigns in the Balkans is sufficiently notorious to need no special mention.

Whatever may have been the secret springs of the Macedonian troubles, there is no doubt whatever that it was the Young Turks who finally precipitated the catastrophe. Although atrocious massacres were engineered by both sides it was the Turkish massacres of the Bulgarians at Kotchana on August 1, 1912, and of the Serbs at Berana a few days later, coupled with the fact that the forthcoming grand manœuvres of the Turkish army were known to be arranged to take place at Adrianople in the following month, and the subsequent announcement that a large army would be concentrated in Thrace, that at length aroused public opinion in the Balkans to definite action against the hated Turk. The reforms proposed by Count Berchtold on behalf of Austria-Hungary and the joint Note of the Powers inviting the immediate discussion of measures for the amelioration of the condition of the Christian inhabitants of European Turkey were like pouring oil on the flames ; for the Balkan States had already decided to take the matter into their own hands, and to act without the sanction of, and in direct definace of,

* " The Balkan Imbroglio," *Fortnightly Review*, November 1915, p. 909.

Europe. They were no longer prepared to trust to the assurances of the Powers—assurances that had so constantly been made, but which, it was notorious, were never likely to be acted upon unless Austria-Hungary were given a free hand to decide the destinies of the Balkans—and they were ready to act entirely in their own interests without considering those of the guardian Powers, who had never succeeded in carrying out a common policy.

The formation of the Balkan League has been directly attributed to King Ferdinand and M. Venizelos.* The former was working industriously on behalf of the Greater Bulgaria ideal, not without the secret support of both Austria-Hungary and Russia, which was accorded to him from entirely different motives ; whilst the latter, emboldened by the success of the Italians, and realizing the importance of sea-power in a conflict with Turkey—a weapon that Greece was well able to use with advantage—thought the time opportune for a decisive move upon Thrace. The attitude of the Balkan States in finally coming to a common agreement was further regulated by the fact that Turkey was engaged in a war with Italy, and it was hoped that this factor would materially lessen the difficulty of attacking their hereditary enemy. But when the favourable opportunity for action occurred, Italy and Turkey were already nearing the conclusion of peace, and the whole situation had to be considered *de novo*, and the strategical and political plans carefully revised.

* M. Gueshoff, who was at one time Prime Minister of Bulgaria, reveals much of the inner history of the negotiations leading to the formation of the League in his Apologia for the part taken by Bulgaria. This book, " The Balkan League," is worth attentive study. M. Gueshoff makes it clear that Bulgaria was coquetting with Turkey with the object of coming to an understanding with the Porte, but that the subsequent action of the Young Turks rendered such an agreement impossible. The Serbo-Bulgarian agreement was finally approved by King Ferdinand " in the course of an audience in the train between Oderberg and Vienna " on October 11, 1911, and a treaty was signed on March 14, 1912. This treaty was aimed at Austria and Rumania as well as against Turkey, for the two parties mutually agreed by a secret annex to aid each other in the event of an attempt by any foreign Power to occupy Macedonia and Old Serbia, and the treaty was placed under the " ægis of the empire which had guaranteed the integrity and inviolability of Bulgaria." The Græco-Bulgarian Treaty was concluded on May 29, 1912, and an understanding was subsequently arrived at with Montenegro, although no written treaty was actually signed.

Each of the four partners in the Alliance had a somewhat different *arrière-pensée*, but all were determined to take the settlement of the Balkan Question out of the hands of Europe, and to demand a solution in which they should be adequately compensated. Bulgaria, and to a large extent Greece, had in view the expulsion of the Turks from Europe and the capture of Adrianople and Constantinople. Serbia was above all anxious to safeguard herself against Austria-Hungary, to obtain possession of Old Serbia, and to secure a port upon the Adriatic; whilst Montenegro was determined to check the Austrian advance along the Adriatic littoral and to establish herself at Scutari.

Turkey herself did not realize the seriousness of the position until it was too late, doubtless retaining a belief in the efficacy of the European Concert, and believing that the Great Powers would not allow matters to drift into actual warfare. The European Powers had so frequently intervened in Ottoman affairs that there seemed every hope for a drastic change, even at the eleventh hour.

But in adopting this attitude the Ottoman Government did not realize how hopelessly the Great Powers were divided, although apparently united; nor how Austria-Hungary was anxious for, though ostensibly opposed to, war. Nor did Turkey thoroughly appreciate the fact that the great mass of the Russian people was eagerly awaiting the coming triumph of the Allies, or realize that her friend Germany was perfectly indifferent to the course of events, or at least was not opposed to Austrian aims, because she believed that the German-trained Turkish army would be able to secure a decisive victory over the Balkan Allies.

The indifferent attitude of Germany at this critical period can only be explained upon two assumptions. German statesmen were convinced that the Ottoman troops would be able to give a good account of themselves; and they were secretly in favour of the coming war, as they believed that Austria would again be able to secure the *pièce de résistance* of the Balkan dish, as she had done after the Russo-Turkish War of 1878. The miscalculations of German policy on this occasion were sufficiently notorious to excite remark even at that time. Writing on October 13, a few days after war had broken out, *The Times* correspondent at Berlin stated that " one can hardly remember a crisis in which Germany deliberately and successfully assumed so modest a part. The Government, which did not until lately believe in war, refused to take any initiative whatever, replied with an almost unkind indifference to the diplomatic communications of the Balkan States, offered probably no advice at all to Turkey, and merely expressed the hope that if there should be war it might be localized." The modesty of Germany on this occasion, so directly contrary to Teutonic methods, is easily explained on the assumption mentioned above.

The few weeks immediately preceding the outbreak of war were occupied by the diplomatists of Europe in incessant activities and in attempting to discover some formula satisfactory to all parties. It was a period of extreme tension in European affairs, for both in Russia and Austria there were strong parties who were anxious to see the Balkan States engaged in a war with the Turks : the Russians, because they firmly believed that the Allies would be able to inflict a crushing defeat on the Turks ; the Austrians, because they saw an opportunity for picking the plums out of the Turkish pudding. There were certain almost incalculable factors that had nevertheless to be taken into account. On the one hand, the possible defeat of Serbia might lead to Russia's intervention and precipitate a general European conflict ; on the other, the success of the Allies might cause the intervention of Rumania on behalf of Turkey, or the active interference of Austria, to prevent the growth of the Serbian kingdom.

Rumania was sitting on the fence keenly watching the course of events, but it was not definitely known on which side she would ultimately descend. The Germanic Powers believed that she was pledged to their interests, and that the announcement which had been made two years previously, that Rumania in the event of any hostile move against Turkey on the part of Bulgaria would mobilize all her forces on the Bulgarian frontiers, still held good. A declaration of this nature, undoubtedly made at the instigation of Germany, who had hitherto been able to induce Rumania to play an important part in the strategical diplomacy of the Fatherland, could not be lightly brushed aside. On the other hand, it was believed in Russia that Rumania had been persuaded to remain neutral, and that the recent appointment of King Charles as a Russian Field-Marshal was a pledge that the Danubian kingdom would not attack Bulgaria. Russia's calculations, based on the assumption that Rumania had been alienated by the Bosnian annexation, proved the sounder.

Meanwhile the proposals of Count Berchtold hastened the catastrophe. The Balkan States realized that it was necessary to act before the European Powers had finally decided on the nature of their own reforms, and on September 30 a decree was signed at Sofia summoning men who had served with the colours for the preceding twenty-five years, and raising the Bulgarian army to a strength of about 400,000 men. An order for mobilization was issued at Belgrade, and a similar step was taken at Athens, although the King of Greece was absent from the country. From that date events moved with a rapidity that was bewildering to the Chancelleries of Europe, used to procrastination and the slow processes of diplomacy. On October 8 Montenegro hastened matters by declaring war on her own account, on the 13th Greece, Bulgaria, and Serbia presented their ultimatum, and on the 17th Turkey declared war on the four Allies.

Previous to the actual outbreak of hostilities *The Times* correspondent at Constantinople, who was particularly conversant with the effect of Count Berchtold's proposal, wrote that " this, or rather the appeal to Europe to support it, has not only supplied the numerous Turkish enemies of Mukhtar Pasha's Government with their most dangerous weapon, but has given those elements in the Balkan States which desire either territorial expansion for themselves or the amelioration of the lot of their kinsfolk within the Turkish Empire the impression that Austria-Hungary will support them in exercising pressure upon the Turks. Count Berchtold's intention was, doubtless, of the best, but war and especially a Balkan War ' is hell ' and the road to hell is paved with good intentions." But the attitude of Austria was not disinterested and the impression she had created amongst the Balkan States was not destined to lead to the fulfilment of altruistic schemes of reform. In Vienna it was believed that the whole war was being deliberately engineered by Russia. " In spite of the theoretical unanimity of the Powers," wrote *The Times* correspondent on October 1, " their action has been too disjointed and their miscalculations of the situation during the last twelve months have been too gross to afford much hope that they can intervene effectively at the twelfth hour in favour of peace. Rightly or wrongly, it is believed here that the Balkan States are deriving encouragement from the unofficial attitude of Russia." There is no cause for wonder, therefore, that when the official attitude of the Powers was finally decided upon their representations came too late to impress the Balkan peoples with either their sincerity or with the ability of the Concert to control the situation effectively.

The Russian Foreign Minister, M. Sazanov, who was then in England, although he made urgent and categorical representations in favour of peace, was unable to counteract the impression produced by the enthusiastic demonstrations that had taken place in Petrograd; whilst the semi-official communication, issued at Berlin on October 1, which conveyed a threat to the Balkan States, was treated with contempt. " It may be hoped," said Herr von Kiderlen-Waechter, " that the certainty of winning glory at most, and no accession of territory in the event of victory, will, even at the last moment, have a soothing effect upon the Balkan States. Russia, as well as France, has given it clearly to be understood that she desires the *status quo* in the Balkans to remain undisturbed, and Austria-Hungary and England are of the same opinion. In such circumstances it is not easy to see with what purpose the Balkan States are anxious to go to war." The statement of the European Powers, conveyed to the Bulgarian Government by the Austro-Hungarian and Russian Ministers on October 8, the day on which Montenegro declared war, that the Concert had undertaken to deal with the question of Macedonian reforms, came too late, whilst the further announcement, that " they would not allow any modification of the territorial *status quo* in Turkey," was merely ridiculous, viewed in the light of subsequent events.

The events of the Balkan War—the crushing defeat of the Turks, the capture of Adrianople, the march upon Constantinople, and the retreat of the Turks to the Chatalja lines—are matters of recent history that do not concern us. The fight of the Cross against the Crescent, to use the flamboyant phrase contained in King Ferdinand's address to his army, had everywhere resulted in the rout of the Turks and, it may be added, in the defeat of European diplomacy. In the face of such sweeping victories the declaration of the Powers as to the territorial *status quo* could have little meaning, because effective European control of the situation was impossible under the menacing circumstances then existing. Doubtless both Austria-Hungary and Germany would have welcomed a return to the *status quo ante bellum*, but the victory of the Allies was a Slav victory, and was interpreted in many quarters as a victory of the Triple Entente over the Germanic Alliance. A return to former conditions could only be achieved through the agency of a general European war, for which Germany was not then prepared. She had played her cards badly and was obliged for the time being to abide by the results of her own miscalculations. " The issue of the Balkan War upset the calculations of Vienna, Budapest, and Berlin ; the extent of their misconception may be studied in Marshal von der Goltz's illuminating little essay on the Turkish defeat." *

Nothing could extricate the Germanic Powers from the bog into which they had fallen save a policy of intrigue, engineered so as to cause the victorious States to quarrel amongst themselves. For this purpose Bulgaria, the spoilt child of the Balkans, was encouraged to make demands upon her allies that would be impossible of acceptance, in the hope that through the support of Austria she would be attached finally to the Germanic Powers should she, as was believed, emerge successfully from the fratricidal strife. They therefore made every effort to destroy the Balkan League, and succeeded in their immediate object.

The chief obstacle to the conclusion of peace between the Balkan Allies and Turkey at the beginning of 1913 had been the demand of the League for the cession of Adrianople and the obstinate refusal of the Turks to consider such an eventuality ; whilst the situation was still further complicated by the attitude of Rumania, who now claimed territorial compensation from Bulgaria as the price of her neutrality

* " The Balkans, Italy, and the Adriatic," by R. W. Seton-Watson, p. 23.

during the war. The Turkish Cabinet for some weeks declined to give way, but the representations of the Powers at length producing their effect, the Grand Vizier, the veteran Kiamil Pasha, was preparing to yield when he was driven from office by a *coup d'état* engineered by Enver Pasha and his associates. This occurred on January 23, 1913, when a military deputation headed by Enver forced its way into the Council Chamber whilst the Cabinet was drafting a reply to the Powers and demanded the resignation of Kiamil. The Commander-in-Chief, Nazim Pasha, who had bravely gone out to meet the intruders, was assassinated on the threshold, together with two or three other officers, and the leaders of this military revolution were able to dictate the policy of the Turkish Government, whilst Mahmud Shevkat Pasha became Grand Vizier.

The change of ministry occasioned by this event brought matters to a deadlock, and the Conference in London, which had been called to arrange the terms of peace, broke up on February 1 without having reached any definite agreement. The armistice therefore came to an end. Bulgaria attacked the Adrianople forts and the Montenegrins and Serbians continued the siege of Scutari. Adrianople fell on March 28, but the stubborn attitude of Montenegro, backed by Serbia, lengthened the war—for King Nicholas, in spite of the fact that the Powers had absolutely agreed, in deference to Austria and Italy, that Scutari should not be handed over to the Montenegrins, still obstinately refused to recognize the new conditions that had arisen. Even a naval demonstration on the Montenegrin coast failed to convince the King that there was not the least chance of territorial expansion in that direction, and the capitulation of Scutari on April 22 even strengthened his resolve to maintain his defiant attitude. Finally, the announcement that Austria-Hungary might be permitted to take isolated action as the mandatory of Europe convinced him that Russia was unable to offer effective support, and the old king, realizing that Montenegro was abandoned to her enemies, yielded to the inevitable on May 5.

The Russian attitude at this critical period was clearly expressed in an official communication issued by the Russian Foreign Office on April 10, which reveals the fact that German and Austrian pressure had been only too successfully exerted at Petrograd. " The principal object pursued by the Government at the time of the military successes of the Balkan Allies," stated the communication, " was to assure for the victors the fruits of their victories in the largest possible measure." This in itself was, of course, a notable triumph for Russian diplomacy in face of the German opposition to any alteration in the *status quo* in the Balkans, and was a recognition of the growing power of the Slav element. " That object," continued the statement, " has been attained as the result of complicated and difficult negotiations, for the Allies could not look for success except through the non-intervention of the Powers. . . . The localization of the war was only possible on two conditions—first, the renunciation by the Great Powers of individual territorial and other advantages; secondly, the renunciation of any individual action on their part. These negative conditions implied a third and positive condition, namely, the revision of the situation created by the war and its reconciliation with the interests of the Great Powers—interests which they could not renounce, and the adjustment of which could only be effected by the European Concert. In these circumstances the Conference of Ambassadors in London was convoked. That Conference had just completed the heavy task of determining the frontiers of North and North-Eastern Albania in opposition to the interests of Serbia and Montenegro with their very natural tendency towards expansion. On the other hand, there were the interests of the Albanians protected by Austria and Italy, who considered the *status quo* in the Adriatic of such vital importance as to admit of no argument on the subject."

With the withdrawal of the Montenegrin claims owing to the unanimous opposition of the Powers the Balkan War came to an end, and a most dangerous situation was temporarily overcome. The strong feeling that existed both in Austria-Hungary and in Russia, among all classes of the population, in favour of a more active policy might easily have led to a European explosion, and there can be little doubt that if the Balkan Allies had not achieved their victories with such startling rapidity the Russian Government, however desirous of refraining from military intervention, might have been forced, by a popular movement such as that which swept Russia into war in 1877, to take up the cause of Slavdom and to enter definitely upon hostilities on the side of the Balkan Allies.

On April 21, 1913, the allied States accepted the mediation of the Powers, after an armistice had been signed on the previous day. It was now necessary for them to come to an agreement among themselves. At this juncture, however, the Balkan States proved to the world that, so far from being actuated by purely altruistic motives in their war against Turkey, they were ruled by greed and governed by the desire of snatching as much territory as they could at the expense of their immediate neighbours. The sacred principles of nationality for which they had been fighting were of small account, and within a few days of the signing of peace it became apparent that they were prepared to follow the example of the Great Powers and to snatch whatever territory they could in the general scramble for the adjustment of territorial claims. Disputes immediately occurred; bitter rivalries were revealed; the forces that were maintained in the occupied districts quarrelled with each other, and bloody conflicts, sometimes almost reaching the importance of pitched battles, took place between the contending parties. To the Greeks, with their Hellenic tradition and their memories of the ancient glories of Athens, and with their privileged position as traders and merchants in every city of the East, the Bulgarians, a nation of peasants but recently delivered from bondage, were little better than bloodthirsty cut-throats; whilst to the Bulgars, realizing for the first time their newly found power, both Greeks and Serbs appeared to be but nations of robbers and bandits.

The opportunity for the nefarious policy of Austria-Hungary —backed, it cannot be doubted, by secret influences emanating from Berlin—was unique. A fratricidal strife would weaken the power of the Serbs and perhaps pave the way for the final triumph of the Bulgars, who were already drifting towards the German orbit and were encouraged in their new attitude by the Austrophile leanings of their German sovereign, the Coburg prince who, although of mixed German and French descent, found his chief interests at Vienna and Budapest.

After the London negotiations had been broken off the secret aims of German diplomacy had been revealed to Bulgaria as an encouragement to her in her opposition to Serbia. It is stated, on no less an authority than that of Dr. Dillon, that offers had been made to King Ferdinand which would have irretrievably bound him to the German coach. "A significant fact, for which I can vouch—it is, of course, well known to King Ferdinand, although it has never been divulged before—" states Dr. Dillon, "is that when M. Daneff broke up the London Conference and the Bulgarians, having taken Adrianople, were about to push through Chatalja and march on Constantinople, the two Central Powers signified their acquiescence in the capture and retention of the Turkish capital and Thrace by Bulgaria. And to my knowledge the eventuality of this annexation, without anticipation of the details, had been carefully thought out and prepared for in Sofia several years before. A splendid reward like this, which would bestow all Macedonia, Thrace, Salonica, Kavalla, and Constantinople upon the Neo-Byzantine Tsar, appealed with irresistible force to the grandson of Louis Philippe. And to secure it was King Ferdinand's steady aim. What neither he nor the politicians of Sofia would seem to have taken into account is the ultimate aim of his protectors. What Austria and Germany really had in view was not merely the command of a formidable Balkan army and the support of the united States of the peninsula, but the concrete fruits which these possessions would bring within their reach. Bulgaria's real part in the business would be solely that of proxy." *

By whatever means the Central Powers achieved their immediate aims the second Peace Conference which met in London on May 20 was unable to come to an agreement as to the division of the spoils, and although a treaty of peace was signed with Turkey on May 30, the Balkan States were finally left to settle their differences among themselves by means of direct conventions with each other. This decision of the Powers was tantamount to giving the former Allies a free hand to fight it out among themselves. It was at this crisis that the Tsar made a final effort to prevent the internecine struggle with which the Balkans were threatened and offered to act

* *Fortnightly Review*, May 1915, p. 764.

as arbitrator between the contending parties. "I wish to make it known," he announced, " that the State which begins this war will be responsible before the Slav cause, and that I reserve to myself all liberty as to the attitude which Russia will adopt in regard to the results of such a criminal quarrel."

Meanwhile the new Grand Vizier, Mahmoud Shevkat Pasha, who had shown some signs of acting independently of the revolutionary clique who then ruled Turkey, was assassinated, it is supposed by the orders of Enver Pasha ; and the official chief of the Young Turkish party, Prince Said Halim, was appointed in his stead. The opportunity of the Turkish "Napoleon" had at length arrived, for Enver succeeded as Minister of War and got ready for the violation of the Treaty of London by making preparations for again obtaining possession of Adrianople. The spirit of the new administration, if such it may be termed, has since been shown in the assassination of the Sultan's heir, who was known to be bitterly opposed to the policy of the Young Turks. An incident which occurred prior to the outbreak of the present hostilities is worth notice here as another instance of that policy of terror inaugurated since Enver reached the pinnacle of power. The meagre details of this affair which are available show that Prince Izzedin had asked the Turkish ministers to his house to discuss the situation. Enver Pasha, like the other guests, had been pledged to secrecy, but nevertheless had the effrontery to bring with him General Liman von Sanders, the head of the German military mission. The Prince, annoyed at the intrusion, maintained silence until Enver asked General Liman von Sanders to explain how Turkish intervention would be beneficial to the Ottoman Empire. A dispute occurred and Enver and his protégé rose to leave, when, the former touching his pistol menacingly, the Prince drew his revolver, fired several shots, and wounded both Enver and Sanders. Whatever truth there may be in this account, there can be no doubt that something of the kind actually occurred.

The result of the Second Balkan War, which began on June 30, 1913, was an even greater blow to the Germanic Powers than had been the sweeping victories obtained by the Balkan Allies during the critical days of the winter of 1912–13. There is not the slightest doubt that prior to the actual hostilities, which were commenced by the Bulgarians,* both German and Austrian statesmen believed that Bulgaria would be strong enough to crush her former allies ; nor can there be any question that the latter Empire had determined to intervene at the earliest possible moment should the Bulgarians be unable to defeat their Serbian enemies.

In order to work up a case against Serbia, Austrian statesmen did not scruple to employ the most nefarious means to attain their ambition. Three separate attempts were made to provoke a war with Serbia. The first of these, the notorious Prochaska incident—the case of the Austrian Consul at Prizrend whom the Serbians were accused of having insulted and even mutilated—was intended to prepare the way for an Austrian invasion. The Austrian Press was unanimous in demanding redress for an outrage which had never occurred, and public opinion was roused to boiling-point by the unchecked attacks upon Serbia that appeared in every Austrian newspaper, inspired by the Ballplatz and by those who were insidiously working to bring about a war with that country. M. Prochaska returned to Vienna, and subsequently stated that he had received official instructions to work up an " incident " in order that a plausible *casus belli* might be manufactured.† During this crisis, Mr. Steed, who was then *Times* correspondent at Vienna, received a visit from a high Austrian officer, who came directly from the Chief of the General Staff to sound him regarding British views about the policy of a joint attack upon Serbia and Russia as the surest means of ending the Southern Slav question.‡

No sooner was the Prochaska bubble pricked than Austria-Hungary attempted to bring about a war over the Scutari question, but this danger was ingloriously averted by the Powers acceding to the Austrian demands. Then, when the Second Balkan War had ended in the decisive defeat of Bulgaria,

---

* M. Gueshoff seeks to prove that the original outbreak was caused by irresponsible parties and was not owing to the orders of the Government. M. Danev's Russophile Government was certainly opposed to war and telegraphed to Petrograd asking for Russian intervention, but events had moved too rapidly, and racial animosities ran too high, for any effective steps to be taken.

† " The Balkans, Italy, and the Adriatic," by R. W. Seton-Watson, 1915, p. 25.

‡ *Ibid.*, p. 24.

GERMANY, TURKEY, AND THE BALKAN WARS 189

Austria-Hungary approached both Italy and Germany with proposals that they should engage with her in a " defensive " war against Serbia—proposals that were decisively rejected by Italy.* These proposals, which clearly reveal the desire of Austria to crush the kingdom that stood between her and the Ægean, were made on the day before the signing of the Treaty of Bukarest, which ended the strife in the Balkans, and for the time being the Vienna Government accepted the situation, but for a few months only.

There is little reason for surprise that the Second Balkan War was so easily engineered under the then prevailing circumstances. An acute observer in the Balkans wrote that the whole peninsula was " one vast madhouse, where sanity seems ridiculous and folly wisdom. MM. Pashitch, Venizelos, and Gueshoff are in the position of warders who have to shout with the rest in order to retain some measure of influence, though they are striving on parallel lines, if not jointly, to prevent the ruin of their work by internecine warfare." That ruin having been determined upon at Vienna and Budapest, there was small hope of preventing the war, but at the last moment two serious mishaps upset the Austrian plans and caused the Germanic Powers to regret that they had so seriously misjudged the chances of their Balkan protégé. The first was the intervention of Rumania; the second, the attack by the Turks. Bulgaria, being caught in a trap, was unable to perform the duty of crushing Serbia that had been assigned to her. The Rumanians, breaking away from the Germanic alliance, marched on Sofia; the Greeks and Serbians, after sweeping victories, pressed forward into Bulgaria; and the Turks, under Enver Pasha, recaptured Adrianople—and definitely stayed there.

The last event was brought about through the energetic initiative of Talaat Bey, the Minister of the Interior, who, finding that the Turkish army could not march for want of equipment, demanded and, what is more remarkable, secured four millions sterling from the Director of the Ottoman Régie.† Armed with these funds, the Turkish army marched on Adria-

* *See* the speech of Signor Giolitti in the Italian Chamber of Deputies on December 5, 1914.
† Dillon.

nople and drove out the small Bulgarian garrison—and the Greater Bulgaria of King Ferdinand's dreams ceased to exist.

The settlement of Balkan affairs was finally arranged at Bukarest, and was the occasion of a pretty little diplomatic comedy played by King Charles and the Emperor William. The latter, having plainly intimated to Austria-Hungary that he would not support her should she be involved in a war with Russia—for which the Germans were not then fully prepared—as a consequence of any attack upon Serbia, and to Russia that if she attacked Austria-Hungary, notwithstanding her abstinence from active intervention in the Balkans, he would fight on the side of his Austrian ally, stepped in and assumed the rôle of unofficial arbitrator and adopted the virtuous attributes of a peacemaker. The part played by Germany at this crisis would have delighted the honest broker Bismarck, but the German Emperor had not the skill of the Iron Chancellor and was in reality merely making the best of a bad job and securing for himself whatever laurels still remained to be garnered from the bloody fields of Balkania. King Charles politely telegraphed his felicitations to the Kaiser in words that have as little meaning as most official congratulations of this nature, but which, doubtless, were pleasing enough to the recipient. " I offer you," he said, " my most sincere and hearty congratulations on the splendid result, for which not only your own people but all the belligerent States and the whole of Europe have to thank your wise and truly statesmanlike policy. At the same time your mentioning that I have been able to contribute to what has been achieved is a great satisfaction to me. I rejoice at our mutual co-operation in the cause of peace."

The net results of the two wars for Bulgaria were: (*a*) the loss of about one hundred thousand officers and men, the devastation of a great part of the country, and a serious economic crisis; (*b*) the expenditure of about forty million pounds; (*c*) the loss of the greater part of Macedonia, which she had determined to annex, and the establishment of Greece and Serbia in that province; (*d*) the final loss of Adrianople and a great part of the fertile province of Thrace; (*e*) the loss of eight thousand square miles of Bulgarian territory, which had been handed to Rumania. The net result so far as Germany and Austria had been concerned was an enormous loss of prestige and the erection of a strengthened Slav barrier on the road to the East. Against this the only practical advantage that had been gained was the formation of an "independent" Albania and the introduction of another German prince upon Balkan soil—Prince William of Wied, an officer in the Prussian army, who, having been selected as Albanian sovereign, maintained a precarious foothold on the outskirts of his dominions—the new outpost of *Deutschthum* in the Near East—until the outbreak of the present war.

The signing of the Treaty of Bukarest on August 10, 1913, gave Sir Edward Grey an opportunity of making an important statement with regard to British policy in the Near East—a statement which in the light of subsequent events may be regarded rather as a pious aspiration than as a correct presentation of the then position of affairs. It may have been correct, as Sir Edward Grey said, that there was then no rift in the European lute, but the implication that all was going well in the best of diplomatic worlds, which the unprejudiced hearer would naturally draw from his statement, was certainly not justified by the course of events. Official telegrams and official congratulations only represented the official mind, and it was largely the Chauvinistic and Pan-German elements who were then directing the policy of the Fatherland and of the Austro-Hungarian Empire upon paths which were directly leading to war. Sir Edward Grey's speech, the charming telegrams exchanged between the King of Rumania and the German Emperor, the telegram of thanks sent by King Ferdinand, were in reality but the polite observances of polite individuals who disliked the rough-and-tumble of the political jugglers who were driving Europe into war. In spite of the Foreign Secretary's denial the Great Powers were certainly divided into two hostile camps, and no soft words or diplomatic phrases could hide the fact from those who had studied the course of German policy in the Near East. Diplomacy, working by set formulas and polite phrases, could no more eradicate the deeply rooted antagonism between Slav and Teuton and between the Entente and the Alliance than could Mrs. Partington's broom sweep back the advancing waves of the Atlantic.

Sir Edward Grey stated that the Ambassadors' meetings which had been held in London since December 1912 had been adjourned for a much-needed rest, but that the Concert of Europe was nevertheless firmly established and that there were no differences tending to divide the Great Powers into opposing camps. The Powers, he said, had set to work to defeat the established axiom that a Balkan war must involve one or more of them, by localizing the war and preventing its spread into other quarters. It was found, he continued, that if two questions were left out, namely, the future of Constantinople and of Asiatic Turkey, they might agree, providing they came to an understanding regarding Albania and the Ægean Islands, the latter in the occupation of Italy and Greece. This agreement was arrived at by compelling Serbia and Montenegro to refrain from making claims that would conflict with Austro-Hungarian interests and by establishing Albania as a separate principality. As to the Ægean Islands, the Foreign Secretary stated emphatically that British interests were intimately concerned; though they were in reality as vitally connected with Serbia and Montenegro and with the establishment of a strong Slav barrier in the Balkans as were Russian interests concerned with the future of Constantinople.

Although the defeat of Bulgaria and the partial dismemberment of European Turkey seemed to be a set-back to German policy, Teutonic influence was so firmly established at Constantinople that within a few months the Germans had regained much of the ground that they had lost. At the end of November 1913 it was announced that a new German military mission was about to proceed to Constantinople under the control of Gereral Liman van Sanders, well known for his Pan-German sentiments and his hostility to France and Russia, and accompanied by several officers charged with the reorganization of the Turkish army. All the officers thus detached from the German forces were to receive commands, it was alleged, in the Turkish army, whilst von Sanders was to be given the command of the First Army Corps stationed at Constantinople.

This news created a great sensation in well-informed circles, for it became apparent that the Young Turks had definitely accepted the Germanic cause and that Turkey was to be attached more firmly than ever to the Teutonic orbit. Entente diplomacy did not remain inactive in this matter, but the initiative of making representations was left to Russia because that country seemed to be the most directly menaced by the course of events. M. Kokovtsov, who went to Berlin on behalf of the Russian Government,[*] was assured that the intentions of Germany were perfectly straightforward, and on December 9, 1913, Herr von Bethmann-Hollweg, in the course of a statement in the Reichstag, dwelt upon the excellent relations between Germany and Russia. Nevertheless a few days later the German officers, dressed in Turkish uniforms, arrived at Constantinople, and on the evening of the same day the Ambassadors of the Triple Entente made a combined communication to the Grand Vizier and demanded information regarding the objects and powers of the mission. But the German mission was already firmly established in the Turkish capital, and formed one of the most powerful factors in solidifying German influence and in persuading Turkey to adopt the cause of the Teutonic Powers; and although it was announced that General Liman von Sanders would have no high command, there could be no doubt whatever as to the real significance of the mission. In this manner Germany prepared for the coming struggle and notified to the Powers of the Entente her determination to control the course of events at Constantinople.

[*] " D'Agadir à Sarajevo," by Pierre Albin, 1915, p. 84.

CHAPTER IX

PAN-GERMANISM AND AUSTRIA-HUNGARY

THE awakening of national and racial ideas was the direct outcome of the French Revolution. Up to that momentous period Europe, and especially Germany, had been dominated by dynastic rather than by racial ideas ; and the national movements that subsequently swept across the Continent, upsetting political policies, changing territorial boundaries, vivifying the ideals of slumbering democracies, and turning principalities into kingdoms and kingdoms into empires, was directed and encouraged by a few visionaries and enthusiasts whose political influence was in inverse ratio with their national insight and racial foresight.

The leaders of the new national movements, such as they were, in Germany, in Italy, in Austria, and in Russia were a feeble folk unknown beyond their immediate circles and comparatively harmless to affect the deeply rooted dynastic principles of their respective Governments. It was in France alone that the movements for the emancipation of nationalities from the political bonds in which they were swathed made any apparent progress ; for the days of Mazzini and Garibaldi, of Tolstoi and Turgeniev, of Kosciusko and Kossuth, of Kara-George and Petrovic Njegos,* of Hecker and Karl Schurz,† and of the giants of the German nationalistic revival, Moltke and Bismarck, had not yet dawned, and the spirit of nationalism, democratic or autocratic, was still imprisoned in the fetters from which it was destined to escape.

Within Germany, to paraphrase the words of Lord Durham, two States were striving within the bosom, not of a single nation, but of an autocratic political system. It required

* The national Serbian poet.
† Leaders of the abortive revolutionary movement of 1848.

the torch of the Revolution and the sword of Napoleon to set free the forces that were to change the political destinies of Europe. Contemporaneously, however, with the birth of the idea of political freedom within the ethnic boundaries of the smaller nationalities there arose two imperious and overwhelming ideals which directly conflicted with the aims of the leaders of the lesser races—Pan-Slavism and Pan-Germanism. With the latter, in so far as it concerns the Austrian Empire, we must now deal.

Austria, in the words of the Russian Chancellor Gortschakov, spoken over sixty years ago, was not a State; it was a Government—dominated, it may be added, by German influences. Even to-day, when the Dual Monarchy, composed of the combined German and Magyar oligarchies, dominates the territory stretching from the Erzgebirge to the Transylvanian Alps and from the Tyrol to the ancient republic of Ragusa, Austria scarcely deserves to be called a State. She is rather a collection of warring nationalities, bound together for mutual support and protection but likely at any time to be thrust apart by new political conditions or by fresh external influences.

Ten nationalities live under the rule of a single Emperor and of two Governments, each pursuing its own national aims and following its own particularist interests with a total disregard for the common good of the whole Empire, but with a lively faith in the paramount importance of their own special aims. Yet in spite of divergent aims and irreconcilable national ideals, the partners in this incongruous collection of States, this "ramshackle Empire" as it was impolitely but correctly termed by Mr. Lloyd George—each fearing the other and each striving after its own good to the exclusion of any common policy—have on the whole pursued one common defensive aim because they feared the outside world and distrusted the forces of Pan-Slavism and Pan-Germanism alike. They have not in the main been anxious to dissolve the galling partnership inside the House of Hapsburg or to tread the perhaps far more dangerous paths of political independence. As Mr. Namier has stated: "Austria is only a Government. She has been, not a home for nationalities, but an hotel or boarding-house. They have quarrelled, they have hated one another, they have abused their managers, they have cursed their fate, and yet up till now most of them were by no means particularly anxious to move out. Only to its three least numerous national groups, to the Italians, the Rumanians, and to the Serbians, who had their own homes just beyond the borders, was Austria a prison." *

Until the year 1866, when the Magyars were admitted into an almost equal partnership, German influence prevailed throughout the whole of the Austrian Empire; but since that political revolution, although Austria-Hungary has become more and more attached to the foreign policy of the new Empire in the North, other factors have acquired an ever-increasing influence—Magyar and Southern Slav—which have made the internal and external policy of the Empire far more complicated and difficult than when Vienna alone controlled its destinies.

We are not here concerned with the origins and growth of Pan-Germanism. That movement, which had its beginnings in the particularism of Prussia, who imposed upon the rest of Northern Germany her own peculiar forms and rapidly conquered the provincialism of the other German States, with the solitary exception of German Austria, was at first concerned with the welding together of the German Empire, and only at a later period assumed its more Chauvinistic and aggressive forms. Yet it must be recognized that one of its chief aims has been to create a situation which would force German Austria to enter the German confederation in order that the dangerous elements that form the present Austro-Hungarian State might ultimately be attached by economic, if not by political, bonds to a great Central European Empire. The masses of Germans settled in the Magyar and purely Slav provinces of the Empire were to be the leaven that was to leaven the whole lump, the political evangelists of the new German creed, the propagators of the fresh doctrines that had been added to the original Pan-German religion, and the secret workers in the national German cause.

An examination of any good ethnographical map of Austria-Hungary reveals the extent of these German oases dotted like plague spots over the face of Moravia and Galicia, placed in the midst of the Magyars, sweeping in compact masses over

* Namier, p. 123.

the boundaries of Bohemia, firmly planted in the centre of Rumanian Transylvania, and to a less extent encroaching upon the territories of the Serbs. In the Pan-German plan these Germans were to be attached firmly to the German Empire and were to control the political destinies of the States in which they were settled; for, as Herr Class, the President of the Pan-German League, stated at a meeting held at Brunswick during the crisis of the Balkan War,* " Our methods are not actuated by the interests of the House of Habsburg or of the Danubian Monarchy, but by the fact that *the German Empire and Austrian-Germanism have identical interests*, and by the necessity of maintaining unimpaired Austria's character as a Power *dominated by the German element*." No statement could better illustrate the aims and objects of the Pan-Germans with respect to the territories of the Habsburg monarchy.

"Germany for the Germans!" was the cry of the new Nationalistic party, and Germany, so far as the Pan-Germans were concerned, comprised all the territory watered by German rivers—the Elbe, the Moselle, the Maas, the Oder, the Vistula, and above all the Rhine and the Danube, from source to sea. In the fourth decade of the nineteenth century, when Germans were for the first time awaking to a consciousness of their national destinies, the great strategist Moltke had proclaimed the doctrine that German rivers should be contained within the political boundaries of the Fatherland and that Germans should be settled at the mouths of the Danube as the advance guard of *Deutschthum* in the Near East; and the industrious propagation of this doctrine—riverine Pan-Germanism—was one of the main objects of the party who eventually secured the political direction of the German Empire.

The Slav peoples of Austria-Hungary were to be swept down the Danube and pushed into national reserves like Kafirs or American-Indians, wherever they came into contact with the forces of Germanism; they were to be placed anywhere and everywhere so long as they were driven out of the sacred riverine boundaries of the new Fatherland. The frontiers were to be settled by Germans, chosen for their military proficiency, who, like the military settlers in Kaffraria, were to keep the hordes of Slav barbarians at bay. Austria-Hungary

* December 1, 1912.

was to be deluged with a flood of Germans, whose duty it would be to displace the useless Slav elements, who were a perpetual menace to the spread of Germanism and, owing to their barbarism and lack of polish, were an affront to Teutonic culture. Either peaceful penetration or conquest by the sword was the Pan-German order—but in any case a conquest, or an assimilation, of the inferior peoples by the all-embracing Germanic nationalism.

Professor Ernst Hasse, a deputy in the Reichstag and Director of Statistics at Leipzig, one of the most prominent leaders of this movement, preached the doctrine of military frontiers, first culled from the *Alldeutscher Blätter* of October 7, 1894,[*] and suggested that upon the western, northern, and southern boundaries there should be established a military " glacis," solely inhabited by Germans of pure blood, well tried, prompt to execute the commands of their superiors, and as obedient to discipline as the Cossacks. These military confines, like those which had protected the Russians against the Tartars, were to be settled by army officers, to whom, in recompense for their services, would be assigned sufficient and fertile lands. These boundaries, needless to say, were not necessarily the political frontiers of the present German Empire.

The policy of German settlement in the Danubian countries was coeval with the rise of the Hohenstaufen and Habsburg monarchies, but it was not until the middle of the nineteenth century that it received its impress as a political movement, or rather as a means for propagating German influences in countries where the population was mainly of Slavic origin. It was Friedrich List, the celebrated economist, fired by the belief that economic and not political bonds must precede the formation of a great German Empire, who first definitely directed attention to the Danubian countries, when formulating his system of founding trading settlements which would take German goods and in return supply the raw products necessary for German industries. " The banks of the Danube," he wrote in 1842, " on the right and on the left from Pressburg [†] as far as the mouth, the northern provinces of Turkey,[‡] and

---

[*] *See* " Le Pangermanism," by C. Andler, p. 26.
[†] The eastern limit of the purely German territories.
[‡] Serbia, Wallachia, Moldavia, etc.

the western shores of the Black Sea offer to German emigrants an abundance of unoccupied and naturally fertile land." *
Dreaming of the future federation of the Germanic kingdoms and principalities into one State, he doubtless foresaw the extension of the Teutonic political system along the German rivers and the formation of a great Germano-Magyar Empire, stretching to the Adriatic and the Black Sea. Both List and the young officer Moltke were equally convinced of the future extension of Germanism in South-Eastern Europe.

The idea of creating this Greater Germany of the Rhine and of the Danube gradually spread in Pan-German circles until no writer who wished to earn his laurels in the Pan-German cause ventured to oppose this demand for a share in the Austrian bundle of sticks. Thus Professor Paul de Lagarde, one of that tribe of doctrinaire educationalists who have since led Germany by the nose, wrote some years ago that " the provinces that we should demand from Russia should be sufficiently large to enable us to establish there, in Bessarabia and to the north-east of Bessarabia, as subjects of King Charles,† all the Rumanians, both those of Austria and of Turkey," with the evident idea of clearing Transylvania of its Rumanian inhabitants in order to make way for settlers of pure German stock; and again speaking of Hungary, with ill-disguised contempt, as " a bundle of impossibilities," he asked, " Is it not our duty to aid these peoples and these tribes to disappear? The Jablunka must no longer hear anything but German, and it is necessary that our fleet should be extended in the south so that there no longer remain any of the lamentable nationalities of the Imperial State " of Austria-Hungary. All were to be swept away, or at least De Lagarde proposed that the Slovaks, the Slovenes, and the Czechs, like the Redskins of North America, should be imprisoned in reserves from which they should be forbidden to move. " The Germanization of Austria," he wrote, " quite apart from *the question of the political use of Austria as a German colony*, is, from the standpoint of the Foreign Office, ' a vital question.' " It has indeed become more difficult since the revival of Magyar nationalism,

* " Sämtliche Schriften," vol. ii, p. 209.
† Then regarded as the faithful vassal of Prussia.

but, he added, "it must be made possible if Germany is to exist." *

Dozens of lubrications of this nature, written by men presumably sane but nevertheless obsessed by the dream of spiritual and political dominion, might be quoted; but the policy of assimilation by means of emigration need only be illustrated further by one single quotation from a book bearing the significant title "Krieg," which was written in 1906. "Let us organize bravely," said the author, "*great forced migrations of the inferior peoples*. Posterity will be grateful to us for our action. . . . To all enemies who shall succumb through their attitude in barring the road against us there must be assigned 'reserves' *into which we shall drive them in order to obtain the necessary territory for our own expansion*." † These statements, however ridiculous they may appear, are symptomatic of the Pan-German attitude towards Austria; and though, as M. Andler says, "one may pass from book to book with great laughter," ‡ this laughter is tempered by the reflection that such dangerous and almost incredible nonsense was the mental food of hundreds of thousands of Germans and represented the ideals of those who were forcing the German Government to advance upon every avenue of expansion.

The movement was born largely of the sense of superiority innate in every German, produced by successful military adventures. As long ago as 1868 Prince Napoleon, who had been paying a visit to Germany, noticed this tendency to regard other nations as barbarians. "The Prince has seen nothing," wrote Lord Lyons, "except in the United States, like the contempt in which foreign nations are held in Prussia. Austria is not considered worth taking into account at all." § Even Englishmen fell under the fatal spell and assumed that the vaunted superiority of the Germans had some foundation in fact. No less acute an observer than Sir Robert Morier, who was a firm friend of Prussia although opposed to Bismarckianism, wrote of German development as being "indis-

* *See* "Deutsche Schriften," 1903, pp. 112, 391.
† "Krieg," by Klaus Wagner, 1906.
‡ "Le Pangermanisme," by C. Andler, p. 25.
§ "Life of Lord Lyons," p. 193.

solubly linked with the cause of human progress," and in a specially interesting letter written to Lady Salisbury in 1896 stated that "the German race, even in its least developed type, is as superior to the semi-barbarous Magyar and the debased Slav and Rumanian races as the Englishman is to the New Zealander [Maori, of course]. The fact which is never sufficiently considered in regard to the German element in Austria is that the German population is not restricted to the purely German provinces, but is diffused and permeated throughout the entire Empire, and that it is the only race thus diffused; there is no town throughout the Empire (the Italian provinces alone excepted) in which you will not find that the industrial class is either German or of German origin. Austria's Austrian mission is one to be mainly fulfilled by the German element in Austria." *

With the growth of Prussianism and all for which it stands, Sir Robert Morier subsequently found occasion to modify his views. Ten years later he addressed a letter to the Crown Prince Frederick, at the period when it was believed that Germany was again about to attack France, which shows remarkable insight into German character and was, in effect, a warning against the military and Chauvinistic tendencies of Prussian policy. In this letter, penned on the morrow of De Blowitz's celebrated article in *The Times*, Sir Robert Morier wrote that "there is no denying that the malady under which Europe is at present suffering is caused by German Chauvinism; a new and far more formidable type of the disease than the French because, instead of being spasmodical and undisciplined, it is methodical, calculating, cold-blooded, and self-contained. As yet the perception of this fact is only beginning to break upon the subconsciousness of Europe, so persistently have the friends of Germany—and, as your Imperial Highness well knows, myself amongst the number—argued and insisted that the unity of Germany once established, Europe would have Chauvinism crushed out of it." † After protesting against the projected attack upon France, Morier continues in words that may well be regarded as prophetic: "An individual may, under the dæmonic impulse of superhuman cynicism,

* "Memoirs of Sir Robert Morier," vol. ii, pp. 75–76.
† Morier, vol. ii, pp. 346–7.

laugh to scorn the opinion and conscience of contemporary mankind, and still more of posterity. I can conceive an Attila chuckling even on the brink of the grave at the thought of living in the memory of future generations as *Gottes Geissel* (Scourge of God); but a nation cannot afford to enjoy the luxury of cynicism, cannot risk to place itself outside the pale of the opinion of mankind, because a nation never dies, and the conscience of mankind never dies, and when the orgies of successful force have spent their strength the day comes when it has to live not only with its own recollections but with those which mankind has preserved of it. . . . The action of Germany, therefore, in the case supposed would be stamped with a pedantic ferocity, a scientific cynicism, an academic cruelty which history would never forget and mankind would take a long time to forgive." How terribly this indictment of German policy, sent to the father of the future Emperor, the German husband of Queen Victoria's eldest daughter, applies at the present moment, when the world is reeling before the savage blows of Teutonic barbarism!

Pan-Germanism as applied to Austria is not of recent growth. Austria, forming the avenue of expansion towards the Near East, was marked down for inclusion within the German Fatherland at a period long anterior to the more recent aggressive utterances of the Pan-Germans; and only the fact that Prussia overreached herself when the movement for German union first assumed definite shape saved the Austrian provinces from incorporation in the new Empire that was in course of formation. Prussian claims to the hegemony of the whole of Germany, Northern and Southern, were too insistent to be ignored by Austrian statesmen, and the House of Habsburg, with its centuries-old prestige, refused to enter the splendid parlour arranged by the parvenu Hohenzollern kings.

The movement for the union of the two Germanies was definitely formulated for the first time at the Congress of Frankfort, which met in 1848 and attempted to bring about the consolidation of the German Empire. The dominating thought in the minds of those who assembled at Frankfort in that year—a few weeks after the Magyar revolution had threatened the overthrow of the Austrian Empire and after the Austrian troops had been driven from Milan and Venice; but two months after the celebrated Metternich himself had been obliged to flee in disguise from Vienna; and after the revolution had for the time being triumphed in the Grand Duchy of Baden, in Hesse-Darmstadt, in Württemberg, in the Duchy of Nassau, and in Berlin itself, that great nationalistic movement which was destined to drive the German nation upon other paths than those intended by its leaders—was the reorganization of Germany as a federal State. Upon this point all were agreed. Every deputy was decided to rescue Germany from the slough in which she had stagnated since the year 1815. It was indeed a truly national movement for which they stood, admirable through its power and its sincerity, and one which animated almost the whole of Germany and led the peoples of Upper and Lower Austria, of Styria, of the Tyrol, in all loyalty to the House of their hereditary sovereigns, to ask for their reunion with the German Empire, which seemed to be at length in process of formation.

But in spite of this unity of aim there was no agreement as to methods. There was indeed a pious aspiration that Prussia and Austria might work harmoniously within the same confederation, but the eternal jealousy between Northern and Southern Germans forced the leaders of the revolution into two opposing camps and led them to press the claims of the Hohenzollerns and Habsburgs respectively to the leadership in the proposed German Empire. On the one hand, Unionists like Heinrich von Gagern looked for the predominance of Prussia in the new Empire; on the other, Austrian statesmen like Schwarzenberg, whilst anxious to conciliate the discordant elements, were indisposed to abandon the claims of the House of Habsburg to the hegemony of Germany. The claim of von Gagern that the mission of Austria was to civilize the East, and that to do that she must retain full liberty of action and must concentrate her forces, whilst Germany should be united to Austria "but distinct from her," was rendered impossible of achievement by the conflicting interests of the various partners in the proposed federation; and the unity of Germany remained an unaccomplished dream under the circumstances then prevailing.

The conditions laid down by the Prussian King, Frederick

William IV, in the following year were equally impossible of realization. After having declared that he would not repudiate the Constitution which had been agreed upon at Frankfort, on condition that it was accepted by the other German sovereigns, he suggested that it was not at all necessary that Austria should be excluded, and stated that the Greater Germany, such as had been dreamed of by Schwarzenberg, could and should be constituted, but that Austria should neither have nor exercise a preponderating position. " Her effective rôle was to render Germanic influence dominant in the Slavic countries, in Italy, and above all in the East," * and not to exert any preponderating control within the German confederation.

The years 1848-1849, when the idea of a united Germany first took definite shape, would require a special volume to themselves if the prolonged struggle between Prussia and Austria for the controlling voice in the proposed union of Germany were to be adequately described. It was a fight between the comparatively new Power that was soon to dominate the whole of Northern Germany and the decaying Austrian Empire, which even then was becoming more and more dependent upon its subordinate nationalities and was rapidly drifting towards disruption unless either Magyars or Southern Slavs could be definitely won over to the side of the hereditary monarchy. The great Hungarian leader Kossuth correctly diagnosed the political situation, and although the following words were written a few years later, they equally apply to the state of affairs in 1849. " The Vienna Court will not give way," wrote Kossuth, " but is embarking upon new and desperate experiments. In the meantime the difficulties with which it is faced are constantly increasing. Its power keeps on diminishing, and at last a moment will arrive when it will have to fulfil all that Hungary desires merely in order to save the Habsburg dynasty." † In fact the German element in Austria was finding itself unable, in spite of the Austrian sympathies of some of the South German States and the prestige of an historic past, to exercise the supremacy which they desired in the Assembly at Frankfort. On January

* Quoted from Debidour's " Histoire diplomatique de l'Europe."
† Kossuth's " Memoirs," p. 649.

14, 1849, six weeks after the abdication of the Emperor Ferdinand and the succession of his nephew, the present Emperor Francis Joseph, the delegates at Frankfort came to the momentous decision, by 261 votes to 224, that Austria should be excluded from the new Empire that was in process of formation, and a little later, on March 28, they offered the Imperial Crown of the new Germany to the King of Prussia. Frederick William, however, convinced that the national ideal was but the revolutionary idea under another form, refused to accept the crown unless it were offered freely by the German princes themselves, and for the time being the danger that Austria anticipated was averted because the German rulers were hopelessly divided upon the question.

Without entering upon the somewhat intricate history of the Frankfort Parliament it may be stated that its proceedings showed that the cleavage between Austria and Germany was incapable of settlement, and from that period the two countries became more and more antagonistic. The Austrian Premier, Prince Schwarzenberg, worked resolutely to crush the pretensions of Prussia by gaining the support of the German princely houses, who, mindful of their long hereditary attachment to the House of Habsburg and distrustful of the parvenu Brandenburgers, were, on the whole, opposed to the formation of a new empire in which Austria should not be represented. Whilst the King of Prussia decided to summon the princes to Berlin, Austria called them to Frankfort, where the Austrian Plenipotentiary, Count Thun-Hohenstein, made it clear that Austria had decided for the moment to abandon all idea of the union, but was nevertheless desirous of re-establishing the ancient Diet of the Empire. On August 8, 1850, the reconstitution of the Imperial Diet was voted, Prussia was checkmated, and the temporary triumph of the Habsburgs over the Hohenzollerns seemed assured. The triumph of Austria, however, was only secured by sowing the seeds of the future Austro-Prussian War, which was definitely to bring Austria within the Prussian orbit.

In November 1850 occurred a revolutionary outbreak in Hesse. Whilst Austrian troops marched into the Duchy on one side, charged with the task of quelling the revolt, the Prussians entered on the other. Schwarzenberg seized the opportunity of humiliating the Prussians. Assembling an army of 180,000 men, he ordered Prussia to evacuate Hessian territory within twenty-four hours. At Berlin, where no preparations had been made for war, the action of Austria was received with dismay; Prussia gave way, and on November 29 the famous Convention of Olmütz was signed. This Convention was a national humiliation for Prussia but a temporary triumph for Austria. Schwarzenberg's policy, summed up in the famous epigram, " Humiliate Prussia, then destroy her," was fulfilled in its first part, but subsequent events and the rise of Bismarck eventually led to the humiliation of Austria. As a matter of fact, Austria hesitated to strike at the psychological moment, and the " crushing of Prussia," which should have been undertaken in 1850, was postponed until it was too late. In the words of Count Beust, the Convention of Olmütz was in reality " not a Prussian humiliation but an Austrian weakness."

Such, in brief, without entering into the details of the quarrel between the Germanic Powers, is the outline of the events that led to the abandonment of the movement for the union of Germany. Nothing had been achieved save a permanent estrangement between Prussia and Austria, only to be settled by the arbitrament of the sword, and the sowing of the seeds of the future Pan-German movement. It may be truly stated that this movement was born at Olmütz, cradled at Sadowa, and nursed to maturity on the battlefields of Alsace-Lorraine.

The failure of the Frankfort Parliament to bring about the union of Germany was directly due to causes operating within the Austrian Empire. When the Austrian Government had consented to send delegates from its German provinces to the Parliament of a united Germany, the question was naturally asked what would be the position of the Austrian monarchy in a union of the German States. So far as Austria was concerned only two solutions were possible. Either the German provinces of Austria should be included in the proposed union—a solution that found favour with the majority of those within the present German Empire who desired the presence of Austria within the confederation—or the whole of Austria, with its vast non-German population, would have to be attached to the new federation. As to the first solution, Austrian statesmen were naturally averse from splitting the monarchy into two halves, one of which would be subjected to a double allegiance, whilst the other would remain under the direct control of the House of Habsburg. As to the second solution, the Radical enthusiasts of Northern Germany, whose ideal was the formation of a purely German Empire, would never tolerate the inclusion of a miscellaneous collection of Czechs, Magyars, and Southern Slavs within the sacred fold of the new German State. From the first, therefore, it was obvious that there were insuperable difficulties in the way of agreement and that Pan-Germanism, as it then existed, was incapable of realization. The difficulty was rendered greater by the internal state of Austria and the seething revolution which characterized every province of the "ramshackle" Empire.

To understand this internal revolution, which in the two decades preceding the final struggle between Austria and Prussia flamed everywhere into active rebellion, some attention must be given not only to the racial constitution of the Austrian Empire but to events that occurred immediately before and after the meeting of the Parliament at Frankfort. At the period in question the ruling race, as is the case to-day, was in a minority and exercised an autocratic but, as events proved, precarious sway over the comparatively inert masses of non-German peoples who formed the majority of the population. The Germans maintained their traditional ascendancy within the Empire under the guidance of that prince of diplomatists Metternich, who, as the most active supporter of reaction throughout Europe and the main upholder of autocracy in Austria, had been able to govern the Empire successfully for a period of nearly thirty years. Metternich upheld the doctrine enunciated by the liberal-minded but reactionary Joseph II, who on his accession had stated that "all provinces of the monarchy must form a single whole, and, in all, the forces of the people must be directed towards a common aim—the power of Austria." As Joseph's chief instrument for this achievement was the introduction of German as the universal language of State throughout his dominions, so Metternich's principal tool in holding together the discordant elements in

Austria was the use of German influence and German culture as the unifying power within the Empire.

The position of Austria prior to the Frankfort Parliament was racially much what it is to-day—that is, the Empire was divided amongst four principal stocks, all inextricably mixed in certain districts but all sufficiently distinct and settled in compact masses to form nationalistic elements capable of uniting in their own territories for political or racial purposes.

These four stocks are: (*a*) The Teutonic occupying Upper and Lower Austria, the Tyrol, Salzburg, Carinthia, and large portions of Bohemia and Silesia, as well as being scattered in large communities in other parts of the Austrian Empire. (*b*) The Latin, of whom are the Italians—who were, of course, a large element, as Austria then occupied a considerable portion of Northern Italy, but who are now confined to the territory bordering upon Italy and to the coastal districts of Istria and Dalmatia—and the Rumanians inhabiting Transylvania. (*c*) The Slavonic, divided into Northern Slavs and Southern Slavs. Of the former, the Poles inhabit a large part of Galicia and Silesia; the Ruthenes occupy the greater portion of Galicia, the Bukowina, and the north-eastern districts of Hungary; and the Czechs and Slovaks of Bohemia, Moravia, and North-Western Hungary. Of the latter, the Slovenes form a compact wedge between the German provinces and the Croats and Serbs of Croatia-Slavonia, Bosnia-Herzegovina, and Dalmatia. (*d*) The Magyars, who now exercise a dual control of the monarchy in common with the Germans of Austria proper. It was the national awaking of these groups in the inevitable reaction against the repressive and unitary policy of Metternich that largely prevented the realization of the ideal of a united Germany under Austrian hegemony.

It is not possible to give more than a bare and unsatisfactory outline of the stirring events that heralded the reawakening of the Slav and Magyar world. The earliest symptoms of the coming revolution occurred in Hungary, where the linguistic and literary revival among the Magyars rapidly undid the work of Joseph II, prepared the way for the overthrow of the Metternichian system, and culminated in the great revolution of 1848, when but for Russian aid and the opposition of the Southern Slavs, Hungary would have achieved complete independence. Yet contemporaneously with the outburst of nationalism that heralded the Hungarian Revolution occurred other racial movements within the limits of the Empire that threatened its stability and were in direct conflict with the Germanizing tendencies of the Vienna Government.

In Bohemia the national movement, confined in its earliest stages to a small group of patriots, was at first Bohemian in the true historical sense, because both German-Bohemians and Czechs were working together for a common end. The pretensions of the Germans and the purely racial tendencies of the Czechs ultimately led to the cleavage which occurred in 1848 when a Slav Congress met at Prague and voiced the aspirations of the Northern Slavs. In Hungary too the predominant race—the Magyars—under the inspiration of brilliant political leaders and a notable literary revival, claimed to exercise complete autonomy within their own State; and the fiercely nationalistic attitude of the Magyars, who would not brook the co-existence of any other national culture within Hungary, largely accounted for the ultimate failure of the whole movement owing to the fact that other nationalities became as bitterly opposed to the Magyar claims as they were enthusiastic for their own racial ideals. As will be shown later, the fierce and intolerant nationalism of the Magyars and the particularism of the Czechs have been one of the main factors leading to the present conflict. Non-Magyars have been goaded into madness by the intolerant policy of the ruling caste in Hungary.

But the most important symptom of the impending catastrophe which was to plunge Austria into a state of anarchy, and finally to end in the creation of the present dual system of government, was the increasing unrest amongst the peasants of all races, who were rebelling against the exactions of feudalism far more than against the political disadvantages under which they suffered. The rising of the Poles in 1846, originating in a political movement at Cracow, was defeated by the scythe and the flail of the Ruthenian peasants far more than by the guns of the Austrian troops. The former fought against their hated landlords—the latter merely on behalf of their Austrian masters.

The year 1848 saw Austria, in common with the greater

part of Europe, under the influence of the revolutionary movement that not only seemed about to overthrow the Empire but likely to end in the establishment of separate kindgoms or republics within the territories of the Habsburgs. On March 3 Kossuth made his famous declaration against the Austrian system. "From the charnel-house of the Vienna Cabinet," he exclaimed, "a pestilential air breathes on us, which dulls our nerves and paralyses the flight of our spirit." The Hungarian rising was the signal for revolution in other parts of the Empire. Vienna fell into the hands of the revolutionary party; the "Young Czechs" at Prague drew up a petition embodying nationalistic and liberal demands and subsequently proclaimed a separate constitution; the Italian provinces broke out in insurrection; Milan and Venice rose against the Austrians; Sardinia took up arms on behalf of the insurgents; revolution broke out in Galicia; and everywhere, in spite of the particularist ambitions of the revolutionary leaders, the doctrine of "the fraternization of the Austrian peoples" against the unifying German element was openly preached.

But in the enthusiasms of the moment the crucial question of the position to be occupied by the conflicting nationalities in this fraternal union was overlooked, and the revolution, weakened by the irreconcilable claims of the various nationalities and the want of unity between the different races, was overcome, and the disruption of Austria prevented by the very forces that were most active in working for their own national independence. Kossuth and his adherents, who were in direct sympathy with the German Radicals in Vienna and Frankfort, aroused the antagonism of the other races who preferred the German ascendancy to the Magyar yoke. By pursuing the Machiavellian policy of setting race against race the German element in Austria at length triumphed over the forces of disruption and the Habsburg monarchy was again dragooned into some semblance of order.

These events, and the disinclination of the Habsburg Germans to sink their individuality in a new German Empire beyond the boundaries of Austria, defeated the immediate aims of the Pan-German Party but paved the way for the subsequent extension of the Pan-German ideal into wider and less particularist channels. The new Pan-Germanism which was born of the Prussian defeat at Olmütz now looked forward to a greater empire than had at first been dreamt of, and eventually aimed at the control, political and economic, of the whole of South-Eastern Europe.

The failure of the revolution in Austria was followed by ten years of reaction and by seven years more of constitutional experiments. In Prussia it was succeeded by the period of unbending autocracy during which Bismarck schemed for the aggrandizement of the Hohenzollerns at the expense of their immediate neighbours and laid the foundations of German unity on the solid rock of autocratic privilege. The two wars of 1859 and 1866—which by expelling Austria both from Italy and from Germany made possible the unity of both countries—rendered internal political reform essential if the monarchy were again to be saved from revolution and disruption.

Previously to the latter event Austria made a last endeavour to secure unanimity in Germany by summoning a meeting of princes to Frankfort and requesting Prussia also to be present. Anton von Schmerling, the Austrian Minister, as a preliminary step arranged for a meeting between the Austrian Emperor and the King of Prussia, which took place at Gastein on August 2, 1863. Bismarck, who accompanied the Prussian sovereign, refused his adhesion to the proposed congress, and the conference which followed at Frankfort was held without Prussia being represented. That meeting, which revealed the ascendancy of Austria among the smaller German States, also demonstrated that nothing could be accomplished so long as Prussia stood aside; for the Austrian proposals were designed far more to secure the permanent ascendancy of the Emperor in the councils of the Confederation than to bring about the unity of the German race. The rock upon which this final attempt to secure the unity of Northern and Southern Germans was wrecked was the Austrian proposal that in the event of any of the German States, having possessions beyond the boundaries of the Confederation, being attacked—such, for example, as Austria—the Confederation as a whole should support the State that had been attacked. The congress broke up without having achieved any definite results, and Bismarck, who had made up his mind that the question of German unity could only be settled by the exclusion of Austria, was left free to prepare for the coming war. The issue was forced by the developments of the Schleswig-Holstein question, which led to an open breach between the two Powers and to the ultimate collapse of Austria on the field of Königgrätz (Sadowa).*

Although by nine votes against five the German States had declared in favour of Austria, the military superiority of Prussia was crushing. The lessons of Olmütz had not been forgotten. Austria, reeling from the blow, was forced to make what terms she could, and henceforth Germany, already imbued with the idea that Prussia alone could secure German unity, consented to the exclusion of Austria, who had forfeited, if not the sympathy, at least the confidence of the other German States.

The result of the Seven Weeks War was the famous compromise between Austria and Hungary known as the *Ausgleich* of 1867—a year that may be regarded as the starting-point of modern Habsburg history. Unable any longer to secure the predominance of the Germans throughout the Empire, the Imperial House sanctioned the experiment of dualism and the formation, within the Empire, of that unitary national State which every Magyar statesman had sought to erect, during the last three hundred years, out of the chaos of conflicting nationalities that inhabit modern Hungary. The underlying principle of the *Ausgleich* was that in each of the two sections into which the monarchy was henceforth to be divided German and Magyar were to be supreme over Latin and Slav.

Unfortunately, from the German point of view the experiment has not been a success. Whilst the Magyars have imposed their will, more or less successfully, upon the races that were attached to the new Hungarian kingdom, and have ruled the Southern Slavs by means that have made modern Magyar

---

* The war between Austria and Prussia caused much distress to Queen Victoria, who became at length aware of the ultimate designs of the Prussian Government. Clarendon wrote on April 6, 1866: "The missus is in an awful state about German affairs." Queen Victoria was now desirous of siding with Austria, and was prepared to take the steps that should have been urged when Prussia attacked Denmark a few years previously, but this time Lord John Russell held back.

policy hateful to all lovers of liberty and nationality, the Germans, on the other hand, when seeking to pursue the same drastic policy with regard to the non-Germans in the Austrian portion of the Empire, have been frequently checkmated by the opposition of the other nationalities, particularly the Czechs, so that Austria became a bear-garden in which racial and linguistic disputes paralysed the whole internal policy of the State. Count Beust is stated to have remarked to his Hungarian colleague when the *Ausgleich* was under consideration: " Take care of your barbarians; we will take care of ours " ; but Austria was in reality incapable of the task.

Weakened by the eternal conflict between German Austria and Hungary, it was in the field of foreign politics that the German bureaucracy, who had so long been supreme in directing the policy of the Empire, were obliged to give way before the combined demands of Bismarck and his faithful henchmen, the Magyars. German Austria ceased to count in the foreign policy of the Austro-Hungarian Empire, which became more and more directed by the natural affinity that existed between the policy of Germany and of Hungary. The German-Austrian provinces became the connecting-link between Hohenzollern policy and Magyar ambitions, and, owing to constant internal strife, were unable to withstand the insistent demands of both. " The system," states a writer in the *Round Table*, speaking of the Dual Monarchy, " was contrived as a just balance between two equals, but this was completely deranged by the breaches made in the German hegemony in Austria, and with every decade it became more and more clear that the machine would only work when one scale was high in the air. For a whole generation Hungary not merely controlled the whole foreign policy of the Monarchy—notably under the great Andrassy, and under Kalnoky, and even the indolent Goluchowski—but also directly interfered from time to time with the internal constitutional arrangements of her partner." *

This fact cannot be too clearly insisted upon, for not only does it explain the paramount influence that has long been exerted by Germany over the foreign policy of the Dual Monarchy, but it also illuminates the attitude of Hungary towards the policy that was driving the Monarchy to the

* *Round Table*, No. 17, p. 90.

Ægean Sea. It was not to the special interests of German Austria to advance in that direction so long as the great port of Trieste and the Istrian and Dalmatian coast-lands were attached to Austria; but it was entirely to the interests of Hungary, a great inland kingdom whose only outlet to the sea was through the port of Fiume, situated in Croatian territory, to push a wedge, economic or political, in the direction of Salonika. And in the pursuance of this aim Hungary also worked on behalf of the larger schemes of the Pan-Germans, of which she was an unconscious, though not unwilling, adherent.

Having recognized that Germany and Hungary were working for a common aim, though not owing to a common reason, much that seems obscure in modern Habsburg policy becomes apparent. The Magyarization of the Southern Slavs, so persistently carried on, since Hungary herself attained freedom within the Empire, was in itself, from the Magyar point of view, a necessity of the highest importance if the Dual Monarchy were to be preserved in its present form and prevented from becoming a mere confederation of equal States—Czech, Magyar, German, and Serb. The existence of Hungary might even be imperilled as an independent unit should the Southern Slavs unite, within and without the Empire, and erect the great Southern Slav kingdom that will, it is to be hoped, be created as one of the results of the present war. A barrier of this nature placed across every outlet that Hungary might have towards the sea would necessarily be intolerable. Thus it became absolutely vital to the integrity of the Monarchy in its present form, certainly to the integrity of Hungary, that no strong and self-sufficing Slavonic State should be allowed to grow to maturity, either within or without the boundaries of the Empire; and thus the policy favoured by the Archduke Ferdinand, who was supposed on the best possible evidence—the evidence of his own actions—to be working on behalf of a triune instead of a dual monarchy, was anathema both to the Hungarians and to the Pan-Germans, who now aimed at the absorption of the whole of Austria-Hungary.

The German penetration of the Austrian Empire was no new idea. It has already been shown how this method of peaceful conquest by means of immigration has been suggested by many writers, but attention must now be directed to the more definite expression of the same aims. In 1859 the *Augsburg Gazette* stated that " we emphatically declare that if it were not Austria that is the legitimate possessor of these non-German countries, the German nation ought to conquer them at any price, because they are absolutely necessary for her development and position as a Great Power."* And from that date onwards, especially after the failure of Austria to secure the unity of Germany, constant references were made to the desirability of constituting a great Central European Empire, with or without the consent of the Emperor Francis Joseph, in which the Germans should be the predominant race.

It was no longer a question of a purely German State, for Pan-Germanism had taken enormous strides under the influence of Moltke's riverine policy. Thus the redoubtable Daniel Frymann, in his well-known book " If I were the Emperor," after stating that " since Bismarck retired there has been a complete change of public opinion. It is no longer the fashion to say, ' Germany is satisfied.' Our historical development and our economic needs show that we are once more opening our mouth wide for new territory," wrote that after the death of the Emperor Francis Joseph the Germans of Austria must go to the new Emperor and demand that he adopt a Dictatorship. " This Dictatorship," stated Frymann, " should restore a centralized State with an Imperial Diet in which the number of seats should be apportioned according to the amount of taxes paid by each nationality to the State. . . . The Emperor should give the Germans a guarantee that their language should be the language of the Empire, and that wherever they were in a minority their will should nevertheless prevail, because the *Staatsvolk* could not be overruled by a majority. We assume that Germans, thanks to the amount of taxes they pay, would have an absolute majority in the Diet : if this were not the case, the Constitution should arrange that every vote should be of no effect if it were contrary to the German vote."

After which, even if the German Empire had to intervene by force of arms, " our surplus population in the Empire can be directed towards the south-east ; for it is a prime necessity for Germany to ensure in Austria a definite preponderance of

* Pontcray, p. 165.

Germanism where it will bring new blood to the German population." As Daniel Frymann states, Germany's mouth was indeed wide open for territory. But the apotheosis of Pan-Germanism was voiced by an English writer, Sir Harry Johnston, who, then under the temporary glamour of Teutonism, gave definite expression to the eastern aspirations of the Hohenzollerns in an article written in 1905.* " The German Empire of the future will be, or should be," stated Sir Harry, " a congeries of big and little States, semi-dependent in many respects, bound together by allegiance to a supreme Emperor, by a common Customs union, an army and navy for the defence of their mutual interests. This Empire will include the present German kingdoms, duchies, principalities, and republics, and, in addition, a kingdom of Hungary, kingdoms of Rumania, Servia, Bulgaria, principalities of Croatia, Montenegro, Macedonia, a republic of Byzantium, a sultanate of Anatolia, a republic of Trebizond, an emirate of Mosul, a dependency of Mesopotamia ; the whole of this mosaic bound together by bands and seams of German cement. Wherever there is vacant land and a suitable climate German colonies will be established, as they have been in Transylvania and Syria (as also in Southern Russia and the Caucasus). The territories of the German League would thus stretch from Hamburg and Holstein on the Baltic and on the North Sea to Trieste and the Adriatic, to Constantinople and the Ægean, to the Gulf of Alexandretta, to the Euphrates and the frontiers of Persia." Comment on this statement is needless, except that it may be stated that Sir Harry Johnston arranged that in return for this splendid heritage the Germans were to " make sacrifices, surrenders, and sales in various directions "—such, for example, as the Danish portion of Schleswig—and to renounce all idea of the incorporation within their limits of the Low Countries. He concluded his article by the statement that "some of my readers may live long enough to see William II or Frederick IV crowned in Saint Sophia Emperor of the Nearer East."

But so far as Austria is concerned the most remarkable example of Pan-Germanism is to be found in the popular book by Herr Richard Tannenberg, " Gross Deutschland,"

* *Fortnightly Review*, September 1905.

published in 1911, which is "one of the three or four books which it is good to read, that one must read, in order to have a just idea of the prodigious literary rhodomontade of Pan-Germanism." * Herr Tannenberg, who planned the redivision of Austrian territory amongst Prussia, Bavaria, Saxony, Württemberg, and Baden, with a kingdom of Austria and an independent Hungary, states that "the fate of the Germans in Austria is for us a vital question. The German people cannot allow the Adriatic to pass from their control without renouncing their pretensions to be a Great Power." Tannenberg's policy, therefore, was to create a great German wedge stretching from the frontiers of the German Empire to Trieste and the eastern shores of the Adriatic, which should include all portions of the Austrian Empire in which the German element not only predominates but in which there are strong German minorities capable of influencing the surrounding Slavs.

"The Germans of Austria," he states, "have suffered from misfortune. In the first place, the hostility between the Hohenzollerns and the Habsburgs has excluded them from union with Germany; in the second, they have been betrayed by the friendship—still more unlucky—of the Hohenzollerns for the Habsburgs, which in 1909 prevented Austria from declaring war against the Southern Slavs and their allies. To make the situation clear, *a war of the Southern Slavs against Austria in 1909 would have been for us Pan-Germans a happy event*, and that from a double point of view: on the one hand, the Habsburgs would have been convinced that the Germans of Austria alone remained faithful to them; on the other hand, the people of the German Empire would have realized the feebleness of the support of the Triple Alliance. We all know that Czech regiments, *en route* for the Bosnian frontier, cried out 'Vive la Serbie!' rather than 'God save the Emperor Francis!' At Prague the Czechs sang 'Serbia will bring us help,' not in a melody which we love, but as the refrain to a well-known Czech song.... The Austrian Slavs make no mystery of their sentiments."

Herr Tannenberg then proceeds to pay the usual Pan-

* Quoted from the Preface to the French edition by Professor Maurice Millioud. The quotations are taken from this edition, published in 1916.

German tribute to the plan of gradually replacing the Slav population by honest and industrious Germans. "A nation can only maintain its position if it increase," he states. "England has her Greater Britain, America has her America for the Americans. If England has been able to get rid of four million Irish and to send them to America without any great European Power taking offence, it should be possible for us to create in Central Europe a state of things which, thanks to the order and calm which will reign there, will serve as a base for the ulterior development of the German people. . . . Our supreme duty is towards ourselves. . . . It is but a miserable and senile policy to look upon all events that happen beyond our frontiers as not being of any concern to us. Every insult offered to a German student at Prague, every popular riot at Laibach, is an affront offered to German honour and is a sufficient and legitimate reason for us to occupy the territories in question. Let us consider what England or France would do if any of their subjects, travelling as tourists in Egypt or Morocco, were attacked. Why are we not allowed to do the same at Prague? It is a disgrace. Who has the best army in the world?" This redoubtable friend of Pan-Germanism, keenly feeling the humiliating position of his great country, ends his homily with the statement that "Greater Germany will be the work of the twentieth century. An Empire of an enormous ethnical power. We shall fill the centre of Europe. Then we shall be ready to perform our new tasks and to carry out the duties that will be imposed upon us."

Chauvinism of this kind might well be left in oblivion did it not represent the opinions of hundreds of thousands of Germans and were it not that the apostles of rampant Pan-Germanism, in spite of their foolish and almost incredible banalities, had been able to drive the German Government wherever they required. Their writings, which have been circulated everywhere in Germany, have had an immense influence over the conduct of foreign affairs, and it would be as absurd to underrate their significance as it would be to belittle the effect of the numerous speeches of the German Emperor. They have been significant of a deeply seated national disease in which greed and megalomania have constantly struggled for the upper hand. No one can now afford to treat their utterances with contempt or to look upon them with the amused tolerance or complete indifference with which they were too long regarded in this country. When it is remembered that the Germans were constantly proclaiming that they had "*lent* ten millions of their countrymen to Austria," and regarded this loan as "the investment which they have made in the Austrian joint-stock company, so that Germans, as representing a higher culture, may become the basis and cement of the South Austrian amalgam with Central Europe," * there can be no reason to doubt the absolute sincerity of the opinions expressed by the henchmen of the Pan-Germans.

German propaganda in Austria has been most actively supported by the various Pan-German societies which have been so powerful a factor in upholding German influence in the Dual Monarchy. In every portion of the Empire that is threatened by a non-German population there are societies whose duty it is to propagate the German ideas and to serve as centres for German culture. The great societies operating in Austria-Hungary have differed as to their methods. The Alldeutscher Verband (Pan-German League), with headquarters in Germany, has not divided Austria into sections but has worked, by means of its various local delegates, to inculcate its political doctrines amongst the Germans to whom it makes its peculiar appeal, doubtless being fully aware that its operations in a foreign country are little short of high treason against the House of Habsburg. On the other hand, the other German societies have been more or less local in character, carrying on their operations in well-defined territories and mainly concerned with securing the predominance of Germans in Austria and not with the propagation of the Greater Germany idea.

But there have been notable exceptions to this general attitude, and open encouragement has been given to the extremists, who desired the absorption of German Austria in the German Empire, by Pan-Germans living beyond the borders. Thus in 1897 the Pan-German League at Dresden unanimously passed a resolution denouncing the ordinances dealing with languages in Bohemia as "an insult to the whole German nation," and inviting all Germans to oppose Slavonic encroach-

* Pamphlet by Dr. von Winterstetten, published in July 1913 at Munich. Quoted by Vernet.

ments by every possible means.* In Bohemia, the Bund der Deutschen in Böhmen, founded at Prague in 1894, has considerably over one hundred thousand members; whilst a similar society in Northern Moravia has over fifty thousand adherents. In addition to these societies there are at Vienna the Bund der Germanen, and in other parts of the Empire the Alldeutscher Verein für die Ostmark (Pan-German Society for the Eastern Frontier), the Deutsch Nationaler Verein für Oesterreich (German National Society for Austria), and the Deutscher Weltbund (German World-Association); whilst in each province there are the German Popular Councils, composed of militant Germans outside the constitutional parliaments, and the Deutsche Schutzvereine, societies formed to aid German tradesmen and to assist them to capture the trade of their Slav rivals.†

Pan-Germanism in Austria—that is, the idea of the entry of the German-speaking provinces of the Habsburg Empire into the German confederation—by no means represented the views of the majority of the Germans in the Dual Monarchy. On the one hand, the Germans in Hungary, who number about two millions, were not in the least anxious to be left to the tender mercies of the Magyars and Slavs, and were naturally as a whole averse from any movement for the formation of an Austro-German State joined to the northern Empire; whilst on the other hand the great majority of the Catholic Austro-Germans were attached to the House of Habsburg and regarded the Lutheran Hohenzollerns with peculiar dislike.

But there has been formed nevertheless during recent years a considerable party, enemies to the Habsburg State, who have been working in close co-operation with the Pan-Germans across the frontiers. This party has had to walk delicately in the pursuance of its avowed aims, although its more extreme members have not hesitated to utter treasonable threats against the monarch of whom they are subjects. Thus on November 8, 1898, Herr Schoenerer ventured to state in the Austrian Reichsrat that he hoped "to see the day when a German army would enter Austria in order to give the *coup de grâce* to the Austrian Empire; whilst the deputy Rudolf

* "France in Danger," by Paul Vernet, p. 73.
† These details are taken from Paul Vernet's book.

Berger, in an address before the Pan-German League, said on June 20, 1905, that "the Pan-German programme demands that all the territories which formerly were included in the German Confederation should be joined to the German Empire as confederate States." "The Slav waves will impotently dash against the German people," he continued, "when they are once united in the territory of Central Europe. . . . We would not allow ourselves to be frightened even by the hostility of the Court. . . . The change from the ancient and miserable German particularism that formerly existed to the German Empire of to-day was infinitely more difficult than will be the passage from the present régime to the Pan-German Empire which we desire to establish." Again, in the following year an Austrian deputy, Franko Stein, stated in the Reichsrat that "the Austrian dignity and the Austrian State are completely indifferent to us. We have but one hope and one desire, and that is that we may at length be delivered from this State . . . in order to lead a glorious existence under the protection of the Hohenzollerns." *

These statements, if they do not prove the existence of an internal conspiracy against the Habsburgs on the part of a considerable section of their subjects, show at least that Pan-Germanism was a sufficiently strong factor in Austria for its adherents to dare to put forward views that if shared by any considerable party would end in the overthrow of the Austrian State. Professor Andler has estimated that the Pan-German group in the Austrian Reichsrat numbers twenty-one members, and states that "the ambitions, at first confused, of these Austrian Teutomaniacs become clearer in proportion as they take the form of the Pan-Germanism of Germany itself," and he quotes a specially significant article that appeared in the *Gegenwart* entitled "Wird Mittel-Europa nicht Deutsch sein ? " (Shall not Central Europe become German ?).† The writer of this article stated that to establish order in the semi-Asiatic disorder a German Dictator was required, who with an iron fist would degrade "to the rank of provinces Bohemia, Hungary, and Galicia" in a unified Austria ; whilst a fiscal union between Austria-Hungary and Germany would assure

* Quoted from "Le Pangermanisme," by C. Andler, p. 70.
† December 26, 1903.

the overwhelming superiority of the Germans over the twenty-four millions of Slavs, the eight millions of Magyars, and the four millions of Rumanians.

The question of Pan-Magyarism, which is so intimately connected with Pan-Germanism, will be briefly dealt with in another chapter, but before concluding the section on Austria it will be well to examine what part the Magyars felt called upon to play in the internal policy of the Empire. " The provisionary mission which Germanism has confided to Austria-Hungary consists in this," states Wladan Georgevitch, " Austria-Hungary tramples under foot and grinds in pieces the people who fall under its power ; it provokes conflict between different peoples or between members of the same race ; it stamps out national sentiment and sends German colonists to dwell amongst these nations." *

This policy, the *divide ut imperes* of Machiavellian statesmen of all ages, has for many generations been the mainspring of Austrian administration. It was long adopted as the leading policy when dealing with the Magyars, and has in turn been successfully applied by the Hungarians in their relations with the Southern Slavs since the *Ausgleich* of 1867. This doctrine, as followed by the Magyars, was made perfectly clear in the book by Count Julius Andrassy, published in 1897. " We have no longer reason to fear social absorption through the agency of Germanism nor Germanization by the power of the State," he wrote. " The Habsburgs to-day no longer represent in Europe the Germanic idea. That rôle has been undertaken by the Hohenzollerns. But the question of nationality can only be settled by a rearrangement of the relations that exist between us and our southern neighbours. Nothing could render our duty towards the races (of Hungary) more difficult than a situation in which we should be entirely on an equality with our southern neighbours and in which they might feel that we have need of them ; in which they would have the possibility, or believe that such was their duty, to obtain a national organization for their countrymen. . . . Hungary is the natural guardian of the independent development of these southern States (*i.e.* Rumania, Bulgaria, etc.). She does not therefore menace them. In that respect the idea of confedera-

* Quoted by Andler from " Die serbische Frage," p. 155.

tion is just . . . but in order that this projected confederation should last and should be advantageous for us it is necessary that we should be much stronger than our confederates." This idea has been the keynote of Magyar policy, and carries out Bismarck's cynical statement that in every alliance there must be a horse and a rider. The Magyars were determined to ride the Southern Slav horse. Hence the Southern Slav question, owing to the brutal behaviour of the Magyars, has during recent years assumed an importance that was persistently overlooked in this country but which nevertheless was the main cause of the present war. In order to oppose this dangerous policy, Pan-German and Pan-Magyar, and to introduce some stability within the rocking Austrian Empire, the Archduke Ferdinand adopted the cause of trialism, hated alike by Germans and Hungarians.

The Archduke Ferdinand, who thus set to work to checkmate the fatal ascendancy of the Magyars and to oppose the unitary policy of the Germans, was one of the two or three outstanding personalities in modern European history. The influence which he succeeded in acquiring within the Austro-Hungarian Empire is all the more remarkable in view of the fact that when he became heir to the Habsburg monarchy, after the death of the Crown Prince Rudolf, he was practically unknown to his future subjects and had scarcely a friend in the whole of the Empire. Moreover, he had been brought up amidst influence of the most reactionary and almost mediæval kind, his health was known to be precarious, he had been imbued with clerical and anti-democratic teachings from his earliest youth, his education in the art of statesmanship had been entirely neglected, and he was severely handicapped owing to the unpopularity of his father, Karl Ludwig, whose hatred of constitutionalism had been an obsession, and by the discredit which surrounded his brother, the Archduke Otto, whose name seemed to be connected with every important social scandal. In addition, by marrying the Countess Sophie Chotek, the daughter of an impoverished Czech nobleman, he not only acted in defiance of the old Emperor whom he was to succeed and made enemies of practically every member of the Imperial House, but he alienated the Germans and sowed the seeds for future political and dynastic troubles which, had he succeeded to the throne, might have ended in the disruption of the Empire.

Yet in spite of these initial disadvantages the Archduke managed to secure a large and enthusiastic following, who saw in his policy the only remedy for the chaos in which the Empire seemed to be permanently involved. The Archduke Ferdinand, with the possible exception of William II, was " the most masterful member of any reigning house."* Only a man of the strongest personality, of iron will, of inflexible resolve, and unbending determination could have beaten down the opposition with which he was met at every turn in his political career. Through his mother, one of the Neapolitan Bourbons, he inherited the obstinacy of that unfortunate and stubborn race. From his father he acquired nothing but a rigid formalism and hatred of every modern democratic movement. At the supreme crisis in his career, when he was called upon to take his position as the heir apparent to the Austrian Empire, he cast aside, so far as that was possible, every preconceived notion, set himself resolutely to the task in hand, formed his own opinions, formulated his policy, made use of whatever tools he could safely handle, and retained the full measure of his obstinacy modified by an enlightened but dogged determination.

The early years of the Archduke, states a well-informed writer in the *Nineteenth Century*, were spent under conditions that might have been framed for the express purpose of unfitting him for his work as his uncle's heir. He was " as completely out of touch with modern Austria as if he had been in the catacombs." † But the change that was effected, not only in his prospects but in his mental outlook, by the death of the Crown Prince Rudolf also exerted a profound influence over his whole future career. The young Archduke, who had been brought up in monastic seclusion, travelled ; and during his intercourse with men of all sorts and conditions he was led to recognize, even if he did not himself drink at the democratic fountain, that the days of permanent repression of nationalistic forces and racial instincts were quickly passing

* *Round Table*, 1914, No. 16, p. 659.
† "The Murdered Archduke," by Edith Sellers, *Nineteenth Century*, August 1915, p. 283.

and that only a radical change in the Habsburg policy could save his future Empire from disruption when the dynamic forces of incipient revolution should once burst asunder the autocratic bonds in which they were imprisoned. The enigmatic figure of the Austrian Archduke hobnobbing with such a sturdy old democrat as the Australian statesman Sir George Dibbs, and studying under his tutelage the institutions of the most democratic community in the world, cannot fail to impress one with the extraordinary personality of the Habsburg prince who was subsequently to reconcile and enlist under his banner such discordant elements as reactionary catholicism and Christian socialism. The Australians made a profound impression upon the Archduke, and he used to state that they were of all people his *Lieblinge*.*

What the Archduke realized, and realized deeply so soon as he began seriously to study political questions, was that the Habsburg monarchy was drifting to inevitable extinction between the grinding forces of Germanism and Magyarism. The policy to which he set his hand was as a consequence purely dynastic, in so far as he believed that it served the interests of the reigning house. He was neither a German, a Czech, a Magyar, nor a Slav, but he worked to reconcile and to make use of all these elements in building up a strong and powerful Austrian Empire as an efficient counterpoise to the growing influence of the Hohenzollern State across the frontiers. How far this policy was intended to checkmate German designs it would be difficult to say ; but there can be little doubt that had the Archduke lived to carry out his policy—the erection of three equal States within the Empire, German, Magyar, and Slav, towards the last of which would gravitate the Slav elements of the Balkan States—he might have succeeded in checking the inordinate ambitions of German statesmen and have frustrated their schemes for the economic, and possibly political, absorption in the German Empire of the Habsburg territories that still interposed a fragile economic barrier against the road to the East. In any case the Austrian Archduke was deeply hated in Germany, and it was only during recent years that he succeeded in forcing the Hohenzollern Court to terms of comparative amity.

* Sellers.

To carry out his policy—Machiavellian from the German point of view, anti-national from the Magyar standpoint, but nationalistic from the Slav outlook—the Archduke most cleverly rallied to his side the clerical party in the country, always a strong group, popularly supposed to be reactionary and opposed to democratic principles, but nevertheless clearly prepared to accept reforms that would not conflict with the fundamental claims of the Church. In this action the Archduke alienated the sympathies of modern Italy, and it is noteworthy that he consistently refused to cross the threshold of the Quirinal whenever he was at Rome. Moreover, his policy was in the main directed against Italian aspirations in the Adriatic, and was intended to checkmate the claim that this waterway should become *il mare nostro*. The Archduke's policy on this point is well expressed in a book by one of his political satellites, Count Leopold von Chlumecky, the editor of the *Oesterreichische Rundschau*.

According to the programme outlined in that work there were two claims which the Austrian Government could never renounce: access to the Mediterranean and preponderance in the Western Balkans. Chlumecky emphatically proclaimed that " the formation of national or political groups in the Balkans, which would carry into Bosnia, Croatia, and Dalmatia the germs of grave agitations, under the ægis of powerful foreign States, cannot be permitted. Every attempt to detach Macedonia from Turkey without the initiative of Austria, every attempt to constitute an autonomous Macedonia that is not undertaken by us or does not fall in with our own ideas, would bring about grave embarrassments for the Monarchy. Such a State would necessarily endeavour to consolidate itself by attracting towards it the other Balkan peoples and our occupied provinces (Bosnia-Herzegovina); and the Southern Austrian provinces would thus be menaced by a new irredentism. That, however, is but a negative interest. We have in addition a notable positive interest—to maintain open the commercial road to Salonika, which is destined to be the most advanced gateway in the south-east for the commerce of Southern Austria and Hungary. Salonika is our hope for the future." *

* " Oesterreich-Ungarn und Italien," by Leopold von Chlumecky, 1907, pp. 61–63.

In other words, the Archduke's policy and the policy of those who were associated with him was as anti-Italian as it was anti-German, and it would never become German until the Austrian Empire might become an equal partner, in fact instead of in theory, in the Triple Alliance. The policy of Trialism involved the further doctrine of hands off the Western Balkans, and subsequently stood for the erection of an "independent" Albania under direct German and Austrian influence. The Balkan features of this policy were particularly acceptable to the Magyars, who, whilst bitterly opposed to Trialism, were not averse from extensions of territory along the Adriatic.

The Archduke's first steps to secure his ulterior aims were undoubtedly successful. Thrust aside at the Court, seldom allowed to see the Emperor, almost treated as a social pariah on account of his marriage, he accepted the patronage of the Catholic School Union, a body that was not only political but also violently propagandist. Its leaders were strongly tinged with Christian-Socialism and were opposed to Protestantism in any shape or form. They were thus enemies of Lutheran Germany and of the Triple Alliance, as well as of irredentist Italy. The Archduke's attitude, dictated in conformance with a deliberately chosen policy, aroused great resentment in Germany but rallied to his standard a powerful party whose interests were not anti-dynastic, like those of a not inconsiderable section of the Germans, but involved the upholding of the prestige of the monarchy in an Empire that seemed doomed to extinction.

The political progress of the Archduke was further emphasized in 1902, when in coming to the coronation of King Edward he insisted upon being accompanied not merely by representatives of Austria and Hungary, but by delegates from Poland and Bohemia also. His action on this and on subsequent occasions proclaimed him to be a federalist and demonstrated his opposition to the prevailing Dualism.

Up to the period of the annexation of Bosnia-Herzegovina the Archduke had been markedly reserved in his attitude towards the German Emperor. But that action, undertaken, as there is reason to believe, without the knowledge of German statesmen—although a direct affront to Germanism and not in accordance with the then desire for peace, convinced German statesmen that a strong and wilful personality was influencing Austrian foreign policy and that it was both expedient and necessary to come to terms if the Triple Alliance were not to suffer shipwreck upon the Italian shoals. As is well known, a truce was arranged. Within a month of the annexation the Emperor William went to Eckartsau, where the Austrian heir and the German Kaiser met on terms of equality. Henceforth German and Austrian foreign policy became closely allied, because Austria, having been strong enough to act independently, was now given a free hand to carry out her purely Austrian aims without dictation or interference from Berlin. Acting on this assumption, the German Chancellery pretended to be unacquainted with the terms of the Austrian ultimatum to Serbia at the commencement of the present war.

It has been made clear that the policy of the Archduke, whilst in no sense unfriendly to Germany, was nevertheless entirely Austrian in its scope. For this reason the future Austrian sovereign was not a *persona grata* with the Pan-Germans, who foresaw in the possible success of his policy the wrecking of their plans for a Central European German Empire. Nor was his attitude acceptable to the Magyars; whilst at the Austrian Court the future Emperor was regarded with a mixture of fear and contempt. The full story of the tragedy at Serajevo will probably never be known. Who set the wheels of the conspiracy in motion may never be discovered. But there can be little doubt that the removal of the Archduke was far more a German, a Magyar, even a Court interest than it was in the interests of Serbia, who was directly charged with the crime. Although undoubtedly war had been determined upon before the assassination took place, that event formed a convenient pretext for attempting the realization of the German and Austrian aims.

The idea that Belgrade had plotted the murder of the Archduke, fearful lest his policy of a Southern Slav State within the Austrian Empire should eventually lead to the absorption of Serbia and Montenegro, was put forward by Count Forgach, the Austrian Under-Secretary of State, who had been convicted in 1909 of having had documents forged with a view to securing the judicial murder of Southern Slav leaders; but it seems far more probable, in view of the peculiar circumstances surrounding the crime, that it was connived at, even if not actually arranged, by the Austrian police. The Archduke's own remark to his suite after the explosion of the bomb—" The fellow will get the Golden Cross of Merit for this " *—sufficiently indicates that Ferdinand himself was fully aware of the joy with which the news of his death would be received in official circles.

But the most striking testimony to the official premeditation of this crime is afforded by Mr. Henry Wickham Steed in an article in the *Edinburgh Review*. " In the spring of 1910," writes Mr. Steed, " I was at Serajevo during the visit of the Emperor Francis Joseph, and was struck by the completeness of the police arrangements. During the Archduke's visit none were made. Having warned off the police, the military authorities, under the command of General Potiorek, the Governor and Commander of the Army Corps, omitted even to provide a military escort. On the way to the town hall a bomb was thrown at the Archduke's motor-car by a youth named Cabrinovitch, the son of an Austrian police agent who had lately returned from a visit to Belgrade, where the Serbian authorities had proposed to expel him as a suspected Austrian *agent-provocateur*. . . . No police official and no military authority was dismissed, nor, as far as is known, even reprimanded for failure to protect the Archduke and his wife. General Potiorek remained Governor and presently commanded the Bosnian army against Serbia." †

It is absolutely incredible that no punishments should have been made for so flagrant a dereliction of duty as was involved in the withdrawal of police and military protection if the crime had not been deliberately engineered by some most highly placed personage. " Much light," states Mr. Steed, " might be shed on the tragedy of Serajevo and on the preparation of the European War could it ever be known exactly what passed at Konopisht amid the Archduke's rose-gardens during the visit paid to him there by the German Emperor and Grand Admiral Tirpitz in June 1914. We know only the externals of those fateful days. The Archduke and the Duchess Hohenburg left late in June for Bosnia, where the Archduke

* *Round Table*, No. 16, p. 660.
† " The Quintessence of Austria," *Edinburgh Review*, October 1915, p. 243.

was to inspect the 15th Army Corps. It has been asserted, and not convincingly denied, that Count Tisza, the Hungarian Premier, warned the Archduke not to go." Whatever may be the inner history of the Serajevo affair, there is no doubt that the Archduke's death directly removed the most formidable obstacle to the realization of German plans. The Archduke had in the past refused to be a German tool. It is possible that he was still equally opposed to any subserviency to the Hohenzollern policy.* In any case it is certain that his own attitude was purely Austrian and purely dynastic, and as such was anathema to the tremendous forces of Pan-Germanism which had been striving for years to bring about the catastrophe of a general European war. With the removal of the Archduke the last barrier had been swept away.

* The real reason for the "removal" of the Austrian heir will probably never be known, but there can be little doubt that the assassination was arranged by some person, or persons, of the highest rank for "reasons of State." It is variously asserted that the Archduke Ferdinand was suffering from an incurable malady and was likely to go mad, if he were not already mentally unbalanced; that he was the one obstacle in the path of Germany; and that his succession would have been a public humiliation for the Imperial family. A notable article entitled "The Pact of Konopisht," by Mr. H. W. Steed, appeared in the *Nineteenth Century* for February 1916, in which the delight with which his death was hailed at the Vienna Court is made abundantly clear. The fact that it was necessary to issue an official excuse for the totally inadequate arrangements at the Archduke's funeral is a sufficient condemnation of the indecent attitude of the Imperial family towards their murdered kinsman.

CHAPTER X

AUSTRO-GERMANY AND THE SERBS

THE immediate cause of the present war is to be found in the relations existing between Austria-Hungary and Serbia, and the determination of the former so to crush the small and apparently insignificant kingdom which stood between her and the road to Salonika that there should be no possibility of the ultimate success of the Greater Serbia movement. Of all the problems affecting the destiny both of Germany and Austria-Hungary and controlling the Pan-German ideal of a great Central European Empire this was the most knotty and inconvenient. Upon its solution depended the realization of all the plans of the Pan-Germans. The chief obstacle across the path of Germany to Asia, whither the dreams of German philosophers had been turned ever since Moltke wrote his now famous essays, was the two small kingdoms peopled by the Southern Slavs, supported by their powerful abettor Russia and standing as a bulwark against the German invasion. Shut off as they were from the sea and confined within narrow political boundaries, which in no way corresponded to the ethnographic frontiers of the Jugo-Slavs,* they completely blocked the land passage to the East and rendered, so long as they remained independent communities, the complete realization of the *Drang nach Osten* an impossibility.

The question of the future of Serbia was further complicated during the lifetime of the Archduke Ferdinand by the policy followed by that unfortunate prince, whose object, so far as can be fathomed without the aid of full documentary evidence, was to change the Dual Monarchy into a triune empire by granting the large Southern Slav element within Austria-Hungary autonomy and freedom from Magyar control, with

* The Southern Slavs or Jugo-Slavs (Jug in Slav means the South).

or without the co-operation of Serbia ; and thus to create a balance of parties which probably would have strengthened the Monarchy as an independent political unit. This policy was directly opposed to German interests ; for it was obvious that such a State, instead of being subservient to the Northern Empire, might have opposed an effective barrier to German aggression. Whatever may be the true story of the murder at Serajevo there can be no doubt that the Archduke's policy did not correspond with Germain aims. The position was made perfectly clear by the *Armee-Zeitung* in an article written in the year 1909, when it was considered that war was inevitable. " Now we are going to extend our arm also in Serbia," wrote that journal, " and we shall offer to their country *the opportunity of rebirth* and of dying for the Pan-Serb ideal under our protectorate, and of becoming the Great Serbia *under the sceptre of the Habsburgs."* *

The liberation of the Slavs, owing to Russia's action in 1877, was in reality a serious blow to German schemes. The half-formed and tentative designs of the Pan-Germans certainly had not taken their present shape at that period ; nevertheless the interposition of independent communities largely under Russian influence on the route over which Germany seemed destined to advance introduced another factor into the difficult problem and postponed the southward expansion of the German people.

By recognizing the independence of the seemingly incongruous and mutually hostile elements who had hitherto formed a portion of the tottering Ottoman Empire, Europe placed an obstacle in the way of German designs, and as these communities daily grew in strength the problem that unfolded itself before German statesmen continuously became more complex and dangerous. Yet the disunion of Slavdom, the constant conflict between the petty interests of petty States, the incessant fight between the subterranean political influences that dominated the politics of the Balkan kingdoms greatly facilitated Germany's task. As her aggressiveness during recent years has been due largely to this unfortunate disunion so the absence of efficient political co-operation and organization enabled Germany, working by and through Austria-Hungary,

* January 7, 1909.

to direct Balkan policy into the avenues most favourable to her designs. The two serious set-backs due to the collapse of the Abdul Hamid régime at Constantinople and the formation of the Balkan League were successfully overcome. Serbia alone was neither bought nor Germanized.

Before describing the conduct of Germany and Austria-Hungary towards Serbia it will be well to have a clear idea of the nature of the ethnographic barrier interposed between the Germans and the road to the East. An examination of any good ethnographic map reveals the fact that the Southern Slavs stretch in an almost compact mass from the banks of the River Drave, on the north, from the neighbourhood of Varasdin, to its confluence with the Danube, and thence extend across the Drave to the confluence of the Rivers Theiss and Maros, and from that point turn southwards to the Danube and occupy the frontiers of Transylvania. At the Danube the ethnographic boundary extends southward, slightly to the westward of the celebrated Iron Gates, as far as Nish, whence it turns to the south-west through the Sanjak of Novi Bazar, turns again northward, cuts across the south-eastern corner of Montenegro, and then follows the political boundary of that country to the Adriatic. From the neighbourhood of Varasdin the ethnographic boundary will be found to run to a spot a little to the north of Fiume, and then to divide the peninsula of Istria into two halves, and to end on the Adriatic at Pola. Within this area, with the exception of the country bordering Transylvania, where Rumanians, Magyars, and Germans are also extensively settled, the Southern Slavs are predominant. If we also include the Slovenes and the Bulgars—the latter of whom, however, though technically Slavs, having retained few of the characteristics of other Slavonic peoples, may well be eliminated from our survey—the territory of the Southern Slavs extends from the River Drave and the Julian Alps in a south-easterly direction as far as the Black Sea.

But beyond these ethnographic borders there is a semi-Slav area which does not strictly fall within these limits, and in the map issued by the Jugo-Slav Committee in London the area of the Greater Serbia, dreamt of by the leaders of the Serbian people, is somewhat extended and includes territories stretching from beyond the Italian frontier in the west to the present southern frontiers of Serbia in the south, a variation which includes the Bulgarian and Albanian peoples in Southern Serbia as well as the Friuli, who are settled on both sides of the Italian frontiers. This area is surrounded by peoples who are largely opposed to the Slav ideal, the Germans and Magyars in the north, the Rumanians in the north-east, the Bulgarians to the south; whilst in the towns along the Adriatic coast and on some of the adjacent islands the Italians predominate, but are nowhere, not even in Trieste, economically independent of the adjacent hinterland. This vast area, peopled by the Southern Slavs, roughly corresponds to the Austrian Carniola and Dalmatia, with part of Istria, Styria, and Carinthia; the Hungarian provinces of Croatia and Slavonia; and the Imperial provinces of Bosnia and Herzegovina; with the kingdoms of Montenegro and Serbia. It is this area which the Serbs desire to see erected into an independent and unified political state.

Within this territory the Southern Slavs are divided into three fairly distinct groups, all of whom, however, have common ethnographical characteristics and are racially united—the Serbs, the Croats, and the Slovenes: whilst these again are divided into three religious groups; for the Orthodox Church predominates in Serbia, Montenegro, Bosnia-Herzegovina, and parts of Croatia-Slavonia and Dalmatia; and the Catholic Church is the predominant religion in Croatia-Slavonia, Dalmatia, Carniola, Carinthia, Styria, Istria, and Bosnia-Herzegovina. In the last province there is also a large Mohammedan community descended from Jugo-Slavs, who had been forcibly converted to Mohammedanism by their Turkish masters.

For centuries the whole of this territory has been under foreign domination, and the greater portion is still under foreign control. From the downfall of the Greater Serbia—which had been organized and ruled wisely by the national hero Dusan, and then included both Zeta (Montenegro) and Rashka (Upper Drina district), Serbia, Macedonia, Thrace, Thessaly, the Epirus, and Albania, as well as the country northward of these regions as far as the Save and Danube—in the latter part of the fourteenth century to the present time the larger portion of this country has been governed by alien rulers. In the north, the Slovene Duchy was united to Austria in the first years of the sixteenth century, although it had retained a measure of independence until that date, and was colonized by German settlers imported by its Habsburg sovereigns. Croatia also, which up to the twelfth century was an important independent kingdom, finally fell under the control of the Hungarian kings, although it preserved a semi-independence for a considerable period, and was only reduced to the position of a vassal State when Hungary reached the zenith of her power at the end of the fourteenth century. Since that date Croatia, with a brief interregnum, has been under the House of Habsburg, and has lost most of her ancient privileges, although retaining certain political rights and a small measure of autonomy.

With the reawaking in the Croatian national spirit in the fourth decade of the last century the Magyars sought to impose their will upon this unfortunate people and " opposed this national awakening with a kind of frenzied insolence." When the Croatians opposed the Hungarian revolution and crossed the Drave with an army of 40,000 men to aid the Habsburgs in reducing their rebellious subjects their doom was sealed, for the House of Austria repaid their services with the base ingratitude characteristic of the Habsburg sovereigns and disregarded their appeal for complete autonomy. Instead of receiving the reward they had expected they were placed under the hated domination of the Magyars and have since carried on an incessant struggle within the bosom of the Hungarian State.

To the south the Turkish invasion, which at one time reached as far as the gates of Vienna, succeeded in overwhelming the Serbian branch of the Southern Slavs and the terrific and irresistible onslaught of the Ottomans completely obliterated the last vestiges of their independence. Bulgaria, conquered by the Turks in 1393, became a nation of slaves; but Serbia, although broken and subdued, was never so sufficiently conquered that all traces of the national spirit were eliminated. On the contrary this brave and stubborn people managed to maintain a precarious existence under the shadow of the Ottoman throne, whilst the Montenegrins, secure in their mountain fastnesses, were never completely subdued. The conquest of Serbia in 1459 did not eliminate the national consciousness, and until their renaissance in the early part of the nineteenth century the Serbians, though under the Turkish yoke, retained not only their language and customs but also their religion. Bosnia, on the contrary, under Turkish dominion became largely Ottomanized.

But the Turks, who advanced in compelling waves along the river valleys and imposed their will upon the interior districts, were never able to dominate the purely coastal regions, for they were met and opposed by the Republic of Venice, who during the height of her power controlled the seaports along the eastern shores of the Adriatic and retained possession of the whole of Dalmatia, until in 1797 it was ceded to Austria by the Treaty of Campo Formio; whilst the Republic of Ragusa, which was independent mistress of the littoral from Sabbioncello to the Bocche di Cattaro and known as a great commercial Power and centre of arts and letters, remained free until the year 1808, when the Republic was abolished by Napoleon. These foreign masters, Austro-Hungarian, Italian, and Turk, divided between them the former Serbian kingdom.

With the decay of the Turkish power the Serbs underwent a national regeneration. A race which had retained its national characteristics through centuries of oppression, which had neither forgotten its national heroes, its history, its literature, nor its folklore, now experienced new and startling developments—new because for the first time during the long centuries of oppression the Serbs dared to assert their individuality and again to raise the sacred banner of nationality: startling because the reawakening was in direct opposition to the then course of European policy, which took no account of nationality, imposed arbitrary and impossible political barriers in the interests of foreign dynasties, upheld territorial rights based upon historical spoliations, and was not disposed to recognize the claims of the smaller nations to a separate individuality.

The Serbians having the virtues and limitations of a peasant democracy assumed an attitude which was in direct conflict with the interests both of Turkey and Austria-Hungary, whilst their immediate neighbours the Croats, undergoing a similar national transformation in spite of their long historical association with the House of Habsburg, strove to assert their independence within the boundaries of that Empire. From across the frontiers of the then Ottoman Empire the peasants of Serbia, a nation of swineherds according to the prevailing German and Magyar opinion, looked upon the contemporaneous movement in Croatia as an earnest of the future amalgamation of the Southern Slavs. Nevertheless in the then political state of Europe it was recognized that the greatest chance of establishing a Southern Slav kingdom was within the Ottoman Empire itself, where the central authority, constantly weakened by internal dissensions and the reawakening of nationalism, seemed less able to cope with the new insurrectionary movement.

The Serbian emancipation commenced in the year 1804, when the barbarous excesses committed by the Turks against their Serbian subjects caused a general rising under the leadership of Kara-George, himself a peasant, but nevertheless a man of resolution and action and the founder of the present Serbian dynasty. For ten years under his leadership the Serbs maintained a stubborn fight with the Turks, and with the aid of the Russians secured autonomy for the northern portion of the present Serbian kingdom. A little later, in 1815, owing to the reconquest of the country by the Turks two years previously, a second insurrection, under Milos Obrenovic, the founder of the second Serbian dynasty, took place, and a restricted form of autonomy was again wrested from the unwilling Sultan. Finally, in 1833, Serbia became an autonomous principality under the suzerainty of the Sultan, and in 1871, after two campaigns against the Turks, Prince Milan proclaimed the independence of his country, and four years later was able to change the former principality into a kingdom. The long series of intrigues which marked the reign of King Milan, who having at first favoured Russian interests suddenly adopted the Austrian cause, embittered as they were by his unfortunate relations with Queen Natalie and his yet more unfortunate attitude towards his son, were an open and unsavoury scandal that did infinite harm to his native country but undoubtedly facilitated Austria's political aims. Queen Natalie, herself a Russian, naturally claimed the protection of the Russian Court, but the open antagonism between the Serbian king and queen was not unpleasing to the Germanic Powers, for it gave them an opportunity of checking the movement for establishing the internal stability of the Serbian kingdom. The domestic quarrel was intensified by the support accorded to King Milan by the Germanic Powers, for " William II well knew that any decided antagonistic step taken by Milan in regard to Natalie would more than anything else throw him into the arms of Austria, and consequently Germany would thus be able to establish herself firmly in the Balkan Peninsula." * Milan became the tool and secret instrument of Austrian policy in the Balkans.

It is not necessary to follow this unsavoury business to its dramatic conclusion—the forced abdication of Milan and the succession of his son Alexander. The latter, having been reared in a nest of intrigue, learned to despise both parents and was easily driven into the Austrian net.† Unfortunately the young king, without political insight and incapable of withstanding the intrigues of Austria and Germany, fell an easy victim to the charms of his mother's lady-in-waiting, Madame Draga Maschin, whom he married in spite of the opposition of the Serbian people. The climax of the Serbian domestic tragedy was reached when it was discovered that Queen Draga had acceded to the wishes of the Austrian party and was apparently prepared to sell her adopted country for the proverbial mess of pottage. In 1903 the King and Queen were assassinated in their bedchamber, and on the day following the murder Prince Peter Karageorgevitch, who had long resided in exile at Paris, was elected king.

During this period the policy of Austria had been one of determined antagonism to the aspirations of the Serbian people. Nothing could have been more directly opposed to Germanic interests than the erection of a strong buffer State on the road to the East. This point was subsequently

* " The Near East from Within," p. 156.

† Count Zichy, states the writer of " The Near East from Within," " was an extremely clever man, and he at once made up his mind that it was worth while to try, by making use of the undercurrents of the Court, to drive the young King into the embrace of Austria. In order to achieve this object Count Zichy spared neither trouble nor money, and it was principally due to his efforts in this direction that Serbia became inundated with people of Austrian birth. No pains were spared to transform Serbia into an Austrian province." (Pp. 165-6.)

strongly emphasized in a speech by Herr von Bethmann-Hollweg in the Reichstag, on April 7, 1913. "For the future the decisive point is," he stated, " that into the place of European Turkey, whose State life has become passive, there have entered political States which exhibit a quite extraordinary activity and vitality. . . . One thing remains beyond doubt —if it should ever come to a European conflagration, which sets *Slaventhum* against *Germanenthum*, it is then for us a disadvantage that the position in the balance of forces which was occupied hitherto by European Turkey is now filled in part by Slav States."

This illuminating avowal, surely one of the clearest and most incisive statements of German policy, was further emphasized by the following remarks which demonstrate how completely Germany had been deceived by the results of the inter-Slav conflict in the Balkans. " This alteration of the politico-military situation on the Continent," continued the Imperial Chancellor, " has passed through the preliminary stage, and now that it is a fact we should be acting unconscientiously if we did not draw the consequences. I do not say this because I regard a collision between *Slaventhum* and *Germanenthum* as inevitable. It is, however, as well known to the Russian statesmen as it is to us that the Pan-Slav currents, about which Bismark even in his day complained and which caused him uneasiness, have received a powerful stimulus from the victories of the Slav States in the Balkans. Bulgarian victories over the Turks have been celebrated in those quarters as victories of the Slav idea in contrast with the Germanic idea. . . . The lively French spirit regarded the defeats of Turkey as defeats of the Germans, and assumed that both the Balkan States and Alsace-Lorraine would attach themselves to France."

In this speech Herr von Bethmann-Hollweg conclusively showed how unpalatable to the Germanic Powers was the growth of strong Slav States in the Balkans, and disclosed the German policy of weakening the States erected by the Treaty of Berlin. In the pursuance of this aim Austria had continuously opposed the growth of Serbia. By Austrian decree the Serbians were destined to remain a bucolic, inland people, tending their flocks and herds, sending their agricultural products by the natural avenues of trade into the Austrian Empire in exchange for the goods which Serbia was unable to manufacture for herself; deprived for ever of a seaport on the Adriatic, although half the eastern littoral of that sea is inhabited by her Slav brethren; and condemned to economic and political dependence upon the House of Habsburg. Austria in fact " tied Serbia up in a sack " * from which there was to be no outlet.

The injustice and stupidity of this policy became sufficiently apparent when, in spite of every restriction, the Serbians were able to reassert their nationality. Under King Peter the country was undergoing a remarkable transformation, and during the last few years especially the national revival was such as to cause profound uneasiness in Berlin and Vienna. In spite of the infamous conduct of Austrian statesmen in their relations with Belgrade and in spite of a campaign of mendacity and intrigue, backed by forged documents and fed by Austrian gold, Serbia was able to regain her freedom from secret Austrian influences and to rehabilitate in the eyes of Europe her political character, which had been so decidedly smirched under the Milan régime. In spite too of the crushing economic pressure exercised by Austria in order to compel the Serbian nation to accept all the Austrian demands, she was able to resist successfully and to re-establish her economic credit upon a sound basis.†

In the meantime, across the Serbian frontiers, Austria's policy was equally relentless towards the co-nationals who were unfortunate enough to be subjects of the Austro-Hungarian Empire. It has been seen that the Croats, in conjunction

---

* " Austria-Hungary and Serbia," by G. M. Trevelyan, *Fortnightly Review*, 1915, p. 982.

† It may be remarked that the attempt of Serbia to conclude a commercial agreement with Bulgaria was vetoed by Austria-Hungary, and that the Emperor Francis Joseph insisted that Serbia should not buy French guns but instead should purchase the inferior Skoda guns manufactured in Austria, and thus put herself into a position of dependence upon that country in the event of war. When Serbia refused to accede to these demands the Austrian frontiers were closed against Serbian trade. Ninety per cent. of Serbian exports were in the year 1905 sent across the Austrian frontiers, but in consequence of Austria's action the exports decreased enormously, and had not the Serbians reorganized their foreign trade with the greatest energy the country would have speedily become bankrupt. *See* an anonymous article, " The Future of Serbia," in the *Fortnightly Review* for June 1915.

with the other Slavic peoples, after aiding the Austro-Germans to overcome the rebellious Magyars, were placed under their control, and that their territory was added to Hungary to form the Hungarian portion of the Dual Monarchy. It might have been thought that under these circumstances they would have formed an efficient counterpoise to the Magyar element within Hungary, who are in reality less than half of the total population of that kingdom.* But as a matter of fact there was no possibility for an equitable political representation under the Magyars, for every device was resorted to in order to nullify any political influence that might have been exercised by the Southern Slavs. The growing aspirations of the Slavs met with no favour at Budapest, where the Magyar autocracy were determined to crush every attempt at securing equality of treatment within the kingdom, and to prevent the successful accomplishment of the policy of establishing three kingdoms within the Empire favoured by the Archduke Ferdinand. " For Austria, the Eastern question begins at Budapest," stated a writer in *The Times*,† " for Hungary, who has strayed far from the wisdom of Deak,‡ it now begins at Agram ; for the Monarchy as a whole it opens in the territory inhabited by the Serbo-Croatian or Southern Slav race. . . . The Monarchy has seemed to be striving with might and main to make enemies of the Southern Slavs and to

* The population of Hungary according to the census taken in 1910 was divided as follows :

Germans	2,037,435
Magyars	10,050,575
Ruthenians	472,587
Rumanians	2,949,970
Slovaks	1,967,970
Serbs	1,106,471
Croatians	1,833,162
Others	569,255
	20,987,425

It is probable that the number of Magyars is considerably less than those recorded in the official figures, which were carefully manipulated, for owing to pressure many non-Magyars professed that they liked the Magyar language best, and thus, from mere motives of prudence, entered themselves as Magyars. It is probable that the Magyars do not number more than eight millions out of the total. † February 2, 1912.

‡ Francis Deak, 1803–76, who did more than any one else to establish the Dual Monarchy.

cause them to regard with equal aversion the Hungarian tricolour and the black and yellow flag of Austria. The Agram High Treason Trial and the machinations of Baron Rauch ; the Friedjung trial with its trail of exposures that brought home to Austro-Hungarian diplomacy the charge of having worked, wittingly or unwittingly, with the help of forged documents . . . the establishment of absolutism in Croatia-Slavonia at the instance of Hungary . . . have gradually embittered Southern Slav feeling." In fact the policy pursued by Austria-Hungary has been deliberately designed to foster racial strife within the Empire in order to prevent any coalition between the incongruous elements within the Monarchy.

By favouring those who appeared to behave well towards the Dynasty or those whom it was positively dangerous to disregard, by curbing those whose power seemed to be growing and likely in the future to become a danger to the ruling element, by establishing " an equilibrium of moderate discontent " * in which no one race was entirely satisfied and never without jealousy of its neighbours, it was sought to attract the discontented races towards the Crown, as the final dispenser of justice and the arbitrator in internal disputes. However suitable this policy may have been in the past, when the intensive nationalism of to-day was scarcely awake and certainly not sufficiently advanced to counteract the claims of historical continuity and attachment to a long-continued dynasty, it became an anachronism so soon as nationalism became firmly established. When subject peoples became awake to the reality of race and to the imperious ties of a common nationality such a policy only served to strengthen further the newly aroused susceptibilities of races who have but recently realized that political bonds could be burst asunder by effective combination and co-operation. The contempt of the Austro-Magyars for the nation of swineherds † across the frontiers and for the conglomeration of unlettered peasants who were supposed to form the mass of the Southern Slavs, expressed in so many obnoxious and hurtful forms, only led to a closer understanding between the two branches of the Southern Slavs ; and when the Serbs and Croats sunk

* *Edinburgh Review*, October 1895.
† " Die Serben das sind Schweine " is a popular Austrian saying.

their differences and came to a common understanding in the year 1905 the anger and dismay of Vienna and Budapest knew no bounds. The first result was the annexation of Bosnia-Herzegovina : the second was the present war.

The recent history of this portion of Austria-Hungary shows how scandalous and frantic were the efforts to avert the consummation of the Southern Slav programme. Every effort was made to reduce Croatia to a state of complete dependence. The reign of the Ban Khuen-Hedervary (1883–1903) represents the most scandalous period in contemporary Croatian history. Under his administration the seaport of Fiume, which until 1891 was a free port, was by a disgraceful piece of forgery taken from the Croats * and a little later occurred the scandalous trials which were to brand Austro-Hungarian diplomacy with infamy. These two trials at Agram † (1909) and Vienna (1908) and the trial of the Bosnian law student Luka Jukilch, who on June 8, 1912, had attempted to assassinate the Ban of Croatia, were supported by forged documents. In connexion with the last trial many students were arrested, and the police in their excessive zeal to serve their Habsburg masters "discovered" a bomb which, according to "expert testimony," was stated to resemble closely those prepared at Kragujevatz, the Serbian State

* "A Sketch of Southern Slav History" (Jugo-Slav Committee in London), 1915, p. 30. It is asserted that when the constitutional charters of Croatia, Slavonia, and Dalmatia were incorporated with the State archives at Budapest the agreement of 1867 was falsified by the pasting of a slip of paper over the specification of Fiume as *corpus separatum adnexæ rex*. On this point consult "The Slav Nations," by S. P. Tucic, 1915, p. 156.

† The dissatisfaction of the Slav elements in the empire having been vigorously expressed in sympathy with the Serbians, it was alleged that an extensive movement was on foot to wrest Croatia, Slavonia, and Bosnia from Austria-Hungary. Fifty-three persons, mostly merchants and teachers, were accused of high treason and brought to trial at Agram. This trial lasted from March 3 to October 5, 1909, when thirty-one of the accused were found guilty and sentenced to penal servitude. The evidence was unreliable, and an appeal having been lodged against this decision, they were again tried (November 1910) and the former sentences were quashed. These proceedings having naturally been commented upon in the papers, Dr. Henry Friedjung, an author of some note, who had accused the leaders of the Serbo-Croatian party of being in the pay of the Serbian Government, became the defendant in a libel action, in the course of which it was proved that the documents upon which he had based his accusations had been forged—the object, of course, having been to drag the Serbian Government into the controversy and to convict it of complicity in the Southern Slav movement.

Arsenal—a clumsy attempt to drag Serbia into the conspiracy. "The Croatian police," stated *The Times*, "could not be congratulated on their story," which read "like a poor copy of the fabrications exposed during the Agram and Friedjung trials." By tampering with the fount of justice the responsible authorities sought to stem the advancing tide of Slavdom. By tampering with the political privileges still exercised by the Croats they tried to deprive them of all political redress within the boundaries of Hungary itself.

The non-Magyars were disfranchised not only by a high property qualification but by deliberate violence and treachery.* "If we look into the electoral statistics," states Mr. Ellis Barker, "we find that the more Rumanian a country is the fewer voters does it possess. We find further that the larger the constituency is the farther from its centre is placed the solitary polling booth. At election time bridges are often broken down or declared unsafe for the passage of vehicles . . . and all the horses in the outlying villages are placed under veterinary supervision at the last moment. The voting is not secret, but public, and by word of mouth. Non-Magyars are thus publicly terrorized into voting only for Magyar members. . . . At election times Hungary mobilizes her whole army in order to terrorize the opposition voters, and if these insist upon their legal right of voting they are frequently attacked by armed mobs or shot down by the gendarmes and military. . . . According to Danzer's *Armee-Zeitung* of June 6, 1910, Hungary mobilized for the election in that year 202 battalions of infantry, 126 squadrons of cavalry, and in addition had Austrian troops sent from Lower Austria, Styria, and Moravia to Hungary." In view of this testimony and of the well-known fact that non-Magyars experience the greatest difficulty in entering the liberal professions, there is no cause for wonder that the Southern Slav movement made remarkable progress during recent years.† One further fact only need be instanced as an example of Austro-Hungarian

---

* *See* the article by Mr. J. Ellis Barker entitled "The Ultimate Fate of Austria-Hungary" in the *Nineteenth Century* for November 1914.

† It may also be instanced as a further proof of the Magyarizing tendency of the Hungarian Government that in 1907 the use of the Magyar language was made compulsory in the whole of Hungary—on the railways, in the law courts, and in the schools.

policy with respect to the Southern Slavs. In the "Southern Slav Programme" issued by the Jugo-Slav Committee in London, it is stated that "the present war has been made a pretext for the worst abuses. The Jugo-Slav nation has been silenced in the most brutal fashion : almost the entire male population has been called to the colours and placed in the front ranks, where it bears the brunt of every attack, and those who have not been called up have either been imprisoned or interned. Under various pretexts hangings, shootings, and massacres have been the order of the day. More than a hundred thousand persons have been exiled and several hundreds of thousands expelled from their homes. The Zagreb Sabor has not been convoked, the Serajevo Sabor has been dissolved, and the provincial Diets of Dalmatia, Istria, Carniola, Gorizia, Carinthia, and Styria have not been permitted to meet."

Little has hitherto been said about the strategic importance of Serbia in the Germanic scheme of south-eastern expansion. It has been stated that Belgrade, seated upon the Danube at the point where it approaches Serbian territory and through which the main railway to Salonika and Constantinople passes, is the key to the East. The route from Central Europe towards these two ports has since the earliest times been by way of the Danube valley to Belgrade, near which city the River Morava falls into the Danube and along the valley of which runs the high road to the East as far as Nish. Here the western branch, also followed by the railway, ascends the valley of the Morava still farther, and then crosses into the valley of the River Vardar, which falls into the Ægean Sea close to Salonika. *For this reason that port is of the utmost strategical importance to the Central Empires.* The eastern roadway, as well as the railway, leaves the valley of the Morava at Nish, and following the valley of the River Maritza by way of Sofia, Philippopolis, and Adrianople, finally reaches the Goldern Horn at Constantinople. These were the highways trodden by the Romans, and they are the two avenues along which the Germans, unless they are successfully checked, will eventually travel on their way to Asia Minor, Mesopotamia, the Persian Gulf, and Egypt.

The importance of this route, or the alternative way through Rumania, was well shown in an article written by the Vienna correspondent of the *Frankfurter Zeitung*, who stated that " the countries comprising the Triple Alliance, which were formerly agricultural countries, are now becoming manufacturing countries. The question of the unimpeded importation of food and raw material is one of extreme importance for them. A war against England, France, and Russia would result in the interruption of all the sea routes. The one route remaining for the Alliance is that which leads through Rumania, Bulgaria, and Turkey to Asia Minor. The Triple Alliance must be assured that that route must always be open to it. That is the explanation of the energetic and menacing attitude of German diplomacy towards the first rumours of a partition of Asia Minor. The interest which the Empire has in keeping the road to Asia Minor open was set above that of the German capital invested in the Bagdad railway ; and the German military mission to Constantinople is an advantage as precious to Germany as to Turkey. This aspect of the matter explains why Austria and Germany resolutely opposed the internationalization of the Adrianople–Constantinople section of the Orient line. For all the countries interposed between Hungary and Asia Minor one rule must be rigorously laid down : either they must be friends and allies of the Triple Alliance or they must reckon upon the implacable hostility of that Alliance." *

The desirability of acquiring full control of these great avenues has long been recognized by the Germans, and the importance of preventing the establishment of German influence along these ancient highways should have been recognized also by our statesmen had they followed the course of contemporary events with sufficient intelligence and interest. Unfortunately, however, previous to the outbreak of war it was popularly considered that there were no countries in the world with which we. had less concern than Serbia and Macedonia. With the latter we had a sentimental interest on account of the desirability of forcing the Turks to introduce suitable reforms for the benefit of the oppressed population : with the former we had not even that sentimental concern, owing partly to the fact that the British nation was alienated by the

* Quoted from an article by Francis Gribble, entitled " Serbia Irredenta," in the *Edinburgh Review*, July 1914.

intrigues supposed to be the essential characteristic of the Serbian people and only took a morbid interest in proceedings in Belgrade. King Milan and his scapegoat son Alexander effectually alienated our national sympathy.

In addition to the route via Belgrade there was one other that was open to the Germanic advance. This was through the Sanjak of Novi Bazar (now incorporated in Serbia and Montenegro), which under the Treaty of Berlin had been handed over to the military occupation of Austria-Hungary. This strategic highway, which under Turkish rule was largely a roadless no-man's-land, was intended to serve as the Austrian avenue to the Ægean Sea. A glance at the map will reveal a curious gap between the railway from Agram towards the frontiers, which stops suddenly at the Serbian borders, beyond Serajevo, where it would doubtless have been carried forward to join the line from Mitrovitza to Salonika but for a change in Austro-Hungarian plans. The history of Novi Bazar and of the attempts to secure through railway communication by this route is of considerable interest and throws an interesting sidelight upon the mazy course of Austrian policy. That Novi Bazar was at first intended to serve as the outlet towards Salonika is made evident in a Vienna paper, which on April 22, 1871, wrote as follows: " With the occupation of Novi Bazar the situation of Austria is wholly changed. The position in Bosnia is a defensive one against Serbia and Montenegro [in other words, to prevent their access to the sea]: the position in Novi Bazar is an offensive one, an outlet against whoever may occupy the Balkan Peninsula. From Novi Bazar we may threaten Albania, attack Bulgaria from the side and foresee the possibility of a bout towards Salonika. To go to Novi Bazar with the purpose of *remaining* there would have no meaning: Novi Bazar can only be a *station, the first step of a vast political action.*" *

In Italy the position was perfectly well understood. On June 7, 1901, Signor Giovanni Bovio stated in the Italian Parliament that " Austria with her eyes turned now towards Salonika, now towards Scutari, aims at dominating two seas. In either case woe to Italy "; whilst on February 23, 1903, Senator de Martini said: " Austria has taken fresh steps in

* These words were quoted by Signor Tittoni in the Italian Parliament.

the district of Novi Bazar. Do you consider that of small importance? But this is part of Austria's whole plan in the Balkan Peninsula, which aims, through Old Serbia, Mitrovitza, and Uskub, to reach Salonika." Speaking further in the same debate, he said that " Montenegro, in a state of dependency in relation to Austria, can no longer be considered as an efficient bulwark between Dalmatia and Albania. If Austria should occupy Novi Bazar, which forms a wedge between Montenegro and Serbia, her supremacy in Albania would be an accomplished fact."

But Austro-Hungarian policy underwent a modification when it was seen that there was some possibility of acquiring control over the better route through Belgrade, and when in the year 1908 Austria-Hungary annexed Bosnia, the rights formerly acquired over Novi Bazar were abandoned and attention was almost exclusively devoted to securing the easier passage through Serbia.* The superiority of the Belgrade route, apart from all political considerations peculiar to the internal policy of the Austro-Hungarian Empire which need not be touched upon here, had been concisely stated in the *Armee-Zeitung*, the organ of the officers of the Austrian army, three years before that date, when that journal wrote that " the great importance of Macedonia is due to its position as the entrance for the avenues of communication between Central Europe and Asia Minor, with its great commercial and military routes, the line from Morava and Vardar, Belgrade–Salonika, and the line Nish–Sofia–Constantinople, beside which the descent by the Bosnian valley, Novi Bazar–Mitrovitza, becomes secondary. It is to these routes that the Gulf of Salonika owes its importance in the communications of the world: it has, in the relations between the Danubian countries and Asia Minor, a situation analogous to that of the Persian Gulf in the communications between Europe and India."

* The abandonment of Novi Bazar was keenly resented in certain Austrian quarters. "By the occupation of Novi Bazar," stated the *Oesterreichische Rundschau* on June 8, 1908, " a wedge was to be placed between Serbia and Montenegro and a bridge thrown by means of which our influence should push forward 'beyond Mitrovitza,' as the Berlin Treaty says. This bridge is now torn down, the wedge is withdrawn, and the 'beyond Mitrovitza' for ever lost. Thus has the platform by means of which we could have made our economic and political influence felt in Macedonia been abandoned." *See* Signor Tittoni's Speeches.

The writer then proceeds to criticize the state of affairs in Macedonia. "Sooner or later," he says, "the state of things must be changed. This work need neither be confided to the Government at Constantinople nor to one of the small States of the peninsula. If Serbia does not range herself on our side loyally and without hesitation, then it will be necessary to direct against her the sword already out of its scabbard, *for it is only after having crushed Serbia* that it would be possible to undertake an offensive against Macedonia." The writer then outlines what was evidently the plan of the murdered Archduke. "It would seem," he continues, "that there will be effected in a future, more or less near, another grouping of the Powers in the Balkans. An independent Bulgaria and Albania, enlarged with a portion of Macedonia, will maintain the tranquillity of these countries. And what could be more desirable than a Jugo-Slav State including Croatia, Slavonia, Dalmatia, Bosnia-Herzegovina, Montenegro, Old Serbia, and Serbia? It would then be possible that the Dualism of the Monarchy would give place to new constitutional forms." *

Austria has persistently worked on behalf of the Germanic scheme for a roadway to the East, not necessarily in the interests of Germany except in so far as they coincided with her own policy, but on behalf of those of the Dual Monarchy itself. In doing this she has endeavoured, strenuously and imperiously, to break down the opposition of the Southern Slavs and to attach the Balkan States to the Austrian sphere of influence. The chief obstacle in the way, Serbia, was to be swept aside if the Serbian people would not accede to the Austrian demands; and, as we now know, plans were far advanced for this nefarious action when Italy firmly intervened and prevented the impending catastrophe. Surely in the present struggle the Allies should have foreseen and provided against such a contingency as the overwhelming of Serbia and the occupation of Serbian territory by the Germanic forces; but unfortunately steps were taken when it was too late and to-day Serbia lies under the heel of German domination. The one bright spot on the gloomy escutcheon is the presence of the Allies at Salonika.

* Quoted from an article by Charles Printa, " La Bosnia et l'Herzegovine devant la future Conférence," in *Questions Diplomatiques*, February 1, 1909.

CHAPTER XI

THE ADRIATIC GATEWAY

" THE Austrian littoral, with the southern portion of Dalmatia, Ragusa, Cattaro, Trieste, and Pola, should constitute, as Alsace-Lorraine, a *Reichsland* administered by an imperial military governor, territory which would serve as a base for the maritime power of Germany in the Adriatic and Mediterranean." * Thus writes a Pan-German author, expressing the desire of the greater portion of militant Germany for an extension of the Fatherland to the shores of the Adriatic. This idea of the ultimate absorption of Austrian Germany, with the additional Slovene territories that at present bar the way to the Adriatic, has so long been a commonplace of Pan-German policy that it is unnecessary to dwell upon this special aspect of the *Drang nach Osten*. Dr. Hasse, speaking on behalf of the party of which he is one of the principal leaders, has expressed the same idea. Trieste, he stated in 1895, " *is the commercial door opening on the East and the Suez Canal. Trieste should therefore become a German port.*" But this policy is in direct conflict with three national ideals—those of the Austrian Habsburgs, the Southern Slavs, and the irredentist Italians. In the present chapter attention will be devoted more especially to the interests of Italy and the vital necessity, from the Italian point of view, of preventing this extension of Germanic influence to the headwaters of the Adriatic.

In the cross-currents of national policy that gather in the Adriatic and make that sea one of the most important strategic avenues of the modern world there are many political and ethnic shoals and shallows that must be successfully navigated before a definite or even a temporary solution of the Adriatic question can be formulated. The conflict between

* " Oesterreiche Zusammenbruch und Wiederaufbrau," Munich, 1899.

the claims of Italy, Germany, Austria-Hungary, and Southern Slavdom with regard to the control of the Adriatic presents many difficult and delicate problems that cannot be settled on purely ethnographical, strategical, or geographical lines without creating fresh difficulties and sowing the seeds of new complications for the future. So far as Italy is concerned no solution will be satisfactory that does not remove the menace of Austrian and German sea-power, and render the eastern shores of the peninsula secure from maritime attack: so far as the Slavs are affected no solution can be acceptable that does not give them free and unimpeded access to the waters of the Adriatic: so far as the Germans are concerned no arrangement would be tolerated that does not leave a free and direct way through the Habsburg territories to the great commercial port of Trieste, which within recent years has assumed an importance with regard to the Fatherland that can only be likened to the position of Hamburg in the commercial system of modern Germany. With the last question the Allies have no concern. Germany and Austria-Hungary, having thrown down the gage of war, can only expect to be treated as they undoubtedly would have treated those nations unfortunate enough to stand across their path.

If we examine the present situation of the Adriatic we shall see that it represents to-day, as it did during the heyday of the Venetian domination, what must be regarded as the principal commercial avenue leading from Central Europe to the Middle and Far East. All other routes, whether through the Balkan Peninsula to Salonika and Constantinople, or from the mouth of the Elbe by the long sea route through the North Sea, the English Channel, and the Mediterranean, are of secondary importance, because the first connotes a long railway journey with expensive haulage, and the second, so long as British and French sea-power is predominant, necessitates a route that would always be open to interruption in the event of war, as well as a longer and more expensive journey. But the northern ports of the Adriatic, joined as they are by railways to the uplands of Central Europe, present an ideal outlet for the manufacturers of Bavaria, Saxony, Bohemia, and Austria, and offer the best opportunity for quick and rapid transit to the East.

Commercially the Adriatic is of vast importance to Germany and Austria, but as a highway for the countries immediately bordering it the sea is of unequal value. The geographical conditions along the western shores are unfavourable to commercial development. In the north the only natural port is Venice, which, by reason of its historical past and of its recent commercial revival, still retains its proud title of Queen of the Adriatic. In the south the only natural harbour is Brindisi, which, being far from the markets of Central Europe or Northern Italy and owing to its natural conditions, is much less favourably situated as a commercial port and owes its main importance as the place of departure for passenger steamships sailing to Greece, Egypt, and the East. The former, Venice, has been greatly improved during the last decade, and its trade has grown from 400,000 tons in the year 1880 to 3,000,000 tons in 1912, and its development will doubtless be greatly accelerated in the future. The latter can never hope to compete with Venice as a commercial outlet.

Between these two harbours there stretches the long eastern seaboard of Italy, a littoral over three hundred miles in extent, possessing but two comparatively unimportant ports, both small and artificial. Neither Ancona nor Bari, the latter of which has grown into a large town during recent years, can hope to serve the commercial needs of modern Italy. This absence of good harbours on the eastern side of a highly developed country like Italy, whilst being a distinct drawback to commercial development, presents a grievous strategical disadvantage that cannot altogether be overcome by the construction of artificial harbours and dockyards. It is for this latter reason that Italian statesmen have cast longing eyes on the opposite shores of the Adriatic, which presents so many strategical advantages to a maritime Power.

The eastern shores of the Adriatic are a direct contrast to the Italian littoral. From Trieste to Valona there are numerous and easily defended harbours, valuable not only for their strategical possibilities but also for the commercial outlets they offer for the products of the interior, whenever those distressful regions, the Balkan States, may be in a position to contribute their quota to the manufacturing industries of the world, or again able to export the agricultural riches for which they were once famed. From the important commercial port of Trieste in the north, the coveted mistress of the German expansionists, to the Straits of Otranto there is a succession of excellent harbours. Pola, Fiume, Sebenico, Spalato, Gravosa (the port of Ragusa), Cattaro, and Valona (Avlona), possess admirable and well-protected harbours, whilst many other ports, such as Antivari and Dulcigno (the seaports of Montenegro), and Durazzo, the port of Albania, with proper railway connexion with the interior, are capable of development. In fact the exploitation of the whole of this coast, with the exception of the ports of Trieste, Pola, and Fiume, which are already served by railways, depends in the main upon the construction of those necessary commercial feeders.

The eastern coast of the Adriatic, unlike the western littoral, is divided between several governments of different degrees of civilization and of varying stages of commercial development. It has been the aim of Germany and Austria to unite the whole of this region under one stable government, and the aim of Italy to prevent the accomplishment of this design, so fatal to the safety and development of the Italian kingdom. Whilst all three countries have insisted upon the preservation of the *status quo* they have done so not because they believed that a change was not desirable from the standpoint of their own immediate interests but because they feared that such a change would inevitably lead to the dreaded conflict of interests which would bring about the break-up of the Triple Alliance. Austria alone dared to make any decided move—and with fatal and irresistible results. Whilst Italy's interests, so far as the more southerly portions of the coast are concerned, were purely negative—that is, they consisted in preventing any other Power from establishing herself on the coast of Albania,* she had other and direct

* " I answered that in Albania," stated the Italian Minister for Foreign Affairs, Baron Sonnino, when telegraphing to the Italian Ambassador in Vienna on January 7, 1915, " I could perceive only one real interest for Italy, a negative one, consisting, that is to say, in our hindering any other Power from invading it, and that, for the rest, it was a region that had no attraction for us."

interests in the Istrian and Dalmatian seaboard, of unequal, but nevertheless great, value.

To the fate of Trieste and Istria, Italy can under no circumstances afford to be indifferent. Not only is Trieste very largely an Italian city, although of recent years the not inconsiderable Slav element has been increasing at a more rapid rate than the Italian population, but the coast intervening between Trieste and Pola is indisputably Italian. This coastal fringe is backed, however, by a hinterland inhabited by Croats and Slovenes, and does not extend into Dalmatia, although there also isolated Italian communities are to be found settled on the coast amidst a sea of Slavs. The essential characteristic of Trieste being Italian it has long been the aim of Austrian statesmen to counteract the Italian element by introducing German and Slav settlers whenever possible. The great prosperity of Trieste and the rapid growth of the city have afforded excellent opportunities for introducing Slovene workmen. Between 1900 and 1910 the Slavonic population of Trieste increased by no less than 130 per cent.[*] and there are at the present time " nearly 60,000 highly organized and nationally conscious Slovenes within its gates." [†]

Although the population of Trieste is predominatingly Italian, the Italian element has nevertheless had a stiff fight to maintain its position, and in some cases, owing to the attitude of the Austrian Government, it has actually been ousted by the new Slovene element, who, imported by the Government, has more than made good its claim to share in the municipal administration. Some instructive figures on this point are given in an article in the *Fortnightly Review*,[‡] from which it appears that the Slav officials were, previous to the war, rapidly driving the Italians from municipal posts. Thus of 828 employees at the State railway station only 70 were Italians; of 358 postmen but 95 were Italians; of 500 Custom House officers but 145 were Italians; whilst of 4600 State officials in the city 3700 were Slavs. This

[*] " L'Italia d'Oltre Confine—Le Provincie Italiane d'Austria," by Virginio Gayda, 1914.
[†] " The Balkans, Italy, and the Adriatic," by R. W. Seton-Watson, 1915, p. 57.
[‡] " Italia Irredenta," by " Politicus," *Fortnightly Review*, February 1915.

suppression of the Italian element is directly in accordance with the Austrian policy of gradually pushing the Italians across the frontier, and by this means ending the question of Italia Irredenta. By favouring the Slovene element at the expense of the Italians the Austrian Government have endeavoured to rally to their support—especially in the event of a conflict with the Southern Slavs—this small but important section of Slavdom which differs considerably from the Croats and Serbs. On the other hand, the large number of Slovenes in Trieste has encouraged the Southern Slav party to put forward a claim to the inclusion of the city in the new Jugo-Slav kingdom.

To understand the position aright some attention must be devoted to the Slovene branch of the Southern Slav family. Through the territory they occupy pass the two easiest and most direct routes from Central Europe to the Mediterranean, viz. the route from Munich to Trieste via Salzburg and the route from Vienna to Trieste via Graz. The Slovenes, like the Serbs, stand directly across the path to the East, and whilst the Germans have been continuously attempting to secure the economic control of the Slovene lands the Austrians, on the other hand, have not been averse from allowing the Slovenes more liberty than has been given to other Slav peoples—the Slovenes, unlike the Croats, who are subject to Hungary, being under direct Austrian control.* Slovenia as the junction of economic arteries occupies a decisive position in the Pan-German plan, whilst Trieste itself has been termed by no less an authority than Bismarck " the point of the German sword."

The lands inhabited by the Slovenes include Carniola, Gorizia-Gradiska, Southern Carinthia, Styria, as well as the north-western portion of Istria and the country around Trieste. On the north the German rampart extends to the River Drave, whilst an advance guard of Germanism is settled around Gottschee and considerable numbers of Germans, not less than eleven thousand, form a small colony in Trieste. The people who thus stop the German advance to the Adriatic are numerically weak and do not exceed a total of 1,278,000, but they form a compact and distinct unit and do not constitute

* With the exception of about one hundred thousand in Western Hungary.

ethnic islands amongst a German or Magyar population. They are an isolated branch of the Southern Slav family, speaking a dialect distinctly different from Southern Slav, and some years ago it was by no means certain that in the event of the break-up of the Austrian Empire that they would have elected to join the Southern Slav kingdom. Within recent years, however, they have become more and more indentified with the Southern Slav ideal, and there can now be no doubt that they form a strong bulwark flanking the western borders of Slavdom and ready to support the plans of the Southern Slav leaders. Under the influence of the celebrated Bishop Strossmayer (1815–1905), who was the first national leader to break down the artificial barriers between the Serbs and Croats, the Slovenes, in common with the two other branches of the Southern Slavs, began to look forward to a renewal of the Southern Slav kingdom. As the leader in every intellectual enterprise and the founder of the Croatian University, Strossmayer succeeded in stemming the tide of Germanism and in preventing the complete Magyarization of his country, and by his vigorous and enlightened nationalism he enlisted the interests of Europe in the claims of his countrymen to recognition. His influence was such that the Slovenes were gradually drawn towards the policy of which he was the embodiment, and away from the particularist nationalism for which they had hitherto stood. They realized that they would not be strong enough to stand alone and that their position upon the Pan-German road rendered their future a matter of vital concern both to the Italians, the Serbs, and above all to the Austro-Germans and Germans.

The extremists of Italia Irredenta claim that Trieste should be annexed to Italy. Whilst there are obvious objections to this course, not the least of which is the fact that Trieste is entirely dependent upon the German and Slav hinterland for its trade, Italy does not possess any historical grounds for claiming the city, which has been a possession of the House of Habsburg since the year 1386. As Mr. Seton-Watson says, " any attempt to include Trieste within the tariff system of the kingdom of Italy would produce fatal results, and the obvious solution is to proclaim the city as a free commercial port." As a matter of fact this was the proposal submitted to Austria-Hungary before Italy entered upon the war and summarily rejected by the Vienna Government. In Article III of the demands formulated by Baron Sonnino it was stipulated that "the city of Trieste with its territory ... is to be constituted an autonomous and independent State in all that regards its internal, military, legislative, financial, and administrative policies, and Austria-Hungary shall renounce all sovereignty over it. It is to remain a free port."

Upon the question of Dalmatia it is not necessary to enter at any length, because whilst the historical claims of Italy to this portion of the Austro-Hungarian Empire rest upon the acknowledged supremacy of the Venetian Republic, of which modern Italy is the heir, Italians have practically no racial claims to the possession of Dalmatia. Whilst Italians inhabit the coastal towns they are an insignificant minority in the country at large. Educated Dalmatian Slavs still speak Italian as a second language, as educated Greeks do in the Ionian Islands, but the current speech of the shops, streets, and even the quays, and the exclusive speech of the countryside is the native South Slavonic,[*] and in Dalmatia, which is Slav and has been so for over a thousand years, Italy has no ethnographic claims whatever.[†]

But if Italy has no special grounds for claiming sovereignty over Dalmatia itself she has, nevertheless, imperious reasons for exercising control over the numerous islands that exist off the Dalmatian coast—reasons almost as cogent as those which compelled the occupation of Valona at the commencement of the war. Italy cannot afford to watch the continuous growth of an Austro-German navy sheltering in numerous harbours along the Adriatic and ready to sally forth in some future war; and for that reason the possession of the archipelago of Curzola was insisted upon by the Italian Government as one of the payments for its continued neutrality. The demand naturally met with a blunt refusal for, as Baron Burian stated to the Italian Ambassador, "the islands of Curzolari, which dominate Dalmatia, would render Italy mistress of those regions, whilst the Adriatic would become

[*] "Nationality and the War," by Arnold J. Toynbee, 1915, p. 249.
[†] Seton-Watson, *op. cit.*, p. 61.

an Italian sea from the moment that Italy retained possession of Valona."

If Italy's position with regard to Trieste and the Dalmatian seaboard tends to the direct negation of Germanic interests in these regions her attitude with regard to the Trentino is a purely Austrian affair. No direct Pan-German interest would be affected by the return of this district to the kingdom of Italy, for although the retention of this portion of the Southern Tyrol was due to strategical reasons and was primarily intended to expose the plains of Northern Italy to sudden attack, the occupation of the Trentino by Italy would not subject Austro-German territory to the same danger. In the Trentino, Austria has for many years pursued a policy of oppression towards the Italians. As she strived to denationalize the Italians in Trieste by the introduction of a strong Slovene element, so in the Trentino she has endeavoured to destroy the Italian elements by setting against them the Germans. But the solid mass of nearly four hundred thousand Italians in the Trentino has on the whole been able to hold its own, and unlike the Italians in Trieste has not seen the Trentino invaded by the introduction of large numbers of foreign settlers. Pan-German policy has not troubled about the Trentino, which does not, like Slovenia or Serbia, stand across the path to empire.

To understand aright Italian aspirations with regard to Italia Irredenta (unredeemed Italy) and the antagonism of Italian statesmen towards Pan-Germanism three factors must be borne in mind. The first is that since modern Italy awoke to full national consciousness and took her rightful place amongst the Great Powers of Europe the Italian people, realizing the importance of sea-power for a country situated like their own, recognized that they could not afford to allow the Adriatic to become a German sea, and that in this respect their national policy clashed with the avowed objects of the Pan-German Party. The second is that whilst they realized that owing to the peculiar political conditions brought about by the Bismarckian policy of creating discord between France and Italy on the one hand, and between France and Great Britain on the other, and knew that only a close alliance with Austria-Hungary and Germany could prevent the complete isolation of their country, they instinctively felt that such an alliance could only be of a temporary nature so long as the outstanding questions with regard to the Italian populations in Austria remained unsettled. The third is that Italian interests in Albania, both strategic and commercial, were as directly antagonistic to the extension of German influence in this region as they were opposed to the growth of Austrian influence in Bosnia-Herzegovina or to the erection of a strong Slavonic State on the opposite littoral. The relations between Germany and Italy were tempered, therefore, by the reflection that the two Powers could only remain on cordial terms so long as Germany was not opposed to the growth of Italian influence in the Adriatic regions. With regard to Austria, the attitude of Italy could only remain neutral so long as that country refrained from an active policy of expansion towards Salonika. These two primary conditions having been violated, Italy naturally and inevitably gravitated towards the Entente, whose objects were also to checkmate Austro-German ambitions in the Near East.

The results of the Second Balkan War had roused Italy to a realization of the dangers that threatened her owing to the rapid growth of the Slav power, but the erection of an " independent " Albania, although acceptable to Italy, was in reality, owing to the extension of Austro-German interests in the new *opéra-bouffe* State, far more a cause of disquiet than the possible appearance of Serbia upon the Adriatic coast. " Austria or Germany (it hardly matters which)," wrote M. Loiseau, " once established at Valona would strictly limit Italy to the Western Mediterranean and would mean the practical investment of Italy by sea as well as by land by the two allies of whom she is merely the satellite : further, it would mean the commercial ruin of the whole Adriatic coast of the kingdom, rendered incapable of fighting against German influence already so menacing to Italian commerce." *

The gradual cooling of Italy towards the Triple Alliance forms an interesting study in the mutability of all alliances. Without unnecessarily trespassing upon the province of the historian it may be stated that Italy was deliberately thrust

* Loiseau's " L'Equilibre adriatique."

towards the Triple Alliance by Bismarck when he permitted France a free hand in Tunis, a country in which Italy had peculiar commercial and national interests and which she had regarded as marked out for her own activities. The bitterness of feeling engendered by the French occupation of Tunis, coupled with the friction caused by the open support of the Vatican by France, who up to the year 1870 had kept a French garrison in Rome, alienated two nations who should have worked in complete harmony in the Mediterranean. Whilst Napoleon III had been directly instrumental in securing the liberation of Italy from the hateful system imposed upon her by the policy of Metternich, the French Emperor had merely used the kingdom for his own purposes against Austria, and in spite of his eloquent panegyrics on the claims of nationality he had no intention of erecting on the southern borders of France a strong national State that might at some future time become a direct menace to French influence in the Mediterranean. Such support as he gave towards the liberation of Italy was amply rewarded when he demanded and obtained as his price the province of Savoy and the district of Nice. By preventing the final consummation of Italian unity he secured the passive dislike of the makers of modern Italy, Garibaldi, Mazzini, Cavour, and finally Crispi, who were distrustful of the Emperor's policy.

The subsequent extension of French colonialism along the African shores of the Mediterranean and the growth of French naval power removed all cause for gratitude and convinced Italian statesmen that they had more to gain by coming to an understanding with Bismarck than remaining on good terms with France. The extension of French influence in the Mediterranean was particularly galling to Italians because they had been encouraged to look forward to the time when united Italy, as the central Power in that sea, would be in a position to dominate and control not only the North African littoral but the adjacent Adriatic coast and the Ægean Sea as well. Bismarck had directly encouraged Italian statesmen in this attitude. On one occasion he had written to Mazzini that " Italy and France cannot be associated for their common benefit in the Mediterranean. That sea is an inheritance which it is impossible to divide between relations. The empire of the Mediterranean unquestionably belongs to Italy, who possesses on that sea coasts twice as extensive as France. Marseilles and Toulon cannot be compared with Genoa, Leghorn, Naples, Palermo, Ancona, Venice, and Trieste. The empire of the Mediterranean must be the constant preoccupation of Italy, the fundamental thought of the Florentine Cabinet." * It was of course Bismarck's constant preoccupation to keep Italy and France apart, and only too well did he play the cards of providence.

So far as Italy is concerned it was Francesco Crispi, the one considerable statesman whom Italy produced since the formation of the kingdom, who laid the foundations of the Triple Alliance. Born of mixed Albanian and Sicilian descent, Crispi was at first one of the most violent members of the Republican Party; but in 1864 he definitely separated himself from Mazzini and adopted the more sane and statesmanlike policy of the Monarchical Party. In 1877 he was invited by the King, Victor Emmanuel, to proceed on a secret mission to the Courts of Europe, when he suggested to Bismarck an alliance with Germany in the event of a Franco-Italian war, but met with a definite refusal in attempting to obtain the support of Germany against Austrian pretensions in the Adriatic. The time had not yet come for Italy to be caught in the Bismarckian net.

Two years later Germany and Austria formed a defensive alliance against a possible attack by Russia on either nation, and in 1882, Tunis having been annexed by France,† Italy took the momentous step of joining the league which thus became the Triple Alliance and was renewed under different conditions from time to time.

The Triple Alliance was naturally advantageous to all three partners, but whilst to Germany and Austria it offered security against an attack by Russia, to Italy it was a matter of life or death. The new kingdom was completely isolated in Europe and could only secure immunity from attack by coming to an arrangement with one of her potential enemies. It is not necessary to trace the successive stages of the Alliance.

* "Politica segreta Italiana," by Diamilla Mulla, Turin, 1881.
† Crispi's saying, "Tunisia is an Italian colony guarded by French soldiers," should be borne in mind.

So long as the three partners did not violate its underlying but well understood principles it served its purpose; but the growth of Pan-Germanism and the inordinate ambitions of German statesmen, coupled with the gradual but persistent extension of Austrian influence in the Adriatic, alarmed Italian statesmen, led them to review the European situation in order to seek for compensating advantages elsewhere, and brought about a revival of the always present but frequently slumbering irredentist movement aimed against the Austrian Empire. Italy's hatred of Austria was still vigorous, and the advance of Austria in the Balkans, the corresponding increase in her naval power, the only too obvious advantage of Austria securing control of the Adriatic and Ægean, and the ill-treatment accorded to Italian subjects in the Austrian Empire, could not fail to awake in the minds of the Italians desires hitherto repressed but now rendered vigorous by the illicit violation of the spirit of compromise embodied in the provisions of the Triple Alliance.

The annexation of Bosnia, which came as an abrupt and convincing proof that the sanctity of treaties was no longer regarded as binding by Austrian statesmen, compelled all Italians to recognize that their country was being treated with contemptuous indifference by at least one of the parties to the Alliance. It directly led to the counter-move by Italy in Northern Africa, and in a non-official sense to a great extension of the irredentist movement in and beyond the borders of the kingdom. Whilst Austria had been busy pushing her influence along the eastern shores of the Adriatic, extending her commercial influence through the agency of the Austrian Lloyd Company and her political influence with the aid of Austrian Franciscans who were utilized to induce Austrian sympathies amongst the rising generation, Italy had not been idle. In Albania, with which close relations had existed for generations, Italian schools were established and the Italian spirit was further disseminated by the many Albanians who returned from Italy after having been educated in the Italian universities. Commercially, Italian influence was spread by the Pughia Steamship Line and the appointment of new Consular agents. But politically it was furthered by the propagandist societies, which were founded on the lines of the various Pan-German societies and were largely designed to meet and counteract Austrian and German propaganda along the Adriatic.

Within Italy itself the greatest of these societies is the Societa Nazionale Dante Alighieri, which, although only founded in 1889, had nearly 60,000 members in the year 1911, with 208 branches in Italy and 72 branches abroad. The aim of this society, which is expressly concerned with the condition of Italians beyond the borders, is to teach and disperse the Italian language and culture in all parts of the world, to counteract the work of other societies engaged in similar operations in countries where Italians are settled, and to maintain and subsidize numerous schools in the Levant, North Africa, and America.* The Societa Nazionale Dante has not only carried on a most vigorous propaganda but it has been honoured by the presidency of such well-known men as Pasquale Villari, Ruggero Bonghi, and Paolo Boselli, and has certainly been one of the main agencies in keeping before the Italian public the claims of their expatriated countrymen. In addition to this society the numerous Societas di Beneficenza, which are established in every place where Italians are settled, and the various missionary bodies, such as the Associazione Nazionale per Soccorrare i Missionari Italiani, whose work is specially limited to the Mediterranean regions, have been active in the support of Italian policy and Italian culture ; whilst in Italia Irredenta, the Lega Nazionale, established in 1890, has been extremely active in combating Slovene and German influences. In 1911 this society had a membership of over 42,000, maintained or subsidized 210 schools, and supported 153 libraries and kindred institutions.† All these societies were galvanized into life by the growing Austrian and German menace and were direct vehicles for the expression of Italian opinion. Their influence was not, like that of the Pan-German bodies in Germany, sufficient to control the course of Italian policy, but it nevertheless clearly indicated the revival of Irredentism and defined the attitude of a fully representative section of the Italian people towards their two partners in the Triple Alliance.

* *See* the " Anuario " issued by the Italian Colonial Institute, 1911.
† " Italia Irredenta," *Fortnightly Review*, February 1915, p. 266.

The final rupture with the Germanic Powers has been fully dealt with in other books, but the main demands of Italy may here be briefly indicated. As has been seen, Italy was chiefly concerned with the strategic position in the Adriatic and with the status and condition of her co-nationals in Trieste, Istria, and the Trentino. Her occupation of Valona (December 25, 1914) was a masterly stroke of policy, which clearly indicated that the Italian Government was determined to prevent, if possible, the accomplishment of the German design for predominance in the Adriatic, and demonstrated its intention to hold the neck of that sea against the Germanic Powers. From that moment events in Italy moved rapidly towards the abandonment of the unreal and unproductive neutrality from which the country as a whole had become thoroughly averse. The brilliant efforts of Gabriele D'Annunzio to rouse his countrymen to an appreciation of the fact that the supreme hour for Italy had at length arrived, seconded by the fierce enthusiasm of hundreds of orators and supported by the magic name of Garibaldi, struck a chord that met with an instant response.

A wave of enthusiasm swept over the kingdom which can only be compared with the stirring times that preceded the triumph of the House of Savoy forty-five years earlier. Austria again became the national enemy. " It is absolutely necessary," said D'Annunzio, " that this menacing Power should be destroyed and rendered for ever impotent and inert. Latin culture is indispensable to all that is grand and beautiful. And in that glorious sea where Greece once shone in a world of beauty and Rome spake in accents of wisdom and justice the advent of the Germans is a thing that is inconceivable. Italy has a higher mission in life than to become the prey of these insensate vultures. Italians! each day that passes is a day of glory lost ! "

In a last endeavour to prevent the national enthusiasm from sweeping Italy to the gates of the Adriatic, Prince von Bülow, the ablest of German diplomatists, whose cold and calculating finesse was designed to chill the warmest enthusiasms, was sent as special Ambassador to the Quirinal, having expressed the opinion that " Italy will be ruined if Pan-Slavism triumphs," and declaring that her " abandonment of her old-time allies in the present situation would be an unparalled violation of international law, a tremendous mistake, and a crime."

In the meantime Baron Sonnino, the Minister for Foreign Affairs, carried on the prolonged negotiations with the Austrian Foreign Office. On December 9, 1914, he called the attention of the Austrian Government to the fact that the advance of Austria-Hungary into Serbia constituted " a fact which cannot avoid becoming the subject of examination by the Italian and Austro-Hungarian Governments on the basis of the stipulations contained in Article VII of the Triple Alliance," which enacted that " in the case of even temporary occupations " the Austro-Hungarian Government was bound to come to an agreement with Italy and also to grant compensations. " The Imperial and Royal Governments," he stated, " should therefore have consulted us before causing its army to cross the Serbian frontier."

The Austro-Hungarian Government replied by protesting against the Italian occupation of the Dodecanesian Islands, which had been seized by Italy during the war with Turkey and still remained in her possession, and recalling the conduct of Italy on that occasion.

The Italian demands were the subject of a long correspondence, and on February 12 Baron Sonnino, voicing the national opinion that the destruction of Serbia could not be tolerated by the Italian people, addressed a warning to Austria to the effect that any new military action undertaken in the Balkans against Serbia or Montenegro, without previous agreement with Italy, would be considered as an infringement of Article VII of the Alliance and would inevitably lead to grave consequences for which the Italian Government would not be held responsible. The result of this strong action was to secure a temporary respite for Serbia from the attack which was then being planned with the assistance of Germany. The diplomatic intervention of Italy saved the Serbs for the time being.

Finally on March 20 Prince von Bülow stated that " in pursuance of instructions from the Chancellor, Bethmann-Hollweg, after audience with the Emperor William, the Imperial German Government offers to Italy a full and complete guarantee that the agreement to be concluded between Italy and Austria-Hungary should be faithfully and loyally given effect to as soon as peace should be concluded."

But Italian statesmen placed no reliance on either German or Austrian "guarantees," and the final demands of the Italian Government were formulated in a telegram sent on April 8, 1915. These conditions included the cession of the Trentino, with the frontiers which became those of the Italian kingdom in 1811 after the Treaty of Paris in the preceding year; the correction of the eastern frontier so as to bring the cities of Gradisca and Gorizia within the ceded territory; the constitution of Trieste as an autonomous and independent State; the cession of the archipelago of Curzola on the Dalmatian coast; and the recognition of Italy's full sovereignty over Valona and its hinterland. Italy further demanded that Austria-Hungary should " cease completely to interest herself in Albania as comprised within the frontiers traced by the Conference of London," and in return for these concessions promised to maintain complete neutrality throughout the war and to pay an indemnity of £8,000,000 as compensation for Government property situated in the disputed territories.

These terms were not acceptable to the Austrian Government. On May 3, Baron Sonnino forwarded to Vienna a formal denunciation of the Italo-Austrian Alliance, which resulted in the offer of fresh concessions by Baron Burian, the nominee of Count Tisza and of the Hungarian interest, who had succeeded Count Berchtold as Foreign Secretary. These proposals were circulated in Italy as the basis of a new treaty, and a last attempt was made by the Austrophile Party to prevent a declaration of war by undermining the Government of Signor Salandra. The ex-Premier, Signor Giolitti, again appeared at the head of the Neutralists, but on May 13 Signor Salandra resigned, an acute crisis intervened, the King refused to accept the Premier's resignation, and the Chambers, by an overwhelming majority, gave the Government extraordinary powers in the event of war. The final breach occurred on May 19, when Italy declared war on Austria and entered the European struggle on the side of the Allies.

CHAPTER XII

GERMANY AND RUMANIA

RUMANIA, which at present forms the buffer State between Russia and the Central Powers, has long been of peculiar interest to the Germans because it is in a very real sense a strategic outpost of *Deutschthum* in the Near East. Although the rampart of the Carpathians pushes a great bastion into the country, sharply dividing the Rumanian lowlands from Transylvania, the great Hungarian plain and the countries of the Lower Danube are linked together by the celebrated Iron Gates, a narrow waterway where the Danube rushes through a constricted passage on its way to the sea.

Among the claims advanced by the Germans none has been more persistently put forward than the demand that Germans should exercise control over the whole course of the rivers rising in the sacred soil of the Fatherland. As has been pointed out, the great strategist von Moltke demonstrated, long before Pan-Germanism had become the chief Teutonic creed, the desirability of Germany's possessing the mouths of her rivers. This idea, industriously propagated during the intervening years, has since become an obsession of the German people.

The Danube, sweeping on its majestic course from Bavaria, through Upper and Lower Austria and crossing the Hungarian plain, at length pierces the mountains by a gap in the Transylvanian Alps, enters the Balkan peninsula, where it forms the political boundary between Serbia and Bulgaria on the southern side and Rumania on the northern side, and then, in the neighbourhood of Silistria, turns abruptly northward, stopped by the rising lands of the Dobruja,* and flows parallel with the

* This district, mainly inhabited by Turks with a sprinkling of Bulgarians, was assigned to Rumania in 1878 as compensation for the seizure of Bessarabia by Russia.

sea, to fall eventually into the Euxine by three well-defined mouths. Along the northern side of the Danube at this point the Russian territory of Bessarabia, secured to her by the Treaty of Berlin, stretches as the advance guard of the Slav movement towards Constantinople, whilst two of the mouths of this great estuary, the St. George's and Sulina mouths, are entirely within Rumanian territory.

It has been a persistent aim of German policy, by means of peaceful penetration in the economic sphere and through the agency of emigration directed towards the sparsely peopled lands of the Danubian estuary, to secure political influence in this region; but although Rumania for many years was ruled by a sovereign of German ancestry, who might have been expected to favour the plans of his countrymen, German policy has not met with the decisive success that had been expected in this quarter. A number of factors militated against the complete realization of the German plans.

In the first place the relations between Bismarck and the King of Rumania were such that neither worked wholeheartedly in pursuance of the Germanic ideal in the Near East, for although the Chancellor did not lose sight of the ultimate aim of German policy he was in no hurry to force the pace. Bismarck, exercising the political caution for which he was famous, never co-operated actively and openly in the movement for the Teutonic advance towards the Black Sea and was resolutely opposed to any premature adventure in this direction; whilst King Charles, although of Hohenzollern blood, knew that his dynastic and personal interests were too deeply concerned with the maintenance of the political and economic independence of his adopted country to permit of any open co-operation with Germany which might lead to domestic upheavals within his Rumanian territories. Although he may have spoken of himself as a solitary outpost of Teutonism placed on the frontiers of Slavdom, he never regarded himself as an agent of Pan-Germanism but rather as an upholder of Western culture in a backward land. Rumania was his family domain—not the antechamber of any future Germanic empire.

The proximity of Russia compelled a cautious and diplomatic policy, whilst French influence, always strong with a semi-Latin race, was sufficiently powerful to exercise a considerable and steadying attraction over the Rumanian people. But primarily German influence, which became so strong in other parts of the Balkan Peninsula and eventually succeeded in drawing Rumania within the German political orbit, was kept at bay and moderated by the sturdy and independent spirit of nationality manifested by the subjects of the new kingdom. Having clearly defined ambitions, expansive and intensive, they were sufficiently strong to counteract any attempt on the part of Germany to exercise full political and economic control. The Germans so far as they influenced Rumania did so on sufferance and as a counterpoise to Russia.

In order to appreciate correctly the peculiar and almost unique position of Rumania, both at the present time and during the last fifty years, an acquaintance with recent Rumanian history is requisite. Into the question of the origins of the Rumanians it is not necessary to enter. They are to-day living where fifteen centuries ago their immediate ancestors were settled, and no people, during the long course of their troubled history, has been able to destroy the essential unity of the Rumanian nation. "'The water passes, the stones remain,' and the hordes of the migration period, detached from their native soil, disappeared as mist before the sun. But the native Roman element (the basis of the present nation) bent their heads while the storm passed over them, clinging to the old places until the advent of better days, when they were able to stand up and stretch their limbs." * For this reason the strongly developed Rumanian nationality has more or less successfully withstood Teutonic intrigue, whilst owing to the fact that a greater Rumania exists beyond the boundaries of the present kingdom, both in Russia and in Austria-Hungary, the intensive nationalism of the Rumanian people has been strengthened by dreams of national expansion—whenever the time shall arrive for decisive action.

When the Ottoman flood swept on its devastating course through South-Eastern Europe the Rumanians, in common with the other Balkan peoples, fell under Turkish domination, but they always retained a measure of independence under their

* Quoted by M. D. Mitrany, in the excellent Oxford pamphlet on Rumania, from "Über den Ursprung der Rumänen," by Traugott Tamm, 1891.

own princes.* Unlike the Bulgarians, they never suffered the Ottoman yoke to be fixed firmly to their shoulders, and with the aid of Russia they managed to preserve their precarious position as tributary States on the outskirts of the Turkish Empire. With the increase of Russian power a new danger threatened the provinces of Moldavia and Wallachia, the modern Rumania, for in the long conflict between the Turk and the Muscovite Rumania formed a debatable ground, sometimes under the control of the one, sometimes under the domination of the other; as Russia, continuously advancing on her way to the Bosphorus, looked upon Rumania as the most convenient stepping-stone towards Constantinople.

For centuries Russia has been trying to reach the open sea and has unceasingly endeavoured to acquire control of the narrows which connect the Black Sea with the Mediterranean, or at least to secure free egress into European waters. Hence the position of Rumania, as the buffer State between Muscovite ambition and Turkish dominion and the eventual goal of the Teutonic advance, was most precarious should the balance of power in Europe become seriously affected either by the renaissance of a great Central European Power or by the unchecked growth of the Russian Empire. With the elimination of Turkey as a serious factor in the year 1878 the position of Rumania, as the meeting-place of two opposing ideals, was not affected, and it became necessary to choose definitely which of the two opposing interests she should adopt. Leading Rumanians, and especially King Charles, became convinced that the vaulting ambitions of Russia could only be successfully opposed by an alliance with the two Germanic Powers; for the nearer and more pressing danger could best be avoided by strong and resolute action directed against the Muscovite movement.

"Owing to her geographical position," wrote the King to Prince Bismarck in March 1880, "Rumania is destined to play an important part in the settlement of the Eastern question, and as she is the defender of the mouths of the Danube, the greatest German river, German and Rumanian interests tend

---

* Except during the Phanariot period in the eighteenth century, when the Greeks inhabiting the quarter of Phanar at Constantinople acquired enormous influence and eventually imposed upon the Rumanians princes of Greek blood.

to become closely associated. We sincerely desire to support the interests of Germany, especially as such action is in harmony with our economic development. Consequently it will be the aim of my Government carefully to promote the valuable relations with the German Empire, and I hope that my country may count upon the benevolent support of Germany in all future contingencies." A month later Count Andrassy, in writing to King Charles, concisely expressed the then aim of Austrian policy with regard to Rumania. " I am convinced," he wrote, " that the most important interests of Austria-Hungary and of Rumania are identical. In my opinion Rumania and Austria-Hungary are, in their own interest and in that of Europe, obliged to form an effective barrier against the Slavonization of Eastern Europe. It is their common task to prevent the union of the Northern and Southern Slavs. An abandonment of that policy would lead to many perils and eventually to Rumania's disappearance. The interests of Austria-Hungary and of Rumania are identical." It was therefore this necessity for preserving the independence of Rumania which compelled her statesmen to choose between Russian domination and a temporary alliance with the Central Powers, so as to preserve in the Near East a balance of power which would secure the country against foreign control. In this respect Rumania has played a singularly able and perhaps decisive part.

With the outbreak of the revolutionary movement which in the year 1848 threatened to overturn the existing political order in Europe, there arose a new intellectual revival in the Danubian principalities and a reawakening of national consciousness. This revival of racialism was still further increased when after the Crimean War the southern part of Bessarabia, then under Russian control, was added to Moldavia, whilst the question of union between the two provinces still under Turkish suzerainty was mooted. That event, in spite of the vigorous opposition of Austria and Turkey, was finally brought about by the spirited action of the Rumanians themselves, who, realizing that the Powers were hopelessly divided upon the subject, took the patriotic step of electing Colonel Alexander John Cuza prince both of Moldavia and Wallachia—a masterly stroke of policy which was recognized by the Porte in 1861, when the two principalities were given a common name and a common Government. With that date the modern history of Rumania commences.

The rule of Cuza was, however, of short duration owing to internal troubles brought about by the very reforms which were to place Rumania amongst the more progressive countries. French influence, which was then considerable, had been responsible for a reorganization of the administration, for the introduction of political and educational reforms, and for a new national and spiritual revival. But vested interests and the opposition engendered by all such movements proved too strong for a prince whose following was confined to the more liberal elements of the population, and on February 23, 1866, Cuza was forced to abdicate.* The National Assembly then proceeded to the election of a new ruler, and the desire was generally expressed that none but a prince of royal blood should be called to preside over the destinies of the Rumanian people. In accordance with the French leanings of the Assembly the choice fell upon Count Philip of Flanders, brother of the King of the Belgians and grandson of Louis Philippe, but owing to the opposition of France and Russia Count Philip declined the offer, and when French circles put forward the candidature of Prince Charles of Hohenzollern, who was also supported by Great Britain, a plebiscite overwhelmingly confirmed that choice. Nevertheless the International Conference which had met in Paris did not acquiesce in the selection, and it became necessary for the new candidate to proceed with extreme caution. Bismarck, who had been appealed to, thought that the Hohenzollern prince might try the venture as he would always find it " a pleasant remembrance," † and on the whole the position was not very hopeful.

Having crossed Austria, which was then on the point of war with Prussia, incognito, the new Hohenzollern vassal and dependent of the Sultan, who travelled in the second whilst his suite went in the first class, descended the Danube on an Austrian steamer and reached Bukarest on May 23, 1866.

* Cuza, who had adopted the title of Alexander I, Prince of Rumania, was obliged to rule autocratically owing to perpetual conflicts with the Assembly, and was finally surprised by a party of conspirators in his sleeping apartment and forced to abdicate.

† See " The Near East from Within," 1915, p. 124.

Although much capital was made out of the connexion between the two branches of the Hohenzollerns and the close and amicable relations which were supposed to exist between them, the choice of the Rumanians was nevertheless a wise one, because in reality there existed little save in name between the Sigmaringen and Brandenburg branches of the family, and Prince Charles himself was by nature and training unlikely to support German pretensions unreservedly. His family were Catholics and partly of French extraction, being related to the Murat-Bonapartes; whilst the Imperial family were Lutheran and almost purely Teutonic.*

The position of the new sovereign of a State exposed to such constant external and internal perils was not exactly enviable. Only a man of considerable attainments and of more than ordinary strength of character should have attempted the task, and Prince Charles, as he then was, showed himself perfectly able to reconcile the conflicting interests with which he was confronted and to counteract the dangerous intrigues

* The following pedigree clearly shows the close connexion between the late King of Rumania and the Murats and Beauharnais:

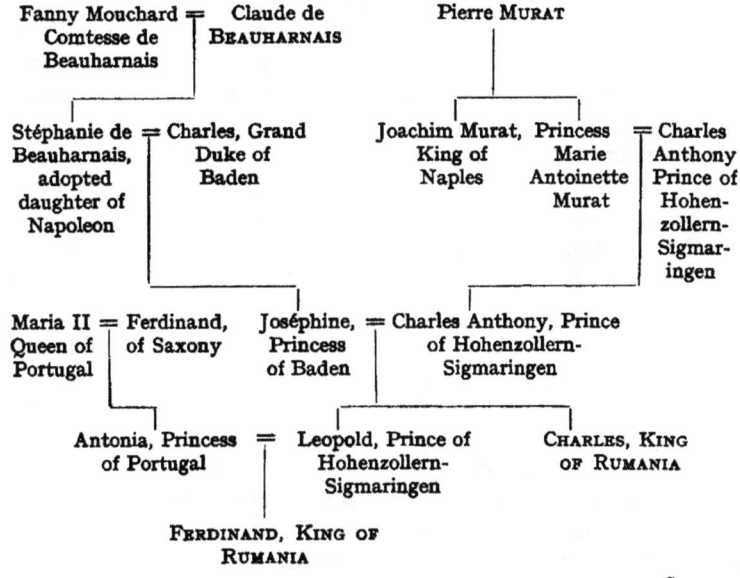

Fanny Mouchard = Claude de BEAUHARNAIS   Pierre MURAT

Stéphanie de Beauharnais, adopted daughter of Napoleon = Charles, Grand Duke of Baden

Joachim Murat, King of Naples — Princess Marie Antoinette Murat = Charles Anthony Prince of Hohenzollern-Sigmaringen

Maria II Queen of Portugal = Ferdinand of Saxony

Joséphine, Princess of Baden = Charles Anthony, Prince of Hohenzollern-Sigmaringen

Antonia, Princess of Portugal = Leopold, Prince of Hohenzollern-Sigmaringen

CHARLES, KING OF RUMANIA

FERDINAND, KING OF RUMANIA

that threatened the stability and independence of his kingdom. He acted with firmness and decision. The position that he occupied called for the exercise of talents of no common order, particularly as his territory was still under the nominal suzerainty of the Sultan. It was King Charles's ambition to get rid of the Ottoman control, and when during the Russo-Turkish War the collapse of Russia seemed imminent, it was the intervention of Rumania which secured not only the independence of his adopted country but also aided in the subsequent Russian triumph.

Although political exigencies attracted Rumania to the German sphere, other factors scarcely less powerful were sowing discord between the new kingdom and the Central Powers. The consequence of the seizure by Russia of Bessarabia in 1878 had been to alienate Russians and Rumanians and to persuade the latter that the chief enemy to be feared was the empire lying beyond the River Pruth. The Austro-Germans were not slow in taking advantage of this situation. Regarding the country as a valuable bulwark against the encroachments of Slavdom, the two Empires sought to direct Rumanian foreign policy into avenues favourable to themselves, and Bukarest became one of the most important centres of Teutonic policy. The ablest diplomatists were sent to the Rumanian capital. Both Prince von Bülow and Herr von Kiderlen-Waechter, who subsequently directed German foreign policy, and Counts Aehrenthal and Goluchowski represented their respective countries in the Danubian kingdom, and Rumania was easily persuaded to regard the two Empires as her natural protectors against Russian intrigue.

The adhesion of Rumania to the Triple Alliance—an event which took place in the year 1896—was the greatest triumph secured by German policy and marked the climax of many years of industrious and secret preparation. Attached as she had become to Germany by economic, financial, and military bonds, Rumania was unable to resist, even if she would, the rough embraces of her clumsy wooers; but, like Italy, submitted with the full intention of regaining her own liberty of action whenever the time should seem most opportune.

In the economic sphere Rumania had gradually become a German domain. Germans flocked to Bukarest and obtained a strong hold over Rumanian industries.* Under their influence industrial, commercial, and mineral concessions were given to German houses, who soon monopolized the greater part of the economic transactions of the kingdom. "One might say, in fact," states a writer in *Questions Diplomatiques*,† " that from the economic point of view Rumania is a dependency of Germany." ‡ This economic conquest was accompanied by an equally determined effort to secure control of the military machine, which, having been created and supported by the French in the first instance, was subsequently to pass into the hands of German instructors, who were not slow in sowing the seeds of Teutonism. The reorganization of the Rumanian army, now a formidable weapon of defence and offence, under the guidance of King Charles, has, however, placed in the hands of his people an efficient machine, which in spite of German influence has never been subservient to Germany. When the German Crown Prince was sent to Bukarest in April 1909 to present to King Charles for his seventieth birthday the baton of a Field-Marshal in the German army, he did not approach a vassal of the German Empire, but an equal who was in a position to direct his national policy as he thought fit. The wooing had become on more equal terms than during the period when Rumania was avoiding the tempestuous embraces of Russia.

It would be difficult to name the primal cause of the failure of German policy after so successful a beginning. The causes have been successive and cumulative with the exception of one, which has for many years aroused the deepest passions of the Rumanian people.

* Although the German population in Rumania is not large, the number of Austro-Hungarian subjects (104,000), of whom many are of German blood, is considerable. German agricultural settlements are to be found in the Dobruja and other portions of Rumania, but are more extensive beyond the political boundaries in Bessarabia, especially in the district between Odessa and the River Kunduk. Such settlements are numerous on both sides of this river and also along the Dniester. This district abounds in German names and was largely settled by Germans between the years 1815–1870.

† "Les Satellites de l'Allemagne," in *Questions Diplomatiques*, August 16, 1911.

‡ In 1911 the import trade from Germany was valued at £7,348,000, the exports to Germany being only £1,320,000; but a vast export trade was carried on with Belgium, amounting to £10,538,000 in the same year. Germany accounts for 37 per cent. of Rumanian imports, whilst Austria-Hungary exports to Rumania another 28 per cent., making a total of 65 per cent. shared between the two Central Powers of the entire import trade of Rumania.

Ethnographic Rumania forms a compact block of territory almost circular in shape, bounded on the south by the Danube but having no clearly defined natural frontiers on the west, north, and east. Beyond the Pruth, which forms the political boundary on the east, lies a Rumanian population within the Russian Empire, stretching as far as and on both sides of the River Kunduk, a territory which between the years 1856–1871 formed part of the principality of Moldavia. Beyond the Transylvanian Alps, which cut across the centre of ethnographic Rumania and form the frontier of political Rumania, lies a great block of territory covering the whole of Transylvania and stretching into Hungary as far as Arad and Grosswardein and into the Bukovina as far as Czernowitz. This territory is settled by a compact mass of Rumanians, with the exception of the district in the bend of the Carpathians which is peopled by Saxons and Zeklers. On the one side of the Carpathians is Rumania and freedom ; on the other side is Transylvania and the political and spiritual domination of the Magyars. It is the fate of their three and a half millions of countrymen beyond the boundaries of the kingdom that has aroused the national aspirations of the Rumanians and excited a deep hatred and distrust of Austria-Hungary.

Although the domination is not German but that of the Magyars—a people who liberated themselves in order to place the noose around the necks of lesser nationalities—the result politically has been the same as if Germany and not Hungary had been attempting to crush the national life of the Rumanians. As a portion of the same political system the Austro-Germans share a common responsibility—and will reap a common reward. It would not be possible to find a more glaring instance of political immorality than is presented in the case of the Magyars, who have deliberately imposed upon others the system against which they themselves revolted. In winning the admiration of Western Europe for the stubborn fight on behalf of the sacred cause of nationality which they maintained against the forces of Austria when revolution shook that Empire to its foundations, they at the same time secured pity and commiseration when, owing to Russian intervention, that rebellion was suppressed. But the part played by the Southern Slavs and the Rumanian subjects of the Austrian Emperor in the suppression of the Magyar Revolution—for they assisted the Austrians both by refusing to join the revolutionaries and by lending the assistance of their arms—has never been forgiven or forgotten by the Hungarians. The Southern Slavs and the Rumanians wished either to receive self-government or to be ruled directly from Vienna, but Austria, always capable of treachery towards those by whom she has been served, chose to place them under the government of Budapest. The Magyars, owing to the peculiar privileges that were accorded to them, were not long in securing an adequate revenge upon those who had opposed their first attempt to secure equality within the Austrian Empire. The Hungarian half of the Dual Monarchy has a population of some twenty-three millions, but out of this number not more than nine millions are of Magyar race—the remainder being composed of the oppressed nationalities who are now looking for freedom from the Austro-Hungarian yoke.

So far as the Rumanians have been concerned the persecution to which they have been subjected has been bitter and constant. "The Magyars monopolize not only the schools and the universities," states a writer in the *Fortnightly Review*, "but Parliament as well. By the Law of Nationalities and by common fairness, Magyars and non-Magyars are entitled to proportionate representation in the Parliament at Budapest. Nevertheless the Rumanians are practically excluded from Parliament. The Budapest Parliament has 413 members. In the Parliament of 1896 there was one Rumanian member; in the Parliament of 1910 the number was five."* The same writer shows, further, the injustice with which the Rumanians are treated in the law courts. "It frequently occurs," he states, "that the Rumanians who do not know Magyar and who have a dispute at law dispute in Magyar by means of interpreters before a Magyar judge who knows Rumanian but who chooses to employ only the Magyar language." The Magyars have deliberately endeavoured to stamp the Rumanians within Austria-Hungary into their own image, and there is no reason for wonder that there has arisen beyond the borders of Hungary and within the modern Rumania so strong a feeling of common nationality and so imperious a desire for a

* "Rumania's Attitude and Future," *Fortnightly Review*, May 1915.

"Greater Rumania," in which all Rumanians may be politically free, that the policies of rulers and statesmen have been modified and that they have been obliged, for their own safety, to withstand alike the pressure of Austro-Germany and Russia.

Rumanian policy underwent a complete change during the two Balkan Wars. Up to that momentous period, although continuously cooling in her attachment to the Germanic Powers, Rumania had given no open sign of her ultimate intentions. But during the First Balkan War she played a waiting game, as she was able to influence, if not to dictate, the terms of peace when the time should arrive for a settlement. The subsequent break-up of the Balkan Alliance and the fratricidal strife between the former allies was Rumania's opportunity for decisive action, yet in spite of tempting proposals from Greece and Serbia she declined to take an active part in the conflict, preferring to obtain by diplomatic action what she could undoubtedly have seized through active hostilities. In this respect King Charles took an honourable and patriotic part, and his attitude on this occasion might have prevented the second war had he only been supported by Austria. The latter Power, however, was bent upon bringing about the dissolution of the League, and was unwilling to aid Rumania and Russia in their attempts to prevent any renewal of hostilities. As is now known, Austria worked ostensibly on the side of Bulgaria but in reality to bring about the downfall of Serbia. Signor Giolitti has stated in the Italian Chamber that on August 9, 1913, the day after the signing of the Peace of Bukarest, Austria intimated her intention of attacking Serbia and was only prevented by the strong remonstrances of Italy and Germany; whilst M. Take Jonescu, the leader of the Conservative-Democratic Party in Rumania, has disclosed the fact that Austria's representative in Bukarest, Count Fürstenberg, was instructed to inform the Rumanian Government in May 1913 that should Bulgaria come into conflict with her former allies, Serbia and Greece, Austria-Hungary would intervene by force of arms on behalf of Bulgaria. This intention of the Austro-Hungarian Government to adopt the Bulgarian cause doubtless influenced that country in the disastrous course upon which she entered when she again plunged the Balkans into the horrors of warfare.

In any case, the attitude of Rumania became clear. The

price of Austrian treachery was the alienation of Rumania from the Central Alliance, and the reward for her own moderation was the rectification of her frontiers to the south-east of the Danube. Rumania was forced out of the German orbit by the ill-advised attitude of Austrian statesmen, who were then prepared to enter light-heartedly upon a European war for the express purpose of crushing Serbia. As M. Maioresco, the Rumanian Minister of Foreign Affairs, plainly intimated, Rumania could afford to wait whilst others quarrelled. On June 9, 1913, he wrote to the King with regard to the proposed alliance with Greece: " With respect to a *rapprochement* with Greece, I postponed my reply until a later moment, when the friction between the Allies should become greater." *

Rumania, in spite of her dangerous position *vis-à-vis* with Russia, became entirely alienated from the Central Powers, and the subsequent journey of the Russian Emperor and Empress to Constantia in the spring of 1914, following upon the visit of the Crown Prince Ferdinand, now King of Rumania, to Petrograd, seemed to presage a close *rapprochement* with Russia. This was the position at the outbreak of the present war, but, as M. Mitrany has stated, " Rumania, when the war broke out finding herself between two countries which had both on different occasions failed to prove their pretended friendship, could not reasonably have been expected to let sentiment influence her policy." The conduct of those responsible for the destinies of Rumania has been in accordance with the national interests, and in this respect presents a striking contrast to the official attitude of Greece, which in striving to preserve neutrality has lost both its independence and dignity. The Rumanian sovereign, supported by judicious and wise statesmanship, has played his part with consummate skill, and the entry of his country into the war on the side of the Allies is not only the most striking testimony to the growing power of the grand Alliance but is also the clearest evidence that the Rumanian people themselves have fully appreciated the international position and its meaning with respect to their own land. The problem of a greater Rumania is now settled, for the hour of destiny has struck.

* " The Balkan League," by I. E. Gueshoff, formerly Prime Minister of Bulgaria, 1915, p. 86.

CHAPTER XIII

GERMANY AND POLAND

In the old days, before Russia, Prussia, and Austria had joined together in an unholy alliance in order to despoil their hereditary enemies the Poles, the worst enemy of Poland was Poland herself. To-day her most deadly foe is Prussia.

It is but natural, perhaps, that the Germans, surrounded by an ocean of enemies of their own making, should endeavour to strengthen the political frontiers of their Empire by Germanizing the disunited elements that surround them. For this purpose it has been the persistent aim of the Prussian Government, and since the foundation of the Empire of the Imperial Government also, to acquire by peaceful penetration a preponderating influence in neighbouring States. Of recent years, especially since the ideal of a Greater Germany has seized hold of the Teutonic imagination, this policy has been pursued with respect to all the non-German countries by which Germany is surrounded. On the west Denmark, Holland, and particularly Belgium were peculiarly suitable for German commercial penetration, whilst in the south Bohemia and Moravia were equally subjected to the insidious German attack. On the east Russian Poland was assailed by a constant influx of German subjects, who formed the advance guard of the Teutonic invasion of the Russian Empire. The economic forces within Germany which drove forth German citizens by the thousand to swell the tide of Germanism beyond the borders of the Empire excellently served the future political policy of the German people. As the tide of emigration slowed down to a small and unimportant stream, when the economic prosperity of the Fatherland had become assured, the forces that were moulding the mental attitude of the German people into a form pleasing to the leaders of Pan-Germanism became more and more pronounced. The growth within the Empire, and the immense and emphatic influence it acquired, of a great body of public opinion that looked forward to the formation of a Greater Germany dominating the whole of Central Europe compelled the German Government to fall into line and to utilize every means for the spread of *Deutschthum*. None of these means of racial propaganda was more useful than the help afforded by the hundreds of thousands of German citizens settled beyond the Imperial frontiers.

Each German colony became the spiritual centre of aggressive Germanism. When established in the midst of a territory peopled by Slavs, as in Russia itself, the colonies were useful for carrying on the political and commercial work of the Fatherland. When settled in the non-German States of the Austro-Hungarian Empire they were able to work quietly on behalf of the Pan-German ideal of a regenerated and unified Germany from which all incongruous elements should be driven or into which they should be assimilated. When established in Russian Poland they formed the buttresses of the German Imperial fabric, protecting the Empire from the erosion caused by the enormous pressure exerted by the continuous westward advance of the forces of Slavdom.

The presence within the Empire of a large and apparently unassimilative foreign population, particularly upon the eastern frontiers, was a constant menace not only to its integrity, but also to the ideal of the new and greater Germany cherished by all Pan-German philosophers. In the old days before the Teutonic ideal became the creed of the vast majority of the German people it would doubtless have been good policy to have conciliated, where it was not possible to assimilate, this foreign and stubborn element, but with the arrogant consciousness born of national strength and of an ever-increasing military power, the Germans came to believe that they would be able to foist upon the unfortunate Poles the full measure of Germanism, to turn Polish patriots into German citizens, to make the unwilling into the meek tools of a rampant Imperialism, and, in a word, to Germanize the Polish provinces of the Empire in the same way that Russia had attempted to Russianize her own western frontiers. The former buffer State between the three great empires was to be as thoroughly crushed out of its original moral shape as it had previously been crushed out of its political outline.

The Germanization of Poland was thoroughly and systematically undertaken. It was felt that if an element which appeared susceptible neither of rejection nor of assimilation were to remain within the German organism it would be necessary not only to remove this foreign obstruction by the introduction of German settlers, whose main task should be to oust the Poles from their landed estates and to drive them from their commercial activities, but also so thoroughly to intimidate it that even if Polish nationalism were not completely stamped out, it would never again dare to lift its head within the sacred frontiers of the German Empire. The position of the Poles had become a question of more than national importance. It struck at the racial supremacy of the Teuton, for if this foreign element were neither assimilated nor destroyed it would for ever remain as a threatening danger upon the eastern borders of the Empire. Although neither Russia nor Austria had succeeded in assimilating the portion of Poland that had fallen to it, the difficulty in their case had been considerably mitigated owing to well-defined geographic or economic conditions. Galicia, separated by the rampart of the Carpathians from the rest of the Austro-Hungarian Empire, was in itself a strategic outpost of that State, sufficiently separate not to be a cause of danger to the central authority. Russian Poland, on the other hand, had become a great manufacturing region and an economic storehouse for the Russian Empire, bound to the rest of Russia by the closest ties of mutual interest, and likely, in the course of time, to secure a separate constitutional existence should the liberal tendencies of modern Russia ever find their natural expression.

But Prussian Poland, barred by no natural obstruction from the rest of Germany on the one side or from the rest of Poland on the other, was too near to the political heart of the Empire to be regarded with indifference, and as the Prussian mind could never adopt a policy of conciliation, the only alternative was vigorous and continued aggression in order that the Slavonic spectre which flitted uneasily beyond the Prussian frontiers might not be welcomed and caressed by the un-German Poles.

Probably of all European peoples the Poles of to-day are the most patriotic—that is, the most deeply attached to the principle of nationality. In spite of the sufferings of a century and a half, the Polish spirit is not crushed. In spite of the fact that liberty has been unknown since the great spoliation, the Poles remain passionately attached to the principle of nationhood. Each persecution, so far from destroying this national sentiment, has tended rather to increase it. Germans might well have taken warning from the experiences of both Russia and Austria, but, unfortunately, the Prussian bureaucracy was incapable of learning. When Bismarck declared that the Poles had lost any right to consideration after their attitude during the revolutionary outbreaks of 1848 he was only voicing the prevailing Prussian opinion. But Bismarck's statement was based upon firmer foundations than a mere desire to impose the Teutonic culture upon others. He learned during the period of his embassy in St. Petersburg, between the years 1859 and 1862, how close was the connexion of Poland with Liberal Pan-Slavism and how ardently the Poles responded to every liberalizing influence within the Russian Empire. He realized that the Poles within the German sphere would not only be a dangerous national element but, which was perhaps far worse, a danger to Prussian bureaucracy, because their political ideals were essentially Liberal and anti-autocratic. The Germanization of Poland became, therefore, a set purpose, and the basis of his policy was twofold—economic and spiritual. The reduction of the number of Polish landlords and peasants by the introduction of German settlers became essential if the Polish menace were to be removed farther from Berlin, whilst the banishment of the Polish tongue from public life and from the universities and schools was necessary if Teutonic culture were to prevail in Eastern Germany.

These two aims of German policy were vigorously upheld by one of those Pan-German societies of aggression which have in the main been able to direct the political activities of the German Government since the last decade of the nineteenth century. Each portion of territory, whether within or without the Empire, that has been threatened by the growth of non-German elements has been taken under the special care of one or other of such societies, and since 1894 the Deutscher Ostmarken-Verein has undertaken the inspiring work of opposing the Poles in East Prussia.

As soon as there were signs of a Polish revival, industrial and political, this society became one of the most active factors in meeting and opposing the threatening danger. Originally formed to combat certain Liberal tendencies which it was thought were shared by the young Emperor, it soon became sufficiently strong to exert pressure at Court in order to compel the Prussian authorities to act in accordance with its wishes. The Deutscher Ostmarken-Verein, which is popularly known as the Hakatist Society, after the initials of its three founders, von Hansemann, Kennemann, and von Tiedemann, had quite recently 54,000 members, divided among 450 branches, and an annual income of 170,000 marks, with a capital of 870,000 marks.* Its peculiar strength lay in the fact that it was supported by every official who wished to curry favour with the authorities and gathered to its fold large numbers of pious Lutherans who were hostile on religious grounds to Roman Catholic Poland. M. Joseph Koscielski, a member of the Prussian House of Nobles, writing in 1908,† states that "Hakatism does, in fact, demoralize visibly and without cessation. What progress it has made at Court it is difficult to ascertain, for the Court is like the book sealed with the seven seals. But, on the other hand, one can see at every end and turn the demoralizing effects of all-powerful Hakatism on the members of the Government," and he shows how the society has been able to compel the German Chancellor to conform to its wishes.

The extremists of all parties are generally those who exercise the smallest influence, at least in countries where there exists a large and moderating opinion able successfully to counteract extreme tendencies. But in Germany it is usually the extremist who has finally succeeded in imposing his will upon the community and has sooner or later dragged the moderating majority into his proselytizing net. It was the extremists who finally drove the Prussian Government to adopt stringent measures against the Poles and to attempt their spiritual,

* Vergnet's "France in Danger," 1915, p. 17.
† See *Contemporary Review*, July 1908.

moral, and economic subjugation. The German point of view is well illustrated in Otto Richard Tannenberg's book "Gross Deutschland," published in 1911.* The redoubtable author would eliminate the Polish element from the German Empire. Adopting from the past history of Poland the idea that only actual "nationals" should be owners of land, he would apply the same lesson to modern Germany. Because after the Battle of Tannenberg—when the Teutonic knights were thoroughly beaten and the eastern tide of Teutonism swept back to its original limits—the Poles, in order to rid themselves of the German incubus, enacted that only Poles were capable of owning land in Poland, Herr Tannenberg suggests that only Germans should be competent to possess land in Germany. "Would it not be a fine thing," he asks, "for such a law to be vigorously applied with us? We should at once be rid of all the *Französlinge* of Alsace, of all the great Polish and Danish landed proprietors. The excellent service which this Polish enactment rendered to Poland can still be seen at the present time . . . and this parallel between Polish and German methods is peculiarly instructive. We are well able to realize what we ourselves have to do."

The Poles, therefore, according to the author of "Great Germany" are to be expropriated, not slowly and laboriously at great expense, as is being done at present, but by simply handing their lands to German owners. Subject peoples can have no rights within the German Empire, for the motto of the Pan-Germans is, "The German Empire is for the German people." Germans and Poles, states Herr Tannenberg, cannot live side by side and enjoy the same rights, and the Poles must be encouraged to emigrate so that good German citizens may occupy their vacated farms and counting-houses.

This policy of expropriation has been tried since 1886, when the Prussian Diet passed a land-settlement Bill granting the Government a sum of 100,000,000 marks for the purposes of (*a*) strengthening the German element in the provinces of West Prussia and Posen and of checking the Polonizing tendencies by settling German peasants and workmen on agricultural holdings; and (*b*) of constructing roads, schools, churches,

* A French edition of this book was issued at the beginning of this year.

hospitals, orphanages, and effecting other improvements. Of the immense sums then and subsequently voted for obtaining this desirable result over £15,000,000 had been spent up to the year 1908 in buying lands in Poland, but as the German settlers were also only too eager to sell their lands to the Government, a considerable portion of this money found its way into German pockets without the colonizing plans of the Government being benefited thereby. On the whole, the results of this attempt to Germanize Poland by economic means have been disappointing to those German patriots who wish to see the Poles driven from the land. In certain districts the Poles have been displaced by German settlers. Thus in the district of Bromberg, where in 1888 there were 524 German villages and 766 Polish villages, there were twenty-five years later 802 German and 488 Polish villages. Again, in the district of Posen there were 674 German and 1461 Polish villages in the year 1888 against 971 German and 1164 Polish villages in the year 1911. But the result of this policy has been that the Poles who have sold their lands at a satisfactory price have generally entered the nearest town, have awaited their opportunity of again purchasing land, and have settled in other districts. To counteract the German settlement scheme the Poles have formed land societies of their own, to enable Poles to buy land at low prices. Moreover, the earlier tendency to sell to the Germans has of recent years been successfully combated by a silent but remorseless boycott of those who have been unpatriotic enough to dispose of their estates, so that it has gradually come about that the economic process at first deemed to be successful has in reality worked to the detriment of the Germans. Figures dealing with this subject are notoriously unreliable. On the one hand, Herr Tannenberg computes in his Pan-German " romance " that by the year 1950 80 per cent. of the inhabitants of Prussian Poland will be Germans; whilst Mr. Beer, writing in the *National Review* * in April 1907, thinks that only about seventy-five thousand acres have passed out of Polish hands, and states that the Polish population is increasing much more rapidly than the German. In any case there can be no doubt that Prussian efforts to Germanize Poland have been extremely

* " Germanization of the Poles," *National Review*, April 1907.

unfruitful. The attempt to dragoon Polish scholars, described on p. 306, only resulted in a strengthening of Polish national feeling, and the process of introducing German settlers has only enabled the Poles to learn many much-needed lessons from their new neighbours, to apply German administrative and agricultural methods to their own estates, and to take all that has been good whilst opposing the political aims underlying German penetration. The Germans, as a matter of fact, have conspicuously failed in their immediate object because Poland is too nationalistic to be conquered by any method short of fire and sword.

The Germanization of Poland has been part of a deliberate policy thoroughly in keeping with the historical spoliations of that country. Nothing has been so greatly dreaded in Germany as the possibility of the re-erection of an autonomous Polish State on the eastern frontier and the spread of liberal ideas within Russian Poland. In the tortuous maze of Prussian policy no fact stands forth more clearly than the utterly unscrupulous manner in which the Germans brought about the downfall of the ancient Polish kingdom, and the way in which they dragged Russia and Austria into their nefarious plans. Whenever there seemed the least chance of a recrudescence of Polish nationality, whenever it seemed at all likely that the Poles might combine their shattered and scattered forces in the sacred cause of nationalism, it was German intrigue that finally succeeded in stopping the movement and thrusting the Poles into the Serbonian bog of political dependence. If in Russian Poland the possibility of more political freedom seemed imminent the German element at the Russian Court proved sufficiently strong to counteract the liberalizing tendencies, and when the Tsar seemed about to confer special political privileges on the Poles the Prussians stirred up trouble in Posen in order to establish the folly of trying to conciliate those who would never be satisfied.

Bismarck himself made the Prussian position perfectly clear in a communication to the British Ambassador in Berlin in 1863. " M. de Bismarck," wrote the latter, Sir Andrew Buchanan, to Earl Russell, " in acquainting me a few days ago of his intention to take measures in concert with the Russian Government to prevent the extension of the insurrectionary movement which has lately taken place in Poland, said the question was of vital importance to Prussia as her own existence *would be seriously compromised by the establishment of an independent kingdom of Poland.* I asked whether he meant to say that if Russia found any difficulty in suppressing the insurrection the Prussian Government intended to afford them military assistance, and he not only replied in the affirmative but added that if Russia got tired of the contest and were disposed to withdraw from the kingdom—a cause which some Russians were supposed to think advantageous to her interests—*the Prussian Government would carry on the war on their own account.*" No statement could show more decisively how Germany has worked to the detriment of the Poles. About the same time the Emperor William I, then only King of Prussia, stated that " it is equally the duty and interest of Prussia to do everything in her power to prevent the establishment of an independent Polish kingdom, for if the Polish nation would reconstitute themselves as an independent State the existence of Prussia would be seriously menaced, as the first efforts of the new State would be to recover Danzig, and if that attempt succeeded, the fatal consequences to Prussia are too evident to require me to point them out." [1]

Here, then, is the keynote of Prussian policy. The Prussian power, having been erected chiefly upon the ruins of ancient Poland, is to be used for all time to keep the Poles not only in a state of political servitude but, so far as possible, in economic dependence and racial degradation also. The economic progress that has been made of recent years has been largely due to the efforts of the Poles themselves, for the Germans in introducing economic reforms in Poland have throughout been actuated by the aim, not to better the Poles themselves, but either to drive them out by German economic pressure or to make them act as willing slaves in the Teutonic economic machine. The emancipation of the serfs in Posen, unlike the subsequent reform in Russian Poland, was not an attempt to win the sympathies of the Polish masses on behalf of the dominating Power, but part of the general process of economic

[1] *See* the excellent article by Mr. J. Ellis Barker in the *Nineteenth Century*, January 1915, entitled " Peace and the Polish Question."

improvement which was to render the peasants more useful to their German masters. The so-called policy of " consideration and concession " which marked Prussian relations with the Poles previous to the year 1830 gave place to the unscrupulous and arbitrary proceedings of von Flottwell when the nobles were deprived of their rights over local administration, such as they were, and a military system of administration introduced.

It is impossible here to describe the full results of German policy. The barbarities of the iron control then introduced led to repeated, though ultimately unsuccessful, local risings, in which the Prussians showed an utter contempt of the elementary rights of humanity. Russian Poland has at times groaned under an iron yoke, but the attitude, though not the severities, of the Russians has at least been justified by the fact that the Poles, being without political insight, have generally claimed the full political extent of the old Polish kingdom—for they have demanded large and purely Russian districts on the ground of historical right, including even Kieff, the cradle of the Russian orthodox faith. The rising in Posen in 1848 was ruthlessly suppressed as soon as the Prussians gained the ascendancy. " All the usages and rules of civilized warfare were totally disregarded by the Prussians. Prisoners were slaughtered, the wounded in the hospitals were killed and in one instance burnt to death. Other prisoners were marked with vitriol on hands and ears. ' I hear German officers and officials,' wrote a High Court official, ' ask each other, with a feeling of horror, whether this barbarity of the infuriated, uncivilized Germans—whether this ferocious desire to murder, which delights in exterminating and tormenting even a conquered enemy, is inherent in the nature of the Germans ? " *

Yet in spite of the severity of the Prussians the Polish element continued to grow, and Europe is to-day faced with a situation that will require the most careful and considerate handling at the conclusion of the present war—that is if Germany is finally beaten. For the Poles have, unfortunately, throughout their troubled and chequered career, shown themselves incapable of a reasoned and restrained policy, and have

* " Poland," by W. A. Phillips, p. 188.

too frequently spoilt their own chances of freedom by excessive demands. " It is impossible for the Poles to forget that they are a nation formerly enjoying independence," wrote the Emperor Alexander I to La Harpe in 1815. " I feel that had I been born a Pole I should reason as they do." The Poles, it is true, can never forget this fact, but they also seem incapable of forgetting that they once dominated provinces in which the population is not Polish, and on this account they make demands that cannot be conceded. " Oh," exclaimed the Emperor Nicholas in 1835, " I know you well ; you are and will ever remain the same. That Fatherland of your dreams has been your misfortune and will always make you unhappy." The same tendencies that existed seventy years ago can be seen in the Poles of to-day. If the Poles demand absolute freedom for a united Poland under a Polish sovereign they seem doomed to disappointment. Although the Italian Chamber has voted a resolution in favour of the restoration of the Polish Republic,* there is no reason to believe that this will come about, for Russian political and economic life is now too closely interwoven into the fabric of Russian Poland for the re-establishment of full political freedom. The only solution seems to be, in the event of Germany's defeat, that Poland should become an autonomous State under Russian suzerainty, when the wealthiest portions of Silesia, including her gigantic coal-mines and ironworks, Posen, and the former province of West Prussia, with Danzig, would again become Polish territory. In the event of the defeat of the Allies nothing can save Poland from absorption in the German Empire.

* At the sitting on December 8, 1915, the Italian Chamber voted the following resolution : " The Italian Chamber, affirming confidence in the victory of the Allies, which will permit of the early restoration of Belgium and Serbia, expresses the ardent wish that the most noble Polish nation, which during past centuries constituted an important factor of civilization by preserving Europe from Tartar and Turkish invasions, and is ordained for a powerful action in view of the peaceful balance of power, may likewise be reconstituted in its unity as a free and independent State."

CHAPTER XIV

THE GERMANS IN RUSSIA

It was long an axiom of British foreign policy that Russia should be looked upon as an octopus stretching forth its tentacles in every direction and spreading eastwards and westwards and southwards at the expense of her immediate neighbours. No country seemed safe from the enormous expansive power which was supposed to be a characteristic of the ugly brute settled upon the banks of the Neva, whose movements appeared to threaten not only the stability of Europe but the integrity of the whole of Asia also. The gradual but constant increase of Russian territory by the absorption of other countries; the spread of Russia eastwards across Siberia to the far Pacific, southwards into Caucasia, south-westwards into the European provinces of Turkey, and westwards into Poland; the increase of Russian influence throughout the Balkans, Asia Minor, Persia, and upon the borders of Afghanistan; and finally the danger that seemed to threaten Constantinople on the one side and India on the other—convinced most British observers that Russia was a dangerous and insidious enemy whose collosal power aimed at the domination of Europe.

Such observers did not perceive the inherent weakness of Russia and failed to understand the true trend of Russian policy. There was another side to this gloomy and alarming picture. The expansive forces that were bringing about the development of Russia were in reality neither so alarming nor so threatening as at first appeared. With the rise of a rival power on her western frontiers the danger, such as it was and if it ever really existed, was removed. New forces came into play. The ambitions of the recently constituted German Empire led to a reversal of Russia's traditional policy of friendship with her western neighbour, and the disturbed relations between Russia and Germany introduced a new factor into the political situation.

These relations form a most interesting and instructive study. On the one hand was a nation, restless, energetic, thoroughly permeated with the idea that its mission was to foist Teutonic ideals and Teutonic culture upon a people who were considered to be vastly inferior in every attribute that makes a nation great: on the other was a vast, unresponsive, almost apathetic body of agriculturists and peasants patiently enduring the yoke of an unsympathetic and partly foreign bureaucracy. Although engaged in a deadly and silent conflict, which during recent years resulted in political cleavage and finally led to war, these two peoples were in reality drawn together by a strong devotion to the monarchical principle and regarded the spread of western freedom and so-called democracy with inherent dislike. The contrast between the ideals of official Russia, which until the end of the last century was the only portion of Russia that really counted in the political world, and Germany was one of degree rather than of kind. The Russians, an intensely democratic and self-contained race, looked upon the Tsar as the embodiment of the whole nation and were encouraged in this attitude by the band of officials whose interest it was to draw from the State the revenues that rendered their position secure and set them apart from the rest of the Russian nation. The Germans also, especially since the memorable events of 1848 when Prussia had deliberately abandoned the path of western democracy, stood for the preservation of monarchical and autocratic government, but under the guidance of their own countrymen and the control of their own officials.

The two nations felt the imperative need of expansion. Russia, subject to vast and subterranean forces, was gradually awakening out of the slumber of centuries, gathering together and consolidating the intensely nationalistic ideals that hitherto had found little vent in the national political life, welding into a homogeneous whole the diverse races and peoples who had from time to time fallen under the sway of the Tsar, and extending its influence into new territories, sometimes peopled by alien nations, but more often settled by kindred races.

The expansive movement, with its spiritual centre at Moscow and its political machinery at Petrograd, gathered force and momentum as the years advanced ; but it was finally checked by three factors which brought an abrupt termination to the period of Russian expansion—the consolidation and rise of the German Empire ; the increase of British power in the East ; and the remarkable and unprecedented growth of the Japanese military and naval power. The first factor, owing to the close friendship that arose between Austria and her quondam enemy Prussia, set a barrier against Russian expansion in the Balkans and prevented the assimilation of the Slavic States of Turkey into the Russian political sphere ; the second prevented the occupation of Constantinople, the natural gateway to the Russian Empire, and the spread of Russian territory towards the Persian Gulf and the confines of India ; whilst the third placed a veto upon the realization of Russian ambitions upon the Pacific. At the same time the creation of a great German navy, second only to that of the strongest naval Power, rendered Russia's position in the Baltic precarious and foreshadowed her ultimate dependence upon German goodwill for communication with Western Europe; whilst the fact that the only outlet to the south, through the Bosphorus and the Dardanelles, was in hands that had always been hostile completely shut off Russia from the maritime activities that were assuredly her due. Hedged round by treaties to which she had been obliged to agree, confined within the vast expanses of a land empire having few outlets to the ocean and apparently economically doomed to stagnation, the Russian people began to realize that their destinies were controlled by other nations and to feel that the great and swelling tide of nationalism might beat in vain against the military, naval, and economic boundaries that had been set up against their expansion. And they also began to realize that of all the forces with which they had to contend that of Teutonism, being the most subtle and insidious, was also the strongest and the most formidable.

The rise of Teutonism brought German and Slav into irreconcilable conflict. German imperialists, basing the economic safety of their empire upon the creation of military and strategic avenues of expansion, like the first Napoleon began to look towards the two roads to empire. To the west they saw across the Atlantic vast territories suitable for white colonization, where a new Germany, peopled by emigrants from the Fatherland, might arise. In South America and especially in Brazil there seemed possibilities of unlimited expansion whenever the fatal Monroe Doctrine, enunciated by the United States and upheld by Great Britain, should be overcome. To the south they perceived vast economic reserves in Africa, where plantation-colonies might be founded and the tropical products needed for German industries might be garnered. To advance upon this western road they forged the naval weapon which in the hands of their Supreme War Lord was designed to break the might of Great Britain. In the east they desired to advance upon overland roads leading to vast commercial and political interests in Asia, and particularly in Asia Minor, Mesopotamia, Persia, and perhaps India; to areas where German commerce might reign supreme and whence might be drawn wealth and recruits to feed the German economic and military machines. One of these roads passed through the Balkans and the other was destined, if the Pan-German scheme should ever reach its full maturity, to go through Russia towards the Black Sea, the Caucasus, and the Caspian. In order to advance landwards the German army was continuously increased until it became the most formidable weapon of offence and expansion ever known in the annals of mankind.

It was precisely this danger that threatened the Russian Empire, and precisely this danger that Russian statesmen at length determined to meet, and if possible to destroy. It is not within the scope of this chapter to relate the story of the political relations between Germany and Russia. These had been almost uniformly cordial until Alexander III, impressed by the essential conflict between German aims and Russian needs, sought the friendship of France in order to obtain some stability for the swaying balance of political and military power.

But the nature of the German advance in Russia and through Russia should be thoroughly studied by those who wish to understand one of the subsidiary factors of the present conflict, because it forms one of the avenues through which the Germans hoped to secure the economic if not the political control of Holy Russia. It was their purpose so to permeate the Russian Empire with Teutonic influences that it should become rotten at its political core, and so to introduce German commercial agents that the economic life of the Russian nation should be completely subjected to German control. For some decades German settlers, under the protection and encouragement of their Fatherland, had been pouring into Russian territory and at the outbreak of the present war the advance agents of Teutonic culture had secured a strong and apparently impregnable position in the Empire of the Tsar. Each German settler, as he took up his abode on Russian soil, became a soldier in the well-drilled army of political and commercial evangelists, subject to the control of the hidden forces that directed his efforts and capable of exerting considerable influence within his immediate sphere of operations. Agriculturist and merchant alike were forerunners of the Germanic ideal. They worked industriously and in the dark for the furtherance of the interests of their Fatherland, and so far from being lost to their country, as Bismarck had suggested, they became the most potent factors in the introduction of German influence amongst the Russians. They were the leaven that was to undermine Muscovite tradition, to counteract the growing forces of Russian nationalism, and in high places to work for the political control of the machine of government. Everywhere, north, south, east, and west, German settlers, merchants, labourers, agriculturists, and educationalists were drilled into battalions of workers in the cause of Germanism, and by means of social, commercial, and political pressure were required to fight the subterranean battles of the Fatherland.

The process of Germanization in Russia had been of long duration. It commenced in the far-off days of Peter the Great, when for the first time the Russian Court fell under the influence of Western civilization, and for the first time the Russian people were subjected to strange and foreign influences. Although Peter was working on behalf of Russian nationalism and although he was the first great exponent of Russian expansion, he was aware, nevertheless, that his countrymen required some outside influence to raise them to the position which, he foresaw, would some day be theirs. Unfortunately the policy of Peter, whilst primarily designed in the interests of his own countrymen, had precisely the opposite effect to what had been intended. Whilst his foreign policy was excellent, because he strove to maintain a balance of power within the German States and withstood the pretensions of Austria and Prussia alike, at the same time cultivating friendly relations with France and Britain, his internal policy was productive of much mischief to the cause of Russian nationalism. It alienated the mass of the Russian people from his schemes of reform and eventually resulted in the formation of a bureaucratic class in opposition to the old nobility, which under succeeding reigns became more and more imbued with Germanic ideas. As a great patriotic sovereign whose chief care was the uplifting of his own countrymen and the suppression of semi-barbaric customs and modes of life, Peter, in building the city that bears his name, made the capital mistake of shifting the centre of Russian political life to a spot far distant from the centre of Russian nationalism. The creation of the new capital amidst the swamps and morasses of North-Western Russia certainly brought his country into closer touch with the western world and with the Baltic regions, in which the wild Letts, Lithuanians, and Esths maintained a fierce and stubborn fight against the advance of Germanism; but it also removed the Court and the new nobility who had been attracted to the side of Peter from the realities of Russian life and created a new political system out of touch with, and far away from, the mass of the Russian people.

It was Peter's desire to enlist the aid of Western Europeans so as to teach his countrymen how to govern themselves, and it was no part of his plan to attract large numbers of foreigners to settle permanently in his country. Nevertheless the eventual result was that the foreigners who had come to teach stayed to govern, and gradually assumed a controlling influence over the Russian Court and over the host of officials who managed the affairs of the Empire. "Intermarriages with members of German dynasties brought to St. Petersburg German princes and princesses with their suites, and gave to a great extent a German character to the Russian Court. Many of the Baltic barons settled likewise in the capital of the Empire, which they considered themselves called upon to rule. Thither flocked from all parts of Germany men whose title to nobility was small or doubtful, filling up all the most advantageous posts, and always pushed forward other Germans who received every preference over Russians." * Moreover the introduction of German scientists and members of the learned and teaching professions into Russia, whilst creating a much needed centre of thought and investigation, nevertheless tended to impose upon Russian soil a body of more or less cultured men bound together by common interests and liable, as eventually happened, to combine for purposes quite foreign to the intentions of their first patron. The Germans of the new régime began to regard themselves as the salt of the Russian Empire. They despised the old Muscovite tradition, they looked down upon the former basis of Russian civilization, and they became hostile to Slavic institutions and to Slavic thought. The Russian Academy of Sciences became a German institution and not infrequently refused admission to the most eminent Russian scientists.†

It was not, however, until a later period that the German invasion began in earnest. Peter's agents of reform had indeed come to occupy high places in the political, educational, and scientific sphere ; German barons had settled in considerable numbers in the Baltic provinces, where they imposed their will upon the Lettish peasantry, and spreading from the Mark of Brandenburg introduced Prussian absolutism upon their Russian estates ; and German merchants, following in the

* On this point consult the excellent account of " Russia and Democracy : the German Canker in Russia," written by G. de Wesselitsky, who for some fifteen years was President of the Foreign Press Association in London.

† This distinguished institution, founded in the year 1725, was composed of the most eminent representatives of science and culture in Russia, but, as M. de Wesselitsky states, it was decidedly anti-Russian in its tendencies. This fact is well illustrated by an analysis of the nationality of its original members, for of those elected during the years 1725-1727 not one was a Russian, whilst thirteen were Germans and the other six were foreigners. The first Russian member was not elected until 1733 and the second not until eight years later. Nevertheless its publications were either in the Latin language or in French, the latter being the language employed by the more cultured among the German residents in Russia at that period and the Court language of the nobles. Recently, however, a large number of publications has been issued in Russian, whilst a not inconsiderable proportion has been written and published in German.

footsteps of the old Hanseatic traders, who from early times had penetrated to the heart of Russia and had founded one of their chief trading establishments at Novgorod,* settled in the Baltic ports ; but their influence was confined to certain aspects of Russian life and in reality had little effect upon the inert mass of the Russian peasantry.

But when a German princess ruled over the destinies of the Russian Empire and imposed her will from the Baltic to the Pacific and from the Arctic Ocean to the shores of the Black Sea, the first wave of German immigration was set in motion. It is not of course suggested that the process of Germanization was at its commencement a settled policy of any one of the German States. Even up to and including the period of Bismarck it can hardly be said that the German invasion was the outcome of a set and deliberate purpose formulated in the secret councils of the German sovereigns, any more than it was the defined and deliberate policy of the German peoples themselves. Bismarck had indeed declared that he had no sympathy for Germans who left the Fatherland. " I am not a friend of emigration," he had once said, " and I fight against it as much as I can. A German who can put off his Fatherland like an old coat is no German for me."

The views of the Iron Chancellor were certainly those of the majority of the German people, rulers and subjects alike,

* The German traders are frequently mentioned in the well-known Chronicle of Novgorod, 1016–1471, an English translation of which was published by the Royal Historical Society in 1914. The first mention of these ubiquitous traders occurs in the year 1188 under the name of *Nemtsy*, which means literally the " dumb " or " incomprehensible " folk, a term applied by all Slavs to all foreigners of Germanic origin, sometimes including Scandinavians. The name is, of course, akin to Kafir, or foreigner. Apart from the establishment at Novgorod, where the Hansa inhabited a special quarter of the town, built a church, guildhall, warehouses, and dwellinghouses, they had other similar establishments at Pleskow, a city on the Velika, and perhaps even a depot at Moscow ; but undoubtedly Novgorod was their most important station. Here the establishment of the Germans was known as the Court of St. Peter, and so rich and prosperous did they become that they adopted the boastful motto, " Who can stand against God and the Great Novgorod ? " Their conflicts with the Russians were constant, and even within the Republic of Novgorod itself they were in constant opposition to the governing authority. But their power was broken under Ivan the Terrible, who ravaged and sacked Novgorod. With the fall of this place their trading settlements at Memel, Riga, Reval, Dorpat, and other places in the Baltic provinces also lost their importance as centres of German trade.

who remained in their own country, and it would be a distortion of history to suppose that the *Drang nach Osten* was either stimulated by the State or favoured by the German princes. It was primarily, until the advent of the present Emperor, the result of economic and political movements and the outcome of the desire of individual Germans to better their position by leaving the poorer provinces of the Empire for what appeared to be the more promising regions of the nearest East. Germans as a people have been loath to venture upon the seas. Although the trading ventures of the Hanseatic merchants carried Germans to distant parts of Europe and led to the establishment of considerable merchant fleets, Germans as a whole turned their faces from the West, during the seventeenth and eighteenth centuries, and left to maritime nations the settlement of the new countries across the Atlantic. But there was a considerable and continuous movement eastwards and southwards along the land frontiers of Prussia and into the Slavonic provinces of the Holy Roman Empire. In the case of Russia, this movement first became pronounced in the reign of Catherine II.

Previous to this period, however, the Germans obtained a strong political position in Russia, partly owing to the dynastic alliances with German princely houses and partly as the result of Peter the Great's Western reforms. During the reign of Anna Ivanova, the daughter of Ivan, elder brother of Peter, who was called to the throne by the Supreme Council in 1730, and ruled through the instrumentality of her infamous paramour Biron, created Duke of Courland, German political influence became pronounced. Biron, the son of one Bühren, a small Courland proprietor, but said by his enemies to have been a groom, gained the favour of Anna, assumed the name and arms of the French Ducs de Biron, and soon swayed Russia through his royal mistress. During his ascendancy a reign of terror existed in Russia, thousands of the old nobility were exiled to Siberia, and a rising for the destruction of the German intruders was suppressed with great brutality. Nemesis, however, overtook Biron on the death of the Empress. He himself was banished to Siberia in his turn and many leading Germans were executed or banished under the reign of Elizabeth Petrovina, the pre-nuptial daughter of Peter the Great, who showed little sympathy with German innovations because she was herself hostile to the Prussians and came under the control of the national party, who for a time obtained the ascendancy. Under Catherine II, however, German political influence was kept within discreet bounds, for although she was the daughter of the Prince of Anhalt-Zerbst, one of the small States to the west of Brandenburg, and was thus from her earliest youth subject to German influences, she espoused the Russian national cause and with two exceptions worked for the interests of her adopted country. These two exceptions were the part she played in the dismemberment of Poland, which was divided between Prussia, Austria, and Russia, and thus introduced a perpetual sore into the political life of all three Empires, and her encouragement of German immigration into the western districts of Russia.

It was Catherine's deliberate policy to introduce into the as yet but partly civilized Baltic provinces and into other portions of Russia a leaven of German settlers to counteract the disruptive tendencies of the disaffected peasantry. Centuries earlier the same policy had been pursued by the Germans, whose knightly order of warrior-churchmen, the Teutonic Knights, which had first been established in the Holy Land at the end of the tenth century, was subsequently invited to subdue and Christianize the country now known as Prussia and to form a bulwark against the unruly Slavonic tribes whose presence was a constant menace to Germanism. The Teutonic Order in turn became the prey of the Margraves of Brandenburg, one of whom, Albrecht, the first Duke of Prussia, became Grand Master of the Order, embraced Lutheranism, renounced his orders, and annexed the knightly territories to his family domains.* The continual conflict between the

* Previous to this period, however, the power of the Teutonic Order had been greatly reduced by the Poles, with whom they came into deadly conflict. At the Battle of Grünwald or Tannenburg in 1410 the knights were decisively defeated, and Polish influence thereafter placed a barrier against further aggression by the German knights. Prince von Bülow has stated that the defeat of the Teutonic Knights was the most " portentous national disaster, as it resulted in the loss of a large portion of the colonization work of centuries, whilst the cession of West Prussia and Danzig to the Poles put an end to the proud independence of this German order of knighthood." German historians have been wont to point to the activity of the Teutonic Knights, as indeed they might, as an instance of successful German colonization. In an amusing anonymous pamphlet issued by the Clarendon Press occurs the following sentence, which, whilst it pokes gentle fun at this German

Teutonic Kinghts, who represented the Germanic element, and the Slavonic tribes ended in the victory of the former within all the Baltic territories, so that the Germans became the ruling element and dominated the whole district. To strengthen this element Catherine introduced large numbers of German settlers and thus initiated that ceaseless flow of German immigration which has since assumed such alarming proportions.

The position of Russian and Slavic agriculturists was rendered still harder under Catherine's reign, because not only was serfdom extended to portions of Russia where hitherto it had been unknown, but the nobility became a class of privileged landowners exercising direct sway over their dependents, whilst the favoured German element benefited by the comparatively mild policy of the Empress towards settlers of German birth. Each German immigrant received about 160 acres of the best land, and to each colony were attached large pasture-grounds and woods. Moreover the colonists were exempted from all taxes and duties, even from military service, and granted self-government within the limits of their settlements—privileges which, as we shall see later, were continued until recent times. "Absolutely useless to Russia, these colonies formed advance guards of the German *Drang nach Osten*." *

From that time onwards there was a constant influx of German settlers. They penetrated into every avenue of Russian political, economic, and social life; established thriving and lucrative businesses, engaged in every department of trade, built and organized factories; and demonstrated to

---

claim, correctly sums up the Teutonic view: "We Germans were in the Middle Ages a great colonial nation. Centuries before the expansion of England, in the days of Henry the Fowler and Henry the Lion, we Germans began that *Drang nach Osten* which carried German farmers, German merchants, German knights, and German monks over the Elbe to the Vistula, over the Erzgebirge to Bohemia, and over the Carpathians to far Transylvania. The illimitable East beckoned, and the romantic soul of Germans cried, 'I come.' But then, alas, there came the Hussite Wars, and next there came the rise of Russia, and later there came still other wars and waves of the backwash of the Slav. For centuries we slept, until our Kaiser came and blew a trumpet-call, 'Eastward-ho, to far Bagdad.' And we heard, and thinking of the Teutonic Knights and many things, we willingly followed." The great castle of the Order at Marienburg has been termed "the grandest mediæval secular edifice in Germany."

* De Wesselitsky, p. 18.

the Russians the benefits of application, co-operation, and persistent endeavour. In the political sphere they acquired an influence which made them the dominating class, and although many became good Russians and had the welfare of their adopted country primarily at heart, vast numbers retained their German sympathies and looked forward to the time when a Greater Germany should be constituted upon the lines suggested by imaginative Pan-German writers. This was especially the case after the foundation of the new Empire when Austria-Hungary had been drawn within the German orbit. It is not possible here to trace the ramifications of German policy in Russia nor to dwell upon the close political connexion that arose between Russia and Germany, or rather between Russia and Prussia, for it was to the latter German State that during the early and middle portion of the nineteenth century Russian political leaders, including the Emperors themselves, were chiefly subservient. But even a brief examination of the position acquired by Germans in Russia reveals the intensity of their effort and the important part they played in directing this close community of policy.

At the outbreak of the war in August 1914 Germans were established in almost every important Russian centre. In Poland they had quietly and persistently ranged themselves in entrenched positions, frequently upon the main lines of communication and at important strategical points,* and always, without exception, in the chief commercial centres.

The thoroughness of the German preparations on the main strategical lines of advance into Russia was exposed in an article in the *Russki Invalid* of December 25, 1914, in which it was shown that veritable German fortresses had been built on Russian soil. "It fell to our troops," states the writer, "to prove by bitter experience the existence of German fortresses within Russia when they were called upon to capture such fortresses as the country mansions of 'Shukla' and

---

* "In 1912 it became known that a native of Germany, a Bielystock factory-owner, naturalized as a Russian, proposed to carry out irrigation work on a lot of land purchased by him in the valley of the Bobr, near the fortress of Osovetz, where conditions favoured a German invasion, and this irrigation programme further contemplated the wholesale settlement of Germans in boundary localities and strategic points."—*Times*, January 15, 1915.

'Porajhneva,' which are distant four and five versts respectively from Vladislav, in our frontier territory of Wirballen. The capture of these fortified posts was no easy matter and occupied five days, from the 18th to the 23rd of October. These fortresses were constructed by their landlord, a German though a Russian subject, in order to be able to hold in check with the minimum expenditure of force considerable Russian forces. They are erections of a sound and permanent type, built in accordance with all the laws of modern fortification; but owing to our criminal confidence in the Germans and our happy-go-lucky system no one took any interest in them. Latterly, and very justly, in Russian life the remark has become prevalent that the most dangerous enemy of Russia is not the German outside Russia but the enemy within our gates." The writer then describes the mansion of "Shukla," a great country house built in the nature of a German barracks, provided with loopholes instead of windows, surrounded by a large cleared space, intersected by a series of canals and by artificial depressions which drew the Russian troops under the enfilade fire of machine-guns posted in the house. Farther on there was an elaborate system of trenches masked by bulrushes in which were wire entanglements. A park had been laid out, in front of which was a thick iron-concrete wall with a high sharp palisade, "behind which were well-made trenches and shelters, which must have been built, according to some of our officers who saw them, a considerable time before they were actually used." In addition there were subterranean passages leading to a dense wood, and to the right of the house another farm "post" connected with the house by a deep trench. These posts not only kept the town of Vladislav "under a murderous artillery fire but also the plain in front of them and the river and high road, thus preventing us from occupying the town or moving through it into Germany. Thus the Germans serve the Kaiser . . . and Russia. Russian 'citizenship' is apparently an empty word." This post was only one of many other similar erections primarily designed for military purposes. Prepared sites for guns have been found at many spots in Russia, France, and Belgium, particularly among the sand-dunes between Heyst and Knocke; and they probably also exist in England.

Apart entirely from the agricultural colonies which formed so many advance depots of *Deutschthum*, they were able, by means of their numbers, wealth, and the commercial pressure they exerted over their rivals, practically to control many of the chief Russian industries. During the last quarter of the century the public were constantly being informed that German peaceful penetration was proceeding like an avalanche and that unless something was done to stop this constant immigration, or unless a national Muscovite movement were to take place, Russia would become, so far as her commercial and political life were concerned, an appendage of the new German Empire. Various attempts were made to stem the advancing tide and to arrest the progress of the Germanic movement, especially with regard to the occupation and alienation of agricultural estates. Attention was called to the matter in the Russian Press, particularly in a monthly review, the *Russky Vestnik*, but so powerful was German political influence within the Empire that inquiry was stifled and attempts to secure redress by legislative enactment were constantly defeated. The immigration into South-Western Russia assumed such alarming proportions that a measure was introduced into the Duma designed to prevent the purchase of Russian lands by German subjects. Stolypin, the Premier, was confident that it would be voted by the Duma " without delay on account of its extreme urgency," but, as with former attempts of this nature, nothing really effective was accomplished.

Considerable attention was devoted to the question in purely Russian centres, and attempts were made to counteract the evil as far back as the year 1890, when Count Tolstoi's [*] administrative changes were carried into effect and measures were taken for the Russification of the German provinces and Finland. But the result was small compared with the effort. Twenty years later German immigration was still attracting attention, both in Russia and other countries. In an article in the French review *Questions Diplomatiques*,[†] M. Pol Kovnike showed that Russia was not off her guard. " The newspapers have lately spoken of a projected law," he wrote, " which is going to be submitted to the Duma relative to German immigra-

[*] Not the novelist and reformer.
[†] "Les Satellites de l'Allemagne," *Questions Diplomatiques*, August 15, 1911.

tion. In certain frontier provinces, as with us before 1870 and still more so at the present moment, the Germans have been filtering in and forming veritable colonies *which flank the routes of invasion*. Rich and prosperous and in close communication with each other, these colonies rapidly increase and soon become flourishing. In time of peace they have already become a danger to the neighbouring population; *in time of war they will constitute a veritable danger for the whole of Russia*. A law will presently restrain this menacing immigration and prevent its possibility. This is no doubt but a small incident in the life of a people, but does it not tend to prove that public attention, even upon questions of less importance, is always turning towards this invading Power which is called Germany? Russia is not off her guard."

In calling attention to this matter on October 16, 1897, *The Times* stated that " the Government has decided to take immediate steps to Russianize, so far as possible, the large German communities in the Volga region and in the western and southern provinces of Russia. At present the German spirit is carefully fostered in these colonies, in which there are no fewer than four thousand schools. The Minister of Education is now going to reorganize these schools with a view to eliminate German sentiment and inculcate Russian national policy among the children." This step was extremely necessary because the German schools occupied a privileged position and their pupils were taught to regard everything Russian with contempt. These schools were supported by the Deutsche Schulvereine, the oldest and perhaps the most important society designed to forward the aims of Germanism in foreign countries, and by other similar bodies. Branches of this society had been established in almost every country where there were German interests to be fostered. In Austria, for example, the society, which was founded in 1880, had 200,000 members, divided into 2500 local centres, with an annual income of 1,177,000 crowns and a reserve of 4,000,000,* whilst in Russia the society was also active. Its propaganda was aided by the publication of numerous school textbooks, the main purpose of which was to exalt the Fatherland at the expense of other nations. Thus in the " School and the

* Paul Vergnet's " France in Danger," p. 77.

Fatherland " it was stated that " Germany's mission in history is to rejuvenate the exhausted members of Europe by a dispersion of Germanic blood," which admirably expresses the main object of Germanic policy in the non-German countries of Europe. Within Russia itself the Germans were anxious to follow the policy adopted in the Polish provinces of Prussia, where German, and German alone, was considered to be the language that should be habitually used by the pupils. In German Poland, for example, the persistent aim of German policy has been to Germanize the pupils, it being compulsory for all over six years of age to do their lessons in the German language. " The Prussian Government," it was stated in a letter to the *Echo de Paris* in 1906, " persists in endeavouring to give religious instruction in German to the Polish children in most of the schools. . . . The school-teachers are exasperated and persecute both parents and children in an unheard-of fashion. The children are locked up, not even being allowed to return home for their dinners. In many schools the teachers have flogged the children until they lost consciousness."

In this connexion it may be noted that Teutonic methods in German Poland show how Russian Poland will suffer in the future should it remain under German control. It would indeed be a case of changing King Stork for King Log, with this difference, that of recent years the former has amended his ways whilst the latter has become increasingly aggressive. In German Poland, for example, it has become practically impossible for any Pole who is not a *persona grata* to the ruling authorities to build a house on his own land, whilst under the law of 1908, generally termed the " Polish Expropriation or Dispossession Act," passed with the object of facilitating the compulsory purchase of such land as may be desired, many Polish landowners have been obliged to part with their family possessions. The operations of the Ansiedelungs Kommission, whilst showing the advantage—to the Germans—of effective organization, are an object-lesson in the soulless proceedings of an oppressive Government bureau. Such methods would doubtless be transferred to Russian soil at the earliest opportunity. The German-Polish scholastic process was equally at work in Russia, though naturally the methods were different, because the Prussian Government was not able openly to introduce the German iron fist into schools that were not under its direct control. The methods were, however, equally insidious, and tended to create an *imperium in imperio* in every centre where these schools were established. At the outbreak of the war another attempt was made to eliminate the German element in Russia, for a bill was submitted to the Council of Ministers by the Minister for Home Affairs, M. A. Maklakov, by which it was designed to prohibit Germans and naturalized Germans from owning immovable property acquired later than June 14, 1870, when, significantly enough, Germany promulgated her convenient and iniquitous law permitting dual citizenship to Germans resident abroad.*

The indiscretions of the Pan-German party were mainly responsible for the attention that was directed to the doings of the German community in Russia. Not only did they openly boast of its numbers and influence, but by a greater indiscretion they published in the *St. Petersburger Zeitung*, the organ of the German party in Petrograd, in the year 1906, a map showing the chief places in Russia where Germans had established themselves.† This map, similar in some respects to those contained in the remarkable Pan-German atlas ("Deutscher Kolonial-Atlas") of Dr. Paul Langhans, issued at Gotha between the years 1893–97, showed the density of the German population in Russia. The map afforded ample evidence of the main trend of German immigration, which was proceeding in two directions from the Prussian frontier, through Poland and along the Austro-Hungarian frontiers to the shores of the Black Sea and north-eastwards through the Baltic provinces to Petrograd. In addition a third important centre of German influence was shown to be upon the Volga, around the important city of Saratov, where flourishing German colonies were settled in the years 1763–5, and had since acquired enormous influence. These colonies, with an estimated population of 120,000 so long ago as 1891, were placed on the direct strategic route to the Caspian and were therefore a menace in time of war. They commanded, moreover, the route from Uralsk to Moscow.

* *The Times*, January 15, 1915.
† Afterwards reproduced in the *Novoe Vremya*, and in *The Times* on January 15, 1915.

An examination of this map reveals many remarkable facts. It shows that with few exceptions the most important centres of the Russian revolution of 1905-6 were also the cities in which the German element was the largest. Apart altogether from Moscow and Petrograd, Lodz and Warsaw, all of which have a large German population, the revolutionaries were specially active in Pskov, Vilna, Bialystok, Kieff, Odessa, Kherson, Kharkov, Astrakan, Saratov, and Samara, each of which cities contains many German citizens. The connexion between the Russian revolution and the Germans is now well established, and as there is no doubt that it was Germany's policy to push Russia into war with Japan so there is no doubt that it was the policy of the Pan-Germans, if not the German Government, to foment insurrectionary movements at the conclusion of that war. The German urban population formed an admirable centre for secret revolutionary intrigue. The production of this map in the year 1906, when Russia was undergoing regeneration by fire and sword and had been heavily engaged in the Far East, doubtless served its purpose in calling attention to the possibility, in a weakened and disorganized Russia, of consolidating German influence in the country. But it also served to awaken the Russian Government to the danger of the German invasion, for it showed in a concrete form the provinces in which the Germans were the strongest. Five provinces and governments were shown with a German population of over 100,000, namely, Piotrokow, Volhynia, Kherson, Saratov, and Samara, and eight others, namely, Kalisz, Warsaw, Courland, Livonia, Petrograd, Bessarabia, Taurida (including the Crimea), and Ekaterinoslav, in which the German population exceeded fifty thousand.

The danger to the State of this greatly extended but also consolidated foreign population may easily be imagined, particularly because the Germans were peculiarly susceptible to secret propaganda. So far as Russia was concerned German influence was utilized by the secret agents of the Fatherland to excite, fortify, and exalt the Asiatic dream of Russian expansion in the Extreme Orient and thus served a direct political purpose, especially as it was backed by the powerful representations of the German Government. For six years, from 1898 to 1904, the same political manœuvres that had been employed by Bismarck to win France to a policy of colonial expansion, which, it was hoped, might lead to a conflict with Great Britain, were employed to arouse the Manchurian ambitions of Russia in order to render a conflict with Japan inevitable, so that Austria might enter upon her Balkan policy and pave the way for German expansion and penetration in that region. The Germans in Russia admirably seconded the efforts of the Berlin Government.

Attention has been directed to the German danger in Russia by many writers, but chiefly by French publicists, who foresaw that German intrigue in Russia might become a menace to the continuance of the Franco-Russian understanding. Thus in 1902 M. Maurice Lair, in his book "L'Impérialisme Allemand," stated that "this Germanic element forms an autocracy imposed upon the poor peasants of Esthonia, Livonia, and Courland," and in describing the German invasion he stated that they "advance as far as Bessarabia and the Crimea. The greater portion, however, do not go so far, but establish themselves upon Polish soil, where they multiply exceedingly. At this moment they possess in the province of Warsaw alone 13,000 landed properties. The whole of Poland is covered with German names, and 450,000 Germans have thus penetrated into the heart of Poland." Another French observer, M. Soubbotine, writing twelve years earlier, in 1890, called attention to the German menace in Russia.* Describing a journey between Vilna and Warsaw, he stated that "the well-being of the Poles, the landed proprietors, and of the Jews, the principal agents in the commercial life of the country, is compromised" by the persecutions of both, "for owing to the gradual elimination of these two economic factors the German element advances here with conquering and irresistible force." "The Germans," he continued, "make themselves strongly felt in the province of Grodno, where the arrogant Teuton, feeling himself perfectly at home, is encouraged by the submissive spirit shown by the Jews and Poles in giving place to intruders. The nearer one gets to Grodno the more one hears the German language generally spoken." Again, in speaking of the environs of Bialystock, one of the most

* "Fragments de Recherches économiques dans l'Ouest et Sud-Ouest de la Russie."

important centres of the woollen manufacture, he says that "the Germans never lose an opportunity of replacing the Jews and the Poles in all branches of agriculture and in manufacturing industries." In Volhynia, the province next to Galicia, he witnessed "German colonists arrive in the country each spring. There are, as a matter of fact," he states, "special agents through whose intermediary during the preceding autumn and winter negotiations have been entered into between the landed proprietors and the expected colonists for the purpose of selling the land. Competent men arrange that these immigrants shall be granted every possible facility for escaping service in the Russian army. There are German colonies of which all the inhabitants are Russian subjects, but which nevertheless have at no time given a recruit to the State. Leading a self-contained existence and governing themselves by their village magistrates, who represent the colonists in all exterior relations, they never enter into intimate relations with the Russian peasants. The colonists are exempted from all contributions and services for which the villages are answerable to the State; their immigration has at the same time completely modified the former relations between landlord and labourer." M. Soubbotine then proceeds to examine the commercial and industrial activities of the Germans. In Bialystock he found that of 85 large factories then in existence three-quarters belonged to foreigners, principally to Prussian and Austrian subjects, whilst the greater part of the remainder were the property of Jews and of Germans who have become Russian subjects. In Odessa there were 269 industrial establishments of which 210 were in the possession of foreigners. As another authority, M. Xavier Chemerkin,[*] remarks, in a suggestive pamphlet describing how the persecution of the Jews opened the door for German merchants, the Jews were replaced not by native-born Russians, "who do not own more than one quarter of the factories," but by Germans. "One can easily understand," he says, writing in 1893, "that the Germans will be sufficiently powerful in the event of war to influence Russian policy, and that they will not refrain to second the interests of the Fatherland. Such is the precipice

[*] "Les Juifs et les Allemands en Russie," 1893.

towards which the Russian reactionaries are pushing the Russian Empire."

As has already been indicated, the persecution of the Jews in Russia during the years 1890-92 and the severe measures taken in Poland directly facilitated the immigration of German settlers. What the Jews and the Poles abandoned they took up. They quietly stepped into the vacant counting-houses and business establishments. This fatal and reactionary policy, for which the Procurator of the Holy Synod, Constantine Pobyedonostev, was largely responsible, was productive of much of the social upheaval in Russia during recent years. As the most intimate adviser of Alexander III and the most bigoted opponent of religious freedom and of Western parliamentarianism, he succeeded in stamping his policy deeply into the soil of Russia and driving away many hundreds of thousands of citizens who were of immense importance to the commercial life of the community.

Many of the Germans in Russia have of course been settled there for many decades. This is especially the case in the purely Baltic provinces, where the small German barons have long ruled over the Lettish peasantry with a heavy hand. Yet in spite of their long residence in Russia a considerable proportion have never thrown off their German sympathies, and although their connexion with the Fatherland may be as far back as the days of the great Frederick, and even much earlier, they have not become Russians. The fact that the German lesser nobility formed a peculiarly privileged class tended to make them clannish and unassimilative. They were cordially disliked by their dependents. " The hatred which the Lettish peasantry in the Baltic provinces," writes a competent observer, Mr. Namier, " feels against the German landowners is unequalled anywhere in Europe. In 1906, during the Russian revolution and exactly seven centuries since the Germans had founded their dominion at Riga, the Lettish peasantry rose against the German nobility, destroying their castles and driving out, though hardly ever killing, their masters. No violence was done to Russian or Polish landowners." * This insurrection might have put an end to the domination of the German barons, but the Russian Government

* " Germany and Eastern Europe," by Lewis B. Namier, 1915, p. 13.

sent a strong force and routed the insurgents. So greatly was public opinion aroused in Germany by this affront to Germanism that large funds were collected for "restoring *Deutschthum* in the German Baltic provinces," and labourers, farmers, and inspectors were sent from Germany to swell the tide of Germanism. This particular business was worked by the *Deutscher Ostmarken Verein*, amongst other societies. The insurrection in the Baltic provinces took place in spite of the efforts of the Russian Government to break, or at any rate to reduce, the power of the German Baltic barons. The numerous privileges and considerable powers which they had exercised in matters affecting educational policy and the administration of local justice were reduced by laws promulgated in 1888 and 1889, when the rights of police and manorial justice were transferred to the central government. About the same period a vigorous process of Russification was initiated in all departments of the administration, in the higher schools, and in the University of Dorpat, which then became the University of Yariev. In spite of such attempts, however, German influence was little modified in these districts.

But it is in the political and bureaucratic world that Germans have been the strongest, for it is precisely in this sphere that German influence has always been most active. Long before German commercial and agricultural penetration became a pressing danger Russia was subject to the control of German bureaucrats, whilst the Russian army was at one time permeated with officers bearing German names, not an inconsiderable proportion of whom were also of strong German sympathies. " A Russian of German extraction once went through the army list with me," relates the Saxon Minister Count Vitzthum in his Memoirs, " and proved to me from the officers' names that the percentage of Germans increases at every grade "— either a tribute to the ability of the Germans themselves or to the influence they were able to exert at Court. " The highest posts in the Army and Diplomatic Service," he wrote, " were filled by Germans, and the numerous sons of the nobility of Courland and Livonia regarded the Russian Empire as an inexhaustible mine of offices and riches." Referring to the growth of the Muscovite party after the Crimean War, Count Vitzthum stated that " the mania for nationality soon found expression in a hatred of the Germans. The Emperors, in choosing their most trusted servants from the sons of the German Knights of the Order of the Sword, had good reason for their selection. In sound judgment, persevering industry, and especially fidelity and honesty, the Germans were infinitely superior to the Russians. One of these Courlanders, whom I had known at Dresden, and who occupied one of the highest posts in the Ministry of Foreign Affairs, assured me that he had warned the Emperor himself of the arrogance of the Russian party. ' If Your Majesty does not check this mischief we shall live to see in your reign a St. Bartholomew's night of all German officials ' " *

German influence in the army was particularly evident during the reigns of Alexander I and Alexander II, the former a pronounced Germanophile and a keen admirer of King Frederick William III of Prussia and his talented Queen Louisa; the latter a grandson of Frederick William, whose daughter had been married to his father, the Emperor Nicholas, keenly sympathetic with all movements for reform and especially with every reform emanating from Germany. During the intervening reign of Nicholas the Germans made little headway.

It was, however, in the Russian Diplomatic Service that German influence was most decidedly felt. During the reign of the first Alexander practically every important post was occupied by Germans or by Russians of strong German sympathies, and the same may be said for the reigns of his successors. Count Nesselrode, who was Foreign Minister for many years and took a leading part in the Congress of Vienna, is stated never to have learned to speak the Russian language. It was Nesselrode who came to the aid of Austria during the revolutionary movement of 1848-9. The German influence was felt everywhere in the Chancelleries. At the Russian Foreign Office it was notorious that officials of German descent managed to secure the plums of the profession, and it is well known that Bismarck, during his earlier career, was offered a post under the Russian Government. Prince Gortschakov,

* " St. Petersburg and London in the Years 1852–1864 : Reminiscences of Count Charles Frederick Vitzthum von Eckstaedt, late Saxon Minister at the Court of St. James's," vol. i, p. 42.

who obtained the neutrality of Austria during the Franco-Prussian War and thus directly contributed to the destruction of the European balance of power, on becoming Chancellor in 1863 decided to purge his department of German influence, but found that his two chief assistants were named von Westermann and von Hamburger ; whilst Prince Schachowskij, who hated and defied " the rotten bureaucracy of St. Petersburg," when appointed Governor of Esthonia attempted to oust the Germans from that government but was himself broken in the struggle.*

Instances of this fight between German and Teuton on the soil of Russia might be multiplied, and the most diverse authorities might be quoted. The whole trend of modern Russian history might be subjected to minute investigation to prove the presence of the German canker. It might be shown that Russia has from time to time bolstered up the Prussian power when it was on the point of collapsing and that, on the other hand, she has aided Austria, with whom her relations were peculiarly liable to misunderstandings, to maintain her position in order to preserve the German balance of power. It might be shown also how, when Prussia finally prevailed in the long struggle within the German sphere, Russia still followed a policy designed to retain the friendship of that Power, largely because Prussia was the only one of the Great Powers which had shown no direct interest in the Balkans, then the absorbing concern of all Russian statesmen. On this point Bismarck had been adamant and it was only the Emperor William who finally alienated Russian sympathies. But the facts of German penetration in all spheres of Russian life are now too well known to need the more dignified historical background that might be supplied, for the results of Germanization have been visible everywhere in Russian political, economic, and social activities. These influences have often been employed for good, but also not infrequently in the exclusive interests of the German Fatherland. Whatever may be the results of the present war, it is certain that the Germanization of Russia has received a final check.

Whilst friendly relations, if not active alliance, with Russia has been the keynote of German policy throughout the nineteenth century, the political friendship between the two

* Namier, p. 16.

countries was tempered, so far as Germany was concerned, by a constantly recurring fear of the latent forces known as Slavism. The community of interests, such as it was, was always overshadowed by the Slavic skeleton in the political cupboard, and though close and intimate relations were the corner-stone of Bismarck's political edifice during the critical period when modern Germany was being founded, such close friendship was only likely to last as long as Russia's relations with Great Britain remained unfriendly. Interrupted by the events of 1878, when Russia began to perceive that Germany's policy was primarily designed to divide the Powers from one another so that the Hohenzollern eagle might secure the political pickings, but again apparently cemented by the compact at Skiernewice in 1884, when the three Emperors agreed that if one of the contracting Powers were to make war on a fourth the other two would maintain a benevolent neutrality,* the arrangements finally fell to pieces when it became apparent that German policy was bent upon the isolation of France and sought to secure the predominance of Teutonic culture throughout Europe. The Pan-German movement in reality sounded the death-knell of all cordiality between the two Empires.

The Pan-Slav movement, which acted as a counter-irritant to the spread of Pan-Germanism in Russia, was in its more modern aspects a revival of an old doctrine which even in the first period of Russian expansion made its appearance as a national and invigorating ideal. "People who decline to leave us any illusions as to the picturesqueness and unself-consciousness of the Middle Ages," wrote the late Mr. Archibald Colquhoun, " now assert that the Pan-Slav made his appearance in the fourteenth century. There is, indeed, evidence that one or two thinkers and writers who were far ahead of their times suggested, at this early period, the advisability of uniting the scattered Slav peoples—the Russians, Poles, Bohemians, Bulgarians, and Serbo-Croats—in a great Slav league, whose principal object should be to resist the Germanic power under the Emperor of the Romano-Germanic Empire. Unfortunately for such a scheme the Magyar nation had

* This, the famous reinsurance treaty of Bismarck, was specially aimed at England, but was only to last for three years.

successfully effected the division of Northern and Southern Slavdom, nor was there any special inclination among the smaller Slav peoples." * It is indeed doubtful whether a Pan-Slav movement embracing the whole of the Slav peoples and seeking to bring them within the political fold exists either in Russia or in any other Slav country as a living political gospel. Such racial sympathy as there is between the various branches of Slavdom is counteracted by deeply seated political antagonisms and no movement analogous to Pan-Germanism exists amongst them. Pan-Slavism as such is weakened by the other " Pan " movements, each of which seeks salvation for its adherents—within Slavdom, it is true, but not necessarily within Pan-Slavism. Pan-Serbism, which aims at welding the Southern Slavs into an empire, the capital of which would be at Belgrade, is balanced by the Pan-Croat ideal, now more or less swamped in the larger Southern Slav movement—which would form into an autonomous State the triune kingdom of Istria, Bosnia, and Herzegovina, enjoying an *Ausgleich* on equal terms with Hungary. Pan-Slavism, on the contrary, implies the uniting of the entire race under the ægis of Russia and has in reality few adherents—though they may increase and probably will—even in Russia itself. In this political sense, therefore, Pan-Slavism is a doctrine which cannot have caused much uneasiness to Germany.

Nevertheless from the German point of view there has long been a standing, and probably increasing, menace in the forces of disunited Slavdom. There is and always has been a triple basis to Pan-Slavism—the political, the linguistic, and the religious. The two latter, gradually mingling as they do with the former, have constituted a real danger for Teutonism. Linguistically the races of Slavdom are closely allied. " Everywhere alike," states Mr. Namier, " the spirit of Slavdom finds its fullest expression in peasant life and its strongest binding link in language ; every Slav, whatever variation of tongue he may speak, is at least able to understand every other Slav." † In the religious sense they are disunited because Slavdom is divided between the Greek and Latin Churches, the former largely predominating.

* " Pan-Mania," by Archibald R. Colquhoun.
† Namier, p. 39.

The aim of Pan-Slavism in its earlier stages was largely religious and was based upon the desire to liberate its co-religionsts from Turkish rule. Its ideal was the establishment of a Holy Greek Empire under Russian protection, with its capital at Constantinople and its spiritual centre at St. Sophia. Naturally such an ideal did not appeal to the Latin Slavs; but should the union between the Greek and Latin Churches ever be accomplished, the religious basis of Pan-Slavism would become a force that would have to be reckoned with. As is well known, this has been the secret desire of the Vatican for centuries and for which during recent years Cardinal Ledochowski, the Prefect of the Congregation of the Propaganda, so industriously worked.

Political Pan-Slavism found its most notable exponent in a book first published in 1869 in the review *Zaria*, which afterwards passed through several editions in volume form. This work, entitled " The Pan-Slavist Doctrine," * was written by Mr. N. J. Danielewsky, a Russian official and the author of many works on economic and political questions. In this book, which may be regarded as the apotheosis of Pan-Slavism, Mr. Danielewsky propounds a federation of Slav States under Russian influence. This federation would consist of the following units : (*a*) the Russian Empire, with the whole of Galicia and Hungarian Ruthenia ; (*b*) a kingdom consisting of the Czechs, Moravians, and Slovaks, with the north-western portion of Hungary—population nine millions ; (*c*) a Serbo-Croatian-Slovene kingdom, consisting of Serbia, Montenegro, Bosnia, Herzegovina, Old Serbia, Northern Albania, Hungarian Serbia, Croatia, Slovenia, Dalmatia, Trieste, part of Carinthia, and Styria—population eight millions ; this is substantially the programme of the Southern Slav party of to-day ; (*d*) the Bulgarian kingdom, with part of Rumelia and Macedonia—population six millions ; (*e*) the Rumanian kingdom, consisting of Wallachia, Moldavia, part of Bukowina, half of Transylvania, and part of Bessarabia—population seven millions ; (*f*) the Greek kingdom, including part of Macedonia, the islands of Cyprus, Crete, etc., and the Asiatic shores of the Ægean

* Fourth Russian edition published at Petrograd in 1889. A French edition with the following title was issued at Bukarest in 1890 : " La Doctrine Panslaviste, d'après N. J. Danielewsky ; résumé par J. J. Skupiewski."

Sea—population four millions ; this is the Pan-Hellenic ideal ; (g) the Hungarian kingdom—seven millions ; (h) the province of Constantinople—two millions. It will be noticed that Poland does not appear in this scheme, which bears a strong resemblance to more recent suggestions for the settlement of European territory after the war. Such a proposal was of course anathema to the Germans, who were particularly incensed by the author's statement that " Russia being foreign to the European world and too powerful to enter the European family is not able to find any other situation worthy of her grandeur and worthy of Slavdom than that of chief of a special political system. She will thus counterbalance, not any single European State, but the whole of Europe. For Russia, that is the advantage and the meaning of the great federation of Slavs." If we examine this doctrine fully we shall see that it nowhere entrenches upon the sacred principles of nationality ; except in two particulars, where the Hellenic kingdom and Rumania, a semi-Latin State, are tied to the Slavic coach. Yet with such a federation of States in existence both Greece and Rumania would have to cast in their lot with Slavdom. This apotheosis of Slavdom is the great danger of the future against which the Germans were preparing.

Pan-Germanism, on the contrary, as applied to Russia was unracial. It aimed at the assimilation of territory that was only partially German and even of districts in which the Germans were but a small minority. Paul de Lagarde, for instance, writing so far back as 1881, stated that " it is necessary to create a Central European Power which will guarantee the peace of all the Continent from the time when the *Russians and Southern Slavs are cleared from the Black Sea, and when we shall have conquered for German colonization large territories to the east of our present frontiers.* We cannot abruptly enter into the war which must bring this Central Europe into existence. All that we can do is to familiarize our people with the idea that this war will eventually happen." *

German policy was therefore one of conquest, a driving away of the Slav peoples and the substitution of German settlers in their place. The ideals of Pan-Slavism were pacific—the formation of a great federation out of territory

* Paul de Lagarde's " Deutsche Schriften," 1905, p. 83.

already peopled by Slavs. Another German author, writing in the following year, suggested that the Prussian frontiers should be thrust back to Bialystock, Grodno, and Brest-Litovsk, and said that " one thing is certain. Prussia at the commencement of operations must march with three great armies upon Warsaw, Vilna, and Riga, and must occupy all the territory to the Dwina. Prussia must undertake an offensive war upon a great scale." * Here again is seen the irreconcilable conflict between militant Pan-Germanism and the political doctrines of the Pan-Slavs. The latter were indeed but little better than swine to the arrogant Teutons. " The Russians are to-day what they have always been," stated the Pan-German leader Friedrich Lange, " a confused mob, without movement and consequently without history ; polished on the surface but sunk in darkness. They are a certain danger for our civilization. . . . Every German action which will advance our influence in these nerveless territories will conquer for the Germans new countries and will presently change them into German lands."† Lastly, as one further instance of the profound difference between the spirit of Teutonism and Slavdom, it should be stated that the leaders of Pan-Germanism were prepared to drive forth peoples of non-German race wherever they stood in the way of the swelling tide of Germanism. Even the Rumanians of Transylvania were to be transferred to other territories so that Teuton settlers could occupy their farms. " The territories which we shall demand from Russia," stated Paul de Lagarde, " should be sufficiently large to enable us to establish there, in Bessarabia and in the country to the north-east of Bessarabia, as subjects of King Charles, all the Rumanians, both those of Austria and of Turkey."

* Constantin Frantz in his " Die Weltpolitik," 1882–83, vol. ii, pp. 60–61.
† Friederich Lange's " Reines Deutschthum," 1904, p. 210.

SELECT BIBLIOGRAPHY

[The more important works are marked with an asterisk]

GENERAL AND POLITICAL

DILLON, E. J. "A Scrap of Paper: the Inner History of German Diplomacy and her Scheme of World-Wide Conquest." xxvii, 220 pp., 1914.
*HANOTAUX, GABRIEL. "Contemporary France." 4 vols., 1903-1909.
*HERTSLET, SIR EDWARD. "The Map of Europe by Treaty." 4 vols., maps, 1875-1891.
MURRAY, GILBERT. "The Foreign Policy of Sir Edward Grey, 1906-1915." 127 pp., 1916.
*ROSE, J. HOLLAND. "The Development of European Nations, 1870-1900." 619 pp., 1914.
*" The Origins of the War." 201 pp., 1914.
SEIGNOBOS, CHARLES. "A Political History of Contemporary Europe." 881 pp., 1915.
TOYNBEE, ARNOLD. "Nationality and the War." 522 pp., maps, 1915.
VERDAD, S. "Foreign Affairs for English Readers." 286 pp., 1911.

PAN-GERMANISM

"J'Accuse," by a German. 456 pp., 1915.
*ALBIN, PIERRE. "D'Agadir à Serajevo." 256 pp., Paris, 1915.
*ANDLER, CHARLES. "Le Pangermanisme: ses Plans d'Expansion allemande dans le Monde." 80 pp., Paris, 1915.
ANDRILLON, H. "L'Expansion de l'Allemagne." Paris, 1914.
BARKER, J. ELLIS. "Modern Germany." 852 pp., 1915.
*" The Foundations of Germany." 280 pp., 1916.
BERNHARDI, GENL. F. VON. "Britain as Germany's Vassal." 256 pp., 1914.
"Germany and the Next War." 280 pp., 1914.
*BEYENS, BARON. "L'Allemagne avant la Guerre: les Causes et les Responsabilités." 364 pp., Bruxelles, 1915 (English translation, 1916).
BLONDEL, GEORGES. "Les Embarras de l'Allemagne." 338 pp., Paris, 1913.
*BÜLOW, PRINCE BERNHARD VON. "Imperial Germany." 284 pp., 1914.
CHAPMAN, J. J. "Deutschland über Alles; or, Germany Speaks." 1915.
CHIROL, SIR VALENTINE. "The Origins of the Present War." (*Quart. Rev.*, October 1914.)
CRAMB, J. A. "Germany and England." 137 pp., 1914.
DAWSON, W. H. "What is Wrong with Germany?" 227 pp., 1915.
DU PONTCRAY, J. "Allemands contre Slaves." 1909.
FIDEL, CAMILLE. "L'Allemagne d'Outre-Mer: Grandeur et Décadence." 78 pp., maps, Paris, 1915.

SELECT BIBLIOGRAPHY

FITZPATRICK, SIR PERCY. "The Origins, Causes, and Object of the War." 124 pp., 1915.
*FROBENIUS, HERMAN. "The German Empire's Hour of Destiny." 137 pp., 1914.
HAUSRATH, ADOLPH. "Treitschke: his Life and Work." 328 pp., 1914.
JOHNSTON, SIR H. H. "The Legitimate Expansion of Germany." (*Fort. Rev.*, vol. 78, pp. 427-33, 1905.)
KOVNIKE, POL. "Les Satellites de l'Allemagne." (*Quest. Dip.*, pp. 223-35, Août 1911.)
LAIR, M. "L'Impérialisme allemand." 1902.
MILLIOUD, M. "La Caste dominante allemande: sa Formation—son Rôle." 145 pp., Paris, 1915.
*MOLTKE, FIELD-MARSHAL VON. "Essays, Speeches, and Memoirs." 2 vols., 1893.
MÜLLER, RODOLPHE. "L'Impérialisme allemand. (*Le Correspondant*, November 25, 1905.)
*"Pan-Germanic Doctrine." 1904.
**"Pangermanisme colonial sous Guillaume II," avec une Préface par Charles Andler. c, 335 pp., Paris, 1916.
REICH, EMIL. "Germany's Swelled Head." 1914.
ROHRBACH, PAUL. "L'Evolution de l'Allemagne comme Puissance mondiale." (*La Revue Politique Internationale*, Juillet 1914.)
"Der Krieg und die deutsche Politik." 100 pp., Dresden, 1914.
*SAROLEA, CHARLES. "The Anglo-German Problem." 1912.
**TANNENBERG, O. R. "Le plus-grande Allemagne: traduction française du livre ' Gross-Deutschland' (1911)." xv, 338 pp., Paris, 1916.
TREITSCHKE, H. VON. "Germany, France, Russia, and Islam." 328 pp. 1915.
*USHER, ROLAND G. "Pan-Germanism." 284 pp., 1914.
VERGNET, PAUL. "France in Danger." xx, 167 pp., 1915.
WILLIAM I, GERMAN EMPEROR. "Correspondence of William I and Bismarck." 2 vols., 1903.
WILLIAM II, GERMAN EMPEROR. "The German Emperor's Speeches." 1904.
WOLF, JULIUS. "L'Allemagne et le Marché du Monde." Paris, 1902.

AUSTRIA-HUNGARY

BARKER, J. ELLIS. "The Murder of the Archduke." (*Fort. Rev.*, vol. 96, pp. 224-41, 1914.)
"The Ultimate Disappearance of Austria-Hungary." (*XIXth Cent.*, vol. 76, pp. 1003-31, 1914.)
BEAVER, MURRAY. "Austrian Policy since 1867." (*Oxf. Pamph.*) 28 pp., 1914.
BEUST, COUNT F. F. VON. "Memoirs." 1887.
CAPEK, THOMAS. "Bohemia under Hapsburg Misrule." 188 pp., 1915.
*CHÉRADAME, ANDRÉ. "L'Europe et la Question d'Autriche au Seuil du Vingtième Siècle." Paris, 1901.
*" L'Allemagne, la France, et la Question d'Autriche." Paris, 1914.
GAYDA, VIRGINIS. "Modern Austria: her Racial and Social Problems." 350 pp., 1915.
*NAUMANN, FRIEDRICH. "Central Europe." xix, 354 pp., 1916.
PROCHAZKA, J. "Bohemia's Claim for Freedom." 1915.
RECHT, CHARLES. "Bohemia and her Position in the War." 14 pp., New York, 1915.

SELLERS, EDITH. "The Murdered Archduke." (*XIXth Cent.*, vol. 76, pp. 281-98, 1914.)
*STEED, H. W. "The Hapsburg Monarchy." 340 pp., 1914.
*WEIL, GEORGES. "La Pangermanisme en Autriche." 296 pp., Paris, 1904.

SERBIA AND THE SOUTHERN SLAVS

"Austro-Servian Dispute: reprinted from the *Round Table*." 1914.
CHIROL, SIR VALENTINE. "Serbia and the Serbs." (*Oxf. Pamph.*) 18 pp., 1914.
CHURCH, L. F. "The Story of Servia." 136 pp., 1914.
*DENIS, ERNEST. "La grande Serbie." 336 pp., Paris, 1915.
FORBES, N. "The Southern Slavs." (*Oxf. Pamph.*) 32 pp., 1915.
GARGAS, SIGISMOND. "La Question bosniaque." Paris, 1915.
*GRIBBLE, FRANCIS. "Servia Irredenta." (*Edinb. Rev.*, No. 449, pp. 41-60, 1914.)
LOISEAU, C. "Le Balkan Slave et la Crise autrichienne." 1898.
"Map of Southern Slav Territory." 1915.
*PETROVITCH, W. M. "Serbia; her People, History, and Aspirations." 280 pp., 1915.
POLITICUS. "The Future of Serbia." (*Fort. Rev.*, vol. 97, pp. 978-86, 1915.)
"Sketch of Southern Slav History." (Southern Slav Library, No. 3.)
*"Southern Slav Programme." (Southern Slav Library, No. 1.)
"Southern Slavs: Land and People." (Southern Slav Library, No. 2.)
"L'Unité Yougoslave: Manifeste de la jeunesse Serbe, Croate, et Slovène réunie." 53 pp., Paris, 1915.
VELIMIROVIC, REV. NICHOLAS. "Serbia's Place in Human History." 20 pp., 1915.
*WATSON, R. W. SETON-. "The Southern Slav Question." 476 pp., 1911.
ZUPANIC, NIKO. "The Strategical Significance of Serbia." 16 pp., 1915.

ITALY, THE ADRIATIC, AND THE TRIPLE ALLIANCE

BARCLAY, SIR THOMAS. "The Turco-Italian War and its Problems." 258 pp., 1912.
BATTISTI, CESARE. "Il Trentino italiano." 24 pp., Milano, 1915.
*BORGESE, G. A. "Italia e Germania." 343 pp., Milano, 1915.
*CASSI, GELLIO. "Il mare Adriatico: sua Funzione attraverso i Tempi." 532 pp., Milano, 1915.
CASTELLINI, GUALTIERO. "Trento e Trieste: l'Irredentisimo e il Problema adriatico." 140 pp., Milano, 1915.
CRANETTI, ENEA. "Trento e Trieste." 60 pp., Milano, 1915.
*"La Dalmazia: sua Italianità, suo Valore per la libertà d'Italia nell' Adriatico." 214 pp., Genova, 1915.
DEGASPERI, ALFREDO. "Noi, gl'Irredenti—déracinismo." 104 pp., Palermo, 1914.
"Il Diritto d'Italia su Trieste e l'Istria: Documenti." 616 pp., Milano, 1915.
DUDAN, ALESSANDRO. "Dalmazia e Italia." 31 pp., Milano, 1915.
FAURO, RUGGERO. "Trieste: Italiani e Slavi." 238 pp., 1914.
FEILING, KEITH. "Italian Policy since 1870." (*Oxf. Pamph.*) 17 pp., 1914.

SELECT BIBLIOGRAPHY

*GRAY, EZIO MARIA. "L'Invasione tedesca in Italia: Professori, Commercianti, Spie." 260 pp., Firenze, 1915.
"Germania in Italia." 36 pp., Milano, 1915.
MANTEGAZZA, VICO. "Il Mediterraneo e il suo Equilibrio." 298 pp., Milano, 1914.
PISCEL, ANTONIO. "Il Conflitto austro-serbo e gli Interessi italiani." 32 pp., Milano, 1915.
*POLITICUS. "Italia Irredenta." (*Fort. Rev.*, vol. 97, pp. 258–68, 1915.)
*" Le Problème italo-slave: la Dalmatia sous la Domination venitienne: l'Etat contre la Population." 71 pp., Paris, 1915.
*SALANDRA, ANTONIO. "Speech . . . in reply to the Emperor of Austria and the German Chancellor." 32 pp., 1915.
SILVA, PIETRO. "Come si formò la Triplice." 36 pp., Milano, 1915.
SULLIOTTI, A. I. "La Triplice Alleanza dalle Origine alla Denunzià." 112 pp., Milano, 1915.
*TITTONI, TOMASO. "Italy's Foreign and Colonial Policy: a Selection from the Speeches . . . of Senator Tomaso Tittoni." xlvii, 334 pp., 1914.
"La Triplice Alleanza: Ricordi, note, appunti di un vecchio parlamentare." 31 pp., Roma, 1914.
TAMARO, ATTILIO. "L'Adriatico-golfo d'Italia. L'Italianità di Trieste." 252 pp., Milano, 1915.
THOROLD, ALGAR. "The Expansion of Italy." (*Edinb. Rev.*, No. 449, pp. 60–79, 1914.)

RUSSIA

ALEXINSKY, GREGOR. "Modern Russia." 362 pp., 1915.
"Russia and the Great War." 358 pp., 1915.
ATACH, F. "Die deutschen Kolonien in Südrussland." Riga, 1904.
*CHERMERKIN, X. "Les Juifs et les Allemands en Russie." 1893.
CHIROL, SIR VALENTINE. "Germany and the ' Fear of Russia.' " (*Oxf. Pamph.*) 20 pp., 1914.
FORTESCUE, G. R. "Russia, the Balkans, and the Dardanelles." 284 pp., 1915.
HAVENS, HERBERT. "Teuton versus Slav." 160 pp., 1914.
*LANE, ADOLF. "Deutsche Bauernkolonien in Russland." (*Koloniale Abhandlungen*, Heft 31.) 28 pp., Berlin, 1910.
LEFÈVRE, A. "Germains et Slaves: Origines et Croyances." 1903.
LEGER, L. "Russes et Slaves." 1890.
QUADFLIEG, FRANZ. "Russische Expansionspolitik von 1774 bis 1914." 259 pp., Berlin, 1914.
ROUIRE, M. "La Rivalité anglo-russe." 1908.
*VINOGRADOV, P. G. "The Russian Problem." 44 pp., 1914.
*WESSELITSKY, G. DE. "Russia and Democracy: the German Canker in Russia." viii, 96 pp., 1915.

POLAND AND LITHUANIA

*EVERSLEY, LORD. "The Partitions of Poland." 328 pp., 1915.
*HILL, NINIAN. "Poland and the Polish Question." 340 pp., 1915.

SELECT BIBLIOGRAPHY

PHILLIPS, W. A. "Poland." 256 pp., 1915.
SZLUPIAS, JOHN. "Lithuania in Retrospect and Prospect." 97 pp., New York, 1915.

THE NEAR EAST AND TURKEY

BARCLAY, SIR T. "The Turkish-Italian War and its Problems." 258 pp., 1912.
BARKER, GRANVILLE. "The Passing of the Turkish Empire in Europe." 336 pp., 1913.
"Balkan States and the War." (*Quart. Rev.*, April 1915.)
*BARKER, J. ELLIS. "The Future of Constantinople." (*XIXth Cent.*, vol. 77, pp. 493-522, 1915.)
*"Germany and Turkey." (*Fort. Rev.*, vol. 96, pp. 1005-15, 1914.)
BECKER, CARL HEINRICH. "Deutschland und der Islam." 31 pp., Stuttgart, 1914.
BENNETT, E. N. "The Turkish Point of View." (*Edinb. Rev.*, No. 444, pp. 278-96, 1913.)
BLUM, JEAN. "L'Allemagne en Orient après la Guerre balkanique." (*La Revue Politique Internationale*, Août 1914.)
BUXTON, NOEL E. and C. R. "The War and the Balkans." 112 pp., 1915.
CHIROL, SIR VALENTINE. "Pan-Islamism." 28 pp., 1906.
COOK, SIR EDWARD. "Britain and Turkey: the Causes of the Rupture." 1914.
"The Crisis in the Near East." (*Quart Rev.*, January 1913.)
DILLON, E. J. "The Downfall of Turkey." (*Contemp. Rev.*, vol. 106, pp. 713-32, 1914.)
DUCHESNE, A. E. "Asia and the War." (*Oxf. Pamph.*) 16 pp., 1914.
"Eastern Problems and British Interests." (*Quart. Rev.*, No. 436, pp. 270-90, 1913.)
*EVANS, SIR ARTHUR. "The Adriatic Slavs and the Overland Route to Constantinople." (*Geog. Jour.*, vol. 47, pp. 241-65, 1916.)
GRIMME, HUBERT. "Islam and Weltkrieg." 24 pp., Munich, 1914.
*GROTHE, HUGO. "Deutschland, die Türkei, und der Islam: ein Beitrag zu den Grundlinien der deutschen Weltpolitik im islamischen Orient." 43 pp., Leipzig, 1914.
GUESHOFF, I. E. "The Balkan League." 141 pp., 1915.
*JACKH, ERNST. "Deutschland im Orient nach dem Balkankrieg." 159 pp., Munich, 1912.
JAIRAZBHOY, CASSAMALLY. "The Suicide of Turkey." 31 pp., Bombay, 1915.
MARRIOTT, J. A. R. "The Problem of the Near East." (*XIXth Cent.*, vol. 77, pp. 337-51, 1915.)
*NAMIER, LEWIS B. "Germany and Eastern Europe."
*"Near East from Within." 256 pp., 1915.
**NEWBIGIN, MARION. "Geographical Aspects of Balkan Problems in their Relation to the Great European War." 243 pp., maps, 1915.
*PEARS, SIR EDWIN. "Forty Years in Constantinople." 390 pp., 1916.
PRICE, CRAWFURD. "Light on the Balkan Darkness." 122 pp., 1915.
RAMSAY, W. M. "The Revolution in Constantinople and Turkey." 340 pp., 1916.
SCHAEFER, CARL ANTON. "Deutsch-türkische Freundschaft." 43 pp., Stuttgart, 1914.
*SKUPIEWSKI, J. J. "La Doctrine Panslaviste." Bukarest, 1890.

"Strategy of the Balkan War." (*Quart. Rev.*, January 1913.)
*SYKES, SIR MARK. "The Caliph's Last Heritage: a Short History of the Turkish Empire." 638 pp., 1915.
SYUD HOSSAIN. "Turkey and German Capitalists." (*Contemp. Rev.*, vol. 107, pp. 487–94, 1915.)
*TUCIC, SERJAN. "The Slav Nations." 192 pp., 1915.
"Turkey in Europe and Asia." (*Oxf. Pamph.*) 22 pp., 1914.
*WATSON, R. W. SETON-. "The Balkans, Italy, and the Adriatic." 79 pp., 1915.
WOODS, H. C. "Communications in the Balkans." (*Geog. Jour.*, vol. 4, pp. 265–93, 1916.)
*YOVANOVITCH, V. "The Near Eastern Problem and the Pan-German Peril." 47 pp., 1915.

RUMANIA

"The Attitude of Rumania." (*Quart. Rev.*, April 1915.)
C., R. T. "Rumania and the War." (*British Rev.*, May, June, 1915.)
*IORGA, N. "Histoire des Roumains de Transylvanie et de Hongrie." 2 vols., Bukarest, 1916.
*MITRANY, D. "Rumania: her History and Politics." (*Oxf. Pamph.*) 39 pp., 1915.
POLITICUS. "Rumania's Attitude and Future." (*Fort. Rev.*, vol. 97, pp. 804–16, 1915.)
PRAHOVAN, ALBERT. "La Roumanie en Armes." 56 pp., Paris, 1915.
*WATSON, R. W. SETON-. "Rumania and the Great War." 102 pp., 1915.

BULGARIA

*"Aspirations of Bulgaria: translated from the Serbian of Balkanicus." xxvii, 249 pp., 1915.
DILLON, E. J. "Bulgaria and Entente Diplomacy." (*Fort. Rev.*, vol. 97, pp. 755–66, 1915.)
O'MAHONY, R. J. K. "Bulgaria and the Powers." 56 pp., 1915.
WAGNER, HERMENEGILD. "With the Victorious Bulgarians." 308 pp., 1913.

MACEDONIA AND GREECE

ANDRÉADÈS, A. "The Macedonian Question from the Greek Point of View." (*XIXth Cent.*, vol. 77, pp. 352–61, 1915.)
DRAGANOFF, P. "Macedonia and the Reforms." 1907.
NEWBIGIN, MARION. "Macedonia: the Balkan Storm Centre." (*Scottish Geog. Mag.*, vol. 31, pp. 636–50, 1915.)
TOYNBEE, A. J. "Greek Policy since 1882." (*Oxf. Pamph.*) 35 pp., 1914.

ASIA MINOR, SYRIA, MESOPOTAMIA, AND THE BAGDAD RAILWAY

*AINSWORTH, W. F. "Narrative of the Euphrates Expedition." 2 vols., 1888.
*ANDREW, SIR W. P. "Euphrates Valley Route to India." 1882.
"Memoir on the Euphrates Valley Route to India." xii, 267 pp., map, 1857.

SELECT BIBLIOGRAPHY

AULER PASHA. "Notes on the Construction of the Hedjaz Railway. (*United Service Mag.*, October 1908.)

AZOURY, NEGIB. "Le Réveil de la Nation arabe dans l'Asie turque." Paris, 1905.

BELL, GERTRUDE. "The Desert and the Sown." 347 pp., 1907.

*BONACCI, GIULIANO. "La seconda Fase della grande Guerra: nel Medio Oriente attraverso il Ponte balcanico. (*Rivista Coloniale*, vol. 11, pp. 17–34, 89–113, 1916.) Map.

CESARI, CESARE. "L'Asia turca : la futura Questione d'Oriente." 110 pp., Roma, 1914.

**CHÉRADAME, ANDRÉ. "La Question d'Orient : la Macédoine : le Chemin de fer de Bagdad." xv, 397 pp., Paris, 1903.

*CUMIN, LOUIS. "La Question du Chemin de fer de Bagdad." 400 pp., Lyon.

FIRTH, J. B. "The Partition of Asia Minor." (*Fort. Rev.*, vol. 97, pp. 795–803, 1915.)

FRASER, LOVAT. "The Baron and his Bagdad Railway." (*Nat. Rev.*, vol. 59, pp. 606–19, 1912.)

FRASER, DAVID. "The Short Cut to India." 381 pp., maps, 1909.

GERAUD, ANDRÉ. "A New German Empire: the Story of the Bagdad Railway. (*XIXth Cent.*, vol. 75, pp. 958–72, 1312–26, 1914.)

HABIB SHIHA. "La Province de Bagdad." 1908.

HAMILTON, ANGUS. "Great Britain and the Bagdad Railway." (*United Service Mag.*, pp. 344–53, 1908.)

*"Problems of the Middle East." xvi, 484 pp., 1909.

*ILITCH, ALEXANDRE. "Le Chemin de fer de Bagdad." 240 pp., Bruxelles, 1914.

JEBB, LOUISA. "By Desert Ways to Bagdad." 311 pp., map, 1908

KOEPPEN, F. VON. "Moltke in Kleinasien." 1883.

LE STRANGE, G. "The Lands of the Eastern Caliphate." 1905.

LUIGI, GIUSEPPE DE'. "La Linea di Baghdad." 15 pp., Milano, 1913.

LYNCH, H. F. B. "The Bagdad Railway: the New Conventions. (*Fort. Rev.*, vol. 89, pp. 771–80, 1911.)

NETTANCOURT-VAUBECOURT, J. DE. "Sur les grandes Routes de l'Asie Mineure." 1908.

NEWCOMBE, S. F. "The Bagdad Railway." (*Geog. Jour.*, vol. 44, pp. 577–80, 1914.)

NICOLA, A. "Il Problem della Razza e la Colonizzazione della Mesopotamia." (*Espansione Commerciale*, vol. 30, pp. 53–61 *et seq.*, 1915.)

O'CONNOR, T. A. "The Bagdad Railway." (*Fort. Rev.*, vol. 95, pp. 201–16, 1914.)

PARFIT, CANON J. T. "Twenty Years in Bagdad and Syria." 122 pp., 1916.

PERTHIUS, COUNT DE. "Le Désert de Syrie." 1896.

PRATT, EDWIN A. "The Rise of Rail-Power in War and Conquest." xii, 405 pp., 1915.

*PRESSEL, W. VON. "Les Chemins de Fer en Turquie d'Asie." 1902.

"Progress of the Bagdad Railway." (*Geog. Jour.*, vol. 41, pp. 244–9, 1913.)

*ROHRBACH, PAUL. "Die Bagdadbahn." 86 pp., Berlin, 1911.

*SAROLEA, CHARLES. "The Bagdad Railway and German Expansion." 1907.

SCHMIDT, HERMANN. "Die Eisenbahnwesen in dem Asiatischen Türkei." Berlin.

SELECT BIBLIOGRAPHY

SPRENGER, A. "Babylonien, das reichste Land in der Vorzeit und das lohnendste Kolonisationsfeld für die Gegenwart." 128 pp., Heidelberg, 1886.
TOYNBEE, A. J. "Armenian Atrocities." 117 pp., 1915.
TRELOAR, SIR W. P. "With the Kaiser in the East." 1915.
WILLCOCKS, SIR WILLIAM. "The Irrigation of Mesopotamia." 1905.

PERSIAN GULF

BOEHM, SIR E. C. "The Persian Gulf." 1904.
*CURZON OF KEDLESTON, EARL. "Persia and the Persian Question." 2 vols., 1892.
DUNN, A. J. "British Interests in the Persian Gulf." (Central Asian Society.) 1907.
*FRASER, LOVAT. "India under Lord Curzon and After." 496 pp., 1911.
JOUANNIN, ANDRÉ. "Les Influences étrangères dans la Golf persique." (*Bul. de l'Asie française*, p. 23, 1904.)
LANDON, P. "Basra and the Shatt-ul-Arab." (*J.R.S.A.*, vol. 63, pp. 505–19, 1915.)
LONG, E. E. "England—and the Persian Gulf." (*Emp. Rev.*, vol. 29, pp. 294–9, 1915.)
ROUIRE, M. "La Rivalité anglo-russe au XIXe Siècle en Asie: Golfe Persique." 1908.
*"*Times* History of the War: Persian Gulf Number." (Part 29.) pp. 91–120, 1915.
YATE, LIEUT.-COL. A. C. "The Proposed Trans-Persian Railway." (Central Asian Society.) 32 pp., 1911.

INDEX

ABADA, 72 n.
ABERDEEN, Lord, 55, 116
ABDUL HAMID, Sultan, 11, 65, 68, 99, 152, 158, 159, 160, 162
ABDUL MEJID, Sultan, 152
ABU MUSA, 91
ADANA, 39, 65, 74, 75
ADEN, 83
ADRIANOPLE, 41, 124, 127, 176, 190, 245
    Capture by Bulgarians, 181, 183
    Recapture by Turks, 189
ADRIATIC SEA, 34, 250 et seq.
    Compared with Persian Gulf, 78-80
    German aims, 250 et seq.
    Italian policy, 253 et seq.
ÆGEAN ISLANDS, 192
AEHRENTHAL, Count, 163, 169, 274
AFGHANISTAN, 97
AFIUN-KARAHESSAI, 75
AGRAM, 247
AGRAM TRIAL, 242, 243 n.
AHMED BEG, 95
AHWAZ, 86, 92
Akademische Blätter, 61 n.
ALBANIA, 34, 162, 163, 192
    An autonomous kingdom, 191
    Italian interests, 259, 262
    Protection of Christians, 109 n.
ALBIN, PIERRE, 193 n.
ALBRECHT, Duke of Prussia, 300
ALEPPO, 36, 36 n., 38, 39, 61, 65, 74, 75, 76, 111
ALEXANDER I, Tsar, 39, 43, 313
    And the Poles, 290
ALEXANDER II, Tsar, 42 n., 142, 313
ALEXANDER III, Tsar, 294, 311
ALEXANDER I, Prince of Rumania. *See* Cuza
ALEXANDER, King of Serbia, 11, 238
ALEXANDER, Prince of Bulgaria, 142

ALEXANDER THE GREAT, 34, 40, 43
ALEXANDRETTA, 11, 36, 38, 68, 75, 112
    A German port, 68
ALEXANDROPOL, 80
ALGERIA, 41
Alldeutscher Blätter, *quoted*, 31, 198
ALLDEUTSCHER VEREIN FÜR DIE OSTMARK, 220
AMANUS MOUNTAINS, 74
AMASIA, 62
AMPTHILL, Lord. *See* RUSSELL, Lord ODO
ANATOLIAN RAILWAYS. *See* ASIA MINOR
ANCONA, 252
ANDLER, C., 198 n., 200, 221
ANDRASSY, Count, 135, 136, 139, 142
    And Rumania, 271
    "Andrassy Note," 120
ANDRASSY, Count JULIUS, 222
ANDREW, Sir W. P., 36 n., 56; *quoted*, 55
ANGLO-GERMAN AGREEMENT, 71-72, 73
ANGLO-PERSIAN OIL COMPANY, 71, 80
ANGORA, 62, 63, 64
ANNA IVANOVINA, Tsarina, 299
ANNUNZIO, GABRIELE D', 264
ANTIOCH, 36, 36 n., 56
ANTIVARI, 253
ARABIA, 57, 75
    Caliph in, 75 n.
ARAD, 276
Arcona, German cruiser, 87
ARDAHAN, 136, 144
Armee-Zeitung, *quoted*, 232, 244, 248
ARMENIAN MASSACRES, 133, 136
ASIA MINOR
    British Consuls in, 136
    German protectorate, 31
    German settlements in, 31

INDEX

ASIA MINOR—*continued*
  Germany and, 17 *et seq.*
  Railways, 36, 60, 63, 64, 75, 104, 156
  Routes, 34–5
  Russian campaign, 1877, 125 *et seq.*
  Strategic importance, 33 *et seq.*, 48, 49
ASSHUR, 33
ASSURBANIPAL, 34
ASTRAKHAN, 41, 43
Augsburg Gazette, quoted, 23, 215
AULER PASHA, 76 *n.*
AUSGLEICH OF 1867, 212
AUSTRIA
  And Bosnia, 163–7
  And Turkey, 162 *et seq.*
  Ausgleich of 1867, 212
  Gladstone and, 119
  Pan-German societies, 220
  Pan-Germanism in, 194 *et seq.*
  Policy of Trialism, 227
  Races, 195, 208, 233, 241
  Revolution in, 207, 209 *et seq.*
  Seven Weeks War, 212
  Southern Slav movement, 241 *et seq.*
AUSTRIAN LLOYD COMPANY, 262
AZERBAIJAN, 94
AZOF, SEA OF, 38

BABYLON, 25, 33
BAGDAD, 33, 34, 35, 38, 39, 42 *n.*, 65
BAGDAD RAILWAY, 11, 30, 32, 36, 39, 47, 50 *et seq.*, 58 *et seq.*, 81, 87, 88
  Amount expended, 65
  Basra section, 69, 71, 80
  British agreement, 71
  Construction, 62 *et seq.*
  Conventions, 68–9, 70
  France and, 66, 74
  Importance to Germany, 47, 53 *et seq.*, 61
  Khanekin branch, 80
  Kilometric guarantees, 65
  Length, 75
  Route, 74–75
  Russia and, 70, 74
BAGHTCHE TUNNEL, 74
BAHREIN ISLANDS, 71, 72, 83, 86, 87, 90, 91

BAKU, 80
BALBI, GASPARD, 38
BALFOUR, Rt. Hon. ARTHUR, 88, 139
BALKAN LEAGUE
  Formation, 171 *et seq.*, 177
  Dissolution, 185
BALKAN MOUNTAINS, 35, 124
BALKAN WARS, 173 *et seq.*
  Austria's attitude, 185–6
  Conference in London, 184
  Germany's attitude, 175–9
  Results, 190–1
  Russia's attitude, 183–4
BALLIN, Herr, 45, 66
BARI, 252
BARING, WALTER, 123
BARKER, J. ELLIS, *quoted*, 244, 288 *n.*
BASRA, 38, 39, 42, 42 *n.*, 55, 56, 65, 71, 79, 80, 86
BATUM, 80, 136, 144
BEACONSFIELD. *See* DISRAELI
BEER, Mr., 286
BEERSHEBA, 76 *n.*
BEIRUT, 36, 76, 106, 109, 110, 111, 112
  University of St. Joseph, 110
BELGRADE, 11, 35, 39, 45, 245, 248
BENNER, 94
BENNETT, E. N., *quoted*, 175
BERANA MASSACRE, 176
BERCHTOLD, Count, 176, 180, 266
BERGER, RUDOLPH, 221
BERLIN CONGRESS, 128 *et seq.*
  And Christians in Turkey, 109
  Plenipotentiaries, 139
  Results, 141–6
BERLIN MEMORANDUM, 1876, 120
Berliner Handelsgesselschaft, 156
Berliner Tageblatt, *quoted*, 72, 106, 172
BESSARABIA, 37, 143, 274
BETHMANN-HOLLWEG, Herr VON, 193, 265
  On Pan-Slavism, 239
BEUST, Count, 135, 206, 213
BIALYSTOCK, 309, 319
BIEBERSTEIN, Lieut.-Col. ROGALLA VON, 47
BIGHAM, CLIVE, 18 *n.*
BIR, 38
BIRON, Duke of Courland, 299

INDEX

BISMARCK, Prince, 54, 120, 127, 129 n. 211, 223, 239, 260, 261, 309, 314
   And Berlin Congress, 132 et seq.
   And emigration, 298
   And French colonialism, 19, 260
   And Poland, 283, 287
   And Rumania, 122, 268, 270, 272
   And Russia, 20, 313, 315 n.
   And Trieste, 255
   And Turkey, 149, 150, 153-4
   His Embassy in Russia, 283
   Letter to Mazzini, 260
BLACK SEA, 35
   Russia in, 117
BLOWITZ, DE, 129, 129 n., 201
BOHEMIA
   Revolution in, 209
   Pan-Germans in, 220
BOKHARA, 41
BONA, 41
BONGHI, RUGGERO, 263
BOSELLI, PAOLO, 263
BOSNIA-HERZEGOVINA, 46, 119, 124, 259
   Occupied by Austria, 143
   Results of annexation, 167-8, 262
   Seized by Austria, 163-7
BOVIO, GIOVANNI, 247
BRATIANO, JOHN, 122, 140
BREST-LITOVSK, 319
BRINDISI, 252
BRITISH IMPERIALISM, 50-52
BROMBERG, 286
BRUNNOW, 119
BRUSSA, 41
BUCHANAN, Sir ANDREW, 287
BUKAREST, TREATY OF, 189, 190, 191, 278
BUKOWINA, 37, 276
BULGARIA, 46
   And Balkan Wars, 175 et seq.
   And Berlin Congress, 142
   And Russo-Turkish War, 123
   Bulgarian atrocities, 123-4
   Manifesto, 1876, 124
BULGURLU, 74
BÜLOW, Prince VON, 104, 139, 274, 300 n.
   And Mesopotamia, 30
   On relations with Turkey, 157-8
   Visit to Italy, 264-5
BUND DER GERMANEN, 220
BUNDER ABBAS, 86

BUNDER JISSEH, 84
BUNSEN, Sir MAURICE DE, 8 n.
BURGAN, 72 n.
BURIAN, Baron, 257, 266
BURTON, Sir RICHARD, 56
BUSCH, Dr., 150, 155 n.
BUSHIRE, 86, 87, 94

"CALCHAS," 3 n.
CAMPO FORMIO, TREATY OF, 236
CARATHEODORY PASHA, 140
CARINTHIA, 255
CARNIOLA, 255
CARTWRIGHT, JOHN, 39
CASPIAN SEA, 38
CASTRIES, Marshal DE, 41
CATHERINE II, Tsarina, 299
   And German immigrants, 300
CATTARO, 253
CAVOUR, 260
CHARLES, King of Rumania, 122, 126, 175, 180, 190, 268, 270, 272-3, 275, 278
CHARLES-ROUX, F., 41
CHATALJA, 181, 186
CHÉRADAME, ANDRÉ, 5, 6, 9, 65
   Quoted, 7, 13, 14, 46, 66 n., 153, 158
CHERMERKIN, XAVIER, 310
CHESNEY, FRANCIS R., 55
   His Euphrates expeditions, 56
CHIROL, Sir VALENTINE, 169 n.
CHLUMECKY, Count LEOPOLD VON, 226
CHOTEK, Countess SOPHIE, 223, 229
CIVIL SERVICE COMMISSION, 8 n.
CLARENDON, Lord, 212 n.
CLASS, Herr, 12, 197
COLQUHOUN, ARCHIBALD, quoted, 3, 315
CONSTANTIA, 35, 279
CONSTANTINOPLE, 11, 35, 36, 38, 39, 41, 56, 63, 124, 127, 171, 192, 245
   And Berlin Conference, 134
   Emperor William at, 105, 157
CONSULAR SERVICE, 9 et seq.
   Percentage of foreigners, 9 n.
COOK, JOHN M., 101, 106
COPPIN, JEAN, 41
CORINTH, 41
CORFU, 34
CORTI, Count, 139, 140
CRACOW, 209

INDEX

CRETE, 116, 144
CREWE, Lord, 94
CRIMEAN WAR, 115-118
    Causes, 108, 115
    J. A. Froude on, 117-118
    Results, 117
CRISPI, FRANCESCO, 260
    And Triple Alliance, 261
CROATIA
    History, 235 *et seq*., 240-1, 243
    National awaking, 235
CROMER, Lord, 124 *n*.
CTESIPHON, 33
CURTIUS, ERNEST, 25
CURZOLA ARCHIPELAGO, 257, 266
CURZON, Lord, 81, 84, 89, 89 *n*.
    Quoted, 57, 84
CUZA, ALEXANDER JOHN, Prince, 271
CYPRUS, 41, 55, 113
    Convention, 136
    Strategic importance, 136
CYRENAICA, 169
CYRUS, 36
CZECHS, 209
CZERNOWITZ, 276

Daily Mail, 3 *n*.
DALIKI, 72 *n*.
DALMATIA
    Italian interests, 236, 257
    Strategic importance, 257-8
DAMASCUS, 36, 76, 110, 112
    Emperor William at, 105-6
DANEFF, Dr., 186
DANIELEWSKY, N. J., 317
DANUBE, 35, 143, 267
    A German river, 23
DANZIG, 288, 290, 300 *n*.
DEAK, FRANCIS, 241
DECAEN, General, 43
DECAZES, Duc, 135
DE LAGARDE, PAUL. *See* LAGARDE
DELAMAINE, General, 86 *n*.
DELCASSÉ, M., 66, 84 *n*.
DERBY, Lord, 134, 134 *n*., 138 *n*.
DEUTSCH NATIONALER VEREIN FÜR OESTERREICH, 220
DEUTSCHE BANK, 60, 64, 66, 67 *n*., 156
DEUTSCHE SCHULVEREINE, 305
DEUTSCHE SCHUTZVEREINE, 220
DEUTSCHER OSTMARKEN-VEREIN, 284, 312
DEUTSCHER WELTBUND, 220

DEWEY, Vice-Admiral, 14
DIARBEKR, 58, 62
DIBBS, Sir GEORGE, 225
DILLON, Dr., 3 *n*.
    Quoted, 171, 175-6, 186
DISRAELI, BENJAMIN, 115, 118, 119, 128
    And Berlin Congress, 130, 138, 140, 145
    And Cyprus, 136
    And " Peace with Honour," 145
    And Suez Canal, 134 *n*.
    And Syria, 113
DOBRUJA, THE, 267
DODECANESIAN ISLANDS, 265
DON RIVER, 38, 43
DORPAT, 298 *n*., 312
DOUGLAS, Admiral, 84
DRAGA MASCHIN, Queen, 11, 238
DRAVE RIVER, 233, 255
DRUSES, THE, 109
DUBOIS, MARCEL, 41 *n*., 42 *n*., 84 *n*.
DULCIGNO, 253
DUNN, ARCHIBALD J., 61 *n*., 75 *n*.
DURAZZO, 253
DURHAM, Lord, 194
DUSAN, 234

Echo de Paris, quoted, 15
ECKARTSAU, 228
Eclipse, H.M.S., 84
EDESSA, 33
EDHEM PASHA, 63
EDVAL, Colonel, 95
EDWARD VII, King, 227
    And Bosnia, 165-6
    And Koweit, 90 *n*.
EGYPT, 41, 163
    And Berlin Conference, 134
    Napoleon's invasion, 40
    Pan-Islamism in, 97
    Strategic importance, 40, 49, 59-60
EITEL, Prince, 102
El Lewa, 97
ELIZABETH PETROVINA, Tsarina, 299
ELPHINSTONE INLET, 80
ENVER PASHA, 160, 187, 189
    And *coup d'état*, 1913, 161-2, 183
    At Berlin, 160
    Proclaims Turkish Constitution, 161
EREGLI, 74
ERZERUM, 62, 126

INDEX

EUPHRATES, 33, 36, 65, 71
   British navigation, 71
   Early travellers, 38–9
EUPHRATES VALLEY RAILWAY, 54 et seq., 136 n.

FALKOWSKI, JULES, quoted, 55
FARMAN, T. F., 109
FASHODA, 99
FEIZI PASHA, 75 n.
FERDINAND, Archduke, 162, 223, 231
   His character, 223 et seq.
   His death, 229–30
   His policy, 225 et seq.
FERDINAND, Emperor of Austria, 205
FERDINAND, King of Bulgaria, 175, 177, 182, 185, 186, 191
FERDINAND, King of Rumania
   His pedigree, 273
FERRY, JULES, 110
FITCH, RALPH, 38
FIUME, 243, 253
FLOTTWELL, VON, 289
FORGACH, Count, 228
FRANCE
   And Bagdad Railway, 66, 74
   And Syria, 107 et seq.
   And Tunis, 138, 169, 260, 261
FRANCIS I, 106, 108
FRANCIS JOSEPH, Emperor, 142, 162, 205, 229
FRANKFORT ASSEMBLY, 1848, 202, 205, 206
FRANKFORT CONSTITUTION, 204
Frankfurter Zeitung, 67, 246
FRANTZ, CONSTANTIN, 319
FRASER, LOVAT, 84 n., 87, 89
   Quoted, 80 n.
FREDERICK II, Emperor, 104
FREDERICK III, Emperor, 105, 129, 153
FREDERICK BARBAROSSA, Emperor, 21 n., 104
FREDERICK WILLIAM III, King of Prussia, 313
FREDERICK WILLIAM IV, King of Prussia, 204, 205
FRERE, Sir BARTLE, 56
FRIEDJUNG TRIAL, 242, 243 n.
FRIULI, THE, 234
FROUDE, JAMES ANTHONY
   On the Crimean War, 117
FRYMANN, DANIEL, quoted, 215
FÜRSTENBERG, Count, 278

GAGERN, H. VON, 203
GALLOIS, EUGÈNE, quoted, 112
GAMBETTA, LÉON, 110
GARIBALDI, General, 260
GARVIN, J. L., 3 n.
GAYDA, VIRGINIO, 254 n.
Gegenwart, quoted, 221
GEORGE, Mr. LLOYD, 195
GERMAN EMPEROR. See WILLIAM II
GERMANY
   Diplomatic Service, 7 et seq.
GHAZIR, 110
GIOLITTI, Signor, 169, 189 n., 266, 278
GLADSTONE, W. E., 115, 118, 119, 134 n.
   And Asia Minor, 136 n.
   " Bag and Baggage " speech, 119
   On Austria, 119
GOETZEN, Admiral VON, 14
GOLSTROM, Major, 95
GOLOUCHOWSKI, Count, 213, 274
GOLTZ, Field-Marshal VON DER, 30, 45, 155, 173, 182
   On the Hedjaz Railway, 76
   Reorganizes Ottoman army, 152–3
GORIZIA, 255, 266
GORTSCHAKOV, Prince, 117 n., 120, 121, 128, 130, 139, 140, 142, 195, 313
GRADISCA, 266
GRANVILLE, Lord, 134 n.
GRAVOSA, 253
GREECE
   And Balkan Wars, 177 n., 180 et seq.
   And Berlin Congress, 140 n., 141–2, 143–4
   And Russo-Turkish War, 123, 127
GREEN, Sir HENRY, 56
GREY, Sir EDWARD, 14, 70, 71, 73, 80, 161, 165, 168 n., 191, 192
GRODNO, 309, 319
GROSSWARDEIN, 276
GROTHE, Dr. HUGO, quoted, 32, 61
GRÜNWALD BATTLE. See TANNENBURG
GUESHOFF, I. E., 177, 188 n., 189, 279 n.
GWINNER, Herr, 66

HAIDAR PASHA, 36, 63, 64, 74, 75
HAIFA, 36, 100 n., 101, 101 n., 103

INDEX

HAKATIST SOCIETY. *See* DEUTSCHER OSTMARKEN-VEREIN
HAKKI PASHA, 70, 72, 172
HALDANE, Lord, 14, 69
HALIF, EL, 68
HALUL, 87, 91
HAMADAN, 95, 96
HAMAM, 111
Hamburger Fremdenblatt, quoted, 75
HAMILTON, ANGUS, 76 *n*.
HANOTAUX, GABRIEL
    Quoted, 131, 132, 135, 137, 140, 145
HANSA LEAGUE, 298, 298 *n*.
HANSEMANN, VON, 284
HARAN, 65
HARDEN, MAXIMILIEN, 15
HARDINGE, Sir ARTHUR, 10 *n*.
HARLING, Herr, 86 *n*.
HAROUN-AL-RASCHID, 34
HASSE, Herr, 12, 198, 250
HEDJAZ RAILWAY, 36, 75–77
HELIGOLAND, 44, 60
HENRY VIII, 106
HERAT, 43
HERBERT, Sir THOMAS, 92
HESSE
    Revolutionary outbreak, 205
HILDEBRANDT, Lieut.-Col., 59
HIRSCH, Baron, 63
HIT, 33
HOFFMANN, CHRISTOPH, 100–101
HOHENBURG, Duchess. *See* CHOTEK
HOHENLOHE, Prince, 20, 42 *n*., 129 *n*., 139, 140, 153
HOMS, 36, 111
HUNGARY
    And the Southern Slavs, 241 *et seq.*
    Elections, 244
    Population, 241
    Racial elements, 241
    Russian action in, 117
    See also Magyars

INDIA, 41, 55, 60
    German missions, 97–98
    Napoleon's plans, 40, 42
ISKANDERUM. *See* ALEXANDRETTA
ISMIDT, 64
ISPAHAN, 94, 95
ISTRIA, 255
ISVOLSKI, M., 165

ITALY
    And the Adriatic, 251 *et seq.*
    And Bosnia, 168–9
    And France, 169, 260
    And Trieste, 254–5, 256–7
    And Triple Alliance, 261–2
    Dispute with Austria, 266
    Italia Irredenta, 258, 263
    Italian societies, 263–4
    Turco-Italian War, 169 *et seq.*

JACKSON, Sir THOMAS, 96 *n*.
JAFFA, 36, 100 *n*., 101, 103, 112 *n*.
JAUNA, DOMINIQUE, 41
JERUSALEM, 36, 101, 102, 105, 112 *n*.
JOHNSTON, Sir HARRY, *quoted*, 216
JONESCU, TAKE, 278
JOSEPH II, Emperor, 207, 208
Journal des Débats, 84
JUKILCH, LUKA, 243
JULFA, 80
JULIAN, 34, 39

KAERGER, Dr., *quoted*, 31
KALNOKY, 213
KANDAHAR, 43
KANNENBERG, KARL, 64
KARA-GEORGE, 237
KARACHI, 80
KARL LUDWIG, Archduke, 223
KAROLYI, Count, 139
KARS, 126, 136, 144
KARUN RIVER, 71, 72 *n*., 87, 91
KASVIN, 80
KATR, AL, 71, 90, 91
KAULLA, ALFRED, 64
KENNEMANN, Herr, 284
KERMANSHAH, 80, 96
KERBELA, 97
KHANEKIN, 70, 80
KHOR ABDALLA, 90
KHORAMABAD, 80
KHUEN HEDERVARY, Ban of Croatia, 243
KIAMIL PASHA, 162, 183
KIDERLEN-WAECHTER, Herr von, 181, 274
KIEFF, 289
KISHM, 72 *n*.
KITCHENER, Lord, 64, 97
KOGALNICEANO, M., 140
KOKOVTSOV, M., 193
KONIA, 65, 74, 75
KÖNIGGRÄTZ. *See* Sadowa

INDEX

KONOPISHT, 229
KOSCIELSKI, JOSEPH, 284
KOSOVO, 35
KOSSEIR, 38
KOSSUTH, LOUIS, 204, 210
KOTCHANA MASSACRE, 176
KOVNIKE, POL, 304
KOWEIT, 11, 39, 65, 67, 71, 72 n., 79, 83, 87, 88, 90
    British Treaty, 88
    Germans at, 88–9
    Turkish claims, 71, 89
KRAGUJEVATZ, 243
"KRIEG," quoted, 200
KUNDUK RIVER, 276
KUTCHUCK KAMARDJI, 108

LA FOREST, JEAN DE, 108
LAGARDE, PAUL DE
    Quoted, 27, 199, 318
LA HARPE, M., 290
LAIR, MAURICE, 309
LANGE, FRIEDRICH, 319
LANGHANS, PAUL, 100 n., 307
LANSDOWNE, Lord, 91
LASCELLES, Sir F., 21 n.
LAUNAY, Count, 140
LEA, HOMER, 48
    Quoted, 82
LEBANON, 108, 109, 111
LEDOCHOWSKI, Cardinal, 317
LEGA NAZIONALE, 263
LEIBNITZ'S MEMOIR ON EGYPT, 40, 43
LESSEPS, FERDINAND DE, 57
LICHNOWSKY, Prince, 73
LIMAN VON SANDERS, General, 173, 187, 192
LINGEH, 72 n., 86
LIST, FRIEDRICH, quoted, 28–29, 198–9
LOISEAU, M., 259
LOUIS IX, 108
LOUIS XIV, 40, 108
LOUIS XV, 108
LOUIS PHILIPPE, King, 186, 272
LOUISA, Queen of Prussia, 313
LUCAS, Sir CHARLES, quoted, 52
LYBYER, A. H., 38 n.
LYONS, Lord, 200

MACEDONIA
    Anarchy in, 163 et seq., 174 et seq.
    Berlin Congress and, 141
    Ottomanization, 163, 173
    Protection of Christians, 109 n.

MACKINNON, Sir WILLIAM, 56
MCLAREN, D., 61 n.
MACLEOD, Sir DONALD, 56
MADAGASCAR, 40
MAGYARS, 196
    And Rumanians, 276–8
    And Southern Slavs, 214, 241 et seq.
    Revolt, 202, 209
MAHAN, Admiral, quoted, 18 n., 48, 81
MAHMUD SHEVKET PASHA, 161, 187
MAIORESCO, M., 279
MAKLAKOV, M. A., 307
MANGELSDORP, Professor R., quoted, 61
MANGOURIT, M., 41
MARDIN, 58, 61, 62
MARITZA, RIVER, 245
MARONITES, 108
MARSCHALL VON BIEBERSTEIN, Baron, 161, 173
MARTINI, Signor DE, 247
MATOFF, Dr., 175
MAZZINI, 260
MEADE, Colonel, 84, 87, 88, 89 n.
MECCA, 36, 75, 76, 97
MEDIÆVAL TRADE ROUTES, 38
MEHEMET ALI, 25
MERSINA, 36, 75
MESOPOTAMIA, 25, 33, 45, 46 n., 57
    A German dependency, 30
    Importance to Germany, 44, 61
    Riches of, 26, 30
METTERNICH, Prince, 207
MEZERIB, 77
MICHELL, Sir LEWIS, 21 n.
MILAN OBRENOVIC, King, 11, 237
    And Russo-Turkish War, 124
MILLIOUD, MAURICE, 217 n.
MILOS OBRENOVIC, 237
MITRANY, M., 269, 279
MITROVITZA, 247
MOHAMMERAH, 80, 86, 91, 92
Mois Colonial, quoted, 111, 113
MOLDAVIA AND WALLACHIA. See RUMANIA
MOLTKE, Field-Marshal VON, 5, 13, 27, 30, 31, 53, 101, 135, 197, 199, 215, 267
    And Asia Minor, 22–25
    And German influence in Turkey, 24
    And Palestine, 23
    And railways, 22, 62

MOLTKE, Field Marshal VON—continued
  And Rumania, 24
  His mission to Turkey, 24, 152
  His riverine doctrine, 13
MONROE DOCTRINE, 18, 294
MONTENEGRO
  And Balkan Wars, 180 et seq.
  And Russo-Turkish War, 124, 127
  And Scutari, 178, 183
  Berlin Congress and, 143
MORAVA RIVER, 245
MORIER, Sir ROBERT, 200, 201–2
MORLEY, Lord, 69
  Quoted, 70
MORTIER, General, 40
MOSTIMIE, 75
MOSUL, 58, 62, 65, 75
MUHAMED FERID BEG, 97
MULLA, DIAMILLA, 261 n.
MURPHY, Major C.
  Quoted, 86
MUSCAT, 71, 83, 84, 92
  British treaty with, 83
  French at, 84
MUSURUS PASHA, quoted, 56

NAMIER, LOUIS, quoted, 195, 311, 314 n., 316
NAPOLEON I, Emperor, 36 n., 43, 44, 236
  And Egypt, 40
  And India, 39 et seq.
  And Mesopotamia, 39
  And Persia, 43, 94
NAPOLEON III, Emperor, 56, 117
  And Italy, 260
  And Syria, 109
NAPOLEON, Prince, 200
NARBONNE, M. DE, 43
NATALIE, Queen, 237
National Review, 3 n.
  Quoted, 72
NAUMANN, Pastor, quoted, 106–7
NAZIM PASHA, 183
Near East, quoted, 103
NEBUCHADNEZZAR, 34
NESSELRODE, Count, 313
Neue Zeit, quoted, 62
NEUFELD, KARL, 97
NEWBIGIN, MARION, 35 n.
  Quoted, 35
NEWBERY, JOHN, 38

NICHOLAS I., Tsar, 116, 313
  And the Poles, 290
NICHOLAS II, Tsar
  And Balkan Wars, 186–7
NICHOLAS, Grand Duke, 121, 125
NICHOLAS, King of Montenegro, 183
NIEBUHR, KARSTEN, 25
NIKOLAIEFF, Dr., 175
NINEVEH, 33
NISEBIN, 61
NISH, 11, 35, 245
NORTHCOTE, Sir STAFFORD, 56, 127
NOVGOROD, 298
NOVI BAZAR, 11, 233
  Occupied by Austria, 143
  Strategic importance, 247, 248 n.
Novoe Vremya, quoted, 93, 95
Novosti, quoted, 105

ODESSA, 35, 275 n., 310
OENSET, Captain, 95
OLMÜTZ, CONVENTION OF, 206, 211
OMAN. See MUSCAT
ORMUZ, 79, 92
OSMAN PASHA, 125, 126
OTRANTO, 79, 253
OTTAIR, M., 83
OTTO, Archduke, 223
OUBRIL, Baron d', 139

PALESTINE
  German colonies in, 100–103
  German Emperor in, 99 et seq.
  Jews in, 113–4
  Moltke and, 23
PALGRAVE, W. G., 56
PALMERSTON, Lord, 56, 81, 116, 119
PAN-GERMAN ATLAS, 100 n., 307
" PAN-GERMANIC DOCTRINE," 3, 26
PAN-GERMANISM, 1 et seq., 50, 318
  And Africa, 10, 17
  And Asiatic Turkey, 26 et seq.
  And Austria, 194 et seq.
  Moltke and, 22 et seq.
  Pan-German societies, 220
PAN-ISLAMISM, 96–7
PANITZA, Dr., 175
PAN-SLAVISM, 28, 315 et seq.
PARFIT, Canon, quoted, 102
PARIS, PEACE OF (1856), 117
PASHITCH, M., 189
PAUL, Emperor, 42
" PEACE WITH HONOUR," 145
PEREIRA, MM., 63

INDEX

PERSIA
    German consuls, 94
    German plot in, 93–96
    Importance to Britain, 67
    Napoleon and, 43
    Peter the Great and, 42
    Railways, 70, 80
    Russia and, 70
    Strategic routes, 78
    Swedish gendarmerie, 94, 95
PERSIAN GULF
    British treaties, 90–91
    Compared with Adriatic, 78–80
    French influence, 84
    German influence, 78–92
    German plots in, 85 *et seq.*
    Great Britain in, 91 *et seq.*
    Strategic importance, 78, 80, 81 *et seq.*
PETER, King of Serbia, 238, 240
PETER THE GREAT, 41, 299
    His policy, 295–6
    His will, 42 *n.*
PHILIP OF FLANDERS, Count, 272
PHILIPPOPOLIS, 245
PHILLIPS, W. A., 289
PICHON, M., 172
PIROT, 127
PLESKOW, 298 *n.*
PLEVNA, 124, 125, 126
POBYEDONOSTOV, CONSTANTINE, 311
POIGNANT, GEORGES, 111 *n.*
POINCARÉ, RAYMOND, 113 *n.*
POLA, 253
POLAND
    Bismarck and, 283, 287
    Expropriation policy, 285–6, 306
    German influence, 280 *et seq.*, 306
    German settlers, 281
    German societies, 283–4
    Italian Chamber and, 290 *n.*
    Rising in 1846, 209, 289
PONTCRAY, M., *quoted*, 167
PORAJHNEVA " FORTRESS," 303
PORTUGUESE EMPIRE
    Decline of, 92
POTI, 80
POTIOREK, General, 229
PRATT, E. A., 22 *n.*, 59 *n.*
    Quoted, 52–3, 62–3
PRESSBURG, 198
PRESSEL, WILHELM VON, 62
    His railways, 63
PRINTA, CHARLES, 249 *n.*

PROCHASKA AFFAIR, 188
PROTHERO, G. W., 17 *n.*
PRUTH RIVER, 274, 276
PUGHIA STEAMSHIP LINE, 262
PUGIN, Dr., 94
Punch's CARTOON ON PERSIA, 85, 87
PURCHAS, SAMUEL, 92

Questions Diplomatiques, *quoted*, 111, 275, 304

RADEK, KARL, *quoted*, 61
RADZIWILL, Princess, 138 *n.*
RAGUSA, REPUBLIC OF, 236
Railway Times, *quoted*, 57
RAS RAKKIM, 91
RAS-AL-AIN, 75
RATHENAU, Herr VON, 66
RAUCH, Baron, 242
RAUWOLF, LEONARD, 38
RAWLINSON, Sir HENRY, 56
RAYAK, 76
REDESDALE, Lord, 166
REPHAIM, 100 *n.*
RESHT, 80, 94
RÉUNION, 40
REUSS, Prince HENRY XXXI, 95
Revue Politique Internationale, 60
Revue des Questions Coloniales, *quoted*, 112
Revue Hebdomadaire, *quoted*, 113
RHODES, CECIL
    And Asia Minor, 17 *et seq.*
    And Rhodes scholars, 21 *n.*
    His interview with the Kaiser, 21 *n.*
RHODOPE MOUNTAINS, 35
ROBERTS, Lord, 3
ROEDERER, PAUL, 109 *n.*
ROGALLA VON BIEBERSTEIN, Lieut.-Col., 47
ROHRBACH, PAUL, 46
    Quoted, 1, 46, 47, 59
ROMAN IMPERIALISM, 51–2
ROSCHER, WILHELM, *quoted*, 27
ROSE, J. HOLLAND, 126 *n.*, 136
ROSE, Sir HUGH. *See* STRATHNAIRN
Round Table, *quoted*, 213, 224, 229
ROUVIER, M.
    And Bagdad Railway, 66
RUDOLF, Crown Prince, 223, 224
RUMANIA
    And Balkan Wars, 179, 189, 278
    And Russo-Turkish War, 122, 126

INDEX

RUMANIA—continued
  And Triple Alliance, 274
  At Berlin Congress, 140 n.
  Bismarck and, 122
  Convention with Russia, 1876, 122
  Gains independence, 143
  German influence, 267 et seq.
  German population, 275 n.
  History, 269 et seq.
  Joins the Allies, 16, 279
  Magyars and, 276-8
  People, 269, 276
  Prince Charles elected, 272
  Russia and, 122
  Von Moltke and, 23
  Trade, 275 n.
RUMELIA, EASTERN, 142
RUSSELL, Earl, 212 n., 287
RUSSELL, Lord ODO, 150
RUSSIA
  Academy of Sciences, 297 n.
  And Bagdad Railway, 66, 70, 74
  British attitude, 291
  Expansion, 291-3
  German " fortresses " in, 302-3
  German immigration, 295, 301 et seq., 308-10
  German understanding with, 315
  Germans in, 291 et seq.
  Germans in Diplomatic Service, 312-4
  Jews in, 310-11
  Pan-German map, 307-8
  Pan-Slavism, 315 et seq.
Russki Invalid, quoted, 97, 302
Russky Vestnik, quoted, 304
RUSSO-TURKISH WAR, 120 et seq.
RUSTCHUK, 124

SABBIONCELLO, 236
SADOWA, BATTLE OF, 212
SAID HALIM, Prince, 187
St. Petersburger Zeitung, 307
SAINT-VALLIER, M. DE, 140
SALADDIN, 34
SALANDRA, Signor, 266
SALISBURY, Lord
  And Berlin Congress, 130, 137, 139, 140 n., 144
SALISBURY, Lady
  Letter to, 201

SALONIKA, 11, 16, 35, 39, 143, 186, 226, 245, 247
  Advance from, 16
  Strategic importance, 248
SAMARRA, 75
SAN STEFANO TREATY, 127, 131
SARATOV, 307
SAROLEA, CHARLES, quoted, 66, 73
SARONA, 100 n., 101
SAULVE, M., 81 n.
SAXONS IN TRANSYLVANIA, 276
SAZANOV, M., 181
SACACHLOWSKIJ, Prince, 314
SCHAFFER, Lieut., 64
SCHENCK, Baron, 7
SCHLESWIG-HOLSTEIN QUESTION, 212
SCHMERLING, ANTON VON, 211
SCHOENERER, Herr, 220
SCHONEMANN, Herr, 95
SCHOTT, GERHARD, 44, 44 n.
SCHOUVALOFF, Count. See SHOUVALOV, Count
SCHWARZENBERG, Prince, 203, 205, 206
SCUTARI, 178, 183, 247
SEBENICO, 253
SELEUCIA, 36, 36 n.
SELLERS, EDITH, quoted, 224
SENNACHERIB, 34
SERAJEVO, 11, 229
  See also FERDINAND
SERBIA
  And Balkan Wars, 177 n., 180 et seq.
  And Russo-Turkish War, 123, 127
  Austrian policy, 231 et seq.
  Berlin Congress and, 143
  Strategic importance, 245
SEVEN WEEKS WAR. See AUSTRIA
SHATT-AL-ARAB, 71, 80
SHIRAZ, 95
SHIRLEY, Sir ANTHONY, 38
SHOUVALOV, Count, 121, 130, 134, 139, 140
SHUKLA " FORTRESS," 303
SHUMLA, 124
SILISTRIA, 124
SIRIM, 72 n.
SIVAS, 62
SKIERNEWICE, 315
SKUPIEWSKI, J. J., 317
SLOVENES, 235
  In Trieste, 254-5, 258
  Their important position, 255-6

INDEX

SMITH, ADAM, 28
SMYRNA, 35, 36, 63, 75, 112 n.
SOCIETA NAZIONALE DANTE ALIGHIERI, 263
SOFIA, 35, 245
SOLIMAN, Sultan, 108
SONNINO, Baron, 253 n., 257, 265, 266
SOREL, ALBERT, 7
SOUBBOTINE, M., 309
SOUTH AFRICA
    Germans and, 17
SOUTH AMERICA
    Germans and, 18, 294
SOUTHERN SLAV MOVEMENT. *See* AUSTRIA, SERBIA
SPALATO, 253
SPEYER, BEIT VON, 9 n.
SPRENGER, ALOYS, *quoted*, 30
STEDINGKS, Baron DE, 42
STEED, HENRY WICKHAM, *quoted*, 159, 188, 229
STEIN, FRANKO, 221
STEMRICH, Herr, 88
STRATFORD DE REDCLIFFE, Lord, 54, 56, 117
STRATHNAIRN, Lord, 56
STROSSMAYER, Bishop, 256
STYRIA, 255
SUEDIAH. *See* SELEUCIA
SUEZ, 42
SUEZ CANAL, 54, 55, 57, 59, 60, 121
    Purchase of shares, 134 n.
SULINA, 24, 268
SYRIA
    French historical claims, 110
    French influence, 107 *et seq.*, 119
    French language, 111
    French railways, 75, 111-112
    Number of French, 112 n.
    Protection of Christians, 108-9

TABRIZ, 38, 80, 93
TALAAT BEY, 189
TAMM, T., 269 n.
TANGANYIKA RAILWAY, 59
TANNENBERG, BATTLE OF, 285, 300 n.
TANNENBERG, RICHARD, 12
    Quoted, 216-7, 285, 286
TAURUS MOUNTAINS, 74
TEHERAN, 70, 80
    German influence at, 93
Temps, Le, *quoted*, 15
TERRIER, AUGUSTE, 41 n., 42 n.
TEUTONIC ORDER, 285, 300

TEWFIK PASHA, 106
THAPSICUS, 33
THUN-HOHENSTEIN, Count, 205
THYSSEN, Herr, 66
TIEDEMANN, VON, 284
TIFLIS, 80
TIGLATH-PILESAR, 34
TIGRIS, 33, 36, 65
Times, *quoted*, 95-96, 104, 105, 157, 179, 180, 241, 244, 305
TIRNOVA, 124
TIRPITZ, Grand Admiral VON, 229
TISZA, Count, 230, 266
TITTONI, Signor, *quoted*, 146, 247 n., 248 n.
TOBRUK, 171
TOLSTOI, Count, 304
TOYNBEE, ARNOLD J., 257
TRAJAN, 34, 39
TREBIZOND, 35, 38
TRELOAR, Sir WILLIAM, *quoted*, 104
TRENTINO
    Italian interests, 258
TREVELYAN, G. M., 240 n.
TRIESTE, 11, 34, 79, 214, 253
    A German outlet, 250, 255
    Italian interests, 254, 256-7
    Municipal organisation, 254
    Slavonic population, 244-5, 258
TRIPLE ALLIANCE, 170, 260, 261-2, 265, 274
TRIPOLI (AFRICA), 20, 169
TRIPOLI (ASIA), 36
TSARITSYN, 43
TUCIC, S. P., 243 n.
TUNIS, 20, 41, 138, 169, 260, 261
TURCO-ITALIAN WAR, 170
Turkestanskaya Viedomosti, *quoted*, 46 n.
TURKEY
    And Italy, 168-9
    Coup d'état, 1913, 183
    German financial influence, 155-7, 172
    German traders in, 157
    Great Britain and, 151
    In sixteenth century, 37-8
    Moltke and, 24
    Ottoman army reorganized, 152, 173, 192
    Overthrow of Abdul Hamid, 160-1, 162
    Railways in, 245, 248
    Routes in, 34-5

TURKEY—*continued*
  Russo-Turkish War, 120 *et seq.*
  "The sick man dying," 116
  The Young Turks, 159 *et seq.*

United Service Magazine, quoted, 114
URFA, 58, 61
USHER, Professor, 3 *n.*
  Quoted, 78
USKUB, 35, 248

VALONA, 34, 252, 253, 257, 258, 259, 264
VARASDIN, 233
VARDAR, 35, 245
VARNA, 35, 124, 125
VENIZELOS, M., 168, 177, 189
VENICE, 79, 236, 252
VERDAD, S., *quoted,* 163, 168 *n.*, 172 *n.*
VERGNET, PAUL, 220 *n.*, 284, 305 *n.*
VESNITCH, M. R., 166
Victoire, La, quoted, 7, 11
VICTOR EMMANUEL, King, 261
VICTORIA, Queen, 212 *n.*
VILLARI, PASQUALE, 263
VINCKE, VON, 25
VINCENT, CHARLES, *quoted,* 112
VITZTHUM, Count, 312
VLADISLAV, 303
VOLGA RIVER, 43, 305, 307
VOLHYNIA, 310
Vossiche Zeitung, quoted, 67

WADDINGTON, M., 139, 144
WAGNER, KLAUS, 175
WATSON, R. W. SETON-, *quoted,* 182, 254 *n.*, 256, 257
WESSELITSKY, G. DE, 297 *n.*, 301 *n.*
WILLIAM I., German Emperor
  And Poland, 288
WILLIAM II, German Emperor
  And Archduke Ferdinand, 227–8, 229
  And Koweit, 90 *n.*
  And Pan-Germanism, 4
  In Palestine, 99 *et seq.*
  Speeches quoted, 12, 13, 106
  Telegram to King Charles, 190
  Visit to Constantinople, 64, 105, 157
WILLIAM IV, King of England, 56
WILLIAM OF WIED, Prince, 191
WINTERSTETTEN, Dr. VON, *quoted,* 219
WONCKHAUS, Herr, 86, 87, 91
WÜRTTEMBURGISCHE VEREINSBANK, 64

YARIEV, 312
YATE, Lieut.-Col., 80

ZANZIBAR, 83
Zaria, quoted, 317
ZEKKLERS, THE, 276
Zeit, quoted, 59
ZICHY, Count, 238 *n.*
ZOBEIR, 65

THE MIDDLE EAST

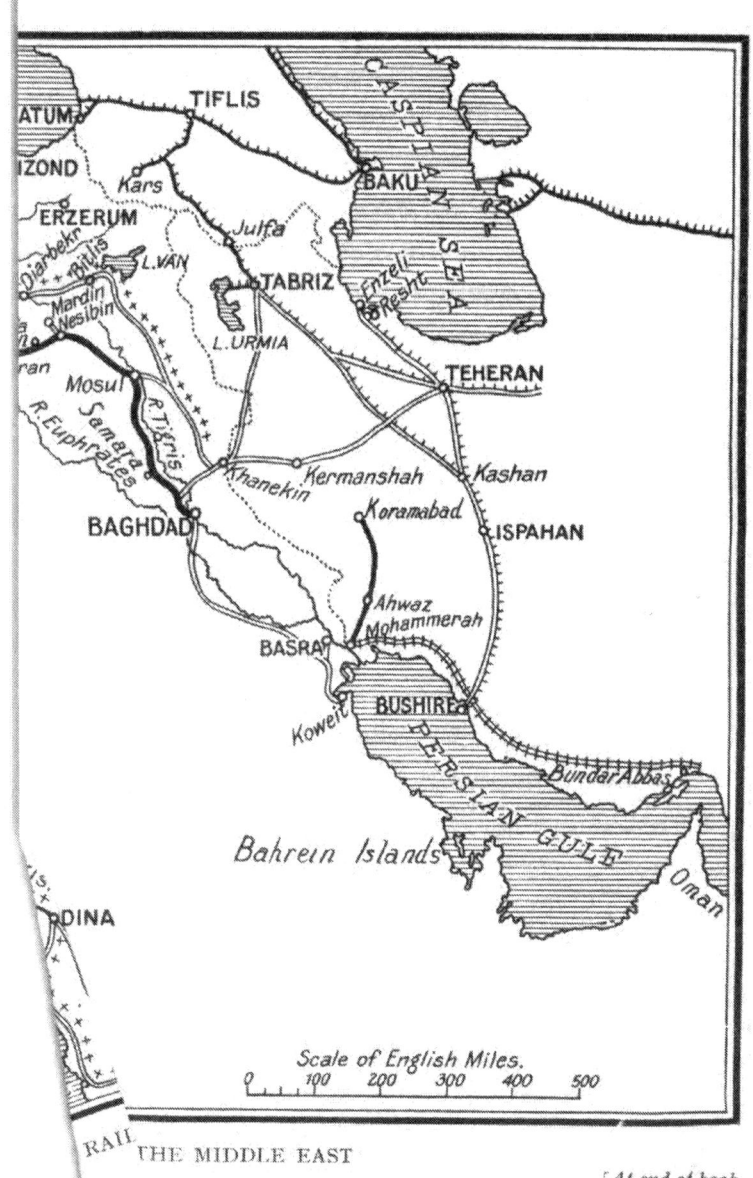

RETURN TO the circulation desk of any
University of California Library
or to the
NORTHERN REGIONAL LIBRARY FACILITY
Bldg. 400, Richmond Field Station
University of California
Richmond, CA 94804-4698

ALL BOOKS MAY BE RECALLED AFTER 7 DAYS
2-month loans may be renewed by calling
(415) 642-6753
1-year loans may be recharged by bringing books
to NRLF
Renewals and recharges may be made 4 days
prior to due date

DUE AS STAMPED BELOW

JUN 24 1991

CPSIA information can be obtained
at www.ICGtesting.com
Printed in the USA
LVHW081552200522
719343LV00011B/606

9 780343 533168